RAY MILLAND

RAY MILLAND

IDENTITY, STARDOM, AND THE LONG CLIMB TO *THE LOST WEEKEND*

GILLIAN KELLY

UNIVERSITY PRESS OF MISSISSIPPI / JACKSON

The University Press of Mississippi is the scholarly publishing agency of the Mississippi Institutions of Higher Learning: Alcorn State University, Delta State University, Jackson State University, Mississippi State University, Mississippi University for Women, Mississippi Valley State University, University of Mississippi, and University of Southern Mississippi.

www.upress.state.ms.us

The University Press of Mississippi is a member of the Association of University Presses.

Any discriminatory or derogatory language or hate speech regarding race, ethnicity, religion, sex, gender, class, national origin, age, or disability that has been retained or appears in elided form is in no way an endorsement of the use of such language outside a scholarly context.

Copyright © 2025 by University Press of Mississippi
All rights reserved
Manufactured in the United States of America

∞

Publisher: University Press of Mississippi, Jackson, USA
Authorised GPSR Safety Representative: Easy Access System Europe—Mustamäe tee 50, 10621 Tallinn, Estonia, gpsr.requests@easproject.com

Library of Congress Control Number: 2025941690

Hardback ISBN 978-1-4968-5914-3 | Paperback ISBN 978-1-4968-5913-6
Epub single ISBN 978-1-4968-5915-0 | Epub institutional ISBN 978-1-4968-5916-7
PDF single ISBN 978-1-4968-5917-4 | PDF institutional ISBN 978-1-4968-5918-1

British Library Cataloging-in-Publication Data available

CONTENTS

Acknowledgments vii
Introduction ix

CHAPTER ONE:
Welsh National Identity and Cinematic Representations 3

CHAPTER TWO:
Stumbling into Acting 36

CHAPTER THREE:
Second Fiddles and Third Wheels: Early Bit Part Player 49

CHAPTER FOUR:
The Brit Effect: Portraying Nobility and Royalty 71

CHAPTER FIVE:
It's a Woman's World: Supporting Paramount's Female Stars 97

CHAPTER SIX:
Reaching a Paramount: The Long Climb to *The Lost Weekend* 159

CHAPTER SEVEN:
Oscar After Party 207

Conclusion 223
Filmography 229
Notes 237
Bibliography 249
Index 255

ACKNOWLEDGMENTS

Firstly, I wish to thank everyone at the University Press of Mississippi for allowing me to publish a second book with them. They were the first publisher to take a chance on an unpublished author with my first monograph *Robert Taylor* back in 2019. That book went on to be shortlisted for Monograph of the Year at the prestigious BAFTSS Awards and has led to some exciting ventures. Special thanks to Emily Bandy, Courtney McCreary, Joey Brown, Kristin Kirkpatrick, and Steve Yates for their enthusiasm and support throughout this long process. Thanks also to my copyeditor Peter Tonguette.

Many thanks to Jenny Reburn, Hollie Price, Ryan Shand, and Melanie Selfe for invaluable feedback and comments on earlier drafts of chapters. Thanks to my best friend, Allison, for always being there and my late friend Colin Watling, who never got to see this book completed.

To my family: Mum, Steven, Barry (and his constant jokes about *Frogs*), Emma and Robyn, I love you all more than words can say.

As always, this book is dedicated to the memory of Gran, Auntie Mae, and Uncle Alan, forever remembered and missed.

INTRODUCTION

FROM WALES TO HOLLYWOOD

> There are very few things that give me greater pleasure than to watch good acting. It exhilarates me and robs me of sleep. On the other hand, really bad acting actually nauseates me.
>
> —RAY MILLAND (1974: 203)

The actor who would become known as Hollywood star Ray Milland was born Reginald Alfred Jones in Neath, Glamorganshire, Wales in the United Kingdom on January 3, 1907.[1] Born into a family with no theatrical background and possessing no youthful acting ambition of his own, when the seventy-nine-year-old Milland died on March 10, 1986, he left behind a screen legacy of almost one hundred and eighty film and television appearances, spanning an impressive fifty-seven years and crossing seven separate decades, from 1929 to 1985. Among other creative roles, Milland often appeared on radio throughout his career and intermittently on stage. In his mid-career, he also sporadically worked as a director: between 1955 and 1969, he directed five films that he also starred in,[2] as well as several episodes of television series (in which he also occasionally appeared).[3]

The first Welshman to win the Best Actor Academy Award, as well as a performer boasting a rich and varied oeuvre from the silent era to New Hollywood, Milland oddly remains a somewhat "lost" or forgotten figure of cinematic history, perhaps due to his omnipresence and capacity to adapt to the changing roles required of him across the years. While the academic study of stars of Classical Hollywood has garnered much needed attention in recent years (see, among others, Girelli 2014; Mercer 2015; Bolton and Lobalzo Wright 2016; Thomas 2018; Kelly 2019; Kelly 2021), this has led to a much more apparent absence of in-depth work on second-level studio luminaries. This book attempts to fill that void, in part, by offering a detailed examination of Ray Milland as one of Hollywood's most durable and fascinating performers of the later studio era.

APPROACHES

What is particularly interesting about Milland's star image and screen work, placed within their sociohistorical, geographical, and industrial contexts, is that despite his almost unique national identity as a Welshman working in the early sound era of 1930s Hollywood and beyond, his origins were not only ignored but completely erased by his home studios, MGM (Metro-Goldwyn-Mayer) and, later, Paramount Pictures, in favor of casting him, perhaps more "safely," as upper-class Englishmen or Americans. Occasionally he portrayed other nationalities, such as Austrian in *Hotel Imperial* (Robert Florey, 1939), but never Welsh. Thus, alongside an intriguing and multifaceted star persona and admirable acting range, it is evident that both MGM and Paramount were unsure how to market their unusual expatriate. Not once did Milland portray a character of Welsh descent on screen and, despite David Berry's assertion that he was one of "the most durable of all Welsh stars in Hollywood," *Circle of Danger* (Jacques Tourneur, 1951) was his "first role in his native country" (1994: 231). However, as is discussed in chapter one, not only does Milland portray an American in this film partially set in his homeland, but one who is oddly confused by British money and customs. Even when Hollywood turned its attention to making films about the nation, such as the phenomenally successful *How Green Was My Valley* (John Ford, 1941), Milland was neither cast nor considered for these roles.

There is much to unpack around Milland's mode of masculinity as a working-class Welshman repeatedly cast as upper-class Englishmen and Americans, as well as his distinct transatlantic identity that was similar to but different from his British-American peers, such as Cary Grant, Stewart Granger, Brian Aherne, and James Mason. Furthermore, the evolution of Milland's complex star image allows broader questions to surface about concepts of Welshness, Britishness, transatlantic stardom, national identity, masculinity, aging stars, and career longevity. As is examined through the deconstruction of Milland's career and image, an untrained actor with a wide range of acting skills who graces the screen with a capacious array of multifaceted performances can make it harder for studios to categorize and promote that star, and for audiences to identify with them on- and off-screen as a result. Since this book is concerned with the constructed star image, performance skills, and characterizations of an individual actor with a vast and expansive career across film, television, radio, and theatre primarily as an actor but also as a director and producer for almost sixty years, it would prove not only impossible but counterproductive to attempt a discussion of each of his roles, unquestionably resulting in a lack of in-depth analysis as well as constructive critical, theoretical, and historical context essential for any star studies examination. Accordingly, this would result in a broad overview or general summary of Milland's career, which can easily be obtained elsewhere online or in print (McKay 2020). Instead, each chapter focuses on a specific facet of Milland's long and varied oeuvre, exploring his work across the years and analyzing the development and execution of his performance skills therewithin. Emphasis is placed on his acting range and ability to maintain a long and successful career without being typecast. This offers alternative images of gender and masculinity while contributing to wider concerns about how we approach male stardom. Additionally, it allows an examination of how mid-level male stars were employed in a Hollywood system more conventionally associated with glamour and machismo, as well as the ways in which Hollywood's studios, with varying levels of success, attempted to position Milland within this context.

Since this book presents a comprehensive study of an individual film performer, the main source of research is the film texts themselves, with specific focus placed on Milland's characterizations and acting skills therein. This is presented through detailed textual analysis of selected screen performances during distinct periods of his career, alongside an examination of his value to transnational and historical media industries, particularly film, in a career that notably spanned the periods from silent British cinema in the 1920s to the New Hollywood of the 1980s. As may be expected for a study on Milland, a large section of the book focuses on his exceptionally lengthy twenty-one-year contract with Paramount, not only highlighting his arduous struggle to become a respected actor but his lower status at the studio in his inequitable pairings with some of Paramount's leading ladies, even when he received top billing. Indeed, Milland only became a star, in the traditional sense, with his sixtieth film, the highly controversial and culturally significant *The Lost Weekend* (Billy Wilder, 1945), to which I dedicate an entire chapter. While the film made him a global sensation, Milland never reclaimed this momentary glory despite working for an additional forty years. Moreover, while his career continued to be varied and diverse, such as undertaking increasingly more antihero roles, it is this film which he has been forevermore associated.

Primary sources such as interviews, magazine and newspaper articles, reviews, official film posters, publicity stills, and letters to the editor of fan magazines, particularly those in relation to the confusion around his identity, are also engaged with throughout. Some of these aid in exploring his star persona, while others illustrate that his Welshness, or suggested lack thereof, was also up for debate with contemporary publications, even in Britain, which erratically labeled him as Welsh, English, and Irish (including by the same journalists in different issues of the same publication). Moreover, his Oscar win saw him gracing the cover of *Life* magazine on February 19, 1946—a rare occurrence for any performer, not least Milland, who is dressed casually in a red plaid shirt. Thus, his star image is not as straightforward as may first appear when presented as upper-class Englishmen on-screen, a role he often played but never truly fitted due to his real identity and background.

Andrew Spicer debates a similar mode of Britishness in his recent monograph on Sean Connery,[4] noting that the working-class Scotsman successfully made the conscious decision to retain his Scottish accent in an industry full of "[Ronald] Colmans" (an identity that was alien to Connery, as it was to Milland). Although initially considered controversial, Spicer asserts that this led to Connery becoming the best-known British star in the world. However, with this success came limitations and Connery has become indefinitely associated with the figure of James Bond. While aiding in his fame, it simultaneously reduced him to the status of a product of a specific period of cultural history and led to his seeking diverse work and independent employment in future decades, never quite managing to become a successful transnational or transatlantic star. The opposite could be said about Milland, who enjoyed a long and productive career across several decades in Hollywood but never achieved the worldwide fame the inaugural James Bond actor did. It also appears that Milland did not crave the level of stardom Spicer declares Connery strived for, which may have contributed to his uneven, and at times unusual, career path.

Both a blessing and a curse, securing an expansive range of roles across genres allows an actor to remain employed and enjoy a long and productive career not limited to industry trends or the focus of a home studio at a specific time. On the other hand, it can lead to a lack of public recognition or longevity since, despite making appearances in films of other genres, John Wayne is still intensely associated with Westerns and Fred Astaire with musicals. Since the primary concerns of this study are the construction and manipulation of an individual star image, issues around national identity, and Milland's performance skills, any in-depth production histories of the films explored are limited, therefore allowing the focus to remain predominantly on Milland's developing acting skills, his presentation on-screen for audiences, and his interactions with other performers. Accordingly, textual analysis is the primary methodology used throughout, underpinned by concepts and theories from star studies, performance studies, cultural studies, and gender studies.

Since it would be an impossible task to cover the whole of Milland's career in any depth within a single volume, there may be certain films or genres that readers feel are missing or have been overlooked. For example, while some may associate Milland with *film noir*, Milland was never a "noir" star in the same way as performers like Alan Ladd, Humphrey Bogart, or his one-time costar, Veronica Lake. In fact, one of the book's fundamental arguments concerns the challenges filmmakers faced when attempting to typecast Milland since he appeared in a myriad of genres and undertook a vast range of characterizations over the decades, many at the same time. For example, in 1951, Milland starred in four vastly different films. *Circle of Danger* (Jacques Tourneur) is a mystery in which Milland's American character travels to Britain to find out how his brother really died during World War II. In *Night Into Morning* (Fletcher Markle, 1951), his college professor plunges into alcohol-fueled depression after his wife and son are killed by a faulty boiler.[5] *Rhubarb* (Arthur Lubin, 1951) is a zany comedy in which he becomes the guardian of a stray cat that has inherited a baseball team. Finally, the tearjerker drama *Close to My Heart* (William Keighley, 1951) explores the issue of a married couple unable to conceive a child, and Milland's reporter obsessively investigating the background of a foundling his wife is desperate to adopt. By the same token, in 1947, he portrayed a tough cowboy opposite Barbara Stanwyck in *California* (John Farrow); a bumbling college professor alongside Teresa Wright in *The Trouble with Women* (Sidney Lanfield);[6] a British officer hiding from Nazis while disguised as a gypsy oppposite Marlene Dietrich in *Golden Earrings* (Mitchell Leisen); and as "himself" in a skit alongside William Holden in *Variety Girl* (George Marshall), all of which he credibly portrayed. Equally, some may find it surprising that Milland's films with well-known directors such as Billy Wilder (*The Major and the Minor*, 1942) and Fritz Lang (*Ministry of Fear*, 1944) receive little attention. However, the immense importance of his later pairing with Wilder in *The Lost Weekend* has resulted in chapter six being dedicated solely to this film, in which Milland is almost ever-present. As both Wilder's directorial debut and a starring vehicle for Ginger Rogers, *The Major and the Minor* did not significantly advance Milland's career or image, supplying him with little more than the role of romantic foil for Rogers to play off.[7] While it could potentially be discussed alongside *The Lost Weekend* in relation to Milland's work with Wilder, it would draw similar conclusions to the chapter exploring his pairings with Paramount's other leading female stars, thereby taking the focus away from the latter, which was so imperative to Milland's career, and thus diluting the analysis of both. While there is a lot more that can be said about Milland's star persona and screen performances, the majority of his roles receive at least one mention, some fleetingly and others with considerably more space dedicated to them. Moreover, it is worth highlighting here that the lack of attention paid to his on-screen debut in *The Flying Scotsman* (Castleton Knight, 1929) and his television work is intentional. I have written extensively on these aspects of his career elsewhere (Kelly 2022; Kelly 2023a); these journal articles provide additional material on topics not covered here.

THE STRUCTURE OF THE BOOK

Unlike Hollywood cinema and the British film industry based in London, cinema in Wales, as a creative industry and a theatrical space, are vastly understudied areas. A consideration of these aids in positioning Milland within wider cinematic debates, such as the continued struggle of Welsh filmmakers to be recognized nationally and internationally while reflecting Milland's own struggles as a popular performer and individual star persona. His status as the first Welshman to win the Best Actor Academy Award is also a notable element of his identity, an accolade positioning him as both British and, more uniquely, Welsh. This helps set up Milland's position within wider, and still ongoing, debates about Welsh cinema, Welsh performers, and the repression of some performers' real identities, such as the long-hidden fact that the mother of fellow Brit Merle Oberon was of Indian origin.

Through the lens of Welsh identity and Welshness in cinema, chapter one begins by establishing Milland's cultural identity from a working-class Welsh background, which Hollywood did not just underplay but completely erased, initially forcing him to fit the model of upper-class Englishness in the mold of Ronald Colman, an already saturated market representing Hollywood's blindered version of "Britishness." Indeed, aside from lower-class British characters who typically spoke with a Cockney accent, this tended to be the only type of "Brit" that Hollywood recognized, thus obliterating Milland's individuality as an uncommon Welshman and instead forcing him to fit a traditional but limited screen "type" upon relocating to Hollywood. Interestingly, although Milland received no acting training before entering British cinema, he seems less stilted in his British films than in his early Hollywood career, as comparisons with his debut in *The Flying*

Scotsman (1929), in which he plays a working-class steam engine fireman, demonstrates (Kelly 2023a).

Aiming to establish Milland as an important and unique yet vastly understudied performer, chapter one places his on- and off-screen personae into context by exploring his Welsh roots before moving on to consider other Welsh performers and Welsh cinema more generally. A sociohistorical investigation of cinemagoing in Wales from Milland's childhood until the present day then follows. This is another particularly understudied area of research which would have proved imperative to Milland's opportunities in life, career choices, and approaches to his work. An exploration of his Celtic connections and Welsh folklore provides a strong link between myth from his native country and Classical Hollywood stars as ethereal gods and goddesses (Dance 2011; Williams 2012; Williams 2018).

Chapter two acts as a preface to Milland's successful, if undynamic, career at Paramount by exploring his significantly lesser-known years at MGM, the studio which initially brought him to the US. During his time at MGM, and when the studio loaned him to Warner Brothers, Milland was repeatedly cast as Hollywood's stereotypical version of the Britisher as an upper-class Englishman. He portrayed nobility and, on occasion, even royalty, but these characterizations lacked real depth, and he was never cast in a leading role while signed to MGM. Moreover, the studio utilized embellishments such as mustaches and bowler hats to align Milland's image with classical Hollywood's stereotypical depiction of "British" masculinity, but this proved counterproductive since it disguised his youthful good looks, star potential, and leading man possibilities at an imperative stage in his career development. While Milland was undisputedly a handsome leading man, he never achieved the heartthrob or "pinup" status of American peers Clark Gable, Robert Taylor, Tyrone Power, or fellow transatlantic star, Cary Grant. As I have stated elsewhere, while the emphasis on a performer's looks can help elevate them to stardom relatively quickly, it can also be counterproductive in their being taken seriously as a skilled performer. Since Milland arguably was a star, although one who enjoyed second-tier fame, star studies and performance studies will be engaged here, although I have done much of this groundwork in my previous monographs on Taylor (Kelly 2019) and Power (Kelly 2021) so will avoid repeating that here.

Perhaps the most natural and believable British character Milland ever portrayed was Alan Howard in *French Without Tears* (Anthony Asquith, 1940). Based on a 1936 play by London playwright Terence Rattigan, Milland's exuberant screen presence and British sarcasm is perfectly encapsulated on-screen as he plays off fellow British performers David Tree, Ronald Culver, and Kenneth Morgan as one of four Englishmen in France trying to learn the language as quickly as possible. Particularly noteworthy is the drunken scene which takes place after the four stars return to their boarding house after a widespread street party, comically singing and staggering. It is a world away from Milland's stark depiction of drunkenness just a few years later in *The Lost Weekend*. Chapters three and four then consider Milland's early roles at Paramount, which employed some of the characteristics already (unsuccessfully) offered by MGM. Moving on to explore his most important and enduring on-screen pairings, chapter five investigates how, even during what can be classed as his "stardom years," Milland was regularly cast as little more than a supporting player opposite Paramount's actresses Dorothy Lamour, Claudette Colbert, and Paulette Goddard. Even when given top billing, Milland consistently played "second fiddle" to their characterizations, and the chapter examines what this meant for both his reputation and his mode of masculinity.

Chapter six analyzes the most important film in Milland's oeuvre, the well-known but peculiarly understudied *The Lost Weekend*. The offbeat casting of Milland as an alcoholic writer allowed him to embody a more complex, troubled screen image than he was previously permitted and provided him with his (temporary) star-making role. Highly controversial, it is regarded as the first Hollywood picture to take alcoholism seriously and was nominated for seven Oscars, winning the four major awards of Best Picture, Best Actor in a Leading Role for Milland, Best Director for Wilder, and Best Screenplay for Wilder and cowriter Charles Brackett. Thus, the importance of this film in Hollywood history and Milland's career cannot be overstated. The chapter examines the range of performance skills Milland demonstrates in his portrayal of a tormented character during a time of great uncertainty in Hollywood, America and the world.

The final analysis chapter, chapter seven, then provides a link from his most successful role to the end of his long and varied career, highlighting some of his most significant films and characterizations while exploring reasons why Milland was not able to maintain or regain the glory of *The Lost Weekend*—even though his career lasted another four decades. Addressing important questions that otherwise dismiss the study of white male actors from the classical era, this volume suggests new ways of thinking through these types of figures by primarily focusing on Milland's complex national identity, gender, the roles in which he was cast, and how this affected his star image. There have been strong and welcome developments in contemporary star studies in recent years, with a particular emphasis on labor contexts and economic practices. While this is explored in relation to Milland's career, image, and cultural background, the primary focus is on the construction of his star image through his film roles, presenting an analytical balance in the case study of Milland as an undervalued yet highly illustrative example of second-tier stardom.

I now turn to explore Milland's Welshness by considering what it culturally means to be Welsh, the understudied and underrepresented notion of Welsh cinema, and sociohistorical and geographical concepts of cinemagoing in Wales during Milland's lifetime and beyond. Furthermore, discussions of Welsh mythology and folklore illustrate the romanticized status of the country, while providing links to Hollywood stars as modernized mythical beings. Moreover, Milland's background and star image are explored in relation to other Welsh and transatlantic male stars—such as his most obvious forerunner, Ivor Novello, and successor, Richard Burton—while stressing how his mode of stardom and Welshness are both related to and discrete from these other performers.

RAY MILLAND

CHAPTER ONE

WELSH NATIONAL IDENTITY AND CINEMATIC REPRESENTATIONS

When commencing research for this project in 2016, ninety-one years after Milland's birth and thirty years after his death, I was surprised, though not shocked, to discover that the only book published on the actor remained his 1974 memoir, *Wide-Eyed in Babylon*. Written long after the sixty-seven-year-old's "stardom years" were behind him, but while his career was still active, its release date predates the final decade of Milland's life and screen work. Similarly, prior to my recent articles on *The Flying Scotsman* and his television work (Kelly 2022; 2023a), scholarly focus on Milland was limited to a 2014 article by Brooks E. Hefner that explores the "five largely unknown feature films" Milland directed and starred in. These films—*A Man Alone* (1955), *Lisbon* (1956), *The Safecracker* (1958), *Panic in Year Zero!* (1962), and *Hostile Witness* (1968)—are examined in the context of Milland's post-studio career. Hefner suggests these films reveal a growing discontent and "paranoia over the place of the studio star in the post-Paramount environment" (2014: 4). Furthermore, he posits the idea of Milland as star-auteur, offering a reinterpretation of the term auteur within the post-studio era and drawing comparisons with filmmakers such as Jerry Lewis.

More generally, given the distinct lack of material on Welsh cinema and Welsh-born performers, I found it astounding that Peter Stead's niche book *Acting Wales: Stars of Stage and Screen* (2002) features chapters devoted to Milland's Welsh predecessor Novello and successor Burton, as well as many other performers of Welsh decent, but Milland receives no more than a passing reference in a chapter dedicated to Stanley Baker. Milland's prominent place in cinematic history as Wales's first Best Actor Academy Award winner suggests he merits a more extensive discussion in a text dedicated to such a narrow subject. Just over a decade later, the authors of the *Historical Dictionary of British Cinema* list Milland as one of only six "international film stars born in Wales" (Burton and Chibnall 2013: 423), the others being Burton, Baker, Anthony Hopkins, Timothy Dalton, and Catherine Zeta-Jones. Online, Wikipedia's page dedicated to "Welsh male actors" lists 142 performers from the inception of cinema to the present day. Listed alphabetically, aside from Milland, only five actors appear under the letter "M," with Charles Morgan (1909–1994) as his only contemporary. While Philip Madoc, Colin McCormack, and Howard Marks were born during the first half of Milland's career, with the latter now remembered more as a writer than a performer, none achieved the cinematic success Milland enjoyed. The only modern-day actor listed, Rhodri Meilir, was born towards the end of Milland's career and has predominantly appeared in Welsh language parts.[1]

Expanding beyond the acting profession, Culturenet Cymru, a Welsh Assembly-funded body based at the National Library of Wales in Aberystwyth, conducted a poll to determine the one hundred most famous people from Wales. The output, a book titled *100 Welsh Heroes* (Coleman et al. 2004), has Burton listed at number five, thus making him the top-listed performer, followed by Zeta-Jones at thirteen and Hopkins at forty-four. On a more micro level, Wikipedia's page for Port Talbot has a section on notable people born in the area, listing several performers and sportspeople past and present, including Hopkins and footballer Rhys Taylor, who was born in Milland's hometown of Neath in 1990.[2] Milland does not appear on either list; his absence from popular discussions of Welsh cinematic performances, alongside academic and encyclopedic discourses, is striking and suggests that even the Welsh do not celebrate Milland as they do Burton or Hopkins. This parallels actress Deborah Kerr's "English Rose" status and upper-class accent conflicting with her Scottish heritage, thus suggesting a set of class-driven assumptions. Similarly, perhaps due to Milland consistently being given upper-class roles, especially early in Hollywood, Welsh or working-class Brits in general could identify with him much less than they could with Burton and Baker.

While Milland's national identity is habitually overlooked in discussions of the actor, when he is mentioned in scholarly or general accounts of film history, the focus tends to be on *The Lost Weekend*. Indeed, this is the only film Milland discusses at length in his memoir, understandably so since his stark portrayal of an alcoholic won him not only the Academy Award but critical and commercial praise and a wider audience. While some may remember Milland for this role, others might be familiar with the film, especially its innovation (such as the shot of the shadow of the bottle hidden in the ceiling lamp), but struggle to recall the leading actor's name. While the film often appears in explorations of director Wilder's work, references to Milland are frequently brief within these accounts. Likewise, although he has the lead roles in *Ministry of Fear* and *Dial M for Murder* (Alfred Hitchcock, 1954), films which still receive academic attention, both are regarded as "director's films," therefore typically explored in terms of Lang's and Hitchcock's respective bodies of work. Moreover, Milland's costar in the latter is the much more celebrated Grace Kelly (later Princess Grace of Monaco), and he tends to receive a passing reference if he is mentioned at all. While Milland's characterizations provide the foundation for the action to revolve around, as is true for many of his other (long neglected) films, he is habitually and curiously left out of these conversations.

WELSH BEGINNINGS

Milland constructs a romantic view of his early years in the small South Wales mining village of Neath[3] in his memoir, idyllically declaring he was born "on a mountain called Cymla" (1974: 8).[4] Calling the town's Castle Hotel "quite old" back in 1974, the website for this luxurious thirty-room hotel and wedding venue now uses its age to advantage by boasting of being steeped in history.[5] While recent publicity hints that Lord Nelson and Lady Hamilton were regular visitors to the hotel, the mid-twentieth century celebrity couple Elizabeth Taylor and Richard Burton are known to have frequented the hotel. While linking Burton to his Welsh roots, this simultaneously suggests strong parallels between historical royalty and modern film stars.[6]

Although born in a picturesque location, Milland experienced a challenging childhood and lacked a close relationship with either parent. His mother and father separated when he was twelve, and he was sent to live on his Aunt Luisa's farm, where he remained for six years and called his "private paradise [. . .] my base, my *querencia*"[7] (1974: 35). She bred hackneys and Welsh cobs, and Milland became an expert horseman, eventually enrolling at a horsemanship school run by retired officer Major Ramsey, where he learned professional skills crucial to his future employment in the cavalry and cinema.

For reasons not explained, his mother took his three sisters with her when moving in with relatives in Cardigan, almost seventy miles away, but left her son behind.[8] Proclaiming his mother "flighty and coquettish," preoccupied with good manners and her reputation in the community, although not explicitly stated, her marriage split would undoubtedly have caused gossip in the village and may have been a crucial reason why she moved away while his father remained. Viewing his father as neither cruel nor harsh, just incredibly quiet, Milland assumed him "an incurable romantic" who was a little afraid, and perhaps ashamed, of his emotions (1974: 18), the very thing that Milland was later required to develop as an actor.[9] As a working-class man employed within the overtly homosocial environment of a Welsh village steel mill at the turn of the twentieth century (Evans 2000: 20–23; Davies 2006: 637), his father would no doubt have felt obliged to hide his emotions behind a manly façade. He had earlier proven his manliness as a young hussar in the Boer War, taking part in the historical triumph of May 17, 1890, with the relief of Mafeking in Cape Colony,[10] which marked a massive victory for Britain. This links to Milland's assertion that his father consistently sported a "fierce cavalry" mustache, which sounds similar to those Milland wore in several of his early Hollywood films (*Way for a Sailor* [Sam Wood, 1930], *Ambassador Bill* [Sam Taylor, 1931], and *Bolero* [Wesley Ruggles, 1934]), but which detracted from his youthful good looks, making him look older and less attractive than he really was. Although Milland does not comment on this association, it is an interesting point to consider, especially given his early separation from his father and that both served in the cavalry during their youth.[11]

Lacking stability, Milland attended several schools over the next few years and obtained jobs in a coal mine and steel mill—typical occupations for working-class men in the Welsh valleys—but his father found out and sent him back to Luisa's farm. At fifteen, he enrolled at King's College, Cardiff, and claims to have enjoyed his time there for two reasons: blonde student Dorothy Taylor and typing teacher Miss Bassett. Taking shorthand and typing classes to impress them, he eventually achieved eighty words a minute in the former and forty in the latter. We could view this as the first time Milland tried to impress an "audience," as he would soon do when on parade with the Royal Horse Guards and later in the cinema. Moreover, a typewriter proves crucial to his highest success in film, *The Lost Weekend*. He also proclaims to have developed a "fantastic memory," with the ability to read and perfectly memorize ten pages of a script in five minutes (1974: 41), an ideal attribute for an actor. His *Something to Live For* (George Stevens, 1952) costar Joan Fontaine confirms this, stating that not only did they both have photographic memories but could retain lines read aloud to them. She recalls dialogue director Ivan Moffat informing them of script changes just before the day's shooting. The actors were playing gin rummy and requested Moffat read the new lines out, but when he accused them of not listening when Milland shouted "gin" after ten pages, they both recited his words flawlessly (1978: 227).

Paralleling his mother's reasons for leaving home, Milland declares feeling "dissatisfied and restless," longing to go somewhere and do "anything that was different." Successfully passing the entrance exams for the University of Wales in Cardiff, he attended school until the following summer but had no desire to return, leading to "a year of aimlessness" (1974: 49–51). Turning eighteen in 1925, Milland was 6'2" and, to use his own words, as thin as "a tuning fork" when he decided to join the cavalry. His father advised him to join one of the two regiments of the Household Cavalry and, while the Horse Guards was harder to get into than the Life Guards, it had more elegance and class, components which later proved vital to Milland's screen image. Writing a glowing reference to the colonel of the Horse Guards, Major Ramsey advised Milland that he should cover the minimum twelve-year commitment by signing up for four years' active service and eight in reserve. Given the restless nature of his youth, Ramsey perhaps sensed that after four years he may wish to do something else, and Milland later declared him "a wise man" (1974: 52–53). Passing the physical examination in Newport, Monmouthshire, around thirty miles from his home, Milland was called for a three-day interview and examination at the barracks in Albany Street, London. He was accepted and asked to begin at once, thus beginning a new life in England's cultural capital.

Despite leaving his Welsh base and only ever visiting sporadically, Milland's memoir is awash with discussions of Welsh locations, culture, specialty food, legends and myths; his background potentially surprising readers who assumed he was English (or even American). Since scholarly texts on Welsh stars and cinema are extremely limited, I now explore these works and propose what they may inform us about films made in or about Wales while also examining Welsh stars from before and after Milland's time as a cinematic performer. This is preceded by a brief look at cinemagoing in Wales, another vastly understudied area but an important one in terms of the socioeconomic and historical contexts associated with Milland's national identity.

CINEMAGOING IN WALES

Two of the most prolific writers on Welsh cinema in recent years have been Helen Richards (2003; 2005) and Kate Woodward (2006; 2012; 2016). While Richards has written on cinemagoing and exhibition history in South Wales between 1900 to 1960, Woodford has explored more contemporary Welsh cinema, from the 1990s onwards, as well as Welsh art cinema. Exploring the history of filmgoing in Wales between 1918 and 1951, cinema's most popular era, Peter Miskell debates some of the social and economic contributions that cinema made to Welsh society during this time and how it functioned less as a national and more as a local institution in Wales, differentiating it from Britain more generally and making it more surprising that Milland remains so undercelebrated, particularly in Wales. In 1918, the earliest date of the study, Milland was still a child living in Wales, while the final date of 1951 marked the end of his "stardom" years in Hollywood, although not yet the midpoint of his screen career. Thus, while Miskell calls this cinema's period of "greatest appeal," this timeframe also involved considerable shifts in Milland's life and career.

Most cinemas in Britain were British-owned (Miskell 2006: 13), but the British film industry's recovery following World War I appeared grim. In the mid-1920s only 5 percent of films shown in British cinemas originated from Britain, while the majority of the others came from Hollywood (Evans 2000: 58). This rose substantially to 25 percent during the 1930s and 1940s, largely due to the British government introducing protective legislation in 1927 (Miskell 2006: 13), just two years before Milland embarked on his own, somewhat brief, British cinematic career. As Miskell suggests, the globalization of cinema really meant its Americanization, with Hollywood films giving Welsh audiences their first, and maybe only, experience of "American characters, lifestyles and fashions" (2006: 2). If audiences seemed attracted to these films because of their glamour, exoticism, and the foreign ideals they projected, it was for opposing reasons that individual cinemas were popular: they were "so conveniently accessible, familiar, *local*" (Miskell 2006: 2, italics in original). And yet, while working in Hollywood, Milland's star persona was consistently built around ideas of the glamour, exoticism, and foreignness of a generic Britain for American audiences, his voice in particular "giving him away" as British or "Other." Even when portraying American characters, he applied his own accent, occasionally clipping words to sound more Americanized. Certainly, the glamorous exoticism built around Milland as a suave and debonair upper-class Englishman from early on in his Hollywood career defied his origins as a steel mill worker's son from a South Wales mining village.

Wales was a popular location for Hollywood when it was preparing to establish its British markets in the classical era, primarily because of its picturesque locales, while British filmmakers, aware of competition from Hollywood and their lack of funds, began moving outside London to capture "authentic (and comparatively cheap) backdrops." Wales also saw a rise in filmmaking that corresponded with the growth in "cinema palaces," permanent buildings which replaced the old music halls (Berry 1994: 66). Cardiff, Wales's capital city, saw its first permanent cinema in 1909 when the 648-seat The Electric opened on Queen Street. With a population of 164,000, Cardiff had eight cinemas just a year later, when The Electric was refurbished. The moderately prosperous Swansea, the city closest to Milland's home, had only 70,000 residents but also had eight venues in 1910 (Richards 2003). Just four years later, Cardiff's had risen to twenty-one and Swansea's to nineteen. Attending the cinema was a fundamental source of entertainment and recreation for the generations striving to forget the horrors of World War I and the industrial depression (Evans 2000: 58). In February 1931, the opening of the 3,000-seat Plaza Cinema provided a crucial point for the city and included a lounge, two cafés and six shops. Proving enormously popular, within just two months there had been an attendance rate of 100,000, but this popularity led to increased ticket prices.[12] People began visiting the cinema two to three times weekly, thus leading to many more cinemas being built to cope with the demand (Evans 2000: 58).

Miskell queries whether the attraction of cinema, and Hollywood films more specifically, offers quantifiable proof that the Welsh working class were "as willing to embrace the popular entertainment of the new world as they were to rely on local or national traditions" (2006: 4). The 1920s was an important decade for cinema, becoming the predominant mode of "publicly consumed indoor entertainment in Wales" (Miskell 2006: 8), it was also a particularly important decade for Milland. Beginning the 1920s as a teenager called Reginald Alfred Jones, by the close of the decade not only had he adopted the name Ray(mond) Milland to enter the acting profession but had played the romantic lead in two British productions: *The Flying Scotsman* and *The Lady from the Sea* (Castleton Knight, 1929), and was soon to embark on a Hollywood career.

Cardiff Film Society was created in 1948, and in two years its membership had expanded from 400 to 800. Towards the end of Milland's career, a new generation of young filmmakers, who were sufficiently confident in exploring specifically Welsh subjects, began to "confront and debunk myths" (Berry 1994: 347; Stanton 2002). Indeed, the rarely seen 1986 documentary *It Ain't Necessarily So*, from English-born Graham Johns and Jeremy Bubb and released the year of Milland's death, "contrasted the respective public and private lives of Ray Milland and Paul Robeson and challenged perceptions" of the two actors (Berry 1994: 347).[13]

CHAPTER ONE

EARLY WELSH CINEMA

Berry finds it peculiar that, while being labeled both the greatest art form and the biggest mass entertainment of the twentieth century, cinema has long been ignored in discussions of Wales's cultural and Welsh literary tradition (1994: 9). Exploring a century of Welsh cinema, stretching back to the early shorts first seen as novelties and shown as "fairground diversions" or on "music-hall bills," he regretfully informs readers that nearly all the "fascinating silent films" about Wales made between 1886 and 1922 have been lost. Moreover, most postwar television was discarded since it was not thought important enough to be preserved (Richards 2003; Whitehead 2007).

Berry notes that during silent cinema's greatest years of 1912 to 1927, at least twenty-six fictional films, including fourteen or more features, were not only shot in Wales but also set there. Due in part to the industry's technical advancements, British and Hollywood studios were now able to "venture outside" their usual locations (1994: 66). Despite this initial "fertile period" for Wales, only three of the films, all produced by the same company in Cardiff, appear to have survived. Berry considers this loss of films "an indictment of the casual way the UK industry developed," since, for decades, "little intrinsic or aesthetic value" was given to film nor any consideration "in the principality itself" in relation to storage or building an archive. Indeed, he proclaims that Wales considered film valueless beyond its transient first-run box-office receipts (1994: 66).

The most significant of these early films was *A Welsh Singer* (Henry Edwards, 1915), the first feature film set in Wales to highlight the importance of education—especially an education in the English language—as a means of escape. Based on a novel by Welshman Allen Raine, it was directed by and starred Henry Edwards, and is noteworthy for featuring the screen debut of British actress Edith Evans. Several other films made around this time used the words "Welsh," "Wales," "Hills," or "Land" in their titles. Milland even declares in his memoir that he chose the stage name "Mill Land" after the land near his home, when he was told he could not have a name with three Ls, he changed it to "Milland."[14] Other titles include *The Little Welsh Girl* (Fred Paul, 1920), *Love in the Welsh Hills* (Bernard Dudley, 1921), and *Land of My Fathers* (Fred Rains, 1921). Thus, the frequent linking in film titles to the land and nationality strongly connotes typical representations of Wales as being full of rural spaces inhabited by ordinary, working-class people, a theme explored by Milland in his memoir when discussing his background. Again, this brings in ideas around class associations and that, despite his choice of stage name, Milland tends to portray higher-class characters without any real correlation to Wales.

Wales may have a long history and rich folklore (Williams 2003; Branston 2005; Perrins 2019), but Berry calls *The Last King of Wales* (George Ridgwell, 1921) "the only work which apparently attempted to treat Welsh historical legend" (1994: 75). Even here the leading players were English (Charles Ashton) and American (Malvina Longfellow). Surprisingly, Berry notes, the only surviving prewar feature film "of special Welsh interest [. . .] is, curiously enough, *Ivanhoe* (Herbert Brenon, 1913)." Directed by an Irishman and based on Scotsman Sir Walter Scott's novel of the same name, it was produced by Carl Laemmle's innovative IMP (Independent Moving Pictures), a forerunner to Universal, and used Chepstow Castle and its nearby countryside to represent the novel's locations (1994: 77). Scott's novel is actually based in England, thus further indicating the interchangeability of England and Wales in cinematic representations, a lack of distinction which is illustrated throughout much of Milland's (early) film career.

In the 1930s, an "unofficial but very effective code of film censorship" meant that companies were banned from recording the political activities of working-class communities and led filmmakers to focus instead on Welsh miners "as the epitome of the long-suffering working-classes" (Evans 2000: 58; Richards 2005). This resulted in mining becoming a major focus of films based in Wales, particularly those made by Hollywood (Whitehead 2007). Documentaries made in South Wales avoided reference to the area's politics and the miners' unions, instead depicting problems related to unemployment, while permitting "the unemployed to address the cameras" (Evans 2000: 58). Indeed, one of the best-known films to come out of this era was the 1937 documentary *Today We Live* (Ralph Bond and Ruby Grierson).

During the 1940s and 1950s, it was primarily due to its performers that Wales made a meaningful contribution to cinema, while film enjoyed "a postwar boom in the principality" (Berry 1994: 8). During the 1920s there were already 250 cinema buildings in Wales, but this increased to 315 by 1946, the year directly following Milland's Oscar win (Richards 2003). While filmgoers visited the cinema two and three times weekly, Burton, Baker and Rachel Roberts were vital in "helping the British cinema to slough off its middle-class past" (1994: 8). Berry declares 1945 to 1962 a time of "new realism" in British cinema, when the three aforementioned players conveyed a more "trenchant, acerbic British cinema," concentrating on "the factory and solid working-class backdrops, with fairly raw idiomatic language of common coinage" rather than the middle-class persona of the Welsh performers of the 1930s and 1940s (1994: 252). Furthermore, this period "proved crucial, not merely in establishing a new breed of star," as embodied by Baker and Roberts, but in "projecting images of the Welsh which lingered to the 1990s" (1994: 201), the decade in which Berry was writing.

In his exploration of Welsh genre films made between 1948 and 1962, Berry discusses *Tiger Bay* (J. Lee Thompson, 1959), *Valley of Song* (Gilbert Gunn, 1953), *The Small Voice* (Fergus McDonell, 1948), and *Circle of Danger* (1951), the latter starring Milland. While Berry suggests that French director Jacques Tourneur "brought nothing distinct" to the film (1994: 231), the contemporary American publication the *Daily Bulletin* declared the release, originally titled *White Heather*, "an outstanding foreign film" (Anon. 1950: 23). Although Milland never portrayed a Welshman on screen, Berry suggests this film has "a certain curiosity and irony" since it marked his first role in his native country (1994: 231). Milland plays an American perplexed by British money as he ineptly counts out coins to pay his cab outside the War Office in Whitehall, London. There is also a hybridity to his character's name, Clay Douglas, with its American-encoded first name and Scottish surname with Gaelic origins, as he visits England, Scotland, and Wales for the first time in an attempt to discover how his brother died. While *Monthly Film Bulletin* declared that, with "naïve good faith" Milland portrayed "the type of American for whom all English girls are supposed to fall" (Berry 1994: 231)—as indeed Patricia Roc's Elspeth Graham does—the actor's Welsh roots, British accent, and general demeanor significantly complicates this proposal. Indeed, upon viewing the film, it seems implausible that, with no attempt to disguise his natural speaking voice, his character is perplexed by British currency and customs.

While the film's locations encompass various parts of England, Scotland, and Wales, there are four noteworthy places Clay visits in relation to Milland's own biography. Taking these in chronological order in terms of the actor's life trajectory, Clay travels to the Welsh coal mine Coellyd Colliery to converse with the miners (figure 1.1). In 1908, the year directly following Milland's birth, this mine employed 231 men, 96 of whom worked underground. Given the actor's later declaration that Wales was "crawling" with his relatives, all named "Jones" (1974: 18), since the manager at this time was a man called Griffith Jones, it is not inconceivable that the two were related.[15] Moreover, Clay also visits the Windsor Colliery coal mine, located in the village of Abertridwr, Caerphilly in Glamorgan, the place of Milland's birth. Opened in 1895, it closed in 1986, just after Milland's own demise. During Clay's visit to London, location footage shows the changing of the guard at Windsor Castle (figure 1.2), an important ceremony Milland had

Figure 1.1. Milland's American character is given a note to visit a Welsh coal mine located near the actor's birthplace in *Circle of Danger* (Jacques Tourneur, 1951).

Figure 1.2. The Changing of the Guard in *Circle of Danger* (Jacques Tourneur, 1951), a ceremony Milland took part in during his time with the Royal Horse Guards in London.

been part of during his former career as a soldier in the Royal Horse Guards in the 1920s, as is discussed presently. Clay also visits Covent Garden, the location where Milland met his first theatrical performers and changed his career path forever, as explored in chapter two. Milland looks relaxed and at ease as he navigates these various locations, such as London's Hammersmith Broadway and Belgravia, areas that the actor would have undoubtedly known well. Indeed, when Clay ironically points out that the countryside reminds him "of somewhere," viewers familiar with Milland's own past may suggest it reminds him of home.

HOLLYWOOD'S "WALES"

Evans declares the 1920 conception of the Miners' Welfare Fund, which gave financial support for the purchase of materials, seating and projection equipment, the manifestation of "Cinemaization" on a substantial scale (2000: 58). Miners' halls began to operate cinemas which mostly showed films on sport but also some concerning Spain, "in an effort to promote their Spanish Aid initiatives" (Evans 2000: 58). As Evans highlights, although these miners' institutes appeared to present an independent cinema throughout the coalfield, it was not possible for them to "challenge the might of the commercial sector," so in the 1930s these miners' cinemas were required to base their programs on productions from America (2000: 58). Proving their popularity, in the 1930s there were more miners' cinemas in South Wales than in all of Britain's other mining regions combined. In Milland's home county of Glamorgan there were twenty-five miners' cinemas in 1940, twenty-one of which were controlled by workmen's committees. Thus, perhaps another reason for a lack of discussion of Milland in Wales is that he was working in Hollywood during this time when "local communities often reacted forcefully against the perceived cultural and social threat of the American screen" (Evans 2000: 59; Richards 2005).

American companies began setting up studios in London, and by the end of the 1930s were producing social realism films. Films set in Wales but made by US studios created tension between the typical glossy Hollywood productions and depictions of working-class Wales (Whitehead 2007). However, Berry sees these films as "fascinating" and meriting "serious discussion in any history of the Welsh cinema" (1994: 5), including *The Citadel* (King Vidor, 1938), starring Englishman Robert Donat and the American Rosalind Russell, and *Proud Valley* (Pen Tennyson, 1940), starring New Jersey-born Paul Robeson. Berry suggests that both films displayed characteristics of urban life not previously seen on cinema screens (1994: 145). Arguing that

The Citadel is the first of a series of Welsh films which illustrated "the conditions and turmoil in urban south Wales," it is also the first to allude to "the high incidence of silicosis or allied dust and lung disease from the pits" (1994: 150). *Proud Valley* was almost the sole British film of the era to showcase a Black performer, Robeson, as "a sympathetic working-class lead" who proves his valor before forfeiting his own life to save men trapped in the mine (Berry 1994: 166).

Berry asserts that any worthwhile study of films about Wales is obliged to mention the "handful of fascinating mining features" made between 1938 and 1949 (1994: 160). When asked for a definition of Welshness on film, he concludes that most people outside of Wales note the "potent views of industrialized mining Wales and its stoic heroes" presented in *The Citadel*, *Proud Valley*, and *How Green Was My Valley* (1941). These films have "borne the weight of Welsh folk-memory and created a mythic Wales" and are "unlikely to be easily dislodged" from cinemagoers' minds (1994: 160; Whitehead 2007). The most successful of these, *How Green Was My Valley*, won five out of its ten Academy Award nominations, but is the film "most often pilloried" by the Welsh (Berry 1994: 8). Indeed, the only Welsh player in a key role is Rhys Williams, while the primary cast comprises of the Irish Maureen O'Hara and Barry Fitzgerald, Scotsman Donald Crisp, and Canadian Walter Pidgeon. Thus, the most popular or influential films made about Wales during the 1930s to 1940s were made by outsiders who "conditioned the way people outside Wales saw the nation" (Berry 1994: 5; Perrins 2019). For pursuing its inspiration in the era's authentic urban Wales and not instead, "some writer's or Hollywood director's fanciful misconception," Berry urges that Jill Craigie's *Blue Scar* (1949) deserves "a place in the pantheon" (1994: 160) as being among the most important "Welsh" films, one of the few to explore nationalization and which was made by "almost the only British female director" working in the UK at that time (1994: 172). The film explores social issues not only from a working-class perspective, but "challenged the socialists' euphoria about the successful battle for nationalization of the pits and hinted at the schism in the miners' rank in the battle for a five-day week" (Berry 1994: 4; Branston 2005). Being British, Craigie was geographically closer to the Welsh valleys than the American Ford, and her film avoids the sheen of the former; however, having been born in England, she was still an "outsider." In a similar vein, *The Corn is Green* (Irving Rapper, 1945), starring American actress Bette Davis, and *Last Days of Dolwyn* (Emlyn Williams, 1949) are melodramas which explore the Welsh language, cultural tensions, and Wales's dependency on England (and vice versa); each offering "fascinating," but partial, views of the industrial experience of Wales (Berry 1994: 160; Fevre and Thompson 1999).

REPRESENTING "WELSHNESS" ON SCREEN

Cinematic representations of Welshmen are often stereotyped as "good-hearted but gullible miners" (*A Run for Your Money* [Charles Frend, 1949]); "parochial wiseacres given to dispensing local saws" (*The Long Arm* [Charles Frend, 1956]); or "the epitome of the little man so beloved of Ealing and usually exemplified by Mervyn Johns" (*The Captive Heart* [Basil Dearden, 1946]). Berry notes that "of course" the Welsh on-screen are often musical, alongside being "homebodies," "nature-loving and generally law-abiding" (1994: 214).

Throughout his seminal volume on cinema in Wales, Berry mentions several Welsh performers, some of whom also worked in Hollywood, such as Ivor Novello, Richard Burton, Stanley Baker, Anthony Hopkins, and Milland. Highlighting the important "creative contributions" Welsh performers have made to both British and international cinema, he suggests that Baker, most specifically, played a "crucial role in changing the emphasis in British cinema (and the way it was perceived)" (1994: 10). A similar argument can be made for Milland in Hollywood since *The Lost Weekend* is viewed as the first serious screen portrayal of alcoholism. However, Milland's character is an affluent American living off his brother and without a job other than being a "writer" who produces no work. Whereas the "more Welsh" Baker, in both his star persona and film roles, provided a much stronger connection to audiences with his overt working-class associations.

The prolific character actor E. E. Clive was born in Monmouth in 1879 and worked extensively in both Britain and Hollywood. He often portrayed stereotypical British butlers, again blurring the lines between English and Welsh, and featured alongside Milland in *Bulldog Drummond Escapes* (James P. Hogan, 1937). Likewise, Lyn Harding, born in 1867 in Newport, appeared on the stage for four decades before moving into film. Making his screen debut in 1920, he soon starred as Henry VIII opposite Marion Davies as Mary Tudor in *When Knighthood Was in Flower* (Robert G. Vignola, 1922) at Paramount. Berry notes that in the 1930s and 1940s a "clutch of fellow countrymen [...] also featured regularly in rewarding and significant roles" (1994: 111). He highlights Emlyn Williams, Mervyn Johns (father of actress Glynis Johns), Naunton Wayne, and Roger Livesey in Britain and, listed on his own, proving his pioneer status, Milland in Hollywood (1994: 111). Other Welsh performers Berry discusses include Meredith Edwards, Donald Houston, Hugh Griffith, and Clifford Evans, stating of the latter that "no Welsh actor conveyed self-reliance and stolidity on screen better" (1994: 224). Other members of the "repertory company" were Roddy Hughes, Ronald Lewis, and Glyn Houston, while Prestatyn-born Peggy Cummins was the only

Welsh-born actress to work at Ealing under Michael Balcon (Berry 1994: 226). During cinema's silent era, Berry suggests that only two Welshmen could be confidently defined as "bona fide stars": Ivor Novello and Gareth Hughes (1994: 90).

Despite his Welsh origins, Novello, born David Ivor Davies in Cardiff in 1893, was promoted as an exotic "Latin lover" type like contemporaries Rudolph Valentino and Ramon Novarro; all were born in the 1890s and shared a dark beauty popular in 1920s Hollywood. Although he died at the relatively early age of fifty-eight, Novello was not only a popular actor during his lifetime, but a dramatist, singer, and composer. Like many from Wales, Novello came from a musical family. His name is kept alive through the Ivor Novello Awards for songwriting and composing, which have been presented since 1955, while several biographies have been written on Novello across the decades (Noble 1951; Harding 1987; Webb [1999] 2005; Slattery-Christy 2006), along with a book-length academic study (Williams 2003).

Virtually the same age as Novello, the other "bona fide" silent star Gareth Hughes was born in 1894 in Llanelli, Dyfed, less than twenty miles from Milland's birthplace, and died in 1965. While Berry considered Hughes a "now obscure" actor in 1994 (90), the subsequent years have seen Hughes's legacy beginning to receive more recognition. In 2000, Nant Films produced the documentary *Gareth Hughes* (Wil Aaron), written by Stephen Lyons and broadcast on S4C in Welsh and, less than a decade later, Kelvin Guy made the film *In Search of Gareth Hughes* (2009), which had an extremely limited release. In 2000, a memorial bronze plaque calling Hughes a "film star and missionary" was erected in Parc Howard Museum, Llanelli, and in 2010 a blue plaque was mounted at his family home at 38 Princess Street.[16] Thus, Milland's "film star" predecessors Novello and Hughes both have a blue plaque at their birthplace (Novello has additional blue plaques in London), as does his successor Richard Burton, but, despite being Wales's first Best Actor Academy Award winner, Milland is curiously without one.

Arguably Wales's most famous actor, but whose career trajectory also includes some questionable additions, Burton was born in 1925 in the small village of Pontrhydyfen in Glamorgan, Port Talbot, the same county borough as Milland. Although belonging to the generation directly following Milland's, Burton's longtime battle with alcoholism contributed to his early death at the age of fifty-eight in 1984, two years before Milland's own demise. As his brother Graham Jenkins notes, Burton spoke only Welsh until he was six years old since the family's "patch of South Wales remained loyal to its mother tongue" (1988: 23). Later, during his time in the RAF, Burton would engage in physical fights in bars with other servicemen either because they were not in the RAF or because they were not Welsh; occasionally it was because they were from a different part of Wales (Jenkins 1988: 50).

Beginning his career as an actor on the British stage, Burton was tremendously serious about his craft and portrayed several major Shakespearean characters throughout his career, including Hamlet and Othello, but saw playing King Lear as an obligation since he felt this was the only interesting Welshman whom Shakespeare ever wrote about, noting that when Lear "lets off steam, when he really lets go, he is utterly Welsh" (Jenkins 1988: 220), apparently something Burton could relate to, while again linking him to ideas around Welshness and masculinity. In the early 1960s, Burton found himself suddenly thrust into the limelight and became an international celebrity overnight after the press revealed details of his torrid love affair with Elizabeth Taylor during the making of *Cleopatra* (Joseph L. Mankiewicz, 1963).[17] Milland never became a celebrity in the same way, his "forgotten" status potentially due in part to his relatively quiet private life, while it is Burton's volatile relationship with Taylor and his alcoholism, rather than his film work, that has allowed him to remain in the public consciousness (for more on stars' private lives and enduring stardom, see Kelly 2019). However, proving his critical accomplishments as a screen actor, between 1953 and 1978 Burton was nominated for an impressive seven Academy Awards, although he was never the recipient of the coveted award, while Milland won for his only nomination.

Despite his instantaneous global fame and extensive work in Hollywood, Burton retained a strong connection to Wales throughout his life, thus enabling him to stand apart from his English peers in Britain and Hollywood; I argue that Milland would have successfully done the same if he had been given the chance at the start of his career. Indeed, Milland discusses Wales and Welsh traditions favorably and in explicit detail throughout his memoir, making it noteworthy that Hollywood immediately removed his national identity as a working-class Welshman. Indeed, most of those I engaged with throughout the research and writing process informed me, when they had heard of Milland at all, that they had no idea he was Welsh, an aspect of his persona long underrepresented, as explored in this chapter .

Although wishing to be buried in Wales, Jenkins notes that Burton's widow, Sally, had her husband buried in Switzerland for tax reasons. However, a memorial service took place at Bethel Chapel in South Wales on August 11, 1984; Jenkins recalls a simple display of red carnations resting on a Welsh flag beneath the pulpit while the minister spoke of Burton's love of Wales, noting that he never forgot his roots or the "rock from which he was hewn" (1988: 244). Suggesting his own restlessness and lack of firm base in either Wales or Hollywood, when Milland died in Torrance, California, he had instructed there be no funeral and his ashes be scattered in the Pacific Ocean, which they were.

Alongside Milland and Burton, Pontrhydyfen was also the birthplace of Burton's *Zulu* (Cy Endfield, 1964) costar Ivor Emmanuel, while Stanley Baker, who had once been Burton's understudy on stage, also hailed from Glamorgan. According to David Berry, Baker was perhaps British cinema's first "virile artisan, proletarian hero and anti-hero." Worlds away from the "likeable but insular, naïve or gullible" Welshmen depicted by Meredith Edwards and Mervyn Johns in the 1940s, Baker and Burton represented a certain "strain of Welshness, constantly playing or suggesting the abrasive loner with a turbulent, dark side" (Berry 1994: 200). Thus, representation of class and masculinity were vital to these performers and far removed from the suave upper-class roles handed to Milland when he arrived in Hollywood. Baker was important to British cinema; his identity as a tough working-class figure on-screen was far removed from the upper-class, suave persona that Milland was often required to display in Hollywood. Andrew Spicer calls Baker "the actor who was a potentially viable British tough guy" whose "working-class South Wales physicality had never allowed him to play gentlemanly leads and his success had come from playing brutes" (1999: 85). Interestingly, both Baker and Milland hailed from working-class mining villages in Glamorgan; Baker being born in Ferndale in the Rhondda Valley, only a forty-minute drive from Milland's home. Moreover, like many men living in this location, Baker's father was a coal miner while Milland's was a steel worker. Physically, however, in his youth Milland was more delicate: he was tall, slim, and had moved to Central London to join the Royal Horse Guards in his late teens, thereby going through rigorous training to improve his posture on horseback and on foot.

Although portraying working-class characters in the two British films he made before going to America (a train fireman in *The Flying Scotsman* and a fisherman in *The Lady from the Sea*), Milland was trained in diction to help him lose his Welsh accent and cast as several upper-crust gentlemen and even royalty during his first years in Hollywood. As Berry indicates, before the 1950s, the most successful Welsh actors were the ones predominantly noted for prototypically English roles and mannerisms, such Naunton Wayne's "dapper, sometimes dyspeptic and frequently bemused sidekick"; the "booming nasal delivery and straight-backed military bearing" of Roger Livesey; and "ex-Guardsman" Milland, who was "adept at playing American or British heroes but usually only if they occupied the higher social rungs" (2014: 252). Milland certainly did not occupy the "higher social rungs" in his British productions, although during his initial years in Hollywood, he tended to be cast as upper-class characters in a place where being British was viewed as more exotic and exciting. This changed with the popularity of Baker and Roberts, whose films exemplified working-class stories that cinematic audiences tended to identify with more.

Writing in 1994, after the reduction of UK film production, Berry notes that a minority of Welsh performers were finding steady work in substantial film roles, with Anthony Hopkins "towering above all others in reputation and recent box-office clout" (Berry 1994: 420). A few years prior to this, Hopkins had won his first Best Actor Academy Award for *The Silence of the Lambs* (Jonathan Demme, 1991) and the "ultimate acclaim" of his profession as he "grew in stature" (Berry 1994: 420). The same can be said of Milland forty-five years earlier when his Oscar for *The Lost Weekend* put him in the record books as the first Welshman to win the award. Moreover, while Hopkins's win was unusual given the little amount of time he is on-screen, as is discussed in chapter six, Milland is almost ever-present in *The Lost Weekend*: he is required to simultaneously captivate and repulse the audience as his character experiences a variety of physical and emotional states, all expertly crafted by the actor.

SPORT, MUSIC, AND WELSH NATIONAL IDENTITY

The subtitle of Miskell's book on cinemas in Wales, *Pulpits, Coal Pits and Fleapits*, refers respectively to the "chapel-going, Nonconformist, Liberal Wales"; the central "industrial economy [. . .] peopled by a large working class" predominantly supporting the Labour Party; and the unflattering name given to early cinemas to describe their lack of hygiene (2006: 3). As Miskell notes, cinema neither promoted class consciousness and political activism nor celebrated Welsh identity, culture, and language, and was depicted as being secular, commercial, and mostly American entertainment. Consequently, the popularity of cinemagoing in Wales indicates that the cultural values generally associated with Liberal or Labour Wales were not as widespread as they may have appeared (Fevre and Thompson 1999; Barlow et al. 2005). Although there remained an interest in the more traditional areas of music, sport, and politics for the Welsh people, these were "not all-pervasive" (Miskell 2006: 4).

Cinema was just one form of entertainment during a time of extreme economic and social stress, and by the start of the twentieth century rugby had already become "something of a national obsession" (Miskell 2006: 6), becoming "the game of the masses and the classes, and a focus for national pride and expression" when it arrived in Wales in the 1870s (Evans 2000: 60). Organized sport became "an important outlet for the depressed regions of Wales, acting as a focus for national sentiment and a safety valve in turbulent times" (Evans 2000: 62). Towards the end of the nineteenth century, football, also known as soccer, made a hasty advancement throughout Wales, with its first professional team in the 1910s and numerous triumphs in the 1920s, including Cardiff City winning the FA (Football Association) cup in 1927 (Evans 2000: 61–62). Football has recently overtaken rugby as the most popular sport in Wales, but during the Depression years, many clubs were compelled to drop out of the leagues. With two-thirds of the local workforce unemployed, people watched the team train but could not afford the admission charges to see the games (Evans 2000: 62). Cricket also gained prominence in Wales during the inter-war years, and in 1921 Glamorgan entered the first-class county championships.

In the early twentieth century, the expansion of sport functioned as both a method of "self-expression and entertainment," and the focus of local and community identity (Evans 2000: 60). Thus, for most Welshmen sporting achievements were a meaningful and "vigorous representation of identity" (Evans 2000: 60). Indeed, rugby and boxing provided Wales with local heroes, with Miskell declaring that they held "a powerful grip on men's imagination," particularly when a local man was competing for a world title. Although Milland played rugby in school at Radyr and had taken part in boxing tournaments while in the army, his success as a leading Hollywood star, despite his "world champion" status as an Academy Award winner, does not seem to have created the same interest and pride from the men in the Welsh Valleys as the more virile sportsmen or more masculine actors, like Stanley Baker or Richard Burton, did. This could, in part, be related to acting still being viewed at the time as an occupation primarily for women, or that film acting was not a tough enough profession to hold the interest of the physical laborers, who would no doubt find sportsmen more relatable and acceptable to support in such a homosocial environment (Evans 2000: 20–23; Davies 2006: 637). Moreover, since Milland portrayed a range of upper-class Englishmen with money, breeding, and education in his early cinematic roles, he would have been much less identifiable with working-class Welsh audiences than if he had been a sportsman, or even played sportsmen or working-class characters on-screen.

Aside from sport, music is the cultural activity most associated with Wales (Miskell 2006: 7; Fevre and Thompson 1999). Milland explores this topic in detail near the start of his memoir, declaring that every Welsh street had several houses with brass plaques advertising its resident as a music tutor, while all boys in Wales were required to undertake music lessons, another kind of performance. Jenkins's[18] book on Richard Burton frequently alludes to his brother's unflinching affection for his home country and its strong associations with music and sport, while a published collection of the actor's diary entries contains the words "Wales" 232 times, "Welsh" 420 times, "sport" 104 times, "rugby" 142 times, "football" 170 times, and makes mention of "music," "singing," and "song" a total of 238 times (Burton 2012). Highlighting rugby and not acting as Burton's first love, Jenkins proposed rugby as "the highest expression of Welsh culture," while Burton was "suited to the game by build and by temperament" (1988: 26). Likewise, when cast in a stage production of *Camelot*, Burton was "appalled" when informed he need not sing in the role, declaring that a Welshman in a musical who does not sing would be classed as a traitor back home (1988: 113). Although not a musical star, Milland appeared in a handful of musical films. He performs a dance number with Anna Neagle in *Irene* (Herbert Wilcox, 1940), plays the piano in several films, and portrays musicians in some non-musicals, including *The Uninvited* (Lewis Allen, 1944). In *Let's Do It Again!* (Alexander Hall, 1953), a musical remake of *The Awful Truth* (Leo McCarey, 1937), Milland portrays a composer who plays piano and drums, and does some (limited) singing, while music is also significant in *Lady in the Dark* (Mitchell Leisen, 1944). The female leads Neagle, Jane Wyman, and Ginger Rogers, respectively, execute most of the musical numbers, however, with Neagle and Rogers being celebrated dancers. Milland's contribution is less active, aligning him with the audience and allowing him to adopt the "male gaze" at the female performer's body while she dances, thus placing him in a more masculine and dominant position. Although Milland slow danced with women in several films, it was not as spectacle as in *Irene*. Furthermore, his piano playing was not a performance for the nondiegetic audience like pianists José Iturbi, Oscar Levant, or Chico Marx. It helped to demonstrate that Milland could do "a bit of everything," allowing him to be comfortably cast in various roles while implying that he had no true specialism or specific talent he was known for.

(THE LOSS OF) A COMPLEX NATIONAL IDENTITY

Steve Blandford (2000) notes both an "orientalism" of Wales as an "exotic other" and the sense of it being absorbed into England and becoming invisible. The latter is certainly true of Milland's cultural identity since, as noted, rather than playing up his distinct identity as a Welshman in Hollywood, he was most often cast as Englishmen and Americans, nationalities represented by many other contemporaneous actors, with any sense of his Welsh lineage eradicated. Thus, while Milland's 1974 memoir is rich in tales of his childhood in a small mining village, his recollections of speaking the Welsh language, and discussions of the country's ancient and mystical folklore, many audience members, or even studio personnel, may have been unaware of his true national identity.

While Alan Phillips's *North Wales Cinemas: Past and Present* (2018) is littered with errors, it does include some noteworthy archival photographs of North Wales's cinemas during their heyday, alongside images depicting the premises today, which makes for some unappealing comparisons.[19] Between the 1960s and 1980s, many buildings were converted into bingo halls, some later becoming nightclubs and several now occupied by either supermarkets (primarily Co-op and Tesco) or Wetherspoons pubs. This is a sad situation since, as Miskell points out, cinemas were as central to Welsh communities in the early twentieth century as chapels or miners' institutes. The sort of society cinema epitomized at this time is "American Wales," a term coined by Alfred Zimmern in 1921, which suggests America's version of Wales rather than authentic Wales (a similar argument can be made for Hollywood's interpretation of Scotland in *Brigadoon* [Vincente Minnelli, 1954]). Miskell reiterates that Hollywood's mass appeal in Wales is "compelling evidence of the existence of an 'American Wales,'" with film-going experience reminding us that it was "at least as firmly rooted in the culture of Wales as it was of America" (2006: 187).

Welsh-born filmmaker Christopher Monger emphasizes the magnitude of the size and scope of US cinema, asking how other countries' filmmakers can "compete for screen-time, let alone an audience"; more specifically, he ponders how a "tiny country like Wales [can] hope to make an impression" (2000: 7). Likewise, Ruth Elroy (2016) presents Wales as a leading example of minor cinema. A similar argument can be made for a Welsh actor like Milland, whose initial move to Hollywood in 1930 meant he was competing for roles with a variety of new and established performers, of both US and European descent, who were already working there. When Monger refers to himself as "an Anglo-Welshman in LA" and declares that in 1999 he felt "excluded and invisible" (2000: 9), we can only imagine how Milland must have felt almost seventy years earlier as one of the first British, and specifically Welsh, expats of Hollywood's early sound cinema.

Monger calls it vital to explore the people and conditions which created national and international cinema, its intended and actual audiences, those who feel represented by it, and those who do not (2000: 10). When a talent scout for MGM invited Milland to Hollywood from the UK, the studio already had an international array of actors, with European stars such as the Swedish Greta Garbo high on its roster. Although Milland's Welsh origins offered the chance to tap into a national identity mostly unexplored by Hollywood and boasting a long and complex history, including its own language and wealth of legends and folklore, he was never cast as a Welshman on-screen.

AN (UN)COMMON WELSHMAN

In her 1975 memoir, Milland's *The Bachelor Father* (Robert Z. Leonard, 1931) costar Marion Davies refers to Milland as "very pleasant" and recalls him talking about "England and Ireland" (1975: 129). While this apparent confusion between Wales and Ireland is understandable from an American's perspective, especially when writing over forty years after the event, even the contemporary British press was confused about which of the four nations the actor came from. *Picturegoer* in the 1930s alternated between calling him English, Irish, and Welsh across the span of several issues. Suggesting that audiences may not buy into his multiple screen characterizations of upper-class Brits if they knew the truth, it highlights that the "true story" of emerging stars provided to the press by studios perhaps was also greatly embellished (Slide 2010).

In December 1936, *Picturegoer* referred to Milland as a "handsome young Englishman" (6), while less than a year later, the same publication carried a biography filled with inaccuracies which asserted that Milland was born in Drogheda, Ireland (1937a: 32). Reprinted several times in subsequent issues, the profile further incorrectly states that Milland was born in 1905 (it was 1907), that he was 5'11" (he was 6'2"), and that he had dark eyes (they were blue). The erroneous statement that his birth name was Jack Millane (1937a: 32) is accompanied by the only accuracies of the profile: the color of his hair (dark) and the name of his wife (Muriel), without which it may be presumed that these "facts" were attributed to Milland but belonged to another actor. What makes the errors particularly noteworthy is that just a month prior, the magazine had published a full-page article dedicated to Milland, in which Max Breen calls him "the young Welsh actor, now making good in Hollywood," while giving his height as a more accurate, but still not exact, 6'1" (1937: 21; Milland 1974: 52). As far back as May 1931, the US publication *Screenland* ran an article on performers they believed were heading for Hollywood stardom; above an image of Milland appears the heading "charge it to Irish luck!"; *Screenland* also states he was born in Ireland, this time with his birth year listed as 1906 (1931: 46).[20] Further highlighting Hollywood's tendency to subsume Welsh into English national identity, the same article refers to fellow Welshman Ivor Novello as an Englishman (1931: 39).

Breen's article also claims that while Milland was working as an extra in British cinema he went by the name "Spike Milland." However, none of his British films, nor those from the start of his Hollywood career, bill him as anything other than Ray or Raymond Milland. Milland's memoir does not mention his ever being called "Spike" but goes into detail about the origins of his stage name, thus suggesting that "Ray(mond)" and "Milland" were paired together from the start. Remarkably, Breen then explores the confusion over Milland's origins, stating that "he seems to have been born in Neath, Glamorganshire, South Wales, and also in Drogheda, Ireland, his real name being Mullane or Millane," neither of which is confirmed by the author. Furthermore, while Breen states that we can discount that Milland was ever a juvenile on stage (1937: 21), six years previously the same publication had correctly noted that he had gained "stage and screen experience in London" before moving to Hollywood (1931a: 46). Breen also declares that despite rumors that Milland had run off to sea and "sailed round the world as deck-hand," he had, in reality, made only a few trips to Jersey and back on a potato boat (1931: 46). Neither version is exactly accurate.

While studying at Radyr, Milland was employed part-time as a messenger for a shipping company owned by his mother's cousins and located in the "wild and perilous dock area known as Tiger Bay" (Milland 1974: 41), a district covering Butetown and the Cardiff Docks. Milland recalls walking around the wharves reading the names of far-off places, such as Santos, Hong Kong, and Sydney, from the sterns. During his school summer holiday, he worked on one of the company's carriers, traveling to Piraeus, the port city of Athens, Greece, before transferring and traveling back along the north coast of Africa. His jobs included checking cargo lists and writing up advanced payments for the crew before they went ashore (Milland 1974: 42); thus, before boarding he knew he would shortly return to Wales. While it is true that Milland did sail (partway) across the world, it was a return trip arranged by his employer, not a rebellious escape. Milland's experience was vastly different from the oft-repeated, and hugely romanticized, story of Bristol-born Cary Grant running away to join the circus. Furthermore, while Breen suggests that this "global trip" was a story Milland had "fed" MGM (1937: 21), it would be more credible to propose that MGM "fed" the story to the public, since Breen's words suggest MGM's publicity department employed gullible and unworldly personnel, which was evidently far from the case (although perhaps as a fan magazine writer he did not want to admit this).

As Anthony Slide (2010) has explored, as well as controlling and manipulating the images of the performers it had under contract, MGM heavily censored fan magazine content about its performers before publication. Breen adds that Milland finally settled down to work at "his uncle's training stable," where he planned to ride in the Grand National (1937: 21). When Milland lived with his maiden aunt (there was no uncle), his height (which, even in his youth, was over six feet) would have made this profession, requiring a lifetime of commitment and training, a strange choice. However, on his aunt's farm he learned excellent horsemanship, which set him in good stead for getting into the prestigious Royal Horse Guards, an important part of his life that is surprisingly absent from Breen's article.

Potentially the most factual part is when the author notes that, even early on, Milland displayed "all the earmarks of a somebody" who "carried himself easily and with distinction," wore tails evidently purchased from London's Savile Row,[21] and possessed a voice of "pleasant timbre with a slight Welsh lilt to it" (Breen 1937: 21). Thus, at the end of a confusing and oddly inaccurate article, Breen praises Milland's star potential and labels him as (somewhat) Welsh. This is interesting since Breen notes both Milland's Welshness and "upper-class" signifiers that seem more associated with Englishness. Milland's voice was a vital component of his star appeal and was highlighted by a *Picturegoer* reader in a 1937 letter to the editor titled "Voice attraction" and signed "Milland Fan." The reader declares that "with the exception of English stage stars who have become film actors (e.g., John Gielgud) I think Ray Milland has the most pleasant and clearly pronounced speech in films," concluding that "after hearing so much American accent [sic] it is a relief to see a film with him in a chief part" (1937b: 28). This suggests that the reader liked the tone of his voice, making it distinct from his American counterparts, but does not state whether it was the Englishness of it or its unusual hints of Welshness that they most enjoyed.

An intriguing article published in the US magazine *Motion Picture* in 1939 bore the title "Welsh—But No Welsher." It contains extensive quotations (allegedly) from Milland, wherein he asserts himself as British by birth while identifying as Welsh. He expresses the belief that the Welsh are "the only true Britons," contesting that the English have been "contaminated by crossbreeding with Normans, Angles, Saxons and such Johnny-Come-Latelys as the Danes." To support his argument, he cites botany and natural history textbooks from England, highlighting the consistent alignment between Welsh spelling and the British mode, thereby affirming the unique connection between the Welsh and the notion of British identity (Underhill 1939: 88). This stands in direct contrast to Hollywood's notion of British identity as English. Author Duncan Underhill points out that language and its various forms hold a peculiar allure for Milland as a multilingual adventurer (1939: 88), despite Milland's disclosure in his memoir that he ceased speaking Welsh in childhood. Perhaps as a way to prevent alienating American fans, Underhill emphasizes that Milland strongly disapproves of what he labels "Actors' English" spoken by the leading men of the "fashionable West End" and instead regards "unaccented American speech from both coasts of the continent" as the ultimate embodiment of refined English. Reflecting on the isolation Milland later discussed in his memoir, the article notes his perceived lack of warmth and diversity in Hollywood's social circles, highlighting that he prefers to "mingle with strangers" who are unaware of his celebrity status and are not compelled to immediately categorize him and treat him based on his fame (1939: 88).

In 1934, *Picture Play* magazine featured an article on Milland titled "Dashing Adventurer," portraying his life as "exciting, devil-may-care" and "more colorful and unusual than any part he has played on the screen" (Dillon 1934: 60). The author, Franc Dillon, describes Milland as "mild-mannered, soft-spoken, a gentleman in every sense of the word," with a "charming smile," before discussing his marksmanship and horseman skills. Perhaps surprisingly, his birth in Wales is not mentioned until the final paragraph on the second page. The article is illustrated by a photograph of Milland in his Royal Horse Guard uniform, a studio portrait, and a picture of him smiling while wearing a sailor's cap. The latter is accompanied by a caption noting his involvement in *Hands Across the Table* (Mitchell Leisen, 1935), starring Fred MacMurray and Carole Lombard, although he did not ultimately appear in the film.[22] The article ends by noting that Milland realized his days of adventure were over when he was at a party and remembered his prior commitment with his wife to buy an oven. An article with striking similarities was published in *Screenland* in 1940. It portrays Milland as an intrepid adventurer and calls his life "more fascinating than fiction." The piece opens with the whimsical suggestion that a fairy godmother "bent over the Welsh crib of new-born" Milland, giving readers a peek into his "romantic life story." It includes childhood photographs alongside the image of him in uniform seen in *Picture Play* six years earlier. Drawings of a boat and an airplane are featured in the article, adding to the allure of his life as a daredevil, while a contemporary photograph of Milland depicts him as "gallant" (Zeitlin 1940: 33).

In 1943, *Photoplay* published an article titled "Portrait of an Individualist," which included a list of lesser-known facts about Milland that "only his best friends know." These included Reginald as his birth name, Neath as his birthplace, and the fact that he "reads the encyclopedia at random"

(Asher 1943: 49). When Milland transitioned to television with the weekly sitcom *Meet Mr. McNutley*, an article in the *Radio-TV Mirror* highlighted his upbringing in Neath, noting that "boys are sturdy and stocky" there, but also emphasized his fondness for "fine books and first editions" (Atwater 1953: 53). This is accompanied by a full-page color photograph of him in casual attire, using a telephone while standing in front of a bookcase filled with matching leather-bound volumes. Furthermore, it includes three candid black-and-white images of Milland with his wife and children on the opposite page.

The anecdote with which Milland opens his memoir, about his return to Neath amid his Hollywood success to attend the funeral of his former school principal, illustrates his awareness of the gap between his career in America and the experiences of his former compatriots who remained in Wales. He recalls that no one really spoke to him and that he felt very much like an outsider on his return. His lengthy journey—a flight to London followed by a 150-mile drive to Wales—proves his dedication to his former teacher, especially since he notes that only two of his schoolmates attended the ceremony. Indicating the smallness of the village, and how little it had changed over the decades, Milland lists some of those in attendance, their professions standing in for full names: Old James the Baker, Williams the Police, and Davies the Butcher, noting that "in front of them I still felt like a schoolboy" (1974: 13). This also links to masculine identity and work, with acting viewed as an "unmasculine" profession, especially for a man from the Welsh valleys. It additionally suggests the residents may have considered they had nothing in common with Milland, since they were uneducated in the acting profession and unsure how to talk to a (now Hollywood) actor despite his once being "one of them." Indeed, his memoir opens with a description of a Hollywood party, where he sat alone at the bar wasting time before his plane to attend the funeral. Thus, although worlds apart both geographically and culturally, Hollywood and Wales are tied together in the persona of Milland. Furthermore, his being detached from others at both events, and choosing to share this isolation with readers, suggests he felt he did not belong to either world but perhaps also to both.

WELSH MYTHS AND CELTIC CONNECTIONS

While Milland's Welsh identity is almost entirely removed from his screen image—most notably in the annihilation of his Welsh surname since Jones was an extremely common Welsh family name—his memoir explores Welsh traditions including its folklore, myths, unique foods, and his own Welsh roots, in minute detail. Particularly interesting is his description of how to create a traditional Welsh breakfast, which he calls "the most appetizing dish in the world" and "an absolute delight." His comprehensive recipe—how to cook the individual components, where to place them on the dish, the significance of the seaweed used in the country's traditional laverbread, an "ancient food made from a special kind of seaweed found only on the Welsh coast and certain parts of Japan"—both belies the number of years since he was last in Wales and bolsters the fact that despite his time away from the country he held onto his roots (1974: 12). Milland's Welsh background and Celtic connections may explain why he was such an excellent storyteller (Aldhouse-Green and Howell 2017); his autobiography awash with observations and anecdotes linking him to the strong Welsh tradition of storytelling. It also helps to explain how he was able to take on an eclectic range of roles in films of varying quality and across diverse genres throughout his long-sustained career, while making each characterization truly his own.

The subtitle of Philip Freeman's 2017 book on Celtic mythology, *Tales of Gods, Goddesses and Heroes*, could refer to the link between mythical stories of the distant past and early cinematic stars, a connection Michael Williams extensively discusses in *Film Stardom, Myth and Classicism: The Rise of Hollywood's Gods* (2012) and *Film Stardom and the Ancient Past: Idols, Artefacts and Epics* (2018), which explore classical Hollywood stars in relation to ancient myths and idols. Moreover, Williams's book-long study of Milland's Welsh predecessor Novello is aptly titled *Ivor Novello: Screen Idol* (2003). Similarly, in 2011, publicity photographs from the John Kobal Foundation were exhibited at London's National Portrait Gallery under the exhibition title "Glamour of the Gods: Hollywood Portraits." Displaying classical era cinematic stars in stark black-and-white photography and dramatic poses aided in projecting them as otherworldly or ethereal beings; an accompanying book was released the same year (Dance 2011).

While most people today are aware of ancient Greek gods and heroes such as Zeus and Hercules, as well as Norse gods like Thor (perhaps due to modern cinematic representations), the Gaulish god Lugus, Irish warrior Cú Chulainn, and magical Welsh queen Rhiannon are less celebrated (Freeman 2017: x). In the first century BCE, Caesar crossed the channel twice to attack Britain during the war in Gaul, while in the next century the conquest of Britain was left to the emperor Claudius and the Romans. Years of ruthless battle forced the Romans into northern Britain and Hadrian's Wall. The British Celts were later restrained and became crucial to the empire, their language, stories and gods enduring under Roman rule until the fifth century AD and the invasion of the Saxons and other Germanic tribes. These ancient stories not only survived but evolved, most notably into "the great Welsh tales of the Middle Ages" (Freeman 2017: xiii). Welsh mythology consists of four loosely connected medieval tales combined as the *Mabinogi*, "fascinating and sophisticated stories" with roots stretching back into ancient Celtic traditions but which also "stand on their own as part of the broader European tradition of the time" (Freeman 2017: 165). The first tale is The Prince of Dyfed, based on Prince Pwyll who ruled over the Welsh kingdom and traded places with Arawn, king of Annwfn, for a year. Linking to this Celtic mythology, Milland once more proves his memoir to be unconventional through his comprehensive examination of Wales's "preponderance of surnames beginning with the letter *P*" because, centuries ago, the country did not use surnames. Instead, he continues, "every man was known as the son of his father, and this relationship was signified by the word *ap*, which meant 'son of.' Thus, you got 'William ap Rhys,' which became over the years William Price. Or 'John Pritchard,' which had been 'John ap Richard'" (1974: 21).[23]

The story of Pwyll and his masquerade as King Arawn links Milland not only to his expert horsemanship but also his career as an actor, a profession based around convincingly pretending to be someone else, while also making (fictional) love to other men's wives. Moreover, Milland was often called upon to portray royalty early on, such as a prince (*We're Not Dressing* [Norman Taurog, 1934]) and a king (*Ambassador Bill*); in the latter, his king masquerades as a commoner, thus adding more complexity and layers to his characterization since Milland was a working-class actor playing a king who pretends to be a commoner whilst still being a king. The other interlinking stories of the *Mabinogi* are Branwen, Daughter of Llyr, Manawydan, Son of Llyr, and Math, Son of Mathonwy. In the latter, Mathonwy rules over the Kingdom of Gwynedd, located approximately three hours from Milland's birthplace and, like a suspenseful Hollywood plot, recounts a tale of murder, passion, love, desire, and deception. Indeed, one could imagine Milland portraying a character like Mathonwy on-screen from the mid-1940s onwards, with similarities easily being drawn between this ancient tale and his antihero roles in the likes of *So Evil My Love* (Lewis Allen, 1948) and *Dial M for Murder*.

Surviving medieval manuscripts depict legends of magic and giants, great kings like Arthur, and women and poets in possession of supernatural powers. Although European literature of the time was a strong influence, Freeman calls these Welsh stories "uniquely and wonderfully Celtic" (2017: xiii). Traditional tales were preserved in the Welsh language for centuries, and although "through war and campaigns of cultural assimilation" the English and French tried to force the Welsh to abandon their heritage, Freeman eagerly declares it fortunate they did not prevail (2017: xiii). He argues that we should not ask who the Celts *were* but who they *are*, since "the Celtic people with their unique languages and cultures still survive" in Welsh towns and villages, and remote areas of Ireland and Scotland; the mythology of the Celts lives on for us all through music and stories since Celts sang and told stories in their native languages (2017: xiii).

Milland poetically says that in its lonely moments, the Celtic mind is "a tumbling sea of love and compassion and romanticism and neurotic hates." Exploring ubiquitous myths about his homeland, he calls Wales "a land of music and mountains and mystery. The land of the ancient Brythons or, if you prefer, Britons." Suggesting he fully endorses these myths and felt connected to them, he nonchalantly declares that each Welsh village has a witch, whom people visit for "the fulfilment of strange and devious desires" (1974: 8). The witch in his village was known simply as Bron and spoke only Welsh. Returning for his headmaster's funeral, not only was he shocked to see that she looked only slightly older after forty years, but he was unexpectedly able to converse with her entirely in his native tongue. Milland's romanticization of this experience and his past in Wales help add to the exoticism of his star persona as "Other" in Hollywood, but with a peculiar lack of "Welshness" in his characterizations and star image. Thus, it seems either Hollywood was ignorant of his Welsh background or tried to hide it since it did not correlate with the sophisticated upper-class persona they wished to create for him.

Within film studies, Rikki Morgan-Tamosunas notes in an article on Spanish actor Paco Rabal that while myths fundamentally relate stories about "supernatural beings, like stars, their significance and impact lie in the ways in which they articulate cultural values and beliefs" (2004: 54). The author adds that Rabal's consecration as a "myth" reflects his charismatic appeal and powerful screen presence but that the "other-worldly connotations" of his "mythical" status paradoxically almost merge with his popular image as a man of the people (2004: 54). Milland's rustic, working-class Welsh background and the proletarian characters he played in his early British films *The Flying Scotsman* and *The Lady from the Sea* stand in direct contrast to the suave characters he often portrayed in Hollywood, including both heroes and the antiheroes of *So Evil My Love*, *Dial M for Murder*, and *Alias Nick Beale* (John Farrow, 1949); in the latter, Milland embodies perhaps the most infamous mythical character of Western culture, Satan. Reprising this role in *King of Kings* (Nicholas Ray, 1961), he voices the character of Satan in an unseen and uncredited role; however, given his by-then strongly identifiable voice, it appears the casting was designed to be recognized rather than anonymous, much like the voice of Orson Welles in the many documentary films he narrated.

These unusual characteristics were juxtaposed with more ordinary figures, including doctors who are medical practitioners (*The Doctor Takes a Wife* [Alexander Hall, 1940], *Untamed* [George Archainbaud, 1940]), scientists (*The Thief* [Russell Rouse, 1952]), and college professors (*The Trouble with Women* [1947], *It Happens Every Spring* [Lloyd Bacon, 1949], *A Woman of Distinction* [Edward Buzzell, 1950], *Night into Morning* [1951], and the television series *Meet Mr. McNutley/The Ray Milland Show* [1953–55]); for more on this series see Kelly 2022). Even when Milland portrays an ordinary man with a regular job and routine life, extraordinary events occur that alienate and/or exclude his characters from their typical everyday existence, even if only for the duration of the film (particularly evident in *It Happens Every Spring*, *Night into Morning*, and *The Thief*). This correlates with Richard Dyer's theory of stars being at once ordinary and extraordinary; being like us, and therefore relatable, but also not like us, making them interesting enough for us to want to watch on-screen (1998; see also de Cordova 2001). The myth of stars as gods, goddesses, and idols of the "silver screen" certainly plays into this theory.

TRANSATLANTIC STARDOM

Since Milland was a transatlantic star working in Hollywood for much of his career, comparisons can be made to similar British performers including Milland's closest English equivalents Cary Grant and, from a slightly later period, James Mason, along with other Welsh actors who ventured to Hollywood both before (Novello) and after (Burton). His American counterparts can also be considered, most notably James Stewart, whose evolving appearance from the 1930s to the 1950s is strikingly comparable to Milland's.

Although sharing a nationality with later stars Richard Burton, Stanley Baker, and Anthony Hopkins, in terms of contemporary actors, Milland shared some commonality with several English-born actors who achieved immense success in Hollywood. Physically he was most like English actor Stewart Granger, six years Milland's junior and the same height. They even appeared together on-screen late in their careers, in the quintessentially British *The Royal Romance of Charles and Diana* (Peter Levin, 1982), with Granger starring as Prince Philip, Duke of Edinburgh, and Milland as a royal servant, hinting at both his lower-class origins and his real-life position as protector of the British royal family as a member of the Royal Horse Guards over five decades earlier. Granger's screen debut came shortly after Milland's when he played an extra in the 1933 British musical *The Song You Gave Me* (Paul L. Stein). Like Milland, for several years Granger had many uncredited roles or bit parts, and in the nine years leading up to 1942, the only time he received a screen credit was for the comedy *So This is London* (Thornton Freeland, 1939). His first substantial role, and the one cementing him in the minds of the British public, was in the historical drama *The Man in Grey* (Leslie Arliss, 1942) opposite Margaret Lockwood, Phyllis Calvert, and James Mason, Britain's top male star at the time. Granger plays the hero to Mason's brutal antagonist who famously uses a horsewhip to beat Lockwood's character to death.

Mason's similarity to Milland is evident in their overt sense of Britishness in both British and American cinema, their vocal intonation and the eclectic range of heroes and antiheroes they portrayed across several decades. Standing at t 5'11", Mason was considerably shorter than Milland and had a more intense, brooding, and almost dangerous sexual appeal paired with darkly beautiful features that made him resemble a Byronic hero. Continuing to work as they aged, both transitioned comfortably from leading roles to character parts, allowing them extensive and enduring careers. With more than 150 screen credits each, they both transitioned to television in the 1970s and worked until their deaths in the 1980s. Interestingly, the trajectory of Mason's 1940s career closely echoes that of Milland's from the 1930s. Consequently, while Mason is often considered somewhat of a pioneer of British cinema (Thomas 2018), it can be strongly argued that Milland paved the way for him in the previous decade, although Mason is celebrated as a British star more than Milland who moved to Hollywood before really establishing himself in Britain. While Mason made more films in Britain than in Hollywood—writing about his great dislike of the American film industry in his autobiography (Mason 1981)—one of his best-known Hollywood films is *North by Northwest* (1959), which was directed by the Englishman Alfred Hitchcock and costarred Cary Grant.

Born in Bristol, England, in 1904, not only were Grant's vocal tone and intonation extremely similar to Milland's—particularly in the 1950s, when they had spent decades in America—but both arrived in Hollywood during cinema's early sound era. While Grant was immediately signed to Paramount, Milland initially signed with MGM, where he was underused and often loaned to other studios. While both actors were given bit parts and played secondary roles to more established stars for years, Grant received a screen credit for his debut film, *This Is the Night* (Frank Tuttle, 1932), and publicity photographs depict him in romantic poses with costar Thelma Todd, suggesting Paramount's eagerness to instantly promote him as a new romantic lead. Three years Milland's senior, Grant retired at the age of sixty-two, a decision perhaps in part due to his becoming a father for the first time, but also suggesting he recognized he did not have the capability proven by Milland to make the transition from romantic lead to aging patriarch and character actor. Grant lived for another two decades and, while continuing to make public appearances as a mature man, he never made another feature film after his final appearance in *Walk, Don't Run* (Charles Walters, 1966). Milland was able to make a smooth transition to supporting roles across film and television, consequently enjoying an additional two decades on-screen before both actors died in 1986. Yet Grant is remembered as a leading icon of cinema, and is the subject of a number of academic studies, coffee table books, filmographies, and biographies, including three very recent additions (Eyman 2020; Glancy 2020; Naremore 2022). Milland, however, has been strangely overlooked by biographers, scholars, and audiences while Mason and especially Grant remain familiar names in popular culture.

Characteristics shared by Milland and Grant are undoubtedly their suaveness and timeless sartorial style, promoting attractiveness and class while reflecting their Britishness through key indicators such as tailored Savile Row suits. In his cameo in *Variety Girl* (1947),[24] Milland mocks his screen persona when dressed in a by-then familiar tuxedo and top hat, telling fellow performer William Holden, "I'm always suave and debonair." Contrastingly, Holden wears an American-coded cowboy outfit, his light hair and lightly colored outfit almost blending into the background, while the much taller Milland in his stark black tuxedo and hat draws the eye.

Although suaveness is often viewed as a positive characteristic, it can have negative connotations of being overly confident, arrogant, or even supercilious, while sometimes being hard to pinpoint; the same applies to being (too) debonair. Thus, when we watch Grant fall off his chair in *My Favorite Wife* (Garson Kanin, 1940) or embody a blundering paleontologist in *Bringing Up Baby* (Howard Hawks, 1938), the aloofness and superiority often attached to suave or debonair men are undermined and we see him as more human, flawed, real, and, consequently, more likable and relatable. The same is true of Milland portraying bumbling professors in *The Trouble with Women* and *It Happens Every Spring*; his reliance on glasses, overt clumsiness, stuttering, and high-pitched voice when agitated add a more down-to-earth appeal to his sometimes-lofty screen persona. In opposition to this, Milland's suaveness permitted him to play dangerous and threatening characters, such as seductive men planning murders in *So Evil My Love* and *Dial M for Murder*, and his urbane Satan in *Alias Nick Beale*. Consequently, Milland's antiheroes are more threatening than Grant's in the likes of *Suspicion* (Alfred Hitchcock, 1941), where, although strongly indicated, his character's murderous tendencies remain unsubstantiated by the film's conclusion, suggesting the stereotype of the suave, upper-class Hollywood villain who is evil but charismatic, thereby darkly exciting for viewers. However, before that the untrained and unambitious actor moved from London to Hollywood, as is explored in the subsequent chapter.

CHAPTER TWO

STUMBLING INTO ACTING

Obviously not grasping the extent of work required to become a cavalryman in the Royal Horse Guards, Milland calls the initial two months of his military training "a nightmare." He had to show aptitude with a lance, saber, and thrusting sword, and proficiency with a range of guns and signals while "mounted on a seventeen-hand horse with a mind of its own" (1974: 54). Added tasks included infantry drills, marching, map-reading, caring for and feeding at least one horse, and the maintenance of field and ceremonial harnesses. The upkeep of personal equipment was also vital, including four mandatory uniforms of utilitarian stable dress, active service uniform, dismounted dress uniform, and mounted ceremonial uniform, including their necessary array of intricate individual components. At the age of nineteen, under the rule of George V, Milland became a full-fledged trooper in His Majesty's Household Cavalry (1974: 56).[1]

Although his London-based life was far removed from his Welsh childhood, the regimental nature of military training would be invaluable for long days of shooting on sound stages and locations when he became an actor, particularly since he often experienced two hours of immobility when on guard. Furthermore, several of his on-screen characterizations were either active in the military or had a military background. Milland details that a "full guard"—the changing of the guard at Whitehall—always occurs when the reigning monarch is residing at Buckingham Palace. It was during this event that Milland drew his first audience, although they were not there to see him specifically. A ceremony that continues to this day, the changing of the guard draws crowds of (mainly) tourists, gathering in the small courtyard between Horse Guards Parade and Whitehall to see one guard replacing another (Milland 1974: 59). Like acting, this group performance demands precision acquired through intensive training and rehearsal. Profoundly steeped in tradition, it is still one of the most habitually British events experienced by those visiting London and is immersed in ideas around class, the empire, and the unified nature of the United Kingdom rather than its individual nations. Obviously not a specifically Welsh tradition, this further hints at a loss of Milland's Welsh identity while helping promote his "transatlanticness" upon relocating to the US. Milland explores his work in the calvary at length in his memoir, suggesting he was proud to be part of this British institution; the London location perhaps made him feel more British than merely Welsh, and thereby led him to adopt a stronger sense of Britishness, or even Englishness, even before the studios began manipulating his persona.

As the title of this chapter suggests, it was around this time that Milland "stumbled" into acting after a fellow cavalryman confided that he was in love with an actress he met at a cocktail party and convinced Milland to go with him to an establishment in Covent Garden to help with the girl. Like the script for a Hollywood film, Milland's chance visit to a bar mostly frequented by theatrical personnel was a major turning point in his life and career when he was introduced to professional stage performers. He admits to being "poleaxed" and "completely ensnared" by the ballet dancer Margot St. Leger, who was in rehearsal for a Stanley Lupino show.[2] In a statement both reflecting Milland's tendency to romanticize and simultaneously revealing his eloquence and Welsh background rich in storytelling, he proclaims the room "became the Garden of the Hesperides. She [St. Leger] was Diana and Atalanta and Pallas Athene. And I felt like a farmer" (1974: 74). Despite associating himself with farmers, close to his own identity, his relating the redheaded dancer to Greek mythology rather than Welsh legend implies discomfort with his background while surrounded by sophisticated performers in central London, who, as he often did on-screen, represented the means of escaping into a more glamorous world.

Being unfamiliar with the theatre, Milland was unaware the room was filled with famous British stage performers, including Margaret Bannerman, Phyllis Dare, and Enid Stamp-Taylor. Attempting to circulate the room but feeling out of place, he declares, "These people were strangers [. . .] strange and sort of glittering," and, aligning himself with the audience of a stage performance, he declares that he could only watch from afar (1974: 77).

Returning to his barracks in the early hours of the morning, he crucially notes being unable to sleep after witnessing this "different world" (1974: 78)—a world he would never have experienced if he had remained in South Wales, or even in his barracks that evening.

So fascinated by this newly discovered "world," Milland not only continued to frequent the establishment but accompanied St. Leger to several theatrical parties. At one of these parties he met American actress Estelle Brody, who had initially come to England to star in a stage play but remained in Britain and achieved stardom as "the comic Clara Bow" at Elstree, the studio known as the British Hollywood (Warren 1983: 36). Milland recalls that when Brody asked if he was going to spend the rest of his life in the army or if he might consider becoming an actor, it created a "restlessness [...] and the beginnings of discontent" in him, making him overtly aware that he had never seriously considered his future or even "given much thought beyond tomorrow" (1974: 78). What is interesting is that it is the glamour and parties Milland finds seductive at this point, rather than the work of acting, which he still knew extraordinarily little about. Having had extremely limited contact with the theatre, Milland admits to having only attended four plays in his life by then. In this sense, acting may seem a surprising choice for him to have pursued.

The first play he ever saw was *The Only Way*, starring English actor John Martin-Harvey, when he was ten; he recalls only boredom from this experience (1974: 78). Nearly a decade later, on his nineteenth birthday, he and his friends attended *The Silver King*, featuring Tod Slaughter, at the Bedford Theatre in London's Camden Town. Clearly not taking the experience too seriously, or demonstrating any aspirations to work on the stage, Milland notes arriving full of beer and oysters, a dozen of which could be bought in the street for a shilling (1974: 78). True to his Welsh roots, Milland spent most of his recreational time and disposable income on music, particularly opera and ballet. While his taste reveals a preference for modes associated with refinement and high culture, he discloses his earthier appetite for the stage by declaring that the London Palladium had "the greatest variety show in the world." Attending regularly, he was enthralled by "the individual brilliance of the performers, the marvelous American humor,"[3] and would "ache from laughing" at comedy duo George Burns and Gracie Allen (1974: 78–79). After signing with Paramount just a few years later, Milland costarred with Burns and Allen three times, in *We're Not Dressing* (1934), *Many Happy Returns* (Norman Z. McLeod, 1934), and *The Big Broadcast of 1937* (Mitchell Leisen, 1936).

Following his introduction to the theatrical world, if only its public facing persona, the repetitive nature of army life began to irritate him. Restless and edgy, he became short-tempered by the "rote and tradition" which only increased his desire for escape (Milland 1974: 79). However, he was yet to experience the work that also goes into acting, with its repetitive nature of learning lines, rehearsing, and performing the same show each night. Similarly, cinematic acting includes learning lines, rehearsing, and multiple retakes, before moving almost immediately to another, sometimes extremely similar, film.

During a state visit for the king of Afghanistan, Milland was part of the procession which started at Victoria Station and included the British royal family. During a break, he met up with Brody and some friends at the bar Bunch of Grapes, near London Bridge. Dressed in full military regalia, including a saber which made sitting impossible, Milland met his first Hollywood star: Constance Talmadge (1974: 80).[4] In the summer of 1928, now finding the prospect of another two years of army life "unbearable," Milland decided to leave the cavalry. After undertaking three years of service, it was possible then for a soldier to pay £40 and obtain an unconditional discharge, much like buying out a Hollywood contract. Submitting his application in June and, aware the procedure would take a month, Milland informed Brody he would be available for acting work in August. She recommended he read aloud whenever possible, and to do so while sitting on his hands, since he moved them around too much. She further advised that he speak as slowly as possible since he currently spoke "like lightning." Astounded by this analysis, he proclaims that "nobody had ever told me about myself before. It was a peculiar sensation" (1974: 83). Released from the army, he rented a room in Half Moon Street, just off Piccadilly. Brody advised him to visit Elstree Studios in Borehamwood, Hertfordshire, where she showed him around (Milland 1974: 85). Thus, it was American actress Estelle Brody who got Milland inside his first (British) film studio.

BRITISH BEGINNINGS AT ELSTREE

Many British performers made their cinematic debut at Elstree and, as the actress and dancer Anna Neagle[5] highlights, the studio had a unique status as "the only British film *colony*" (1983: 6, emphasis in original). Although the start of Milland's cinematic career was rather unspectacular, his early work may have taken on more significance had he stayed in Britain, gained more experience, and established himself there first. Cary Grant also started his career at Elstree and features as one of only three stars on the cover of Patricia Warren's book about the studio. Given Grant's limited work for Elstree, it seems surprising that he would appear on the cover; however, his familiar star image may have been used to create more interest in the book. Furthermore, given Grant's status as a highly recognizable international star with British roots, he may help to generate a much wider readership than many lesser-known performers who remained in Britain for the duration of their careers.

When J. D. Williams, W. Schlesinger, and Herbert Wilcox built Elstree in 1925–26, it was called British National Studios (and later ABPC and Thorn EMI). Due to the founders' financial issues, Glasgow solicitor John Maxwell took over in March 1927 and renamed it British International Pictures (BIP). Having entered the film industry in 1912, Maxwell already had fifteen years' experience in film production behind him and endeavored to ensure that BIP could compete with Hollywood and Germany's leading studios by building a vertically integrated company, incorporating film production and distribution through Wardour Films and ABC Cinemas. Warren calls Maxwell a "canny, clever Scot" who had a vision and the courage to invest his skills and money to develop the studio, thereby the British film industry forever owes him a debt of gratitude (1983: 20).

Maxwell signed up young British director Alfred Hitchcock and, in February 1929, Hitchcock's *Blackmail* and Milland's debut film, *The Flying Scotsman*, both went into production at BIP, thus demonstrating the studio's ability to successfully move from silent to sound cinema. Although BIP produced some high-budget films, its output comprised mainly of productions with low or medium budgets, often comedies and musicals. This mixing of budgets appears to be a deliberate mimicking of Hollywood, demonstrating Maxwell's clever approach to following other successful film production models. For example, the "Quota Quickies" were substandard films akin to Hollywood's B-movies (Chibnall 2007), steadily produced to comply with the Cinematograph Films Act of 1927, which stated that 20 percent of all films shown in British cinemas had to be British in origin (Warren 1983: 31). These films, including *The Flying Scotsman* and Milland's second film, *The Lady from the Sea*, were mainly intended for home audiences, rather than international distribution.

By 1928, the pre–World War I idols were being replaced by the next generation of Britain's "young screen heroes," including Brian Aherne, Jack Buchanan, and John Longden, while supporting actors still tended to be recruited from the stage; Ivor Novello kept a "foot in both camps" so that he could eventually move from Elstree to Hollywood (Warren 1983: 34). While several British performers, including Milland, Aherne, Cary Grant, David Niven, Madeleine Carroll, and Victor McLaglen, soon relocated to Hollywood, Maxwell conversely secured several Hollywood stars to appear in his British productions, including Lionel Barrymore, Tallulah Bankhead,[6] and Anna May Wong, the latter proving particularly noteworthy in Milland's early cinematic career.

Recounting his first time on a studio lot, Milland hyperbolically recalls getting lost and finding himself in "a cavernous place that looked like an airplane hangar" and was lit by "at least a thousand searchlights" which were "absolutely blinding" (1974: 85). Realizing he was surrounded by around 150 "very beautiful" people in evening dress in what seemed to be a nightclub, his eyes were drawn to a couple dancing. He discovered they were Jameson Thomas and Anna May Wong, proclaiming that the latter took his breath away and was "the most exotic-looking creature" he had ever seen (1974: 85). They were rehearsing for the "now famous" 1929 film *Piccadilly* (E. A. Dupont, 1929) (Warren 1983: 40). When Milland showed great interest in the film, Brody convinced its casting director to give Milland some crowd work, which he only got because he owned a dinner jacket and could be on the lot by 8 o'clock the next morning.

Echoing his recollections of the Hollywood party and Welsh funeral opening his memoir, Milland declares that on the set of *Piccadilly* nobody spoke to him or even approached him. Finally, another man in eveningwear asked what they were meant to be doing as it was also his first time on a film set, but Milland was unsure. He learned the man was Jack Raine, who had worked in the theatre for a decade and was married to West End star Binnie Hale (Milland 1974: 87). Notably, *Piccadilly* also marked the cinematic debut of Milland's future costar Charles Laughton (*Payment Deferred* [Lothar Mendes, 1932] and *The Big Clock* [John Farrow, 1948]). A RADA-trained actor, Laughton had performed on the stage since 1926, and here he appears briefly as a problematic customer unhappy with his meal. Warren suggests Maxwell must have been pleased with his "ambitious international line-up" (1983: 40) since, although *Piccadilly* is about London life, nightclubs, and slums, it stars the Chinese Wong and Polish American Gilda Gray and was directed by the German Dupont. Until then, Dupont had only directed one other British film, the opulent *Moulin Rouge* (1928), which some sources, including IMDB, erroneously list as Milland's debut film.[7]

While working on *Piccadilly*, Milland observed how often one was required to wait around. He recalls analyzing his fellow extras, all of whom appeared intensely bored, when the film's casting director and American film director Denison Clift approached him. Requiring two actors to travel to Scotland to portray house guests, Milland declares that Clift instantly offered the roles to himself and Raine. Taking a sleeper train to Pitlochry, north of Edinburgh, that night, they were paid six guineas for two weeks' work (1974: 87), which converts to just over £400 in today's money and the exact cost of his rented room in Piccadilly. Unable to recall the name of the film, but knowing it starred Nigel Barrie, Milland claims it was never released; in fact, with the rain being so bad on location he is unsure if it was even made (1974: 87). Although Milland did appear in a 1929 film starring Barrie, the semi-silent *The Plaything*, what is unusual about his recollection is that this film was made at Elstree Studios and again directed by Castleton Knight. The most perplexing part of the story, however, is that surely Milland would have remembered that Barrie's costar was his close friend and mentor, Estelle Brody.[8] After this mysterious trip to Scotland, Milland proclaims that he returned to London to again question his future since he saw those in the film industry as "not of my world" and acting "a most insecure calling" that was rampant with "exhibitionists" (1974: 88), a statement he is evidently excluding himself from, thereby still assessing the profession from the position of an outsider.

"THE SHARPSHOOTER"

Milland obtained Frank Zeitlin as an agent and, after around a month of no contact, Zeitlin sent Milland to Elstree to work on BIP's *The Informer* (Arthur Robison, 1929).[9] Although they had already engaged a German sharpshooter to do the film's trick shooting, he had instantly been hit by a bus when arriving at London's Victoria Station after looking the wrong way before stepping into the road (Milland 1974: 88–90). *Piccadilly*'s casting director had remembered hearing about Milland's army-trained gunmanship, and when director Arthur Robison asked if he was a professional marksman, Milland recalls, "little me, remembering my three and a half years in the cavalry, said yes" (1974: 89).

Studio director Joe Grossman handed Milland a Belgian Browning .22 caliber automatic rifle which held twelve L. R. cartridges, while Robison drew a chalk circle around a coin at the other end of the room and instructed him to fire at it as rapidly as possible. Requesting a practice shot after explaining all firearms behaved differently and that he had never held this gun before, Milland fired before checking the bullet. He noted the direction was perfect, but the shot was around an inch too high. He then fired the other eleven bullets with Grossman, Robison, actor Moore Marriott, cameraman René Guissart, and writer Walter Mycroft watching. Milland declares he had a sworn statement signed by each of them that all eleven shots had made "a hole you could have covered with a quarter. It had taken no more than ten seconds. I couldn't have done it again. Nobody could" (1974: 91). Proving his skill with a gun, he was engaged and began work the following day.[10]

Halfway through production, Milland notes a gesture was made "towards modernism" by filming the second half with dialogue (1974: 92).[11] Although British filmmakers continued to make silent films, dismissing sound as a fad,

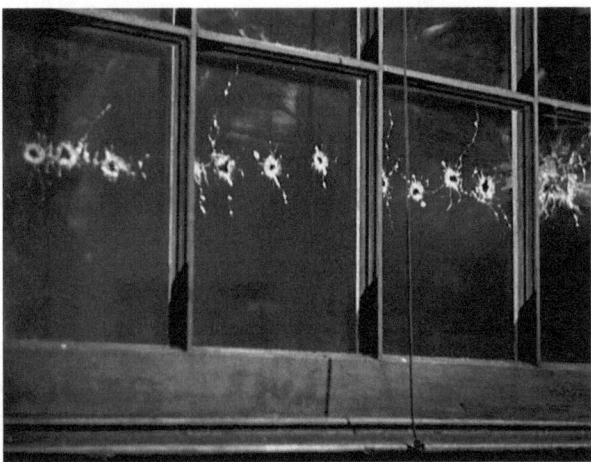

Figure 2.1. Milland's first film work was technical, in the off-screen and uncredited role of "The Sharpshooter" in *The Informer* (Arthur Robison, 1929).

by 1929, some 80 percent of the films shown in Britain were "full talking" pictures from America, thus proving silent cinema was becoming outmoded. Since performers' voices would be heard on-screen for the first time, Milland sarcastically notes that adding dialogue to *The Informer* was extremely confusing since the plot was a purely Irish story, yet it had a German director, a Scottish assistant director, and a French cameraman. Leading man Lars Hanson was Swedish, leading lady Lya de Putti was Hungarian, and supporting player Carl Harbord was Anglo-Dutch. With "The Sharpshooter" being "a Welsh farmer," in the words of Milland, "this wasn't Irish stew—it was bouillabaisse mixed with goulash" (1974: 92).

For his uncredited role in the film, Milland was required to shoot the Browning across a twenty-foot window in a way that replicated machine-gun shots, which he needed to achieve in one take since it would take half a day to replace the glass (Milland 1974: 93). Once more, seemingly in the right place at the right time, while filming this stunt he was introduced to director Castleton Knight. Filming *The Flying Scotsman* on the neighboring stage, Knight was seeking a new leading man after Cyril McLaglen broke his leg on the way to the studio, persuading Milland to try out for the role of a train fireman. Undertaking a screen test during his lunch break, Milland panicked about his lack of acting experience but was informed later that day that he had the part; this meant he had to do the rest of his sharpshooting work during his breaks (1974: 95). Although not seen on-screen, Milland's marksmanship is displayed through the neat row of bullets shot through a windowpane in the opening scene (figure 2.1).[12] Rather nonchalantly, Milland claims his film career began when he walked onto a film set full of curiosity, was given a role as an extra, and was then requested by chance to perform a stunt based on his military training. Furthermore, his serendipitous encounter with Knight, along with McLaglen's broken leg, led to him securing his first role as a romantic lead, but this narrative strongly suggests his lack of drive and commitment to the profession at this time.

A SOUND PERFORMANCE

Warren notes that, while John Maxwell was "quietly preparing the ground for the eventuality of the success of sound," it "arrived with a bang" in 1927 with Warner Brothers' Vitaphone[13] production of *The Jazz Singer* (Alan Crosland), starring Al Jolson. The following year, *The Singing Fool* (Lloyd Bacon, 1928), another Jolson vehicle at Warner Brothers, became the first major American sound feature film presented in London (1983: 43). While British producers were dismissive of sound as merely a passing fancy, Maxwell was innovative and sent his general manager to the US to purchase sound equipment, cameras, and expertise (Warren 1983: 43). This led to a race to produce the first British film featuring sound, while the added complications of different recording systems and trade show dates has led to conflicting claims as to which was the first film to feature sound. Among those with claims to being the first are *The Crimson Circle* (Frederic Zelnik, 1929), *White Cargo* (J. B. Williams, 1929), *Wolves* (Albert de Courville, 1930), and *The Flying Scotsman*, although the industry tends to regard Hitchcock's *Blackmail* as Britain's "entry into sound film production" (Warren 1983: 43). Milland echoes Warren's claims by stating that during breaks in *The Flying Scotsman* he visited other sound stages to see films being made, but he incorrectly calls *Blackmail* Britain's "first all-talking film" (1974: 97). While it did include sound, the first all-talking British picture was *The Clue of the New Pin* (Arthur Maude, 1929). Initially meeting Hitchcock on the set of *Blackmail*, the two men worked together only once, twenty-five years later in Hollywood, with the big screen production of the stage play *Dial M for Murder*.

In April 1929, before permanent sound stages were completed, BIP installed crude phonograph recording equipment in two temporary studios,[14] where Hitchcock directed *Blackmail* and Milland starred as Jim Edwards in *The Flying Scotsman*.[15] Calling his first attempt at acting "the damnedest collection of bilge" that still followed him forty-five years later when writing his memoir, Milland suggests the preliminary attention he received as a performer brought "nothing but shame. I didn't want to go anywhere or be seen by anyone. Certainly not by the boys in B Troop," his military unit (1974: 95). While adjusting to work often associated with femininity, and an unusual career choice for a former soldier, he also felt uncomfortable replacing Cyril McLaglen since he was "one of England's most promising film stars" and the brother of actor Victor McLaglen, a member of the Royal Cavalry during World War I (1974: 95).

Since I have written extensively on Milland's performance in *The Flying Scotsman* elsewhere (Kelly 2023a), I will not linger on it here. However, it is worth noting that Milland calls his cinematic debut as a "roughneck fireman [...] eight weeks of embarrassment," partly due to his ignorance about acting or "theatrics of any kind" and the inclination to hide his emotions, particularly in front of strangers (1974: 96), a trait he appears to have inherited from his father and a typical male attitude at the time, especially given his working-class background. But he remembers Knight as a kind and understanding man who helped him through the process and was grateful for the twenty-five pounds a week which, adjusted for inflation, is around £1700 today.

He must have done better than he assumed, though, because just two weeks later he was signed to a six-month contract at twenty pounds a week for twenty-four weeks to make *The Lady from the Sea* (1929), costarring Moore Marriott and Mona Goya, and again directed by Knight. Having been released on DVD in 2014 by the now defunct Network, it is more readily available to view today, but in 1974 Milland notes he did not think it was ever released as he had never seen it.[16] Since this was his final British film before leaving for Hollywood, he may have missed its UK and European release windows. Critiquing his early acting, Milland suggests the film brought "his true talent to the surface, which turned out to be the size of a sardine" (1974: 96). However, as one of Britain's earliest full talkies, it contains stilted and labored performers from most of the players, as the whole industry grappled with this innovative technology. Nevertheless, winning the role of romantic lead in his first two films is no mean feat and suggests Milland's early star potential, even if it was not yet fully developed. As one of Hollywood's leading studios, MGM must have seen sufficient potential in him to sign him so early in his career, even if the pairing proved to be something of a disappointment.

Milland benefited from the start of his career coinciding with the shift to sound, particularly since his voice became such an important and recognizable part of his star persona, although it certainly needed work at this stage since it is slightly too strained and pronounced to sound natural. In opposition to his casting in Hollywood, here his working-class fisherman, Tom Roberts, is seduced by the upper-class Claire le Grange (Goya) and, despite having a loving woman waiting for him, he gives into temptation. As

Figure 2.2. Milland's fisherman is seduced by Mona Goya's upper-class character in the British film *The Lady from the Sea* (Castleton Knight, 1929).

figure 2.2 demonstrates, Milland began showing early signs of acting traits that became familiar elements of his star persona in Hollywood, particularly the use of his eyes and eyebrows to convey a wide range of emotions. Here his facial gestures imply Tom's inner conflict as he battles between the guilt of cheating on Rose (Eugenie Amami) and his weakness while being seduced by Claire; Goya's facial expression perfectly contrasts with Milland's and shows her character is entirely in control of the situation. Indeed, she instigates a kiss between the two just before the scene fades out.

At the age of twenty-three, Milland seemed neither convinced of his skills as a performer nor possessed any real desire to act. He decided that if he did not show any ability within six months he would quit, and upon learning that the owner of the "theatrical" Covent Garden establishment, Bobby Page, was putting money into a touring company he decided that would be an excellent opportunity to test his theory. He was given the juvenile lead in the American drama *The Woman in Room 13* and, after just three weeks of rehearsals, it opened in Southport, Lancashire, England. Despite the nerves of performing for a live audience, Milland recalls the first show went well but the second was a disaster. In an anecdote that suggests the plot of a slapstick comedy, he remembers another performer had kicked the carpet on the stage onto the footlights when they exited, so he was instructed to work his way downstage and kick it back. As he did so, however, he caught his foot on the light and fell straight into the orchestra pit, much to the audience's amusement. Additionally, having lost two teeth in an army boxing match, Milland wore a bridge; during his final line ("You have defiled me"), the bridge flew out and landed loudly in a copper bowl on the stage, again causing the audience to break into hysterics (1974: 103). Nonetheless, one theatrical notice concluded that there was an "extraordinary performance by a young actor named Raymond Milland. Extraordinary," but it is unclear whether the reviewer meant extraordinary positively or negatively. Two weeks later, the company let him go on the grounds that he was too tall and accident-prone (Milland 1974: 104), but the experience allowed him to gain some much needed, if brief, stage experience.

Undertaking acting and dance lessons, Milland also succeeded in seeing respected London drama coach Kate Rorke, if only briefly. With a vastly different mindset to fellow Welshman Richard Burton, upon being handed a copy of *Richard III*, he declared that "Shakespeare is not my idea of entertainment. As children in school we found it incomprehensible, but we had to wade through it and the scars still remain" (1974: 105), a belief many readers may also hold. When Milland had concluded his reading, Rorke asked about his prior occupation before informing him he "better get mounted again" (1984: 106). A few weeks later, again serendipitously, Milland was taking a dance class at Max Rivers's School of Dancing in Regent Street when André Charlot, of Charlot's Revue, invited him to audition for his new show at the Hippodrome Theatre at 9 a.m. the following day. Milland was handed a contract with the promise of £15 a week and the chance to appear in two more of Charlot's shows (Milland 1974: 108). However, he never appeared in the show, and, after another fortuitous meeting, it would be thirty-five years before he appeared on stage again.

HOLLYWOOD CALLING

In yet another fateful coincidence, Milland recalls that the day after he signed with Charlot, he was at the Carlton Hotel when he was approached by MGM's Robert Rubin, who recognized him from *The Flying Scotsman*. Asking Milland to visit the MGM offices in Great Tower Street that night, Rubin and Sam Eckman listened attentively while Milland talked about himself, nodding to each other when he had finished. He later discovered that Rubin was the vice president at MGM, while Eckman was the general director of MGM's British activities. Asking if he would like to come to Hollywood on a contract starting at $175 a week for nine months, with the chance of a rise, he was informed he would get first-class transport both ways as well as sufficient travelling expenses (Milland 1974: 110). Milland recounts being in a daze and telling them he would give them his answer the following day. Finding himself outside the Empire Theatre in Leicester Square, he went in and watched a film starring Charles Bickford and Kay Johnson, although he could not recall the name.[17] Sitting through the film twice, he studied it in extreme detail, noting, "I devoured every tree, every street, every set, and every face. I kept marveling at the prospect that I could be seeing these very places and people in a matter of weeks," and recalls asking himself, "Could this be happening to Reggie? This incredible day?" (1974: 110). Recounting the events for his 1974 memoir, it is interesting that Milland is unable to recall the name of the film but remembers the stars forty-five years later, thus demonstrating the impact performers have on audiences and their importance to the industry. Furthermore, the fact that he still considered himself "Reggie," despite now using a stage name, demonstrates the on-screen/off-screen paradox of an actor (Dyer 1998), while suggesting he still did not feel part of the theatrical world.

Having not yet signed his contract with Charlot, he decided to sign with MGM instead and was told to be ready to leave for Hollywood in two weeks. Sailing from Southampton, England, he arrived in New York for the first time on July 20, 1930.[18] Traveling overnight on the Twentieth Century, he boarded *The Chief* to Los Angeles and was met by Jerrod Asher of MGM's publicity department. The studio had booked him a room at the Ambassador Hotel for a week, after which time he was on his own. Foreshadowing his most famous role in *The Lost Weekend*, he had forgotten about Prohibition and tried to order a whiskey and soda at the Plaza Hotel on his first night in the US. Meeting up with the ship's entertainers, he brought a bottle of Scotch in a brown bag but became violently ill upon returning to his hotel. Waking the next morning looking and feeling like "a frayed shoelace," he declares it was almost a year before he had another drink (1974: 114), a common thread in his memoir and, apparently, throughout his adult life. Nevertheless, he was in Hollywood and signed to major studio MGM, if only temporarily.

Milland's transition from young soldier with no interest in acting to amateur performer intent on gaining experience, to eventually "devouring" every aspect of a film is depicted in his memoir as both extremely fast and dependent on numerous fortuitous opportunities, whether they are completely based in fact or not. However, we do know that he arrived in the US in 1930 and began working at MGM shortly afterwards.[19] Thus, the next chapter explores Milland's initial period in Hollywood, examining his (limited) performances at MGM, and loan-outs to Warner Brothers, before his temporary return to Britain when, despite bringing him overseas and without giving him the chance at a decent role, MGM decided not to renew his contract.

CHAPTER THREE

SECOND FIDDLES AND THIRD WHEELS
EARLY BIT PART PLAYER

Having explored concepts of national identity around Welshness, cinemagoing in Wales, and cinematic representations of Welshness and Wales in chapter one, chapter two set up prominent events in Milland's life and career before his preliminary move to Hollywood. The current chapter focuses on the actor's brief employment at MGM, between 1930 and 1932, evaluating the limited range of roles he was awarded during this time. In particular, it identifies the lack of exposure and character development Milland was allowed during his employment, which seems at odds with a studio that actively brought him over from Britain after securing the role of romantic lead in his first two British films. This peculiar lack of promotion suggests that perhaps the studio did not know what to do with him or how to cast him after signing him, resulting in Milland's option being dropped just two years later and his temporary return to Britain.

During Milland's first stint in America, his lack of familiarity with the country comes through in his shock at discovering that to get anywhere in the US requires driving for an extended period, commenting that "if this had been Europe I'd be in another country by now" (1974: 116). He also observes that when a foreigner first visits the US, they are struck by the fact that "some Americans speak more attractively than others to a foreigner [. . .] they all speak exactly the same language. American. But some are pleasanter to listen to" (1974: 124). Although true of all countries, particularly Britain if we consider the many regional accents in and across England, Wales, Scotland, and Northern Ireland, this comment proposes that Milland viewed Americans' use of English to be different from his own and how he had previously experienced it. Upon moving from South Wales to Central London, he must have been aware of the eclectic range of regional accents his own country was made up of. While his observations may seem unusual to us today, given the prevalence of US accents we regularly hear in films, television, and on the internet, since Milland arrived in the US just as sound cinema was taking off, he would have been unaccustomed to hearing such a diverse range of US accents. Moreover, his strong bond with Estelle Brody most likely resulted in his growing accustomed to her regional accent as the baseline of how Americans speak, just as upper-class English was Hollywood's default for the collective "British" accent. This also meant that coming from Britain, and specifically Wales, his voice was more distinct than the majority of those already working in Hollywood, eventually becoming key to his star persona, although, peculiarly, not at MGM.

On his first night in Hollywood, MGM personnel took Milland to dinner at the famous Brown Derby restaurant. Speaking like a starstruck fan or tourist, he highlights his ordinariness and outsider status—heightened by his first visit to Hollywood—by asserting that he is unable to recall what he ate since he was too busy watching "the parade going on" around him (1974: 116). Reinforcing his ordinariness, while linking concepts of Welsh mythology to Hollywood stars as ethereal beings, Milland remembers seeing people he "never really believed existed," recalling intricate details about them almost forty-five years later. While Joan Crawford was "beautifully dressed" and Corinne Griffith "breathlessly lovely," the way he describes some of the other "gods and goddesses" of the silver screen suggests the extent to which the Hollywood machine manipulated on-screen images to give stars their otherworldly appeal, as well as elevating Milland above the status of an unquestioning ardent fan. While noting cowboy star Tom Mix was much shorter than expected, he calls Wallace Beery "gross-looking" and "shambling." Most tellingly, he failed to recognize Jean Harlow off-screen, describing her as a "rather common-looking girl with platinum hair and a surly expression" (1974: 116–17). Despite his transatlantic journey, it was fellow Brit Victor McLaglen, with his "joyful smile and rollicking walk," whom Milland was most enthusiastic about, asserting that "*there* was a man" (1974: 117, emphasis in original).

Although Milland attended the premiere of the Greta Garbo vehicle *Romance* (Clarence Brown, 1930) at the Pantages Theatre that evening, he declares "the show at the Brown Derby was better" (1974: 117). These words strongly indicate that even their appearance in the restaurant was a performance, further underscoring the façade of Hollywood stardom and the industry's distinctive version of modern folklore. Indeed, Milland learned that these luminaries did not frequent the premises and were only there because of the premiere; the rest of the time, the restaurant catered predominantly to "tourists and gawkers" (1974: 117). Stopping near Hillcrest to observe the lights of Beverly Hills, West Hollywood, and Los Angeles, Rubin announced to Milland that everything they saw belonged to Ramon Novarro since he was Hollywood's reigning romantic lead at the time (1974: 117). Again, indicating the industry's fickleness, MGM's extensive promotion of Novarro as the "Latin lover" variety of male pinup was their attempt at replacing leading star Rudolph Valentino, who had died prematurely in 1926 at the age of thirty-one. Despite his British roots and birth name David Ivor Davies, Milland's Welsh predecessor Novello was comparably marketed to Valentino. However, like so many, his reign in Hollywood proved fleeting.

MOVIE READY?

Milland's first Hollywood screen test was for Cecil B. DeMille's *The Squaw Man* (1931), the director's third version of the film and the first to incorporate sound. Although the test was directed by Mitchell Leisen, with whom Milland later worked several times, and would have been a good start to his US career, nothing came of this test. Shortly afterwards he was given a bit part in *Son of India* (Jacques Feyder, 1931), starring Novarro and Madge Evans, cast as a subaltern in the British army in India who is "suave, smooth, and murderous with women" (Milland 1974: 121). Although these characteristics became familiar traits of Milland's star persona, he admits to being "terribly nervous and self-conscious" since the role seemed better suited to Ivan Lebedeff or Cesar Romero, and he was fired before shooting commenced (1974: 121). During a dress rehearsal, director Jacques Feyder had bellowed from his elevated position on the boom, in a voice "loaded with ridicule and venom" as he asked Milland where he ever got the idea he could act, and questioning which "clown in the casting office had been responsible for foisting on him such a cretinous imbecile." He then demanded Milland return to whatever job he had in whatever country he had come from and not waste the time of directors like him (Milland 1974: 122). For a young man in a foreign land and in a profession still relatively new to him, this must have proved a humiliating experience and evidently still affected him decades later.

Feeling homesick and implying he was still questioning if acting was for him, Milland found a job helping at the stables at Sunset, which he was more comfortable with. However, his claim that "a big, rangy thoroughbred gelding who could jump over a house but was completely mad" had later killed actor Monroe Owsley (1974: 124) is implausible since contemporary sources agree that Owsley died of a heart attack, following a car accident, on June 7, 1937.[1] Furthermore, Owsley's death was overshadowed by the death of twenty-six-year-old superstar Jean Harlow on the same day.

Although MGM had several American actors already under contract and specifically brought Milland over from Britain, casting director Benny Thau demanded that Milland learn how to speak like an American and lose his "limey accent," a derogatory term for a British person. While Milland stresses that Herbert Marshall, Ronald Colman, and Clive Brook were Hollywood stars in part because of their British accent, they had already been stars before moving to Hollywood and had parts written specifically for them, whereas Milland had to adjust to fit the roles he was given (1974: 125). This decision appears counterproductive after not only bringing another Brit to Hollywood—Milland's examples were all English—but a Welshman. Being trained to speak American by a voice coach from Alabama led to him acquiring what he recalls as "the damnedest Southern accent ever heard north of the Panama Canal" (1974: 127). It seems particularly peculiar that MGM expected him to adjust his excellent speaking voice, one of his most unique and appealing features, to become a poor imitation of the numerous Americans already employed, such as his counterpart Robert Montgomery who, interestingly, was often cast as a Brit.[2] As noted, Milland's Welsh origins offered MGM, and other studios, the chance to tap into a national identity previously unexplored in sound cinema and to exploit his Welshness, something they mysteriously failed to do at any point.

THE MGM YEARS: 1930–1932

Milland finally made his US screen debut in MGM's pre-Code drama *Passion Flower* (William C. DeMille, 1930), starring Kay Francis and Charles Bickford, although he was no more than an extra as an uncredited party guest. Just under an hour into the film, Milland can be seen standing alone in the background, while those around him talk, dance, and drink champagne. His outfit, comprising of a dinner jacket and white tie, clothing that would become a major element of his star persona in just a few years, helps to project the sense of an upper-class background for his character. His

Figure 3.1 Milland moves into the foreground to utter his first line in Hollywood to Charles Bickford and Kay Francis in *Passion Flower* (William C. DeMille, 1930).

hair is slightly messed up, with some strands falling onto his forehead and, although there are several others in this scene, Milland draws the viewer's eye by slightly stumbling around to suggest his character has enjoyed a little too much champagne. Wandering over to the door, he leans on Bickford's shoulder before shaking Francis's hand (figure 3.1). Mumbling in impeccably polished English about having a "perfectly gorgeous time" but having to "trickle along to some silly breakfast party or another," he does not actually leave but turns and wanders back into the room. This dialogue proposes an American writer who assumes this is how Brits, or at least those of the higher echelons of British society, tend to talk and act; while the "Welsh farmer," as Milland often referred to himself, was required to make these lines seem believable if he had any chance of securing more roles.

In the subsequent scene, he leaves with the other guests, clearly even drunker now as he comically searches for the hat he is holding. Re-entering the room to tell Bickford's Dan he found it, Dan humors him by calling him a "good boy" before he remembers he has a letter for Dan. Milland's upper-class accent is punctuated with a slight slurring and stumbling over his words, another indication of his character's drunken state, as he informs Dan that the letter arrived just after he had vacated his London hotel and so he brought it to him. Putting on his hat before leaving, he bids them farewell as Dan thanks him and we hear Milland's off-screen voice reply with

Figure 3.2. Milland's brief, and again uncredited, role as a ship's officer in *Way for a Sailor* (Sam Wood, 1930).

"it's alright." We see the address on the envelope to be the expensive and rarefied The Savoy hotel, confirming his character's privileged class status. Thus, although Milland's Hollywood debut is an extremely brief one with little dialogue (although he has more lines than the other party guests), it allowed him to exhibit strong ties not only to Britain but to London, where MGM had found him. His association with The Savoy, a famously exclusive venue built in 1889, links him to privilege and tradition through its status as an enduring emblem of England's capital city. This brief scene also presents Milland to US audiences in evening clothes for the first time, proving his elegance and refinement, even when his character is a little inebriated, in a comical but stylish foreshadowing of *The Lost Weekend*.

Given cinema's recent transition to sound and its attempts to be taken seriously as an art form, having a character who sounds like Milland in an early talkie would help to add a sense of class and culture to not only the film and the image of the studio but to Hollywood productions more generally, even if in a supporting role as Paramount was doing with Cary Grant. But MGM continued to use Milland in minute bit parts for much of the time they had him under contract, perhaps unsure of how to cast him once signing him up. These early films include *Way for a Sailor*, *Strangers May Kiss* (George Fitzmaurice, 1931), *But the Flesh Is Weak* (Jack Conway, 1932), *Just a Gigolo* (Jack Conway, 1931), and *Polly of the Circus* (Alfred Santell, 1932).

In the first of these, *Way for a Sailor*, Milland has an uncredited part as a ship's officer, a role even smaller than in *Passion Flower*. Nevertheless, since

Figure 3.3. A more youthful looking Milland (far right) grins and chats with Robert Montgomery during his brief scene in *Strangers May Kiss* (George Fitzmaurice, 1931).

the film stars John Gilbert and Wallace Beery, two of the most popular male stars of that period, many audience members would see Milland's short but powerful appearance in this film. He rushes across the deck of a ship during a dramatic storm at sea, trying to coordinate a rescue mission. A woman grabs his arm and stops him to ask about lifeboats and, while replying to her, Milland is shot mostly in profile before looking up slightly and rushing off-screen, appearing extremely busy and efficient after conversing with her for a few seconds. Reflecting hugely different circumstances compared to the party scene in *Passion Flower*, he wears a raincoat with a uniform underneath and an officer's hat (figure 3.2). His single appearance is filmed entirely in a medium two-shot, and he is mostly seen in profile while the camera remains stationary. Milland is on-screen for only fifteen seconds of the film's eighty-five-minute duration, during which time he looks slightly forward only once and speaks limited dialogue; again, he is nothing more than a bit part player. What is most unusual about Milland's appearance here is his thick dark mustache, which he would wear again in several 1930s productions. The mustache detracts from his youthful looks and romantic potential; it was plausibly used here to make him appear older and more authoritative as the ship's officer. Whatever the reason, since Milland documents in his memoir that MGM talent scouts told him he had everything going for him physically, it seems odd to cast him in a small role requiring him to cover his body with a loose-fitting raincoat and his face with a large mustache.

Similarly, in *Strangers May Kiss*, starring Norma Shearer and Robert Montgomery, Milland is again uncredited and has under a minute of screen time. He does, however, converse with Montgomery during his few lines of dialogue. Milland's Britishness is rather ambiguous in the lines he is given, since he sounds Scottish when he calls Shearer's Lisbeth a "lassie" but English when he uses "rather" as a form of yes, as well as "what say?" as a way of asking "what do you think?" Wearing a lightly colored contemporary suit, he converses with Montgomery's Steve while grinning widely and leaning on a chair, one hand placed casually in his pocket (figure 3.3). Milland's character hints at Lisbeth's notorious reputation when Steve asks if he knows her; he responds with a rather telling, "Yes, but not as well as some of my friends do." After introducing the two, he disappears from the scene and from the film. Looking younger sans mustache, and more relaxed in his posture and vocal intonation, it appears that Milland is becoming more comfortable on-screen, and yet he was still being handed extremely limited dialogue and screen time.

The following year, Milland appeared fleetingly in another Montgomery vehicle, *But the Flesh Is Weak*; here, he is dressed in formal white tie and tails and once more portraying a party guest, who grins, nods and mutters his one line of "How do you do?" when introduced to Montgomery's Max Clement. Milland shares the screen with four other performers, aside from Montgomery, who all appear relatively naturalistic in their movements while Milland, conversely, is "mugging" for the camera. He is still a long way off from skillfully using his facial expressions and body gestures in a nuanced fashion, as he does so effectively two decades later in the "silent" experimental film *The Thief* (1952), proficiently using his face and body to effectively "replace" the nonexistent dialogue in conveying the story to the audience. Here, however, it appears that Milland felt that to be considered a "performer" he had to keep moving while on-screen, since he alters his facial expression (eyes, eyebrows, mouth) and the position of his head constantly while observing the conversation in front of him, which is not what people tend to do in everyday situations. Indeed, every line of dialogue spoken by another performer generates a diverse, and far from naturalistic, response from Milland, making it obvious he has not yet learned the skills needed to generate an understated screen performance. Aside from the sartorial outfit, which reflects his character's high social standing and later became strongly associated with his star image at Paramount, what is most notable about this film is that the dialogue was written by fellow Welshman Ivor Novello and derived from his 1928 play *The Truth Game*.

Although William Haines is the only actor billed above the title in *Just a Gigolo*, Milland actually received screen credit this time, billed eighth of eleven players. Listed as "Freddie," his character's name is never mentioned in the film, and it is once more an extremely brief appearance which amounts to not much beyond another role of an extra. Notably, however, in the two scenes he features in, he is seen firstly in a lightly colored modern suit and later in evening wear, both of which would become familiar outfit choices for the actor throughout his lengthy career. He enters the film after about fifteen minutes, along with another man, before trying to kiss a girl. Over six minutes later, he looks polished and suave in evening wear, standing up as a woman leaves his table, thus showing his gentlemanly manners and breeding. Although he exits the film within the first half hour and does not return, what is significant about this film is that the American Haines portrays the sort of character Milland would play repeatedly throughout the next few years: a British aristocrat named Lord Robert Brummel.

Portraying an uncredited church usher and boxing coach in *Polly of the Circus*, starring Marion Davies and a pre-mustached Clark Gable—whom the studio was building up for stardom—Milland receives a collective one minute of screen time. He is first seen boxing with Gable on the floor of a gym; wearing light-colored gym wear, lying on Gable's legs to aid him in sitting up, he is breathing heavily from the vigorous exercise they have undertaken. In this comical scene, Gable calls him a "big gorilla" before throwing his boxing gloves in Milland's face, causing him to fall over. Milland recalls that during this scene, he accidentally knocked Gable's bridge out of his mouth before stepping on it and breaking it. Since the incident caused a two-day delay on the film, Milland feels he "might as well have had leprosy" and claims that Gable never forgave him. Over the next thirty years they regularly saw each other at parties, and even though they belonged to the same golf club, Gable would never take him as a partner (1974: 145). Since Gable was being developed into a major star by MGM, it is possible Milland did not have more substantial roles due to this mishap and the subsequent animosity between the two men. In his other brief scene in the film, Milland is seating people as a church usher when he recognizes Davies's Polly, smiles, and asks how she is before proceeding to the rear of the church as the service begins, the camera then filming him from behind. When the elderly cleaner begins dusting during the service, Milland rushes forward to inform him that it is Sunday. We hear him talking to the older man off-screen, telling him he can come back and dust another day, leading him out by the arm to avoid any commotion. A kindly man, who shows he is less prejudiced towards Polly

Figure 3.4. Milland's first substantial role in Hollywood was as Englishman Geoffrey Trent in the Marion Davies vehicle *The Bachelor Father* (Robert Z. Leonard, 1931).

than most of the other town residents, he is presented as a decent fellow, if a vapid one, since he has no real character development or backstory.

The Bachelor Father (1931) is an important film in Milland's career trajectory as, unarguably, it provides him with his earliest role of any substance in the US; he also deemed it his "first legitimate part" in Hollywood (1974: 127). Milland receives fourth billing after American star and coproducer Marion Davies, and London-born actors Ralph Forbes and C. Aubrey Smith, a former English Test cricketer who became an actor. Milland, at this point still using the name "Raymond," enters around twenty minutes into this ninety-minute film wearing a three-piece suit and tie which make him appear stereotypically British. This is exactly what the role called for, since the plot of this pre-Code film revolves around Smith's Sir Basil Winterton gathering together his three international but illegitimate children for the first time: the American Tony Flagg (Davies), Spanish Maria Credaro (Nina Quartero), and English Geoffrey Trent (Milland). In addition to his distinctive appearance, Milland's dialogue contrasts with Davies's hip young American; he calls the house "rather a jolly kennel this, what?" and, when referring to their father, "the old man isn't up to scratch, right?" Geoffrey comments that "my mater says he's a good deal of a pill," meaning that his mother found their father "hard to swallow," like taking routine medicine, therefore being somewhat unpleasant or boring. Just over an hour into the film, the homesick Geoffrey leaves for England and does not return.

Although a Davies vehicle produced by Cosmopolitan Pictures, a company owned by her lover, William Randolph Hearst, *The Bachelor Father* offers Milland a decent amount of screen time. He is elegantly dressed, wearing a range of suits and evening wear (including a white tie), and, taking advantage of his real-life childhood music lessons, his character writes music and is seen playing the piano. The actor's skilful use of gestures, particularly with his eyes, would become a major element of his acting style in subsequent years; however, in this early venture it is a little overused and still in need of refinement. What is particularly interesting about his appearance here, in contrast to his work in Britain in *The Flying Scotsman* and *The Lady from the Sea*, is that, even though he has retained the harshly slicked-back hairdo of the era, in *The Bachelor Father* he is heavily made-up with evident lipstick and as much, if not more, dark eyeshadow as the two actresses portraying his sisters (figure 3.4). Milland refers to this in the photographic spread contained within his memoir, labeling himself "the girl on the right" in a still image with Davies and Quartero.

Having already encountered difficult film directors despite still being relatively new in Hollywood, Milland writes that Robert Z. Leonard restored his faith in American directors, being "well-mannered and patient" (1974: 127). He found making this film a pleasant experience, viewing Davies as a courageous and generous woman who was mischievous, a little scatterbrained, and with a slight stutter, but who was "kindness itself" (1974: 131). Further suggesting his comfort with those involved in the film, during a picnic he even confessed that as a child he raided the orchard at Hearst's castle in Wales.[3]

On a personal note, but one imperative to his career path, around this time Milland met premed student Rex Ross, who was taking a year's sabbatical in Hollywood.[4] He invited Milland to Pasadena to visit a family called the MacLeods, where Milland amusingly mentions meeting "a lean and flashing dark man" in his mid-twenties he assumed was English since he called him "chum"; he later learned the man was a fellow transatlantic actor and future major Hollywood star, Cary Grant (1974: 133). The MacLeods are pertinent in the story of Milland's life and career because it is through them that he met his future wife, Muriel (Mal), the main reason he returned to Hollywood, and Paramount, after his unsuccessful stint at MGM.

Equating his first encounter with his future wife to being struck by lightning, Milland declares that he missed hearing her name because his world unexpectedly stood still, and he felt utterly lost. Poetically describing the moment in similar terms to his first encounter with dancer Margot St. Leger, he recalls that "the room was empty and there was just her, tall, with dark hair with some silver in it and eyes that truly were sapphire" while he "mumbled some inanities" (1974: 137).[5] In another twist of fate resembling a film plot, he was invited to breakfast at a house in Hollywood which just so happened to be owned by Muriel's family. Aware that his "Welsh charm" would not help him with Muriel's parents, Milland notes it felt like less of a statement and more like an accusation when her father declared him to be English (1974: 139). Since England continues to be seen as the default of Britain, this encounter suggests that, although Milland still considered himself to be a Welshman with Welsh traits, it would be easier to agree to being English when addressing an American to avoid confusion and further explanation of the union, especially when trying to impress the man's daughter. The pair were married less than a year later and, implying Muriel's own family links to Hollywood, one of the ushers was Duke Wayne, who a few short years later would become famous as Western star John Wayne and Milland's costar in *Reap the Wild Wind* (Cecil B. DeMille, 1942) a decade later. Thus, Milland was married extremely early in his Hollywood career and remained married to the same woman for the rest of his life.[6] This may have undermined Milland's romantic appeal, since Hollywood preferred its stars, and potential stars, to remain bachelors as long as possible to aid their romantic interest to (female) audiences, as was certainly the case in 1939 when popular romantic leads Clark Gable, Robert Taylor, and Tyrone Power married actresses Carole Lombard, Barbara Stanwyck, and Annabella, respectively[7] (Kelly 2019; Kelly 2021).

Milland then made three films in eight months: one at MGM and two on loan to Warner Brothers. Of these, he calls *The Man Who Played God* (John G. Adolfi, 1932) the "only one worth any comment," even though he was given a minor uncredited role, and he calls the film "easily forgettable" (1974: 141). His presence is limited to a four-minute scene towards the end after his character, Eddie, has been caught stealing money from his workplace but claims he planned to return it. Threatened with five years in jail, Eddie and his girlfriend prepare to take poison but as he raises the vial to his lips, he is told the company is dropping the charges and he is free. The scene reads like a modern-day *Romeo and Juliet*, only with a happy ending since the young couple are saved in time, but it did allow Milland to prove some (limited) dramatic acting. What made the film important for Milland is that he got to see leading man George Arliss at work, whom he describes as a true professional "completely dedicated to his craft" (1974: 141). Despite

Milland's negative views of his films at Warner Brothers, they prove that he was starting to become capable of more in-depth characterizations, thus able to display a greater range of acting skills. Therefore, his films at the studio are worth closer examination.

ON LOAN TO WARNER BROTHERS

For the pre-Code drama *Bought!* (Archie Mayo, 1931), Warner Brothers paid leading lady Constance Bennett $30,000 a week, more than they had paid any other performer (Hirschhorn 1981: 10). Bennett, the indisputable star of the film, has her name above the title while actress Dorothy Peterson, leading man Ben Lyon, and Bennett's real-life father, Richard Bennett, are supporting players. Billed in smaller letters, Milland enters the film almost halfway through, smartly dressed in a dark suit and tie. His elegant and fashionable Charles Carter Jr. is introduced while mixing cocktails in his vast home as he casually converses with his sister. His surroundings and costume instantly reflect a standard upper-class "rich boy" persona for his character; Milland's hair is once more slicked back, while the addition of dark eye makeup again almost feminizes him. In his next appearance, he wears evening clothes while dining with his parents in their opulent dining room with servants in attendance. Charles is being too attentive to Bennett's Stephanie Dale, intrusively leaning on the back of her chair and grinning at her, a cocktail once more in his hand. These elements combine to radiate Carter's privileged background, high social class and arrogance.

In what would become a common trait for Milland in his films, Carter takes Stephanie dancing, before returning her to her small and basic apartment, a stark contrast to his tastefully decorated spatial surroundings and a strong reflection of the characters' diverse social standing. Moreover, his impeccable evening clothes of white tie and tails look extremely out of place in her barren flat, making him stand out as the one thing that does not quite "fit" and thus foreshadowing their doomed romance. The camera pans from the clock on the mantlepiece to settle on the couple kissing on the couch, Bennett seductively lying down as Milland kneels over her. Moving to another part of the room, Stephanie coldly informs Charles that now that the effect of the champagne has worn off, kissing means nothing and is just silly. As he walks over to join her, almost gliding and in a dreamlike state, Milland uses his face and body to indicate that Carter is in a romantic daze and feels quite different from Stephanie. Grabbing her arms, he calls her "the most fascinating little thing" he has ever known. Standing up just long enough to turn off the light, he sits down and tries to kiss her again, but she refuses. Both performers use their body and vocal intonation to portray their characters' conflicting inner feelings as Charles adoringly declares he is in love and wishes to marry her, while Stephanie very unromantically agrees to the proposal by underwhelmingly stating that it might be nice, while still refusing to kiss him. He grabs at her once more, but she hands him his hat and cane before calmly and solemnly sending him on his way. He leaves in what appears to be a romantic stupor, his grin showing that Carter is selfishly unaware that Stephanie is more interested in elevating her own social and economic status than any romantic connection despite the unenthusiastic nature of her acceptance. After closing the door, she practices aloud "Mrs. Charles Carter," which indicates she is more interested in the title and how the name would sound than in marrying Charles for himself.

Their next scene together takes place in a garden where he is trying to persuade her to have a drink and kiss him again. Although still unmarried, his sexual desire for her is obviously overpowering as he requests that she pretend they are already on their honeymoon, a ruse to convince her to sleep with him. She refuses and reminds him that their wedding is only a month away, but a little later as she stands on her bedroom balcony, we hear the door to her room slam shut. Although we are not shown who has entered, we see Stephanie turning towards the door as she utters Charles's name in surprise, and we then see her from his point of view as the camera approaches her. Initially she tells him to go, but as the camera pans towards the ocean outside, there is a stationary view of the moon on the water as Stephanie's off-screen voice softly says, "Please go. Please go. Please." Her final word trails off as the couple undoubtedly consummate their relationship.

The following morning, Charles is at breakfast when Stephanie joins him. Grinning widely to suggest that he is evidently satisfied from the night before, Charles tells Stephanie that she is wonderful. Establishing the disparity in their emotions and, thereby their incompatibility, the unsmiling Stephanie discloses that she is disgusted with herself. Sensing she has a stronger bond with Charles after consummating their relationship, she reveals to him that her parents were never married, but this information leads to him instantly altering his demeanor. Milland adjusts his expression from the sickly grin of a young man in love who has made his latest conquest to one filled with horror. Charles is appalled by this announcement and begins moralizing, exclaiming that she must be joking before asking what people would think and what the papers would say. Stephanie returns Charles's engagement ring and turns to leave. He informs her that, given his wealth and social position, she would be crazy to ditch him entirely and suggests they go away together without getting married. Slapping him across the face and walking out, Stephanie scoffs at his superior nature and his lack of decency compared to the lower-class people she knows. Looking down at the engagement ring in his hand, he leans against the wall; this is where Charles exits Stephanie's life and Milland exits the film. When Stephanie tells Nick Amory (Ben Lyon) that her parents were never married, he accepts it completely and says it makes no difference to him as he has always loved her. She then confesses to sleeping with Charles but never being in love with him, a revelation that upsets Nick. Informing her that love would have been an honest reason for her behavior, he asks why she did it and she replies that she told herself it was for money and a position. The moralistic, working-class Nick is the one she really loves, and, despite his lack of money and her social and economic aspirations, they end up together, love conquering her desire for position and wealth.

Milland convincingly portrays this rich and privileged young man who believes he can get anything he desires because of his social status. Furthermore, he successfully demonstrates his character's development when Charles ironically rejects Stephanie for being born out of wedlock the morning after convincing her to sleep with him before their marriage. However, Stephanie also uses Charles. While each of the main characters is revealed to be flawed in their own way, in the end only the underdeveloped Nick shows a selfless and unbiased love for Stephanie. Although Milland identified himself as a "Welsh farmer" at the start of his career, he was capable of convincingly portraying the upper-class, spoiled Charles Carter Jr. with the same conviction that the famous and extremely well-paid Bennett plays the penniless Stephanie.

The second, and final, film Milland made while on loan to Warner Brothers was *Blonde Crazy* (Roy Del Ruth, 1931), starring James Cagney and Joan Blondell.[8] Although Cagney's bellhop Bert Harris is the leading man, it is Milland's Joe Reynolds whom Blondell's hotel maid Anne Roberts falls for and later marries. While this character's name is more Americanized than Milland's prior portrayals, Reynolds is nevertheless still upper-class, highly intelligent, and interested in poetry, art, and music. Throughout the film Joe is placed in direct contrast to Cagney's lower-class Bert, a small-time crook who looks like an overgrown child in his bellhop outfit. Joe and Anne meet on a train during a clichéd "meet cute" when she gets a cinder in her eye and, unable to see, tries to sit on the seat Joe is occupying. Shot in profile, he carefully removes the cinder from her eye with one sweep, proudly showing it to her on his handkerchief and introducing himself with a smug grin (figure 3.5).

Joe is introduced while reading the magazine *Tennis*, an elite sport, while dressed in a tailored suit and tie; this instantly suggests he is a studious and

Figure 3.5. The seemingly gallant Joe Reynolds (Milland) shows Anne Roberts (Joan Blondell) the cinder he removes from her eye in *Blonde Crazy!* (Roy Del Ruth, 1931).

intelligent man who is refined, athletic, and appreciates culture.[9] Advocating his wealth and position, thus establishing him in opposition to Bert, Joe informs Anne that the firm he works for is part of the New York Stock Exchange. His erudite nature is echoed in the following scene when, although absent from the screen, Joe sends Anne a book of Robert Browning's poetry which can be read as an incarnation of his personality and presumed values. Jealous of Anne's interest in Joe, Bert demeans him and the poetry, calling him "high and mighty" and a "poetry shark" before reciting from the book in a farcical manner. Although Joe first appears charming as he grins at Anne and asks her to have breakfast with him on the train, there is also something slightly off about Joe, demonstrated predominantly through the way he leers at her with one eyebrow raised as she walks away, followed by the aura of arrogant superiority he gives off when shaking Bert's hand. This foreshadows the cad he will eventually reveal himself to be, slowly being revealed by Milland through a range of subtle gestures and facial expressions which play against the dialogue.

Unlike Bennett's Stephanie in *Bought!*, Anne appears to genuinely love Joe. However, upon meeting his friends and family she feels out of her depth and detached from their world, much as Milland felt when meeting London's theatrical set for the first time. Anne is also pragmatic enough to admit that marrying him will give her a better quality of life. Diegetic church bells ring as Joe and Anne emerge from the church like any other newlywed couple, she in a white gown and veil, and he in a dark tailored suit. They stop and turn to look at each other with wide, excited smiles as Bert watches solemnly from his parked car. The couple then waves to the crowd of gatherers from the backseat of their wedding car as it drives away.

Two minutes later in the film, but representing a year in the narrative, a distressed Anne visits Bert to inform him that Joe has used $30,000 in negotiable bonds belonging to his firm for a deal he thought would make him a fortune; losing it all, he now faces prison upon its discovery. Since Bert has secretly been in love with Anne for years, he visits Joe's office to discuss a planned robbery which will help Joe get the money back. Joe commits the despicable act of reporting Bert's plans to the police, and the foiled "robbery" results in a car chase where Bert is shot at before being caught and incarcerated, while Joe denies any knowledge of the missing funds. In the final scene, Anne visits Bert in his cell to inform him of Joe's spineless double-cross and asserts that she has left him for good. Proclaiming her love for Bert, who, unlike Joe, has never pretended to be anything other than what he is, she kisses him and informs him that she will be waiting when he gets out.

Anne has left Joe because of his contemptible and cowardly behavior, which is never explained but may be due to his jealousy of Anne's continued close connection with Bert, and the two stars are united at the end, their characters penniless but, it is implied, happy since it is clear that Anne feels an honest crook is better than a dishonest one. Indeed, according to Mick LaSalle, Joe's actions were unforgivable for both Anne and the audience since Bert, "the all-out street gangster at least put it all on the line [. . .]. So long as a character had courage and steadfastness, pre-Code audiences could overlook a lot" (2002: 75). Conversely, despite Joe's privileged background, he unforgivably "rats out" Bert to the police and blames Bert for his own criminality while Bert was trying to help him out, if only for Anne's sake.

Patrick McGilligan calls it a "tight, breezy little comedy" that was popular with audiences; when it came to the critics, however, one periodical complained that "[it] makes thievery rather dangerously attractive" (1975: 39). Writing in 1975, McGilligan not only suggests the film is arguably the most enduring work of director Roy Del Ruth but was "gratefully rediscovered by feminists" drawn to the equilibrium that the film establishes between Cagney and Blondell (1975: 39). It was also important in establishing an early "heel" role for Milland, as well as one of his earliest characters with some substance. Although Joe is initially characterized as superior to the film's many other crooks, including Anne and Bert, partly due to his social standing and breeding, he turns out to be the worst of them all. LaSalle calls Joe an "upper-class businessman" and the film's "only despicable character";

the embezzler of the pre-Code being viewed as "the pariah, a child molester among shady types." An embezzler was required to have a job in the first place, "probably a high-paying one," but he just got "greedy, and sneaky." Furthermore, it would be difficult to think of anyone as low as "a sneak who manages to fool the cops and pin the crime on someone else," as Joe does in this instance with Bert (2002: 74–75).

According to LaSalle, Cagney often emphasized that one of the secrets of screen acting was never to relax, because "if you relax, the audience relaxes. Here, his energy is nonstop" (75: 2002). Despite Estelle Brody's previous advice that Milland should slow down his speech, because he spoke "like lightning," the energy on the set of *Blonde Crazy* is highlighted by an amusing anecdote Milland tells when he and Cagney performed a three-page scene, that should have taken three whole minutes to unfold, in just twenty-six seconds. Milland mentions that director Roy Del Ruth looked at Cagney and him with "utter disgust" before remarking that their accelerated speech sounded like "a couple of goddam woodpeckers" (1974: 143). While this is something Milland later controlled, it long remained a recognizable part of Cagney's star persona. Made relatively early in both actors' careers, *Blonde Crazy* was the only time they appeared on-screen together. Although Milland says he got to know Cagney well over the years, they never discussed work and instead had a friendship based on their mutual love of boats (1974: 143).[10]

A FINAL SHOT AT MGM

While top billing goes to Charles Laughton as William Marble and Maureen O'Sullivan as his daughter, Winnie, in *Payment Deferred* (1932), Milland receives fifth billing as Marble's nephew, James Medland, who arrives at the Marbles' London home one rainy evening. At first, it seems Medland is also English since, like Milland's earlier characterization in *The Bachelor Father*, he uses British idioms like "oh rather" and "feeling rotten." However, his question about whether it always rains in England suggests he neither originates from nor lives in Britain. Although we soon find out that Medland has been hunting kangaroos in Australia, it is unclear whether he was born in England and moved to Australia, was born in Australia, or was only there for a short trip. This shows the lack of belonging for another of Milland's characters since Medland appears not to "fit" in either nation. He has a strong upper-class English accent and uses a range of Britishisms, but is paradoxically unknowledgeable about the country's characteristic wet weather, the subject of national amusement.

Figure 3.6. Milland's final moment in *Payment Deferred* (Lothar Mendes, 1932), and his final appearance in an MGM film, as his character reaches for a drink laced with poison.

Before Medland visits, we learn that Marble is deep in debt and has been threatened with dismissal from his job as a bank clerk if he does not pay an overdue bill. There are subtle indications that Medland has money since he has arrived by taxi, a luxury not many could afford during this time of economic crisis and high unemployment. Moreover, he is wearing a stylish overcoat that Marble excitedly declares must be worth at least "a tenner" (£10), at a time when the average wage in the UK was just over £1 a week. Learning that Medland is indeed wealthy, Marble repeatedly tries to borrow money from him while Milland excellently portrays his character's increasing unease as the evening progresses, mainly through subtle gestures such as a raised eyebrow, quizzical looks out of the side of his eye, and the slow raising of his chin, counterpointed by Laughton's theatrical depiction of increased desperation with the dramatic wiping of his brow, exaggerated sweeps of his arms, and overly pronounced dialogue. Following Medland's repeated refusals, the audience receives a privileged view of Marble adding cyanide to a glass of whiskey before handing it to him. In a shot reminiscent of his first British film, *The Flying Scotsman*, when his working-class train fireman nervously reaches for a restaurant bill presented on a silver tray, Milland is filmed from a low angle as he takes the poisoned drink (figure 3.6). Although this marks Milland's final appearance on-screen in the film, and consequently his final moment in an MGM production, his character remains ever-present as Laughton plays out Marble's growing panic and fear of discovery: he repeatedly stares at the spot in the garden where he has buried Medland's body as he mentally deteriorates throughout the film.

Before Laughton signed to Hollywood, Milland recalls seeing him in *On the Spot* on the London stage and stresses the immense talent he exhibited. Noting that just three years later they were appearing together on-screen, it seems Milland either forgot about, or was unaware of, Laughton's (brief) role in *Piccadilly*. He calls the film's German director, Lothar Mendes, charming and possessing humor and patience, which he notes was required not only for dealing with his own inexperience and "lack of talent" but Laughton's "outrageous grotesqueries" (1974: 147). Although he gave a satisfactory performance in his first (albeit brief) dramatic role, MGM dropped Milland's contract just two weeks after filming ended, thus leaving him a jobless expatriate and newlywed. Despite his experiences at MGM and loan-outs to other studios, Milland had "absolutely no belief" in his acting talents and lacked the dedication and confidence needed to succeed in a highly competitive industry (1974: 148). Over the next five months, his only job was in a never-released experimental film for which he received $750, thus averaging just $150 monthly to support himself and his wife. Using the first-class return fare provided by MGM, Milland returned to the UK in hopes that two years in Hollywood may open some doors for him in British cinema (1974: 148).

BACK TO BRITAIN

In another twist of fate, during his eight-day journey back to Liverpool aboard the *Laconia* Milland claims to have met Arthur Barker, who later became one of England's most respected publishers. Barker suggested Milland contact his brother, Vere, a partner in a theatrical agency in London's Regent Street called Connie's Agency. Milland took a room in a small hotel in Piccadilly Circus called Oddenino's (1974: 149), not only situated in one of the most famous intersections in London, arguably even the world, but in the heart of the West End, London's theatre district. However, he could only afford to stay there for three nights before finding a more permanent and less expensive residence in Earl's Court.

Visiting Wales, and possibly recognizing that he had grown up and his life was forever changed, he painfully recalls the visit as "unpleasant"; he found his father reclusive, and Luisa, dramatically aged in just five years. He did not see his mother, who had married an art dealer from Cardiff, but conveys their strained relationship by voicing his relief at avoiding her "bogus affectations of respectability and her denigration of all things bucolic" (1974: 150).

Conversely, he had pined for the very rural surroundings his mother disdained. He reminisces about the simple sights and sounds he missed while in Hollywood, from seeing salmon in the River Usk on the northern slopes of Wales's Black Mountain (y Mynydd Du) to hearing the "simple" and "innocent" sound of church bells on a Sunday morning. Another blow was the death of Bello, the horse he had learned to ride on, and with an "idiot sense of loyalty," he refused to ride during his visit (1974: 150). The loss of Bello suggests the symbolic death of Milland's old life on the farm and a melancholy longing for his lost youth. It could, however, also have been a driving force for his return to America since Wales and the people there no longer held the same appeal.

Meeting with Vere Barker and "Miss Connie" upon his return to London, they agreed to act as his agents for a year. They secured him two roles in early 1933, presumably in the comedies *Orders is Orders* (Walter Forde, 1933) and *This is the Life* (Albert de Courville, 1933), but neither provided him with more than a supporting role. Still, they equipped him with a combined income of £250 (which, with inflation, equates to £18,792 in 2022) and employment in British cinema again. Although these films have proven extremely difficult to track down, the former, starring Charlotte Greenwood and James Gleason, seemed the ideal choice for Milland since the plot sees a Hollywood film company moving into British army barracks to make a film. The latter also has an Anglo-American component, with Gordon Harker and Binnie Hale portraying quintessential British teashop proprietors who move into London's high society after inheriting a fortune from a dead uncle but find themselves entangled with Chicago gangsters. Milland was now playing extras in the UK and having depicted the romantic lead in his first two British films, this must have been frustrating. He then decided to return to California and his wife, but not necessarily to Hollywood.

RETURNING TO AMERICA

Despite his fleeting departure from the US, when Milland returned in August 1933, the country was in the depths of the Great Depression. Foreshadowing the imminent outbreak of World War II in Europe, Milland comments on the substantial power Adolf Hitler was gaining and eerily notes that the saber "rattling and police-state repressions were beginning to worry the world" (1974: 158). Finding an apartment fifty yards from Fairfax, on the south side of Sunset, Milland purchased a Model A Ford coupe once belonging to Olympic swimmer and actor Buster Crabbe. Although it was "a real rattler," he notes that during the Depression people were "glad to sell anything" (1974: 160).

Referring to agents as "very uppity," Milland wryly asserts that it can be easier to get a job in Hollywood than to get an agent. Using the telephone at Laurel Drugstore—situated directly across from the more famous Schwab's Pharmacy, where Milland's *A Life of Her Own* (George Cukor, 1950) costar Lana Turner is said to have been discovered—for three days solid, a couple called Bernard and Meiklejohn finally "condescended" to handle him (1974: 160). Instead of finding the expected publicity shots of young Hollywood stars on their office walls, however, Milland amusingly reveals the photographs depicted an aging Shakespearean actor, a Vaudeville performer, seals, acrobats, and jugglers, and that he heard nothing from them for weeks (1974: 161).

With his career and marriage now in limbo, he would not set up a home with Muriel until he had $3,000 in the bank and "an honest job" (1974: 161). Flat broke, and with his car repossessed, Milland traveled by bus to the Shell Oil offices for a job interview and was hired as the assistant manager for the Sunset and Clark Shell station to begin that Monday. Unveiling yet another improbable twist of fate, Milland claims to have boarded the bus home only to discover he did not have enough money to cover his fare and would have to depart several stops early and walk the remaining three miles. Reading more like the plot of a Hollywood film than a real-life occurrence, Milland describes disembarking four blocks from Paramount Pictures, "the best studio in town," and was a hundred feet from the front gate when casting director Joe Egli came towards him and announced he was just the man he was looking for.

Milland puts the story into context by noting that he had encountered Egli several times while searching for a job over the past few months. But the good fortune of being in the right place at the right time with the right skills in Britain when securing his technical role for *The Informer* and the romantic lead in *The Flying Scotsman* seemed to follow him to Hollywood. The George Raft/Carole Lombard film *Bolero* (1934) needed a man to fill the role left vacant after an unnamed English actor was "stabbed by his boyfriend the night before" (1974: 162). Egli thought Milland would be the perfect replacement and took him to meet the director, Wesley Ruggles, who asked if he could play an Englishman. Milland recalls telling him that he was English, but "could feel Aunt Luisa writhe," before being provided with a script and told to report on Monday morning wearing white tie and tails (1974: 163). If this story is to be believed, after months of trying to secure employment, Milland was handed two remarkably different jobs on the same day and, perhaps most astonishingly, commenced his long and successful career at one of Hollywood's most powerful studios without even trying.[11]

CHAPTER FOUR

THE BRIT EFFECT

PORTRAYING NOBILITY AND ROYALTY

I now turn to explore the frequency with which Milland was cast as nobility and royalty in the initial period of his Hollywood career. This casting as lords, a prince, and even a king is paradoxically at odds with his working-class background and pertinent to the persona Hollywood seemed bent on fashioning for him. Milland's physicality, facial gestures, and particularly his voice are key components of these discussions, with close examination of these elements verifying how Milland's early screen image as a debonair and suave gentleman with perfect diction was formed almost immediately after he arrived in America. Although his voice fluctuates from role to role, as is explored in this chapter, this was in part due to his level of experience at the time and the genres in which he was cast. However, his distinct accent is consistently present whether or not he is portraying a Brit.

A BRIEF HISTORY OF PARAMOUNT

Despite being one of the most powerful studios in Hollywood's classical era, there remain surprisingly few books dedicated to Paramount Pictures; none have been published for decades. One of the earliest accounts is Leslie Halliwell's *Mountain of Dreams* (1976), the title evidently referring to the studio's now legendary logo featuring a mountaintop. As Halliwell notes in the foreword, his book is not a "serious history" of Paramount but instead adopts the "unusual angle" of presenting a vast array of press material, enabling readers to observe a small selection of the immense advertising output of one important studio during "those exciting Hollywood years" (1976: ix). It is worth highlighting here that since the book was published close to fifty years ago, it obviously precedes the internet era, thus the copious illustrations of publicity advertising throughout Halliwell's almost two-hundred-page volume produced during Paramount's classical era would have rarely, if at all, been seen by the public at this time, thereby making it almost a collective archive for contemporary readers.

Whenever a film was sold to an exhibitor it came with a campaign book of publicity material. Although ephemeral, and therefore not meant to be saved, due to the diligence of some collectors, archives such as the British Film Institute (BFI) in London now have a vast collection of these campaign books available to researchers; on occasion, they even appear for sale on internet auction sites such as eBay. These campaign books contained a range of "carefully designed advertisements which could be reproduced, via metal blocks supplied on request for a few pennies," in newspaper and magazine columns (Halliwell 1976: ix). Some of the original metal blocks have also been auctioned off recently, thus allowing individuals to buy into, and literally own, elements of exhibition history. Much has already been eloquently written about the history of the Hollywood studio system by scholars including Tino Balio (1993), Richard Maltby (1995), Thomas Schatz (1997), David Bordwell and Kristen Thompson (2003), and Douglas Gomery (2005), with Paramount's individual history tightly interwoven into this story, so I will not retell it here. I will, however, highlight the importance of the studio and some of the challenges it faced over time, which, in turn, influenced Milland's career as one of Paramount's longest-running contract players.

In 1912, after importing and distributing *Queen Elizabeth* (Henri Desfontaines and Louis Mercanton), starring stage actress Sarah Bernhardt, Hungarian-born Adolph Zukor formed Famous Players in Famous Plays, later Famous Players Film Company, to "exploit the star system and prestigious literary adaptations" and it soon became part of the most powerful studio in Hollywood. Another step towards the creation of the studio system, Famous Players merged with Jesse L. Lasky's Feature Play Company, becoming Famous Players-Lasky in 1916 (Bordwell and Thompson 2003: 68). Following a series of mergers between Zukor, Lasky, and William Wadsworth Hodkinson of Paramount Pictures Corporation, by the late 1920s, Zukor ensured the studio was the largest and most profitable in Hollywood (Otter 1997: 50). Hollywood's first centenarian, Zukor lived to be 103 years old and spent an impressive sixty-four years at Paramount's helm, helping to give the studio its distinct feel and ensuring it was "one of the biggest organizations in the history of the entertainment industry" (Eames 1985: 7).

While many are familiar with the studio's logo of a snow-capped mountain surrounded by twenty-two stars, it is less well-known that each star represented a performer Zukor had under contract at Famous Players. One of them was Mary Pickford, with whom Zukor was sure he had "a big international 'star'—the word was barely coined—in his hands" (Halliwell 1976: xiii), and her importance as "a product of film [with] enormous popularity" cannot be overestimated (Edmonds and Mimura 1980: 53). Referring to the logo, Halliwell proclaims that this "hallowed trademark" connotes the studio's tendency to eschew realism, while historians mostly remember Paramount for "its sardonic high-life romances," since most of its employees came from Europe (1976: ix). Halliwell argues that given the "penchant for smartness" European stars provided the studio with, it is "surprising that the Paramount publicists were invariably so ill at ease with the studio's more ambitious, serious or sophisticated productions" (1976: ix). He suggests that they knew how to sell Bing Crosby and Bob Hope comedies, but "whenever a soupcon of taste was required, as in the case of Preston Sturges, they fumbled it" (1976: ix). While Warner Brothers was recognized for its crime films, Universal for its horror pictures, and MGM for its family-friendly films, Paramount presented a "slightly naughty world" on-screen and enjoyed "harmless suggestiveness" through the performances of its stars like Clara Bow, W. C. Fields, Mae West, and Marlene Dietrich (Halliwell 1976: ix).

Since many of Paramount's influences were European, this made it the least consistently American of Hollywood's studios, thus leading to it being viewed as the most sophisticated (Halliwell 1976: xiii; Cook 2003: 187). In 1918, when Paramount became a staple part of the "growing village" of Hollywood, filmmaker Cecil B. DeMille was the studio's main source of commercial but relatively respectable films and unquestionably the name most synonymous with Paramount (Halliwell 1976: xiii). Highlighting his importance to both the studio and the industry, DeMille was given his own department at Paramount (Kobal 2019; Birchard 2021), "an empire within an empire" which Paramount depended on to create a succession of hits (Halliwell 1976: xiii). While Halliwell suggests that Paramount produced fewer films now considered "classics" than any other Hollywood studio, he finds it admirably maintained "its aura, its personality, its unmistakable impression of the Hollywood dream of life" (1976: x). Despite their longevity at the studio, Milland and DeMille worked together just once, with the historical epic *Reap the Wild Wind* in 1942, a film Halliwell dubs "DeMille's *Gone with the Wind* with knobs on" (1976: 93).

Throughout Paramount's early years, several men worked as head of production, including B. P. Schulberg, who left just before Milland was signed and was succeeded by William Le Baron, a playwright with a university degree—unusual for a Hollywood mogul. He appears to have enforced "quiet good taste" for the studio in the mid-1930s, which evidently involved yielding to the requirements of the Hays Office and the Legion of Decency. Before resigning in 1941, he "tamed Mae West, promoted Bob Hope and encouraged" Billy Wilder and Preston Sturges (Halliwell 1976: xvi). Buddy DeSylva, a songwriter who promoted actress Veronica Lake, the "Road" movies with Hope and Crosby, and superficial World War II musicals, took over, leaving in 1944 without a replacement. With no new executive producer, various producers reported to senior executives Y. Frank Freeman and Henry Ginsbury, who progressively took the responsibility of company management over from the aging Zukor (Halliwell 1976: xx).

German filmmaker Ernst Lubitsch was more responsible than any of the others in creating the "indefinable Paramount style, and the certainty of its European texture" (Halliwell 1976: xxi). A brief list of personnel working for the studio at the time reflects this "European texture" and includes directors John Stahl (German), Josef von Sternberg (Austrian), Rouben Mamoulian (Armenian), Marion Gering, and Anatole Litvak (both Russian). Moreover, Paramount had more contract performers of continental European origin than at any other studio, including French-born Claudette Colbert and Maurice Chevalier, Austrian Erich von Stroheim, Hungarian Paul Lukas, Swedish Warner Oland, Polish Pola Negri, and German Emil Jannings and Dietrich. Instead of referring to them as collectively British, Halliwell highlights Paramount's "strong English contingent," listing Milland alongside Herbert Marshall, Charles Laughton, Clive Brook, Roland Young, C. Aubrey Smith, Henry Wilcoxon, Guy Standing, Gertrude Lawrence, and Victor McLaglen (1976: xxi). While Halliwell argues that American performers like Gary Cooper "always looked slightly out of place" at the studio (1976: xxi), Cooper was actually one of Paramount's most successful performers, along with fellow Americans Jean Arthur, Joel McCrea, and, of course, Mae West. Indeed, in the most recent account of the studio, *Engulfed: The*

Death of Paramount Pictures and the Birth of Corporate Hollywood (2001), Bernard F. Dick declares that several sources erroneously claim that West single-handedly saved Paramount from bankruptcy after the Depression.

In the late 1920s, Paramount's top male stars included Cooper, Charles "Buddy" Rogers, and Richard Arlen, all of whom appeared alongside Clara Bow in *Wings* (William A. Wellman, 1927), which won the inaugural Best Picture Academy Award in 1929. Ten years later, Wellman directed Cooper as the title character in *Beau Geste* (1939), with Beau's younger brother, John, being portrayed by Milland.[1] By the close of the 1920s, the issue of sound in film raised concerns about current stars' voices and whether they would successfully translate into talking pictures. Silent players were given voice tests, with Paramount surpassing Hollywood's other studios by "raiding Broadway" for performers "whose vocal skills were already established," unlike many untrained screen actors (Oller 1997: 51). Paramount consequently signed stage performers Claudette Colbert, Fredric March, and Ruth Chatterton, along with musical performers Jeanette MacDonald and Maurice Chevalier, since sound had "put a new premium on singing ability" (Oller 1997: 51). Cooper, Arlen, Rogers, and Bow passed their voice tests, as did Fay Wray, Louise Brooks, and the newly signed Jean Arthur. Cooper and Arthur had particularly unique voices that added individuality to their star personae in sound cinema. The same is true of Milland, whose speaking voice was a crucial element of his star persona throughout his lengthy career, while his Britishness allowed him a comfortable fit within Paramount's long-established European characteristics.

In rather problematic terms, Halliwell proposes that Paramount films "never hit one between the eyes" since they were "artificial, scorning the real world and its problems" by creating escapism through the "satisfying end product of a dream factory" (1976: xxi). While this judgment may comfortably apply to Milland's screwball comedies of misunderstanding, such as *Easy Living* (Mitchell Leisen, 1937) and *Say it in French* (Andrew L. Stone, 1938), or the unusual *Rhubarb* (1951), about a cat that inherits a baseball team, it defies the stark realism of *The Lost Weekend* or the bleakness of *So Evil My Love*, among his many other pictures with social messages or heavy subject matters. Milland's first film for Paramount, *Bolero*, although somewhat lighthearted, contains war, disease, and death. Even before signing with Paramount, Milland had repeatedly been cast as an upper-class Brit, thus it was imperative to establish the sociohistorical and industrial context of both the studio and more general American history before moving on to analyze Milland's individual roles during this time. Indeed, MGM had already lent Milland out to Fox to play a supporting role in the Will Rogers's vehicle *Ambassador Bill* (1931), in which Milland portrays the noblest of all noblemen: a king.

Wearing a pilot's uniform and again donning a thick mustache, Milland is virtually unrecognizable in this role. A licensed pilot off-screen, his character is first seen landing a private plane before rapidly appearing panicked, his body tensing and his facial expressions conveying alarm as he hides from a group of approaching soldiers. We soon learn that it is a revolution, and although he tells Bill (Rogers) he is a pilot from Berlin, the audience receives the privileged knowledge of his true identity as the country's ruler, King Lothar, and that he is in hiding. That night, trying to remain unseen by the guards, he jumps onto his wife's balcony before kissing her and nuzzling her neck, but the exaggerated way Milland performs these actions suggests he still needed to work on the nuances of his performance. Opening his mouth, he looks at her seductively before walking away with one eyebrow raised, a performance trait he would continuously use throughout his career to varying degrees. Their passionate reunion is interrupted by a group of men chasing and shooting at the king, causing him to flee once more. Since it is believed that Lothar has deserted, his extremely young son is acting as king. A photograph of Milland in an elaborately embellished uniform as King Lothar sits in the queen's bedroom (figure 4.1), which she stares at before bursting into tears to show she loves and misses him. He re-enters the film in the pilot's uniform again to allow him to visit his son safely and is later seen briefly wearing a military uniform, used as a shortcut to demonstrate that he is actively fighting and not the coward people believe him to be. When Lothar is informed that his son is out in the street during the fighting, surrounded by gunfire and explosions and in extreme danger, he rushes to help his family without thinking of his own safety. The film ends with Lothar reunited with his family and reinstated as king, allowing his son to revert to a child without adult responsibilities. With his arm around his wife and the small boy by his side, he looks majestic in his pristine white uniform and truly resembles a king. As a Will Rogers vehicle, Milland is clearly not the star of this film, but he is the most authoritative figure, outfitted in a variety of uniforms and awarded a role that requires exhibiting several layers, which he deals with admirably. Although it becomes obvious that he was still not fully comfortable in front of the camera, with some of his actions appearing rather deliberate, especially during his love scene, Milland does make a believable king through his stance, voice, and overall demeanor. In a more stereotypical and unspectacular role, and again on loan-out, Fox safely cast Milland in the supporting role of British lawyer Neil Howard in *Charlie Chan in London* (Eugene Forde, 1934).

Figure 4.1. Milland looking regal in a framed photograph as King Lothar in *Ambassador Bill* (Sam Taylor, 1931).

REACHING (A) PARAMOUNT

In 1930, just four years before signing Milland, Paramount dominated as Hollywood's most powerful and profitable studio, owning more than 1,000 theatres and with an "international distribution arm stretched across the world" (Gomery 2005: 81). However, 1933 proved to be the worst year of the Great Depression for both the public and the film industry, with fifteen million Americans unemployed and many of Hollywood's top studios suffering severe financial losses (Dick 2011: 53). Although RKO and Warner Brothers lost millions in 1931, it was not until December 1932 that Paramount experienced its lowest financial state, recording an annual loss of $21 million (Gomery 2005: 88; Balio 1993: 15). Lacking an alternative, the studio declared bankruptcy in 1933 since "the company Zukor had built simply had no solution to deal with the Great Depression" (Gomery 2005: 88). However, as Tino Balio explains, bankruptcy and receivership were common during the Depression, and enabled "distressed companies to protect their assets for the benefit of investors" while a plan was worked out on how to pay creditors. A reorganization of the studio allowed all debt to be paid off and enabled Paramount to emerge from the Depression intact (1993: 15). The studio was in receivership for two and a half years and still had a debt of around $95 million in 1935. More encouragingly, though, after a two-year absence, in August 1935 the studio was relisted on the New York Stock Exchange (Gomery 2005: 88).

Barney Balaban was instrumental in returning Paramount to its former glory, even declining a salary at first as he consolidated operations and increased efficiency to help the studio get back on its feet; for quickly stabilizing the company, Douglas Gomery calls Balaban "the answer to Paramount's woes" (2005: 88). Importantly, Balaban looked to other media for new screen stars, and in the late 1930s he signed radio stars Bob Hope and Bing Crosby, who were highly profitable for the studio, both separately and together. Other profitable radio stars who worked for the studio included Jack Benny, George Burns, and Gracie Allen. During his first years at Paramount, Milland worked with all but Hope, although they did appear together on a television special decades later, on April 10, 1972, in a skit spoofing *The Lost Weekend*. Under Balaban's control, Paramount made a profit of $2.5 million in 1939, even without much aid from the European market, which had been understandably disrupted by the war (Gomery 2005: 89). By September 1941, Paramount was again the top studio in Hollywood, making profits of $1 million per quarter (2005: 91), and it was around this time that Milland received his first taste of stardom with *Arise, My Love* (Mitchell Leisen, 1940).

Accordingly, by the time Paramount signed Milland in 1934, the studio already had a "proud and glorious past" which stretched back to the silent era when DeMille, Pickford, Douglas Fairbanks, Rudolph Valentino, and Gloria Swanson all worked there (Oller 1997: 50). Oller sees Paramount as "the very model of efficiency" during this time, when its high quality and diverse films were unmatched by any other studio (1997: 49–50). Thus, its name fitted it, since an online dictionary definition of paramount is "more important than anything else, supreme" (Merriam-Webster 2022).[2] One of the most noteworthy films of this period was DeMille's epic *The Ten Commandments* (1923), the most extravagant picture ever made at that time (Edmonds and Mimura 1980: 115; Blanke 2018). After starring in *It* (Clarence G. Badger, 1927), Paramount player Clara Bow became Hollywood's biggest box-office draw and brought even more attention to the studio (Oller 1997: 50). When Bow's popularity began to wane at the turn of the decade, Paramount signed Carole Lombard and, after she "burst on the screen," nobody missed Bow any longer (Edmonds and Mimura 1980: 186). After gaining a following as the "coin-flipping killer" in *Scarface* (Howard Hughes, 1932), George Raft made his starring debut in *Night After Night* (Archie Mayo, 1932), for which he proposed Broadway performer Mae West for a role (Edmonds and Mimura 1980: 191). West later became a major performer at Paramount, but its top stars in the early 1930s were Lombard, Raft, Cooper, Sylvia Sidney, and the "rapidly rising" Claudette Colbert and Fredric March (Edmonds and Mimura 1980: 192).

Starring Lombard and Raft in the lead roles, *Bolero* was released in February 1934 to "crowds fill[ing] the theatre" (Ott 1972: 115), soon becoming one of the year's most successful films (Eames 1985: 101). Thus, securing a role in such a phenomenally successful film would have gained Milland some well-needed exposure. It was also the first film he made for Paramount, a union that would last over two decades and during which time both parties would encounter many changes including technological, industrial, economic, and sociopolitical. For Milland, it also meant a geographical change since he married the American Muriel Webber in September 1931 and applied for American naturalization in May 1938, stating that he had lived in the US since 1930.

Lombard was on the cusp of major stardom when *Bolero* was released, Paramount having employed her as a featured player in 1930 after her impressive work in *Safety in Numbers* (Victor Schertzinger, 1930), starring Charles "Buddy" Rogers. Although signing another contract with the studio in late summer 1932, Lombard was consistently unhappy with the roles she was given (Morgan 2016: 78). While Milland also features in Lombard's next film, *We're Not Dressing*—both released in early 1934—her subsequent role in *Twentieth Century* (Howard Hawks, 1934) was so significant to her career and the genre of comedy more generally, arguably being the first screwball comedy, that Lombard biographer Michelle Morgan understandably concentrates on this film. Lombard's two outings with Milland merely receive a passing reference (2016: 88), while Milland receives no mention at all.

For his role as a British army officer, which was hardly a stretch for him, Milland was made up by famous Hollywood makeup artist Wally Westmore, who gave him a "fierce military" mustache, almost identical to the one he wore in *Ambassador Bill* and reminiscent of that which he described his father consistently wearing (Milland 1974: 163). For much of the film, he is dressed to reflect Hollywood's stereotypical version of a British gentleman, frequently wearing a bowler hat and carrying gloves and a cane, "essential aspects of bourgeois dress" (Crane 2000: 37), thus indicators of his higher social standing than the American Roaul and Helen. Although his Lord Robert Coray marries Lombard's Helen, their relationship appears more platonic than a passionate love affair, while his disguised looks desexualize Milland and take away from his youthful handsomeness by making him appear much older than his twenty-seven years, as do his stance and gestures

Figure 4.2. Milland as typical English lord in *Bolero*, complete with cane, gloves, bowler hat, and thick mustache (Wesley Ruggles, 1934).

which are often stiff and proper (figure 4.2). This was potentially not only to reflect how American filmmakers and audiences perceived an upper-class Englishman to look and act, but to stop Milland from competing with leading man Raft for the audience's attention since we are asked to identify with and desire his Raoul, with Lombard's Helen acting as a surrogate for us.

In another link to Milland's off-screen life, Raoul and his brother Mike (William Frawley) are coal miners, but the former aspires to become a dancer.[3] Rising to the top of his chosen profession, Raoul takes Helen as his professional partner, and they travel to London to dance. It is there that Annette (Sally Rand) tells Raoul that Helen is receiving a lot of male attention, especially from Coray. Thus, Milland's character is discussed before he enters the film, approvingly described as having "marriage in his eyes and he's not hard to take," declaring that Helen "would be a sap to pass him up." Before being seen, then, through Annette's description, we know that he is rich, attractive, has a high social position as a British lord, and is overall a decent man. As with Cagney's Bert in *Blonde Crazy*, he is the opposite of Raft's Raoul in several ways but proves himself to be much more decent than *Blonde Crazy*'s Joe.

After this initial introduction of Robert's virtues, the scene cuts to show Milland in his first appearance in a Paramount film, as he walks into the nightclub dressed in evening clothes and with a thick mustache. Sitting down at a front-row table, he casually takes out his cigarette case before looking towards the stage as the diegetic music for Raoul and Helen's number begins.

When their dance concludes, a cut to Robert/Milland shows him grinning and clapping; when Helen/Lombard looks over, he smiles and slightly bows his head in polite recognition of her performance. The jealous Raoul is less enamored with his presence, snapping, "He's here. He's always here." When Helen walks towards Robert's table, he immediately jumps to his feet and pulls out her seat in a gentlemanly gesture. While she greets him with a civil, "Hello Bob," he replies with a much warmer, "Hello darling," the combination of the line and Milland's delivery showing that Robert is smitten. Becoming instantaneously shy in her presence, he fiddles with his mustache while mumbling that he could not stay away. He questions why she will not marry him, thus suggesting he has asked her several times, but she continues to refuse. His nervous stuttering as he leans towards her is juxtaposed by her calm and controlled demeanor, devoid of any real emotion and seemingly detached from the situation, thereby giving Helen power over Robert while suggesting their love is one-sided.

Showing his perseverance and financial means to do so, Robert follows Helen to Paris on her dancing tour. She and Raoul are rehearsing in a closed nightclub when Robert walks in, sits down, and silently watches them; his obvious annoyance and jealousy in seeing them together depicted by Milland's facial expressions and gestures, including steadily swinging his walking cane to depict his repressed anger. Despite being six years younger than Raft, Milland's bowler hat, bow tie, cane, and elaborate mustache make him appear much older, uptight, and again desexualized while Raft is more sexually free, dancing seductively in a white silk shirt and tight trousers. It is obvious that Helen loves Raoul from the way she looks at him, touches him, and answers his questions breathlessly, while her looks at Robert seem based more in amusement, her brief touch of his arm appearing sisterly and her answers to his questions, even marriage proposals, determined and controlled, an early hint at the strong women Milland would consistently support as a leading man in just a few years. When Raoul asks if she has a date with Robert, she proclaims a definite "no" but says she could not stop him from coming to Paris; shortly afterwards the two dancers reveal their feelings for each other and kiss before dancing the Bolero of the film's title.[4]

After World War I breaks out, Raoul enlists in the army, declaring he will not dance again until America is victorious, but Helen is disillusioned when she discovers he only did it as a publicity stunt. A harrowing montage with images of war, destruction, bombs exploding, and men dying is then intercut with a very brief shot of Helen and Robert being married, she in a white dress and he in military uniform. Mike calls Robert a "swell guy" as he shows Raoul a newspaper report of the wedding. Sustaining an injury in the war, doctors warn Raoul that his heart and lungs are not strong enough for a dancing career. He tells no one and returns to dancing after the war ends. Helen has retired after marrying Robert, who takes her to see Raoul dance. After his new partner arrives drunk, Mike asks Helen to step in just this once since it is the opening of Raoul's nightclub, which had long been his dream. She asks Robert's permission, but he has no objection. Although Helen informs Raoul that she is incredibly happy with Robert, we see none of the spark or passion that exists between her and Raoul. Watching Helen dance with Raoul for the final time, and it is definitely the final time since Raoul drops dead in his dressing room directly afterwards, Robert claps and smiles proudly and lovingly, just as he did when introduced. Thus, Robert is depicted as an understanding and devoted man who would do anything for Helen, but, like many of Milland's early characterizations, he has no real substance or character development, while his nervous actions, restrictive costume, and general demeanor allow Raft as Raoul to be the undeniable dominant, more masculine star whom Helen shares a passionate love with that is far removed from her stability with Robert.[5]

Although signed for this single picture, a week after *Bolero* wrapped Milland had returned to the studio for a day of retakes and recalls bumping into producer Barnet Glaser while leaving the set. Glaser informed him he was beginning *We're Not Dressing* in two weeks, a comedy starring Lombard and Bing Crosby with a part that would suit Milland.[6] Successfully securing the role, Milland remarks that the film had "the damnedest cast ever assembled outside of *Dinner at Eight*,"[7] and, along with Lombard and Crosby, had Ethel Merman, George Burns and Gracie Allen, Leon Errol, Bob Burns, Jimmy Dorsey and his band, and "a six-foot bear who could roller-skate" (1974: 167).

Milland recalls a crucial moment in his career when he, Burns and Allen began ad-libbing a scene and making it "much better than the original script," leading to director Norman Taurog suggesting to Paramount that they put him under contract. Making a brief call to the front office, he sent Milland to see Al Kaufman who, for reasons not explained, asked Milland if he was Czech. When Milland replied that he was Welsh, thus informing the chief production executive of his national identity before even being signed, Kaufman announced that he had once managed the Welsh singer Madame Clara Novello Davies, whose "flighty" son Milland greatly resembled. He ponders whether Kaufman knew that the boy had "become one of Britain's biggest stars, the darling of the gods in the upper balconies," Ivor Novello (1974: 169). Kaufman signed Milland to his first seven-year contract with options, starting at $175 a week and rising each time his option was picked up. When he announced to Kaufman that he was getting $300 a week for his current film, he was told it may be another six months before he got another role, whereas this contract guaranteed him a steady weekly income and the pair finally reached a compromise.[8] Thus, in yet another occurrence of serendipity, if we are to believe Milland's recollections, he was now officially under contract to Paramount Pictures without even trying, where he would remain for twenty-one years.

We're Not Dressing, released in April 1934 (Ott 1972: 117), is a comedy based on J. M. Barrie's 1902 play *The Admirable Crichton*. Lombard portrays spoiled socialite and yacht owner Doris Worthington, while Crosby's Stephen Jones is a penniless sailor who works for her. The film begins during a pleasure trip on the Pacific where Doris is accompanied by her uncle Hubert (Leon Errol), friend Edith (Ethel Merman), and princes Alexander (Jay Henry) and Michael Stofani (Milland, again billed as Raymond), who pay her a lot of attention because of her money. Doris becomes interested in Stephen but tries to belittle him because of her attraction to a man with a much lower social position; following a verbal dispute, she slaps him and he kisses her, leading to her firing him. After a drunken Hubert runs the yacht into a reef and causes it to capsize, the party ends up on an island, and the only one with survival skills is Stephen. When Doris demands that he fetch food and build shelter for the group, he reminds her that she fired him and tells them that they are on their own. It becomes obvious that the party with money, but no actual life skills, will not survive on the island without Stephen's help, and one by one they come around to his way of thinking, except for the stubborn Doris who would rather starve and freeze than ask him for help.

Due to the limited cast and with much of the action taking place on a desert island, Milland became an almost constant presence on-screen for the first time in his Hollywood career. Although portraying a prince, his character is depicted as being extremely useless and only attentive to Doris because of her wealth. He and his brother are a constant duo, hardly separated for a moment and almost merge into one entity; they are even dressed identically throughout. The others look down on the princes, and they are continually emasculated by the others collectively referring to them as "the boys," which denies them an individual identity and standing as adult males or "real" men. The film is full of comedic moments, and by the end, Doris finally confesses her love for Stephen, having learned her lesson about judging people based merely on their financial wealth or social position, another link to the Depression and the financial straits many faced during this time.

Milland does not take center stage in the film, but his clean-shaven face reveals a more youthful and attractive visage, while his fitted white outfit underscores his physique. Undermining his masculinity and social position, Michael does not receive the respect expected of royalty. Edith (Ethel Merman)

Figure 4.3. Milland (right) raises one eyebrow when his masculinity is questioned, with Jay Henry and Carole Lombard in *We're Not Dressing* (Norman Taurog, 1934).

calls him "gorgeous" and declares she will marry whichever prince Doris rejects, thus reinforcing the brothers' status as one entity and their position as only being there for the women's amusement. Although highlighting Milland's romantic potential, it can also be argued that this was detrimental to his screen presence, since even his character's peers do not take him seriously. However, we learn that the princes are in financial difficulty and pursuing Doris solely for her money; therefore, they are presented as being unethical and undeserving of the audience's sympathy. Moreover, it is strongly hinted that they are not only broke but homosexual and that, just like their outer display of wealth in the evening clothes they constantly wear throughout, their supposed heterosexual interest in Doris is also a façade. While Doris dismisses them as, collectively, "the boys" and a bit of flirtatious fun to keep her amused and fetch her drinks without creating any real romantic entanglement, Hubert dislikes them intensely and degrades them at every opportunity. When his insults are within earshot of the princes, Milland responds with a series of double takes, raised eyebrows, and silent scowls, gestures that would become familiar elements of his screen persona over the years.

Milland appears almost instantly, his Prince Michael engaged in a card game on Doris's yacht. Shot in profile, his serious expression suggests Michael is concentrating intensely on the game while he points his fingers slightly towards the cards he grips. Dressed in a form-fitting pale cutaway dinner jacket, dark trousers, white shirt, and black bow tie, all of which accentuate his figure, he politely stands and smiles when Edith leaves to get a drink. After this, he can be seen in the background in the same position while Merman and Errol perform a musical number in the forefront of the scene. Looking at them stony-faced, he begins exhibiting annoyance as they throw items around, leaning back in his chair to avoid getting hit. Interacting with Doris/Lombard for the first time, he approaches her on the deck with a wide grin and a slight bow, declaring that he and his brother just "cut" for her and he won. Not looking overly thrilled, she asks him to get her a highball, to which he again smiles and bows, militarily turns on his heel and walks briskly off-screen. When Alexander tries to interfere with making the drink, they start to bicker, and Michael tells him to "lay off" since he proposed to Doris first. Although scowling at his brother, the moment he turns around, Milland has comedically altered his expression to a wide grin as he walks towards Lombard with the drink in his hand. When Michael tells Doris that he hopes he has not made the drink too strong, Errol makes a quip insulting his masculinity, with which Milland turns towards him with one eyebrow down and a scowl on his face (figure 4.3), before turning back to Lombard with a plastered-on grin once more.

Michael jealously watches from afar when Doris sits next to Stephen and stares at him while he sings. Taking a superior attitude, which is undeserving given his morally ambiguous situation and his financial straits, he raises his chin and puts his nose in the air before condescendingly declaring that a sailor should not be allowed to parade the deck, leading Errol to quip that there are other "things" that parade the deck (clearly referring to the princes). At this remark, Michael/Milland rocks back on his heels before Edith leads the princes away to defuse the situation. Once they have left, Doris informs her uncle that they are "nice boys" who want to marry her, but there is no passion or romance in her voice, just the sense that she enjoys the attention; her words once more undermine their maturity as grown men. She also appears to have no preference for either and, despite the fact they cannot both marry her, she again appears to consider them as a collective being.

The film's most comical scene occurs when the ship begins to sink and we see the princes standing on-deck wearing life preservers over their eveningwear. They shout through a closed door to inform Doris that she needs to put one on too, but when she informs them that she does not have one Michael/Milland immediately turns his eyes to Alexander/Henry's life jacket before childishly and defensively grabbing at his own, thus showing Michael's selfishness and possessiveness. Although Alexander declares they will save her, the ship begins to tip and Michael/Milland looks left then right before they both run and jump overboard, leaving Doris to fend for herself. If this act of cowardice were not enough to suggest that they do not have any real feelings for Doris, they argue about her while engaged in rowing their tiny lifeboat. Michael tells Alexander that if he had not interfered, he may have already married Doris, to which his brother quips that Michael would have her money then. Michael/Milland stops rowing, a look of annoyance on his face as he throws his hand up in despair and declares that nobody has it now.

As the princes approach the island Michael demands that Stephen, who is already there, pulls them ashore. Having been fired and with no respect for the princes, Stephen utters a "yes sir" before pulling the rope and causing them both to topple into the water. Even more cutting is when Errol sees they got to the island safely and quips that the shipwreck "hasn't turned out as well as I'd hoped." When Michael declares in an overly confident manner that the brothers will look after them all, Edith sarcastically retorts that now she knows they will starve. She may have objectified the princes on the yacht when they were surrounded by luxury, but she is all too aware of their lack of competence when it comes to survival skills. More comical moments follow which illustrate her point, and which would not have been out of place in a silent comedy starring the likes of Buster Keaton or Charlie Chaplin, such as Michael's multiple failed attempts at starting a fire using stones. Stephen informs the princes that he will give them a portion of his food if they collect some wood for a fire, and they wander off. When Michael/Milland returns carrying heavy wood on his shoulder, he is puffing and his hair is untidy, indicating that Michael is evidently not used to undertaking manual labor. Stephen is presented as the opposite of the princes: he is adept at physical tasks, is tough, and looks after Doris because he loves her. When he becomes annoyed by the princes, saying he will break their necks, they back off and, as soon as he raises his fist, run off in a comically terrified manner.

When the party is eventually rescued from the island, Michael pretends he gave Doris the life preserver, but the audience observed Stephen putting it on her while she was unconscious and getting her off the yacht before it sank, while the princes deserted her. When it is obvious that she has fallen for Stephen and that neither prince has a chance of marrying her, they search the telephone book for women listed as "Miss." Finding a new heiress who lives in the affluent Park Avenue, the brothers smile and shake hands, conveying a silent agreement on their next venture. They clearly have no regrets over losing Doris, other than the fact that they lost out on her money; their spineless and comedic actions project a sense of queerness about them throughout the film, an offensive stereotype common in Hollywood films at this time. Thus, despite their good looks, they are no real threat to Stephen, and their uselessness is frequently hinted at or even explicitly stated by those around them. Hubert particularly dislikes them, referring to them as many things including "a crime against nature." Undermining their masculinity, or lack of it, at every opportunity, at one point he states that he does not like them, "they dance beautifully, and probably knit beautifully too", before telling Doris that he could paste them together and she still would not have a man. Thus, even though Milland is almost ever-present for the first time in a Hollywood film, he is never alone and rarely apart from his identically dressed brother. His character is comical and not meant to be taken seriously; lacking any depth, substance, or personality, he is only there as a parasite after Doris's money and to be laughed at. Crosby is the leading man of the film, the alpha male who can survive on a desert island and look after his woman in the process, and although Milland is more conventionally attractive than Crosby, he has to act the fool to allow the audience to believe that Doris would fall for Stephen over the handsome princes who have nothing more to offer than looking good in a tuxedo and knowing how to mix cocktails, which are hardly life skills.

The next time Milland played a lord was in *The Gilded Lily* (Wesley Ruggles, 1934), an important film in his trajectory since this was the first time he had a substantial role in Hollywood and was able to show some character development as the likable "Charles Gray," an out-of-work Englishman who turns out to be the wealthy Lord Granton visiting America incognito. He also receives third billing just after stars Claudette Colbert and Fred MacMurray but ahead of C. Aubrey Smith and Edward Craven. John Douglas Eames refers to the film as "a featherweight comedy [with a] choice cast" that was good for both audiences and exhibitors (1985: 112), while Milland recalls it as a "very pleasant engagement and most successful financially" (1974: 189). Eames suggests that due to her recent Best Actress Academy Award win for *It Happened One Night* (Frank Capra, 1934), Colbert was a hot property at this time, while *The Gilded Lily* demonstrated that Paramount had "much-needed male stars" in MacMurray and Milland (1985: 112), who had both begun their screen careers five years earlier, in 1929. In his biography of Colbert, Bernard F. Dick notes that the film was written specifically for her to cash in on the phenomenal success of *It Happened One Night* as an unexpected multiple Oscar winner; MacMurray's Peter Dawes stood in for Clark Gable's Peter Warne of the former film and Milland's Charles Gray was "a British peer in lieu of King Wesley" (2008: 101), who was portrayed by Jameson Thomas. I would suggest, though, that this appears to be quite a stretch given the different dynamics in this film.

Milland enters the film with his back to the camera in a crowded subway station. When Colbert's Marilyn Davis is pushed by a guard, unlike his

Figure 4.4. Milland's British lord and Claudette Colbert's American stenographer on the beach in *The Gilded Lily* (Wesley Ruggles, 1934).

previous screen incarnation, Charles is the only one to step in, pushing the guard before being punched to the ground. Getting to his feet, he returns the punch before the guard begins repeatedly blowing his whistle. The commotion ends when Marilyn grabs Charles's arm and hurries him out of the station and into the nearest store. It is a rather violent "meet cute" but demonstrates that Charles is a gentleman who is ready to defend a woman even if he does not know her. They soon get to know each other though, and in the next scene he is taking her home after buying her dinner. When he asks if he can see her again, it is only then that she comments that he sounds English. He informs her that he was born in England, making it clear to the audience, if it was not already obvious by his voice, that he is an Englishman. Even though they have clearly spent hours together, it is also only now that he introduces himself, as Charles Gray, a name we will soon learn is an alias. Charles is obviously smitten, and she appears to like him too; they enjoy a day together at a funfair; we see them riding a rollercoaster, on which his ice cream cone comically lands on his face. Afterwards, as they lie on their stomachs on a beach, he appears relaxed and more casual as he makes patterns in the sand with his finger and softly smiles intermittently at her. Milland's hair is no longer harshly slicked back but falls freely onto his forehead; the heavy makeup of his MGM films is gone, which adds to his youthful, clean-cut appeal as a romantic figure (figure 4.4). Charles suddenly confesses his love for Marilyn, who appears excited at the prospect since she keeps moving in towards him, instigating their closeness throughout, but just as he leans in to kiss her, a child trips over him. The boy shouts to his father that Charles grabbed him, while Charles stutters out a proclamation that he never touched the boy. He turns and comically identifies the boy's father as the subway station guard; with a look of horror, he and Marilyn once more link hands and run. Ironically, they share their first kiss at the bench where Marilyn spends her free time with Peter (MacMurray).

As Charles confesses to his father that he wants to marry Marilyn, an American stenographer, it is revealed to the audience that he is the affluent Lord Granton. We also learn that he is engaged to a wealthy British woman in a marriage of convenience rather than a union of love, a repeated trope in Milland's 1930s Paramount films. He leaves Marilyn for a couple of weeks to return to England and sort things out, aiming to return to her free and ready for marriage.

Although Marilyn sees Peter as a close friend in whom she can confide about anything, Peter has secretly been in love with her for a long time. When Charles leaves on the boat to return to Britain, reporter Peter takes a photograph of him, and his true identity is revealed in the newspaper. Marilyn reads the story in the subway before confronting Peter about it. Peter then deceitfully authors stories about her that are not true, saying that she refused the rich and handsome Lord Granton and forced him to go back to England. A montage of images follows showing a range of newspapers featuring Charles and Marilyn as their front-page stories, with a variety of headlines and photographs of the two players. This acts as a shortcut for the mass of publicity generated by Peter, while also establishing how important a figure Charles is to warrant so much media attention, especially given the period. As Dick notes, when Peter uncovers the identity of his rival, he creates "a media blitz, known only in the movies of the 1930s when a romance between a British lord and an American stenographer could drive the Great Depression off the front page" (2008: 101).

It is aboard the ship back to England that Charles is made aware of these stories; as he listens to the captain relaying the newspaper reports, Milland arguably does his first real in-depth screen acting of his Hollywood career. Here, he displays a real sense of character development, no longer just a surface reading of the jolly, rich Englishman who has no financial worries and is only interested in chasing after women. Misunderstanding and thinking that Marilyn is the one behind the stories, he looks bemused and hurt. Leaning on the table, he slouches over and asks why she would do such a thing. Sitting down, he appears agitated as he leans forward with his

Figure 4.5. Rivals for Marilyn (Claudette Colbert), Fred MacMurray's Peter and Milland's Charles reluctantly shake hands in *The Gilded Lily* (Wesley Ruggles, 1934).

eyebrows raised. Getting angry at her, he stands and paces with his hands in his pockets. Hurt, irritated, and feeling betrayed, Charles then sends Marilyn a telegram asking how much it will cost "for a poor little working girl to forget she ever met me."

Upon receiving Charles's telegram Marilyn confronts Peter, who secures her a job as a nightclub entertainer known as "The No Girl," but she proves to be talentless. Marilyn embarrasses herself by trying to sing and dance but the audience, thinking it is a comedy act, laughs and claps for her. A cut to Charles sitting with friends in London shows him dressed once more in smart evening attire, and as he reads about her act in the newspaper he confesses he still loves her; it is obvious here that he holds no malice and is an extremely decent man. Across the Atlantic, Marilyn tells Peter she is still in love with Charles and arranges shows in London in the hope that he will come to see her. He does indeed arrive at the nightclub to see her act, visiting her in the dressing room afterwards and telling her he still loves her. They kiss in a full-length shot, Milland looking desirable in evening clothes of white tie and tails. Peter, who has accompanied Marilyn to London, then enters the room and the two identically dressed men size each other up. The main physical difference between the actors is that MacMurray is much broader than Milland, his newspaperman appearing quite uncomfortable in the restrictive tuxedo, and the way he looks ready to burst out of it suggests a manifestation of his all-American machismo being constrained. By contrast, the more refined Milland, with his delicate features, looks much more at ease in the eveningwear, and given his social position, Charles, as an upper-class English lord, is evidently used to wearing such attire in his everyday life (figure 4.5). The actors were almost the same height, Milland at 6'2" and MacMurray at 6'3"[9] and around the same age, Milland having been born in January 1907 and MacMurray in August 1908. Both had dark hair and attractive features, and were physically a good match for each other, allowing the audience to understand why Marilyn could be in love with them both.

Charles and Marilyn reconnect in London, but when he kisses her passionately under a tree she gets up and begins to pace. Like Constance Bennett's Stephanie in *Bought!*, Charles wants to be with her so much that, when she once again refuses to marry him, he suggests they spend a week in a country inn. Although leading him on and rebutting his proposals, she is offended by his proposition and leaves for New York and Peter's arms, showing that she has finally chosen between the men.

Throughout the film, Marilyn and Peter both betray Charles, and she incessantly toys with his affection. His lack of anger over the newspaper stories and the hoax that Peter initiates against him, and Marilyn takes part in, proves that he is a respectable man with class and decorum, and that he genuinely loves her. Moreover, although she professes to love him, and sensually flirts with him in her dressing room, she knocks him back each time he proposes. He loves her so much that he finally offers to take her away as his mistress if she has no desire to become his wife, but she balks at the idea and leaves. In fact, although Charles was deceptive in keeping his true identity hidden, it was so as not to alert the press and to discover if Marilyn genuinely loved him and not his money. The deception by Peter, with the phony newspaper articles, and Marilyn, by not telling him she is in love with Peter, represent worse deceptions. Thus, in the end the leading lady again favors the earthy, rough and ready all-American over the impeccably mannered and understanding Brit portrayed by Milland.

Dick suggests that Colbert and MacMurray were "a natural fit. The warmth the two of them generated as they sat on a stone bench at the New York Public Library, eating popcorn, filtered into the audience, who thought of them as the ideal couple," until Charles shows up. He concludes that "Milland's Prince Charming was so at odds with MacMurray's common man that audiences hoped Marilyn would make the right choice" (2008: 102), but some audience members may be in doubt that she actually does. It is obvious that the filmmakers are presenting MacMurray's fast talking, confident he-man in his slightly disheveled suits and paper bags of popcorn as the ideal mate for working-class stenographer Marilyn, while Milland's lord is presented as somewhat boring and reserved, stuttering while he speaks and immaculately dressed in tuxedos and tweed suits. It is suggested, then, that Marilyn will have a fiery and passionate romance with Peter, while the same would not be possible with the cool-headed and politely aristocratic Charles. However, Milland had more sexual allure and eroticism on-screen than the average supporting man and, as is discussed in the next chapter, he was permitted the opportunity to prove this through his incredibly sensual pairing with Colbert in *Arise, My Love* (1940), the film that arguably made him a star.

A UNIVERSAL STAR

Milland portrayed one more lord in the 1930s, this time on loan to Universal, where he had a supporting role in the musical comedy *Three Smart Girls* (Henry Koster, 1936), a star vehicle for young soprano Deanna Durbin. Despite signing a seven-year contract, as Kaufman had highlighted, there was a lack of work for Milland. The actor reports that only high-priced contract players were given attention by the studio, while others were "ignored, sort of relegated to a grab bag of reserves, to be used only in case of emergency, practically forgotten" (Milland 1974: 170). Milland mentions that despite receiving a weekly pay from the studio, actors still had to "get out there and make a name" for themselves before they would be noticed; he also believed that being tied to one studio was extremely constricting (1974: 170). Arriving home from a flight one day, he recalls receiving a message from Paramount that he was being loaned to Universal to start on a role at once. Heading to the studio, he met with Joseph Pasternak and director Henry Koster and was informed that he would be replacing yet another British actor. This time it was Louis Hayward, who had been engaged in New York just two weeks prior. While Milland suggests that Hayward had not been seen or heard from since being signed, other sources suggest that he started working on the film but came down with pleurisy four days into filming. Paramount had suggested Milland as a replacement and, as long as he had a smoking jacket and could report to the set the following morning, he was hired (Milland 1974: 173).

The film follows three sisters—Joan (Nan Grey), Kay (Barbara Read), and Penny (Durbin)—who try to reunite their parents after discovering their father Jud (Charles Winninger) plans to marry the much younger gold digger Donna (Binnie Barnes). The sisters hire a penniless count (Mischa Auer) to pretend to be rich and to romance Donna as a way of showing her up for what she really is and prove she is only after their aging father's money. However, in a typical case of mistaken identity, they pick up the wrong man who happens to be a genuinely wealthy lord (Milland) and who plays along with their scheme because he has fallen for Kay. Milland's Lord Michael Stewart is first seen briefly as he signs in at the desk of a hotel, impeccably dressed in an affluently coded tailored suit which fits his frame perfectly. Kay pushes him out of the way to write a telegram and, although she is too busy to notice him, he has most definitely noticed her. Staring at her in a lovesick way, when her pen does not work, he tries to give her one from his pocket, but his assistant intervenes. He then tries to follow her into the restaurant, walking slowly as if floating, but the man with Michael informs him it is time to leave; he looks back at her and it is obvious he is smitten at first sight. Kay does not notice him at all, and although he is given some agency by being the possessor of the gaze during this scene, he soon becomes entangled in the sisters' plans and loses his masculine dominance as a result—a common leitmotif exhibited in Milland's films with Paramount's top female stars, as is discussed in detail in the next chapter.

Reentering the film as he sits at a nightclub bar, he is again impeccably dressed in white tie, tails, a white handkerchief in his breast pocket, and a white carnation in his lapel. The man they have hired is to carry a specific magazine so that the sisters can recognize him. However, upon seeing a friend the count drops the magazine and Michael picks it up from the floor before placing it under his arm as he pays the bartender. Mistaking Michael for the count, Kay walks up to him and pretends to know him. He turns, confused, but when he realizes she is the girl he encountered earlier, he grins widely and asks her to dance. After Kay dances with Michael, she forces Donna onto him and he charms her too, entirely because Kay has requested him to do so. Milland employs a range of subtly confused and perplexed looks while Kay calls Michael a no-good drunkard (clearly referring to the reputation of the count), but as long as he can be near Kay, he plays along and pretends to be the man she believes him to be, even if her opinion of him is low. This scene shows how Milland had started to develop more refined acting techniques, especially in the way he juggles the prop of the magazine to make sure the scene works, along with how he balances Michael's confusion with the situation through a series of wisecracks combined with the occasional outburst that demonstrate his feelings for Kay.

The next morning, Michael requests a local jeweler drop by his hotel room and, as he picks out a ring for Kay costing $7,000, he wears a form-fitting dark pinstriped suit and tie, which accentuate his figure and add to his attractiveness. Michael is obviously becoming serious about Kay extremely fast, requesting the best ring the jeweler has and not even flinching at the cost; money is clearly no object for the affluent Michael. Inviting Kay over on the pretext that he needs more money to take Donna out for an arranged dinner, she falls for his scheme and goes to his room. Given the case of mistaken identity and, believing him to be both a thief and an alcoholic, she locks away his alcohol before putting the key down her dress. She suggests they go for a walk so that she can keep an eye on him, during which he shakes the key out of her dress and sets his watch back so that he misses the arranged date with Donna and has more time to spend in the park with Kay.

When it is later revealed that he is not the penniless alcoholic count they hired, but instead a wealthy lord, Kay takes the news extremely badly and declares that she hates him and his dishonesty because he has failed to get Donna away from her father, adding that if they get married it will be all Michael's fault. When Kay arrives at his rooms, Michael is wearing a silk smoking jacket and white cravat while conversing with his butler, thus reflecting his true position as an upper-class British gentleman of wealth. When Kay runs out crying, Michael immediately calls Donna and asks her to meet him; he gives her two tickets to sail on the *Queen Victoria*, one for her and one for her mother, he keeps a third for himself. When he cryptically tells her that his future happiness depends on this, Donna believes he is talking about her, but we know he is referring to Kay. In a desperate last resort to stop the wedding, Penny runs away and after an altercation with Jud, Donna and her mother decide to sail with Michael, which upsets Kay greatly since she is in love with him. Entering the cabin of the ship, they see a large bunch of flowers, leading Donna's mother to call him "such a gentleman, all the British have such lovely manners" (although Barnes's accent is also obviously British). A note attached to the flowers informs them that he is not sailing with them, but the real count just so happens to have the cabin across from theirs and introduces himself as the journey begins.

Since Kay believes Michael is sailing with Donna, and has therefore lost him, she begins to cry and runs to the front door. In an extremely romantic moment, and a shot that must have required tremendous precision from all involved, she runs right into him just as he walks through the door and they "accidentally" kiss on the impact of their collision. Looking at each other, she wipes away a tear and he smiles before she raises her chin up to him for another kiss. As they kiss again, the butler asks whom he should announce and Milland comically moves both his and Read's heads to allow him to look at the man while still kissing her. Although the plot revolves around several actual and potential romances, the one between Kay and Michael is the only truly developed love affair, and despite this being the film's most romantic moment, it is also a comical one. The film concludes with the whole family, along with Michael (who, it is understood, will marry Kay and become part of the family), meeting the girls' mother at the boat and their parents are united for a typical Hollywood happy ending. Milland proves to be a convincing romantic partner in this film, but he appears much older than Read; indeed, his twenty-nine to her nineteen is a little off-putting as he presents himself as a grown man in opposition to her rather childlike features and demeanor. Read was, however, the oldest of the actresses playing the three sisters, but Nan Grey as Joan appears the most mature in looks and stature, and there seems to be less of an age gap between her and her (underdeveloped) love interest Bill Evans (John "Dusty" King), even though King was also nine years Grey's senior.

Universal was struggling financially at this time, and Milland implies that everything went smoothly on the film except for the long hours which he calls "appalling." Made during a time before the Screen Actors Guild was formed, when a cameraman "conked out" from exhaustion at 3 a.m. one morning, everyone was dismissed and told to report back on set at 9 a.m. After sitting for eighteen hours dressed in white tie and tails, he drove home without even changing and arrived back on set at 9:15, noting in 1974 that this was the only time he was ever late for work during his forty-three years in the profession (174). Given Universal's extreme monetary difficulties, *Three Smart Girls* was released just sixty days after completion rather than the usual three to six months. The film was an immense success, making Universal huge profits and leading to a sequel. *Three Smart Girls Grow Up* (Henry Koster) was released in 1939 with the same director and most of the same principal cast, but without Milland this time.[10] Due to the film's popularity, Milland notes that "Universal was back in the chips [. . .] a little of the glow even fell upon me" (1974: 175).

As this chapter has explored, during Milland's first few years on-screen in Hollywood he was often cast as members of the British aristocracy and, on occasion, even royalty. His polished vocal intonation, clean-cut good looks, and ability to wear evening clothes, military uniforms, and tailored suits equally well helped advance this believable presentation on-screen, while allowing him to credibly portray these characters, even if his acting skills were still in need of work. Although he was repeatedly portraying a "type," due to his British background and physical characteristics, these characters were different enough so as not to merge and become one entity. For instance, while his Prince Michael in *We're Not Dressing* is comical, non-threatening, and rather useless, presented as an attractive but shallow figure only after women for their money, his wealthy lords in *Bolero*, *The Gilded*

Lily, and *Three Smart Girls* are decent men who treat women well, longing to shower them with gifts and affection. Even though Helen marries his kindly character in *Bolero*, she has long been in love with the darkly sexual and passionate Raoul, while Marilyn turns his upper-class Brit down for a lower-class American alpha male in *The Gilded Lily*. As a king in *Ambassador Bill*, he already has a wife and son, which is a necessity of the plot, while he romances and wins the love of Kay in *Three Smart Girls* through his charm, wisecracks, and good looks.

The comedic but romantic appeal he presents in the latter film is the first time we see the more recognizable Milland who would continue to grace the screen across the next decade or so opposite actresses such as Dorothy Lamour, Claudette Colbert, and Paulette Goddard, whether he was playing an Englishman, an American, or a character with an undetermined national identity (but never a Welshman). Indeed, as will become evident throughout the next chapter, these three women were some of Paramount's top stars at this time, and Milland consistently played second-fiddle to them on-screen, even after winning his Academy Award, which many male performers may have objected to doing. Moreover, even when he received top billing, Milland was required to play a supporting role, but he consistently gave both professional and believable performances, no matter the size of the part, the genre, or the leading lady he was cast opposite. This proves both his aptitude and bankability to Paramount, assets that may not have elevated him to the upper echelons of stardom but that kept him employed in quality pictures at the studio for over two decades.

CHAPTER FIVE

IT'S A WOMAN'S WORLD

SUPPORTING PARAMOUNT'S FEMALE STARS

THE FIRST SEVEN-YEAR CONTRACT

Paramount was a studio known for its reliance on "spillover" fame, and stars like the German Marlene Dietrich and French Maurice Chevalier carried their European-earned fame with them when they arrived in Hollywood before it "spilled" over into America (Basinger 1994: 198). Thus, they each brought an already established star image with them, even if this was further altered by Hollywood, as was certainly the case with Dietrich. Moreover, stars already linked to other mediums, such as Bing Crosby and Bob Hope on radio and the Marx Brothers on Broadway, successfully transferred familiar components of their personas to the big screen. Paramount's policy was to make fewer films than many other studios did, using big stars and directors to attract more box-office income but with less investment (Basinger 1994: 198). As with other writers, she highlights Paramount's position as Hollywood's "sophisticated studio," with personnel comprising of "chic European stars" like Dietrich and Colbert, or American women with "great personalities," such as Goddard and Veronica Lake (1994: 201), all of whom Milland was paired with on-screen. Basinger calls the studio's male stars "suave types," naming Milland alongside Alan Ladd and John Lund, while calling the studio's "unsophisticated" comedies those starring Hope, Crosby, and Betty Hutton (1994: 201).

Despite having signed a seven-year contract with one of Hollywood's most powerful studios, Milland certainly did not achieve instant, nor even rapid, stardom. Furthermore, since Paramount was a studio so renowned for its powerful female stars, it was not until the mid-1940s, after fifteen years working in cinema, that Milland started to be given his own big-budget starring vehicles, such as *Ministry of Fear* (1944) and *The Lost Weekend* (1945). What is perhaps surprising, given the career trajectory of most stars, is that even in the films which cast Milland as the leading man, and even the top-billed performer, he is often relegated to not much more than a supporting player and romantic foil to some of the studio's leading female stars, most notably Colbert, Goddard, Dietrich, Dorothy Lamour, and Ginger Rogers. Just looking at the titles of some of his films perfectly illustrates this point, since they include *Alias Mary Dow* (Kurt Neumann, 1935), *The Return of Sophie Lang* (George Archainbaud, 1936), *The Jungle Princess* (Wilheim Thiele, 1936), *Wise Girl* (Leigh Jason, 1937), *The Lady Has Plans* (Sidney Lanfield, 1942), *Lady in the Dark* and *Kitty* (Mitchell Leisen, 1946), *Irene*, and *A Woman of Distinction*, all of which focus on the female protagonist who is helped along, and romanced, by Milland's character. One film title even comically asks *Are Husbands Necessary?* (Norman Taurog, 1942)—the husband in question, of course, being portrayed by Milland.

This chapter investigates this unusual phenomenon by analyzing his three most common on-screen collaborations at Paramount, with Lamour, Colbert, and his most frequent on-screen partnership, with four-time costar Goddard. As is explored, in each film Milland gives a professional and authentic performance while never trying to outperform his costar. Although this undoubtedly enhanced his bankability and durability at the studio, and in cinema more generally, it most certainly also contributed to his long struggle in acquiring a unique identity and forging a distinct star persona that would help him stand out in the competitive realm of Hollywood.

FROM THE JUNGLE TO MEXICO WITH DOROTHY LAMOUR

Between 1936 and 1938, Milland and Lamour were paired together in *The Jungle Princess* (1936), *Her Jungle Love* (George Archainbaud, 1938), and *Tropic Holiday* (Theodore Reed, 1938). The titles of their first two pairings are not their only common point since the plots are exceptionally similar, the latter being made relatively quickly after the former in hopes of replicating its tremendous box-office success. Although their third outing followed their second almost immediately, *Tropic Holiday* places their romance as part of the subplot that takes a backseat to the main stars, Bob Burns and Martha Raye, it also marked the end of their on-screen partnership. The jungle films were not only important in allowing Milland to display a more overt sense of manliness for the first time in Hollywood, through his characterization of an explorer and aviator respectively, but his character (of undetermined nationality) also teaches the sheltered, unworldly native girl—played by the scantily clad Lamour in her soon-to-be internationally famous sarong—how to speak English and what a kiss is, while she similarly teaches him about true love and the simple pleasures of island life far removed from the excesses of Western society he is used to. In the former, Milland is seen shirtless for the first time on-screen, which is repeated in the second film, only this time in Technicolor. While this may be rendered safe by the active physical task of swimming and the hot climate on the island, it is also accompanied by brightly lit close-ups which place him as a passive object of the erotic gaze for both the diegetic (Lamour) and nondiegetic audiences. In both films, the camera films him from below as he lies on a rock in a pinup pose. Thus, Milland was transformed into a new type of leading man through his pairing with Lamour. As noted, however, although these films helped him to gain traction as a more believable and eroticized romantic lead, he is mostly relegated to supporting Lamour as Paramount's latest discovery being built up for major stardom, while each of their pairings tells the story of her character rather than his.

Emphasizing his still minor status at the studio, Milland declares Paramount enlisted him to appear in twelve screen tests as they attempted to find a suitable leading lady for the upcoming film. Proclaiming his delight with their final choice, he calls Lamour "easily [. . .] the best of the bunch" and, rather Britishly, a "smashing young girl, whose figure lent itself beautifully to a sarong" (1974: 175). Previously a singer in her husband Herbie Kay's dance band, Lamour had never acted in a feature film. The song "Moonlight and Shadows" was quickly written for her to sing to Milland in the film, and it went to number one on the Hit Parade.[1] Milland asserts that Lamour had suggested that he would be perfect for the as-yet-uncast leading man, and when the positive reviews for *Three Smart Girls* came in, Paramount agreed (1974: 175). However, Lamour remembers events slightly differently, indicating in her own memoir that she believed Milland had already been cast when she was signed. She does, however, admit her memory to be rather hazy and, quoting from Milland's "delightful" book, she highlights his crediting her with helping him get the role. Her statement, "I frankly don't remember, but if it's so, I'm glad" (1980: 52), exemplifies that autobiographies are not the best sources for information. However it happened, with *The Jungle Princess* Milland was given his first role as romantic lead in a Hollywood A-picture.

Discussing Milland's professionalism, Lamour calls him a "genuinely unselfish actor—a rarity in the film business" (1980: 53). Knowing nothing about camera angles, she notes that she would often turn her face away, while he would "gently take me by the shoulders and adjust me so I was facing the lens" and "even sacrifice his own scenes to get my face in the proper position. That's really something when a performer does that for a colleague!" Most tellingly, regarding Milland's expertise and competence, as well as his encouragement of other performers, she proclaims that he taught her "more about the technique of motion picture acting" than anyone else (1980: 53).

To gain a sense of authenticity, they were sent to live in tents in Brent's Crags in the San Fernando Valley for the duration (Lamour 1980: 54). Moreover, with a sixteen-to-eighteen-hour workday, six days a week, the schedule was extremely demanding, and Milland notes the whole crew, himself included, were terrified of German director Wilheim Thiele (1974: 176). In another example of Hollywood viewing Englishness and Britishness as synonymous, while discussing cultural representation in jungle films, Milland notes that an odd thing about this type of picture was the fact that "the heavies were always Englishmen, wise in the way of slave trading and the robbing of temples," therefore "when they came upon me in the jungle they berated me for letting down the SIDE" (1974: 176, emphasis in original). In yet another instance of the blurring of the actor's national identity, writing as late as 1980, Edmonds and Mimura declare Milland "an English gentleman who had labored rather fruitlessly in the Hollywood vineyard" before being cast in *The Jungle Princess* (214).

Costing around $300,000 to make and grossing around $15 million, when Milland wrote about the film forty years later, he declares it was still being screened in "outlandish places" (1974: 176). Eames calls it an "unpretentious production, a pleasant entertainment and a whopping profit-maker" (1985: 120), and it was certainly crucial in Milland's career trajectory in terms of the development of his screen image since it not only gave him his initial role as a romantic lead in Hollywood, but was the first to truly present him as an object of erotic desire for both the film's female characters and the cinematic audience. The latter is particularly evident in a scene which transpires after he lies outstretched on a rock, attempting to dry out in the sun after swimming in a lake. Dressed only in a pair of light-colored swimming trunks, the camera exhibits Milland's face and body in a range of close-ups and full-body shots while his slightly wet, mussed up hair, and glistening bare chest and shoulders aid in presenting him in a comparable way to a male pinup posing for a still photograph. The camera stays focused on Milland's face, filming him from below as his expression changes from a smug grin to a wide smile, where he displays his teeth, to a sultry gaze at Lamour and,

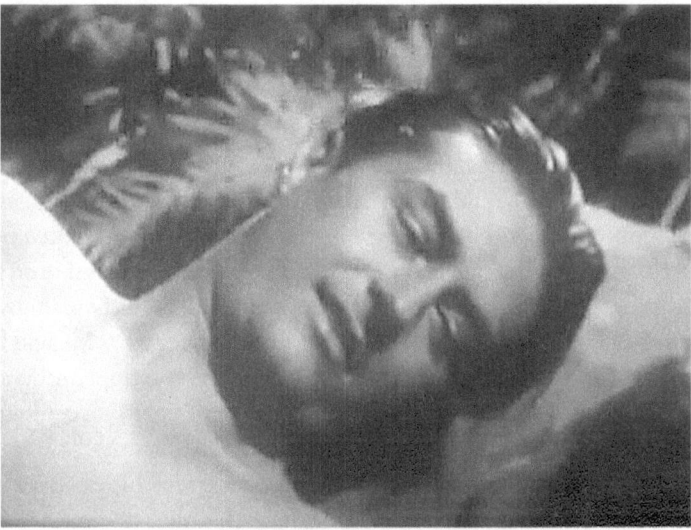

Figure 5.1. Milland's first "pinup pose" in *The Jungle Princess* (Wilheim Thiele, 1936).

by extension, us since he moves his head slightly towards the camera while doing so (figure 5.1). Thus, we see Milland in a vastly different way than he had been depicted on screen thus far, especially in his portrayals of stuffy Englishmen dressed in restrictive tweed suits and cravats. Lamour's Ulah acts as a surrogate for the audience in her appreciation for his attractiveness and, although the film is named after her character, tells her character's story, awards Lamour with top billing (despite it being her screen debut), and made her an instant star, curiously it is Milland who receives the most screen time.

Milland wears three varied outfits in this film. While there are the trunks, rendered "safe" within the narrative of being on a tropical island and undertaking the active task of swimming, for much of the film he is dressed in archetypal safari gear. However, Milland consistently wears his shirt sleeves rolled up past his elbows, a subtle but sensual hint at his manliness through the display of his quite muscular arms, "a typically sexualized part of the male body and principal in distinguishing men from women" (Kelly 2019: 123). Towards the conclusion, he is also seen in more familiar and oft-repeated evening clothes, comprising of a dinner jacket and bow tie, his palpable sartorial style discernible even when dining outside of a small hut on a desert island.

The desirability of Milland's Christopher "Chris" Powell is underscored within the narrative by the two vastly different women who vie for his affections: his sophisticated fiancée, Ava (Molly Lamont), and native island girl, Ulah (Lamour). The former is typically standoffish and reserved in her relationship with Chris and, while their interactions lack any warmth or passion, she wants to hold onto him like a trophy. Conversely, Ulah is primitive and apt to give in to her animalistic urges without the restriction of Western society telling her what is acceptable, which Chris finds refreshing if rather unsettling, given his background. Because of his commitment to Ava, whom he has grown up with and become engaged to as a matter of form, Chris makes nervous attempts to resist Ulah, but it soon becomes apparent that he has fallen hard for the innocent native girl and must let his fiancée know. Permitted by the tropical climate of the jungle setting, there is a notable amount of skin on show from the principal characters for a Code-era film, but even more unusual is the amount of bare skin they have touching since Lamour paws Milland while he is dressed only in trunks and she in a strapless sarong wrapped around her body. This adds to their erotically charged scenes with Ulah's lack of inhibition and low level of edification when it comes to social boundaries.

After the film was complete, a homesick Milland took his American wife on her first European vacation. Following the extraordinary success of *Three Smart Girls*, and with *The Jungle Princess* having just been released, Milland notes that it was Paris where he got his first sense of what it was like to be in the public eye. Calling the French very film-conscious, he notes that magazine journalists somehow managed to find him and that they were "very intense and dedicated" people (1974: 186). Returning to London and showing Muriel the typical tourist sights and where he had worked in the calvary, he notes the six years since he left felt like a lifetime. Staying at The Savoy hotel, a place where he would never have been able to stay when he was living in London but where he had met with MGM's representatives before his first journey to Hollywood, they saw Winston Churchill, Douglas Fairbanks Sr., and the then-current prime minister, Stanley Baldwin, while dining in the hotel's Grill restaurant (1974: 184). He notes there was even a clichéd "real pea-souper" of a London fog which made it pitch-dark at three in the afternoon. With visibility almost impossible, the couple were walking in Embankment when a London "bobby" (police officer) advised them it was not safe to be out in the extremely thick fog, "especially for foreigners." Milland declares to having "bridled a little" at this comment but said nothing, while his excited wife ruminated that Jack the Ripper had never been caught. A seeming in-joke to his later career, Milland refers to the incident as "pure Roger Corman" (1974: 185).[2] Retelling this incidental event in extreme detail several decades later demonstrates not only his familiarity with the local area and its colloquial language, but suggests that his time in Hollywood had made him look like he no longer belonged to Britain, despite having lived and worked there for much of his life.

Two years after *The Jungle Princess*, and with profits still "coming in like lava," Milland and Lamour were "ordered back to the studio tropics" to make another jungle film (Eames 1985: 120). Despite an extremely similar title, one of the key differences with *Her Jungle Love* is that its bigger budget allowed it to be shot in Technicolor, only Milland's second color venture.[3] It proved to be yet another box-office hit, potentially due to its reuse of a popular formula and audiences enjoying the connection between the two leads. The film opens with aviators Bob Mitchell (Milland) and Jimmy Wallace (Lynne Overman) crashing on a remote island during a storm. Bob sustains a nasty head injury, the bloody gash graphically depicted in Technicolor; while Jimmy goes off to search for help, native girl Tura (Lamour) approaches Bob and throws a knife at his head. Discovering he is injured, and therefore not a threat to her, she takes Bob to her cave and tends to his wounds.

As with their earlier pairing, Milland's character has a fiancée, only this time she is back home and frantic when newspapers report his disappearance. Tura remains at Bob's side until he is well, while Jimmy tries to fix the plane's radio to call for help. After Bob's recovery, Milland is again shirtless, this time in full color, while napping in the sun. We see Tura tickling Bob with a flower, saying his name and beating on his stomach to try and wake him. Leaning down towards him, she tells him, in broken English, "Bob pretty." To which he immediately jumps up into a sitting position and asks incredulously if she said he was pretty. When she gives an affirmative smile, he looks insulted, as if she has just undermined his masculinity instead of paying him a compliment. He places a hand on his knee, leans in, and pointedly informs her that men are never pretty, strongly emphasizing the "never" before concluding that it is girls who are pretty and adamantly insisting that he certainly is not.

An adjective associated with girls and women, "pretty" is primarily used to describe visually attractive females who are not quite beautiful. Indeed, Tura appears to associate the word with something aesthetically pleasing, her heterosexual desire for Bob leading her to apply the word to him, much to his dismay. When she then directly asks him if she is pretty, Milland uses his face and subtle but rigid body movements to suggest Bob is caught off-guard by her boldness and that this is not something he often comes across in polite Western society. He awkwardly confirms that she is "very pretty," but her ignorance of social manners and personal space leads her to move uncomfortably close to him. Although he nervously but softly pushes her away, she repeatedly edges closer while Milland shows Bob's uneasiness through nervous laughter and stiff, uncomfortable posture. In another reversal of gender norms, Tura hands Bob a flower. When he automatically attempts to place it in his lapel, the "manly" way of wearing a flower, he laughs anxiously when recalling he is shirtless. Their lack of clothing and exposed skin causes him to fumble around while wondering where to put the flower. He briefly considers putting it in his hair and then behind his ear before reaching over and placing it in Tura's hair. Suggesting female construction of beauty through accessories, Tura asks if she is now "more pretty" with the addition of the flower. He mockingly parrots her before looking down and comically muttering to himself, and the audience, in a naturalistic way, and with raised eyebrows, that she "better stick to her English lesson" as he again tries to create a distance between their heavily exposed bodies.

Milland combines Bob's obvious attraction to Tura and his attempts to distract her from her amorous actions by nervously suggesting they listen to a record on a portable player, teaching her the words to the song "Coffee, Kisses and You." His brief "singing" segment mostly consists of Milland speaking the words of the song, thus standing in direct contrast to the stereotype that all Welshmen can sing, while further distancing him from his national identity, as Hollywood repeatedly did. Finding it hard to give a satisfactory explanation of a kiss, Bob begins confidently enough before starting to get flustered the longer Tura stares at him without comprehending. Scratching the back of his neck to show Bob's discomfort and puzzlement at how exactly to describe it, he eventually demonstrates it by kissing her quickly on the lips. Tura looks shocked and runs to her cave. Kissing her own hand twice in confused wonderment, she grins widely, runs back to him, and demands more kisses, displaying both Bob's virility and setting Milland up as a desirable romantic lead. Understandably now even more nervous as she repeatedly tries to kiss him, Milland shows Bob to be jumpy and panicky as he pushes her away, looks terrified, and squirms with embarrassment. Finally seeing his only escape route as the pond, he jumps in, but she follows him before pushing him down and kissing him underwater, but we are shown that his foot is caught, and he is drowning. Although she manages to save him, she is visibly upset. Weakened and breathless from his struggle, he lets his feelings overpower him. Sitting up to face her, he tenderly tells her it was not her fault, and she puts her hands on his bare shoulders as they both lean in for a kiss. Kissing softly at first and then more passionately, they wrap their arms around each other before he lays her down on the rock, their hair and bodies dripping wet in this highly erotically charged scene. The volume of skin the actors have touching exceeds even their previous pairing, and perhaps even more shocking, given it is a Code-era film, is the fact that the pair remain in a vertical position throughout. By far the most romantic scene Milland had played thus far in his career, it proved that he was a good fit as a romantic leading man with a desirable eroticism that had been virtually nonexistent in his earlier roles as stuffy, almost asexual Brits and may have aided in helping audiences view him as a screen heartthrob.

Figure 5.2. As Milland places a flower in Dorothy Lamour's hair in *Her Jungle Love* (George Archainbaud, 1938), his tattoo is visible for the only time on-screen.

Another noteworthy and unusual element of this scene is that the tattoo Milland got at the age of fifteen can be seen briefly for the first and only time on-screen. In his memoir, he states that getting the tattoo was one of the worst decisions of his life, and the unsanitary conditions in which he received it almost cost him his arm, if not his life. Milland discusses the process of getting the tattoo at length, an adornment which not only seems unusual for an actor of this period but at odds with the upper-class, impeccably dressed British characters he had so often portrayed. If he had remained in his native country, even to work as an actor, the tattoo may have seemed less peculiar since it would have been a better fit with the working-class laborers he portrayed in the British films *The Flying Scotsman* and *The Lady from the Sea*. Not nearly as widespread in the early 1920s as they are today, Milland notes being "absolutely amazed [at the] awesome and fascinating" sight of a tattoo on the back of a ship's first engineer (1974: 43–44); therefore, it seems doubtful that any of the local men in his village or his fellow soldiers had tattoos. Immediately and impulsively deciding to get one himself, after docking in Alexandria, Greece,[4] he chose a design in red, green, and yellow depicting a human skull with blood dripping from it and a snake protruding from the right eye socket and sitting coiled on the top of the skull (1974: 44–45). While Milland places the flower in Lamour's hair, a tattoo in the exact design he describes can be seen momentarily on the outside of his upper right arm (figure 5.2).

After getting the tattoo, Milland recalls becoming feverish, developing a swollen arm that "ached abominably," and contracting a severe case of septicemia[5] (1974: 47). This incident is another indication of Milland's impulsiveness, previously demonstrated through his jumping between jobs before he finally settled on acting and, perhaps surprisingly, remained in this career for over five decades. Ironically, what he described as one of the biggest mistakes of his life was a permanent, and lifelong, reminder of that very mistake. Given that Bob is a flyer, and not an upper-class gentleman or royalty, perhaps meant that the glimpse of the tattoo did not cause an issue with the studio or audiences. Getting the tattoo at fifteen also reinforces the fact that he had no acting ambitions at this time, since he probably would have reconsidered getting something so permanent if he had.

Bob's active masculinity is proven when he and Jimmy improvise a raft out of their wrecked plane so they can leave the island. When the leader of the natives demands that Tura (unwillingly) accompany him to his island, Bob stands erect and defends her against this large and powerful man. However, they are forcefully taken to a cave and tied up. With his arms and legs bound, Bob is forced to be a passive witness to Tura's demise, as he helplessly struggles to get free. However, a sudden earthquake causes the high rock formations around them to crumble, crushing and killing some of the natives while the escapee crocodiles eat others in a rather graphic scene. Bob channels his machismo and becomes the truly active male by dragging himself towards a fire and using the flames to burn the ropes off his wrists; pulling his hands free, he unties his feet in time to save Tura and Jimmy from an approaching crocodile. Although a typical Hollywood "happy ending," it leaves the viewer questioning whether Bob will be able to adjust to island life. Moreover, since the freed crocodiles and falling rock formations have killed most of the inhabitants, this seems a rather large obstacle, especially given Bob's former life of luxury.

Immediately following *Her Jungle Love*, Milland and Lamour were thrown together a final time in *Tropic Holiday*. The exotic location was changed to Mexico, with Louisiana-born Lamour portraying a Mexican woman who speaks broken English. Although again cast as a non-native English speaker, this time she was at least able to converse with Milland's character more than in their previous pairings. What is most unusual about this film, given the tremendous success of their previous ventures, is that the pair are relegated to supporting players, providing a secondary love story to bolster the comedy performances of top-billed stars Bob Burns and Martha Raye. Despite having now built a reputation as a romantic lead, Milland again moves down the credits and receives fourth billing after Burns, Raye, and Lamour. Since the film adds little to their on-screen partnership, and even marked the end of it, it appears a strange decision for Paramount to cast the now established performers in these roles. It would have been a film more suited to their initial pairing, when Lamour was new to acting and Milland was still trying to establish himself as a leading man, like the first pairing of Fred Astaire and Ginger Rogers as the secondary couple to Dolores Del Rio and Gene Raymond in *Flying Down to Rio* (Thornton Freeland, 1933). However, after playing leads in *The Gay Divorcee* (Mark Sandrich, 1934) and *Top Hat* (Mark Sandrich, 1935), the earlier film would have been a step back for Astaire and Rogers,[6] just as *Tropic Holiday* was for Milland and Lamour. Nevertheless, they tackle their roles with dedication and professionalism, which the studio would have been grateful for and was perhaps a factor in why both remained under Paramount's employ for so many years, even if they were never again paired on-screen.

While Lamour portrayed a string of native girls in her first few years on-screen, meaning her accent was rarely heard, Milland's distinct vocal intonations were recognizable enough by this stage to be used as an indicator that it is he who is standing in the shadows before he appears on-screen. Since he is passionately imparting a diatribe of romantic words to Midge Miller (Raye), we are to assume they are lovers, even if they make for an unusual union. However, in an on- and off-screen connection, it soon transpires that Ken (Milland) is a Hollywood screenwriter dictating his latest story to his secretary, Midge. To gain inspiration for his script, Ken has taken a room above a Mexican café, and through the aid of a signed photograph, we learn that he is engaged to the glamorous blonde Hollywood actress Marilyn Joyce (Binnie Barnes).

Immediately after Ken enters the café, waitress Manuela (Lamour) grabs his arm and reminds them they have a date. Milland's confused facial expressions convey to the audience that Ken has no idea who she is or what she is talking about; appearing dazed and silently stunned, suggesting Ken has been caught off-guard, he looks unsure how to react. Finally concluding that she is trying to avoid the man who has been pestering her, he plays along and escorts her outside. She thanks him as they walk, and he grins widely as he does up the tie that was loosely hanging around his neck. Manuela's impromptu singing when they reach the beach obviously fascinates Ken; Milland fixes his eyes on Lamour and keeps his body almost stationary throughout her number, the only slight adjustment to his posture being a slow brushing of his hand up and down his leg as he listens intently. Although this scene allows Milland to show Ken's newfound interest in Manuela, it is clearly constructed to highlight Lamour's singing, Ken becoming the captive diegetic audience for Manuela and a surrogate for the cinematic audience, thereby once more providing support for Lamour.

Milland conveys Ken at his most confident in a darkly humorous scene that demonstrates both his character's wit and cinematic knowledge. He convinces the weaker Breck Jones (Burns) to carry out a hasty plan to recreate the scene from *A Star Is Born* (William A. Wellman, 1937), released the previous year, in which "Fredric March commits suicide by walking into the sea" so that Midge will worship his memory. Interestingly, Ken uses the name of the actor and not the character in his explanation, implying that audiences tend to associate films with performers while signifying the blurring of real and "reel" lives that Hollywood consistently generates. They go to the beach to conduct this unwise scheme after Ken instructs Breck on how to write his suicide note; however, in true comedic fashion, Midge fails to show up. Breck is rescued by a fishing boat, and in another cinematic in-joke, dryly comments that he started out in *A Star Is Born* and ended up in *Captains Courageous* (Victor Fleming, 1937).[7] Both films were released shortly before *Tropic Holiday* and thus would have likely have been fresh in audiences' minds, especially given their popularity, thereby helping regular filmgoers to understand the understated humor of the cinematic in-joke.

Milland's casual dress in a crisp, open-collared white shirt not only reflects the Mexican climate but sets off his good looks and dark hair. When Manuela enters his room to bring fresh papayas, he rushes over while grinning widely and asks her for a date. She refuses after noticing the framed photograph of Marilyn, but we realize the relationship is strained when Ken quips that she would rather be in the spotlight than in the moonlight. This foreshadows the kind of woman Marilyn is: false, manipulative, fame-hungry, self-centered, and attention-seeking—in other words, the opposite of Manuela. Thus, two vastly different women are again interested in a character portrayed by Milland. Since Marilyn has been controlling him and undermining his masculinity, we want him to end up with Manuela. While she sings "My First Love," her way of confessing how she feels to Ken and the audience, he silently looks at her, looks away, and then looks back. Without any dialogue and through looks alone, Milland proficiently conveys Ken's conflicting emotions as he contemplates what to do about Marilyn and his growing feelings for Manuela.

The pair's most romantic scene occurs during another of Lamour's musical numbers. Ambiently lit by firelight, she sits with her back against a tree while he lies on the grass on his stomach and gazes lovingly up at her, suggesting her elevated status and his wish for her to be in the spotlight. Slowly sitting up, he moves beside her while never averting his eyes from her face until they are on the same level, symbolic equals in love. Milland slowly and apprehensively places an arm around Lamour's shoulders, suggesting that Ken is worried Manuela will not reciprocate; but, when she gravitates towards him in an organic manner, his face displays relief and contentment. With both performers now facing the camera, she leans her body against his while continuing to sing. Milland opens and closes his mouth several times, alternating between moving his eyes rapidly around his surroundings and looking down at Lamour from his position beside her. His breathing also gets noticeably heavier and more labored as the number progresses, suggesting their proximity has excited Ken intensely.

However, the scene's intimacy is broken after the musical interlude. The camera pulls back to reveal that he is now looking down, Milland's expression hinting at Ken's agitation and despondence. When she asks what he is thinking, he stares ahead, unable now to meet her gaze while stating in a bemused and quizzical tone that for years he has been sitting behind a typewriter writing scripts that are nothing more than "carbon copies of love." The way Milland spits out the "c" at the beginning of both words not only implies the relentless tapping of the letter on a typewriter but emphasizes Ken's realization that he has inflicted a soulless stereotype on unsuspecting audiences, and how false it all seems to him now that he is experiencing true love for the first time. In an overly dramatic and mocking tone, he recounts the predictable clichés he has penned about moonlight, roses, and stars in a girl's eyes while pondering how he could ever have believed that was love. This confession works on a meta-level since the character within the film is criticizing his work as a successful Hollywood screenwriter, shown through his ability to travel with his private secretary to research and write in Mexico, his boss constantly demanding his finished script for the next stage of production and his engagement to a glamorous Hollywood star. Moreover, by criticizing the falseness of his writing he is also criticizing the film industry in general, many of the films made at Paramount (the studio to release this film), and the screenplay for this specific film since it shows two beautiful people meeting and instantaneously falling in love on a Mexican beach.[8]

Suggesting that real love is nothing like these romantic platitudes, he leans forward and clasps his legs between his hands before embarrassingly stating that someone in love walks around with a silly look on their face. Giving a nervous laugh, he adds, "His heart's full of words and his mouth's full of cotton. And you feel awful." Elongating the final word, when Milland stresses the syllable "aw" he renders it a cry of anguish. With his brow knitted and looking physically sick, he asks her how she feels. When she announces that she does not feel so good he nods in agreement, adding an element of humor to this soul-baring scene. After their mutual confession of love, they lean in for their first kiss as romantic music swells, just the sort of cinematic cliché he says he writes about. However, just before their lips touch, Manuela's young brother appears and tells Ken to keep away from his sister, thus delaying their lovemaking.

Discovering Marilyn has announced their engagement to the newspapers and is flying down to Mexico, he drops weakly onto a table as if needing stability and looks utterly disheveled. Never having proposed to Marilyn, nor having any intention of doing so, she is controlling their narrative as a way of gaining publicity, writing her own "carbon copy" of love. When Midge encouragingly tells him he will think of something, he sounds both helpless and nauseous when asking, in true writer's style, "With what? They serve better brains than mine in a restaurant." As if becoming a performer himself, Ken calmly practices the speech he will give to Marilyn in his empty room, his hands casually thrust in his pockets and his voice strong and definite. Grinning as if impressed by himself, he cockily states, "Boy, that's telling her," before noticing Marilyn watching from the doorway. Employing a comical double take, Milland lets his whole demeanor change the instant Ken notices her. He stutters her name while his entire body becomes unnaturally rigid as if he fears her or at least her power in the industry. The screenwriter has no more clever words as he weakly points at nothing in particular. Making clear she is the dominant party in the relationship, she interrupts every time he attempts to speak, orders him around, and demands he pack because she is taking him back to Hollywood, as if addressing a child or a pet rather than a grown man. She stops at the doorway, looks him up and down, and declares that he looks wonderful, before blowing him a kiss and exiting. Positioning him as the object of the erotic gaze, she talks as if he is merely window-dressing for her, again suggesting a reversal of typical gender roles at the time. Thus, while he can be the breadwinner in his relationship with Manuela but still let her take the spotlight, this is not possible with the self-obsessed Marilyn, who is looking to both effeminize him and own him.

Marilyn and Ken attend a bullfight where he is dressed casually in an open-neck shirt and blazer jacket which allows him to blend in with the locals, while she wears an enormous hat and excessive jewelry that draw attention since she is the only one dressed in such an outlandish way. He looks completely downtrodden while plainly stating that they are not in love and they know it, but instead of talking about their feelings and their obviously fake relationship, she immediately snaps back that the newspapers, and by consequence the public, believe it. Marilyn begins an evidently false speech about being willing to give Ken up for the "little Mexican girl," to which he raises one eyebrow to show surprise and quickly turns towards her as if shocked but believing her. Showing narcissistic tendencies, she then attempts to make him feel guilty by telling him this would make her the laughingstock of the country, in an overly theatrical and completely unbelievable performance that lacks any compassion or true feelings for him. Looking back down, he begins fidgeting, but being a gentleman, Ken announces that he does not want to hinder her career. We are aware she is feeding him a line, perhaps from one of his own screenplays, and quickly snapping out of her performance she coldly replies that they will leave for Hollywood that night. Milland folds his arms and presses his lips together to illustrate Ken's understanding that he has been duped. However, as Hollywood films tend to do, loose ends are tied up, and Ken is left free to marry Manuela.

While this marked the last of Milland and Lamour's films together, she would go on to make similar films with other leading men in the interchangeable role of romantic support, including Robert Preston in *Typhoon* (Louis King, 1940), Jon Hall in *Aloma of the South Seas* (Alfred Santell, 1941), and Richard Denning in *Blue Horizon* (Alfred Santell, 1942), while starring alongside Hope and Crosby in the highly successful "Road" films. This film did nothing to develop Milland's star image; if anything it made him just another generic romantic lead, mainly present to look lovingly at Lamour as she sings several musical numbers. Having made over forty films by this point, Milland's career appeared to be going backwards, here playing a rather inconsequential secondary role. Comedians Burns and Raye are the real stars of the film, while Milland is once more consigned to a good-looking but generic love interest, reminiscent of the dull love stories intercut with comedic scenes in Eddie Cantor vehicles or the Marx Brothers' films at MGM—subplots, the studios reckoned, that were necessary for gaining a wider audience for these comedians. Moreover, the characters Milland plays in the two jungle films are almost identical, just with different names and alternative reasons for being on the island, while *Tropic Holiday* merely alters the location and his character's occupation. Additionally, in each film, his character has a sophisticated but domineering fiancée whom he is not in love with, and when he falls for Lamour's unworldly innocent, he ultimately makes the "natural progression" to protective male and reverses his emasculation.

Along with several other performers signed to Paramount at this time, Milland and Lamour both appeared briefly but separately in Paramount's all-star movie *Star Spangled Rhythm* (George Marshall, 1942); he in a card skit and she in a musical number with two of Milland's other costars, Paulette Goddard and Veronica Lake, in a sendup of their manufactured images: the comedy number "A Sweater, A Sarong and a Peek-a-Boo Bang," which references Goddard, Lamour, and Lake, respectively. While Milland shared the screen once with Lake in *I Wanted Wings* (Mitchell Leisen, 1941), it was

Goddard who became his most regular, and arguably best-suited, costar, with Paramount pairing them in four successful films discussed later in this chapter. I will now explore Milland's partnership with his other three-time costar, Claudette Colbert, which resulted in a broader range of films than his partnership with Lamour allowed.

WAR AND DIVORCE WITH CLAUDETTE COLBERT

Between 1935 and 1941, Milland made three films with Colbert. The first of these, *The Gilded Lily* (1935), is analyzed in the previous chapter because Milland not only has a supporting role in this film but is presented as Hollywood's stereotype of a stuffy upper-class Brit in contrast to leading man Fred MacMurray's rugged, all-American working-class hero. Although giving Milland some much-needed exposure in a big-budget film alongside popular star Colbert, it was their second film together, *Arise, My Love* (1940), released half a decade later, that was, in Milland's words, "a blockbuster and my first real step to stardom" (1974: 202). Eames declares that Paramount "fielded one of its strongest teams" for this film, which drew sizable, enthusiastic audiences (1985: 145). It also received an impressive five Academy Award nominations, winning for Best Writing (Original Story).

Arise, My Love not only sees Milland as more of a conventional romantic lead, but he was cast as an American, with only slight alterations to his looks and vocal intonations from his British characters. Milland gives an overtly complex and varied performance across the film from his initial scene in a prison cell as his soldier of fortune awaits execution at the end of the Spanish Civil War to the highly sensual relationship that his character develops with Colbert's character. The film carefully highlights the complex nature of the couple's relationship as it matures from lust to love, and the sacrifices they make when World War II breaks out, thus helping link the characters to contemporary audiences and their experiences at the time. In fact, throughout production, the script was consistently rewritten to keep up with the war news (Eames 1985: 145). The film concludes with a powerful anti-Nazi message highlighting the genuine issues facing America if and when it joined the war, and why participation was imperative.

Since Hollywood was displaying a violation of neutrality regarding the war, two isolationist senators in North Dakota (Gerald P. Nye) and Missouri (Bennett Champ Clark) demanded an exhaustive examination of propaganda distributed through film and radio which aimed to "influence public sentiment" regarding US participation in the European war (Dick 1985: 89).

This led to Senate Resolution 152, sanctioning a dual inquiry into film propaganda and monopoly. Hollywood's "Big Eight"—Paramount, MGM, Warner Brothers, Twentieth Century-Fox, RKO, Columbia, Universal, and United Artists—clearly constituted a monopoly, so there was nothing particularly subtle about associating propaganda with monopoly. Moreover, the first five studios were vertically integrated, meaning they exhibited their own films in their own theatres. Since these studios made most of Hollywood's anti-Nazi films, Nye and Clark accused them of attempting to pull the US into the war (Dick 1985: 89).

With accusations of violating the Sherman Anti-Trust Act, attempts were made to break up the studios' monopoly and to bring an end to Hollywood's "warmongering." As Dick declares, this also brought Hollywood to an end less than a decade later when studios' monopolies were revised, and exhibition and distribution were made separate entities (1985: 89). Those who viewed anti-Nazi films as a consequence of monopoly and vertical integration saw a direct link between the films and those making them, in other words "foreigners" in a Hollywood that, in Nye's words, "swarms with refugees and British actors" (Dick 1985: 89). Filmed just before America entered the war, but while Europe was already fighting, *Arise, My Love* starred the British Milland and French-born Colbert, with a script cowritten by Billy Wilder, a German in exile. Therefore, it was a key target for such allegations.

World War II was not the only war causing issues, though. While referring to The Spanish Civil War as the war that "dared not speak its name," Dick notes that when it ended in March 1939, Paramount, "that unpredictable studio, was the first to utter it in the opening title of *Arise, My Love*" (1985: 89). Indeed, the opening puts the film into context by stating, "It is Spain and the summer of 1939. The Civil War is over," adding that "of the soldiers of fortune who came from all over the world, only a few remain, waiting to be written off, in a military prison near Burgos." Dick suggests that, although Hollywood had never spoken the war's name before, here it was making a connection between the war that ended in March 1939 and the one that began that September, a connection that historians have continued to make (1985: 20–21).

The film's opening is bleak and sees Milland's pilot, Tom Martin, who has flown for the Republic, playing cards with Father Jacintois (Frank Puglia) in his prison cell shortly before he is to face Franco's firing squad. Dressed in a lightly colored military uniform, Milland sits on the hard floor while the sun casts light on his face through the barred window of the cell. Puglia's dark garb and positioning in shadow not only highlights the bright lighting Hollywood studios used for their leading players but aids in connoting Tom's imminent doom and status as a martyr. Neither acknowledges that another man from Tom's squadron is readying execution outside the window, and Tom employs wit as a coping mechanism for the horrific situation. He slightly jumps when diegetic gunfire is heard off-screen, and his face becomes set and grim. Giving this action believability, Milland uses understated gestures that may be missed in a single viewing and is certainly not deploying any overacted or theatrical convulsions that would read as false.

Throughout the scene, Milland seamlessly shifts between appearing solemn and cracking jokes as a way of adeptly depicting Tom's obvious anxiety. When the padre asks if he can help in any way, he dryly replies that he could deal him better cards. Similarly, when asked if his death is scheduled for five o'clock, he responds sarcastically, raising his voice with mock exasperation as he asks, "Father, where's your tact?"—the actor making it evident that his character has adopted a façade to disguise his fear while conveying this to the audience with precision and nuance. When the padre nervously comments that it is his first execution, he chillingly replies, "Mine too," while staring into the distance in a way that suggests Tom finally realizes the true horror of his situation. Alternating between a two-shot of the men and close-ups of Milland, we see the actor subtly use his eyebrows and mouth to indicate Tom's range of emotions, including anger, disgust, humor, fear, and disdain.

Tension builds as Tom receives a full pardon at the last minute after being told his wife has arrived to take him home. Confused but grateful, Tom tells Jacintois "under the seal of the confessional" that he is not married. Knowing the priest is sworn to secrecy, that the woman is a stranger, and that the commanding officer believes her to be his wife, Milland comically looks between all three with marginally altered facial expressions, since only he has privileged knowledge about each of them. The woman, soon revealed to be a reporter, Augusta "Gusto" Nash (Colbert), in search of an interesting story, runs over and asks Tom for a kiss. Looking dazed and confused, since we know they are strangers, he briefly glances at the padre before raising both eyebrows and tipping his head as if signifying he has no other choice. Bending down, he gives Gusto a long and passionate kiss, to the delight of the commanding officer and the horror of the padre before she finally pulls away, breathless. Milland is dressed in a flying jacket, and his dark hair is longer and unstyled, making him look more modern, more handsome, and younger than the harsh, slicked-back style of his previous films allowed. Positioned between the other actors, and in the center of the frame for much of the scene, the others continually look towards him for reactions, and this naturally draws the viewer's eye to Milland. Moreover, given that he is much taller than the others, his dominant and imposing frame takes up more of the screen, which also aids in attracting the audience's attention.

World War II is first alluded to when Tom asks the officer to say goodbye to Adolf, a very clever rat he shared his cell with and whom he trained to raise its paw "like this," lifting his arm in a sudden and violent Nazi salute. Later, aboard the train, war correspondent Gusto begins to read Hitler's *Mein Kampf* while Tom naps. Becoming increasingly enraged, she finally slams the book shut and throws it out the window of the moving train—an action that, according to Dick, says more than dialogue can (1985: 81). Directly after this, her anger dispels as she smiles at the sleeping Tom, observing him without his ability to look back. However, he soon reveals that he is not sleeping and, with his eyes still shut, comically quips, "If you are counting my eyebrows, there are two," as he both shocks her and takes his dominance back.

Dick highlights that two versions of the film were made for the foreign and domestic markets, one including anti-Nazi dialogue, but the extra work proved unnecessary as days after the film's completion, the Nazi government banned all American films from being exhibited in Germany (1985: 20). Dick feels that scriptwriter Wilder criticized isolationists and appeasement but finds it surprising that the Breen Office retained Tom's remark that he wasted his life on "palooka preliminaries" in Spain before Hitler and Chamberlain "warmed up for the main event," implying that the Munich pact, and not just the Spanish Civil War, prefigured the Second World War (1985: 66). I would add that several sexual references were allowed to remain, a few overtly obvious, which was unusual for mainstream Hollywood at this time. For example, when Gusto and Tom get shot at in their small plane, he seductively tells her they should make the most of what might be the last hour of their lives, beginning with her kissing his earlobe. When he exclaims that she is just his type, she sarcastically replies that after ten months in prison a St. Bernard would be his type and that he is "just hungry," while he seems to nod in agreement.

Slightly later, the camera appears dangerously high while filming Milland in near-transparent bathwater as he shaves and converses with two male friends. When Gusto calls to announce she is coming over, he lets out a whoop and hurries the men out, believing she wishes to consummate their relationship. What follows is an extremely sophisticated scene and one of the best comedic performances Milland ever gave. Indeed, it would be much less effective without Milland's understated gestures, facial expressions, and vocal intonations in portraying Tom's unspoken thoughts, while allowing him to display a wide range of acting techniques in a condensed period. Milland controls his voice well, altering it from low and seductive to high-pitched and panicky in just a few minutes through natural modulation and not an abnormal switch that would sound spurious. Moreover, although the scene may appear to have been included merely for amusement, it does much to inform us about Tom's personality, his desire for control and his rather conventional beliefs when it comes to romance, helping us identify him more as a romantic lead than a cad or mass seducer of women, as previously hinted.

Dressed in a satin bathrobe and cravat, Tom rushes to the door before slowly looking Gusto up and down, informing her in a low and seductive tone that he is at her complete disposal. Placing his hand on the door beside her, he leans in and tries to kiss her, but she marches past, and he almost falls into the door. In this scene of complete misunderstanding, Gusto is innocently trying to find the best position to take his photograph for her publication while he believes she is referring to sex. As the scene progresses, his demeanor changes from seductive and passionate to confused and then horrified as he consistently misinterprets her words and actions. For most of the scene, Milland stands behind Colbert or faces away from her, meaning that we are witness to Tom's evolving panic, while Gusto remains oblivious throughout. She begins by stating matter-of-factly that they should get down to business as he turns from the door and confusingly declares "What, now?" before suggesting they begin with a drink or some music. Refusing, she messes with his hair, saying he looks cuter that way, while he gives a nervous but excited laugh. As she analyses the room for the "best setup," he stutters as he tells her not to be so scientific, a slight raising of his hand moving into a one-shoulder shrug. When she proposes they try a chair, he glances towards the bed as a more obvious choice before stuttering again. Examining the chair, he moves his head slowly as if trying to imagine how they would incorporate the prop into their lovemaking, but when she dismisses it as a little too conventional, he nervously rushes over to pour himself an alcoholic beverage. In the space of just a few minutes, he has moved from potential seducer to nervous wreck in a variety of modulating stages. When Gusto accuses Tom of being coy, he feebly confesses to it all being a little too fast for him, a phrase typically more likely to be uttered by a woman than a man in a romantic situation and highlighting Tom's emasculation and Gusto's complete control. This is reflected in their attire since he is underdressed and vulnerable in a bathrobe and she is in a sharp business suit and heels, suggesting she is in possession of the phallus.

He allows her to physically move him around the room in her attempts to find the "perfect position," forcefully sitting him in a chair before he becomes agitated and defiantly states that he is "afraid I won't like it." In the crux of their cross-communication, which can be interpreted either way, much to the audience's amusement, she tells him that he will like it when he sees it in the Sunday supplement. His eyes widen and he hopelessly declares, "What's been happening in America since I've been in jail?" When she adds that he will be in full color he jumps up and bellows "What?" in complete disbelief, his eyes now exceptionally wide. Just then there is a knock at the door, he moves across the room to answer it before looking back at her with a perplexed look on his face. When a group of men with cameras push past him, Milland allows the tension to physically leave his body, his face loosening up in a sense of relief to show that Tom realizes he has misunderstood the situation. However, this relief is only momentary when he concludes there will be no lovemaking and he sits on the chair with his arms folded and a glum look on his face like a defiant child, barking as they attempt to take his photograph. After the men leave and he fails to seduce Gusto once more, he changes tactics by announcing that he is going to devote all his evenings in Paris to "amour." When she quips "that's a lot of amour," without missing a beat, he grins and retorts that he was in jail for an awfully long time. This ends a particularly shocking scene for a Code-era film, although it is all done through suggestion and aimed at knowing adult audiences. It is through Milland's subtle facial expressions, gestures, and vocal responses to Colbert's words and actions that really make the scene work.

Changing tactics, he pretends to have plans to meet a lady at Maxim's but agrees to do Gusto's interview before his date arrives. In the restaurant, he looks polished and exceedingly handsome in a tuxedo and black tie, and with the camera placed closer to Milland than Colbert, he becomes the dominant one in the frame, suggesting that Tom's masculinity has now been restored. Grinning smugly, Milland sits casually on a barstool, one arm across his waist, his other elbow propped up on this arm, and a champagne cocktail in his hand. When Gusto asks Tom if he was ever a test pilot, he plays the fool by instantly replying, "No, that was [Clark] Gable," causing her to groan. Looking immensely proud of his wit, he turns to her with a grin reminiscent of British comedian Stan Laurel rather than a seductive romantic lead. An obvious in-joke about Colbert's former costar, who made a film called *Test Pilot* (Victor Fleming, 1938) two years earlier, a similar joke occurs later in the film when Tom runs into two old comrades who have reenlisted, and one asks him to knit him a sweater in the shape of Dorothy Lamour. Asking Gusto for tips on entertaining his date, she suggests he take a carriage ride, count to one thousand and then kiss the woman. When Tom's mysterious date fails to appear, Gusto concludes that she has been tricked but is relieved rather than angry.

The following scene opens with Tom and Gusto taking a carriage ride, foreshadowing their first kiss. Although traveling in silence, we are aware that both their mouths are slightly moving, thereby suggesting they are counting to a thousand. She nervously looks around while he stares forward with raised eyebrows, but she is unprepared when he leans over and kisses her, telling him he cheated since she only counted to 910. Through a grin, he breathlessly informs her that he could not wait and, although she repeatedly attempts to exit the carriage, he keeps a firm grip on her. Moaning as he moves towards her, he nuzzles her neck and locks his hands around her waist before declaring that it is too late for her to leave since her pulse is unsteady and her cheeks flushed. When she finally convinces him to let her return to her hotel to work, he fixes his bowtie, crosses his arms like a sulking child, and proclaims that she will not get any work done because she will be thinking of him. Through small gestures in the tight space of the darkened carriage, Milland and Colbert are entirely convincing in demonstrating their characters' strong sexual attraction. However, apart from Tom instigating their first kiss, Gusto again takes control throughout, talking incessantly while he passively listens and sporadically paws at her. She is the one disciplined enough to break off their rendezvous so that she can work. Calling her at her hotel, although we cannot hear what Tom is saying, Gusto laughs excitedly as she reprimands him. We imagine his words are sexually explicit, what may now be labeled "phone sex," but the censors would not permit Tom's side of the call to be included. While tantalizing the audience, Gusto looks shocked when declaring she is using a public phone and abruptly hangs up. Pausing for a second, she begins smiling to herself before moving to the bed, turning off the light, and seductively touching her chest, neck, head, and mouth while contemplating Tom's words, thus suggesting Tom's erotic appeal to her and, by extension, stressing Milland's masculine appeal for (female) viewers.

The pair share a mature adult relationship that is evidently an intimate one, which is unusual for a Hollywood film during this period, at least for respectable, white, middle-class romantic leads. One scene makes it explicit that the unmarried couple have been making love in the Compiègne Forest, where they wake at dawn. Colbert sits with her back against a tree while Milland's head rests across her knee. She is starry-eyed, playing with his hair and calling him "darling," while he looks up and seductively greets her with a good morning. In a low, sensual voice, he informs her there is dew in her hair before leaning in to kiss her. Just as she grabs the back of his neck, the camera pans away to show a deer instead, suggesting a form of censorship.

After a cut indicating the passing of time, three deer now stand where there was one, with two of them kissing to symbolize that the human couple have again engaged in intercourse. When the camera pans back to the performers they are lying on the ground, Colbert on her back and Milland on his stomach. His hair now ruffled, he delicately plays with her wrist while she puts her other hand to her head and exclaims that she feels like she has a brand-new set of senses, having been tone-deaf and colorblind before.

Figure 5.3. Milland and Claudette Colbert enjoy some alone time in *Arise, My Love* (Mitchell Leisen, 1940), just before their characters learn World War II has broken out.

This can be read as Gusto vocalizing her first orgasm after her passionate and fulfilling lovemaking with Tom (figure 5.3). Tom is more subdued but happy, suggesting he is sexually satisfied but more experienced than Gusto, while being proud to have demonstrated his virile masculinity for her pleasure. The performers' size difference is particularly obvious here, the petite Colbert significantly smaller than Milland, whose large hands are around the same size as her head and his elongated body stretching much further than hers in their suggestive vertical positioning. Still lying on the ground, she sensually raises her leg while he kisses her, but he is distracted by several skittish animals running past. He abruptly raises himself onto one elbow just as the diegetic sound of aircraft fills the air. They look up to see the sky full of bomber planes as Tom grimly states that it has begun. A radio is then used as a shortcut to inform us that Hitler has taken Poland, and their lives are now forever changed.

From Tom's escape from jail to this moment, the film could be comfortably considered a romantic comedy, with their relationship developing in a fun but sensual manner. The couple are sailing on the SS *Athenia* when it is torpedoed. The first boat to be sunk during World War II, in September 1939 the ship was destroyed by a German submarine U-30 in the Western Approaches near Britain, killing ninety-eight passengers and nineteen crew members while many others died trying to escape in lifeboats. Therefore, this recent and real-life harrowing event is merged with the fictional lives of the characters. Tom and Gusto escape on separate lifeboats and are frantic and more in love than ever when reunited, their relationship now on a level that is no longer just physical. Milland fills his words with emotion, his voice even breaking on the last word as he hugs her tightly. Announcing he has never loved her so much, Tom forcefully kisses Gusto before turning abruptly and leaving to help on a dangerous rescue mission, showing his bravery and personal sacrifice for the collective good.

Separated by the war, the relationship comes full circle when Tom locates Gusto in the Compiègne Forest in June 1940, where Gusto delivers a powerful speech about America, pride, and never giving up that sounds like pure propaganda or, as Dick calls it, "an interventionalist prayer," with an ending even more anti-isolationist than the shooting script in which Gusto "buoys up Tom's spirits" by noting he can still train fliers even if he can no longer participate himself (1985: 82). Although Gusto's words are similar in the film, she reminds him that the prayer, "Arise, My Love," that he said upon takeoff can no longer be just for him but must now be said for America: "Arise, my love. Arise, be strong" so you can stand up straight and say to anyone under God's heaven: "All right—whose way of life shall it be—yours or ours?" Milland delivers the film's final line, smiling proudly and with love in his eyes as Tom proclaims Gusto has always been the best, again highlighting her importance in the film. Representing the country as a united whole, they are locked in an embrace at the fadeout. Tom has sustained an injury to his hand, and his voice is filled with pain when announcing that they do not want him in England with his compound fracture. Off-screen, Milland failed his wartime medical after sustaining two separate hand injuries shortly before the war, resulting in the ex-soldier, expert gunman, and licensed pilot being rejected from the air force for the lack of functionality in his hand (Milland 1974: 195). In 1938, a poorly positioned camera on the set of *Hotel Imperial* (1939) had caused him to fall from a horse at high speed into a pile of broken masonry, resulting in him sustaining a "badly mangled" left hand, concussion and a three-inch laceration on his head requiring nine stitches. Just months later, he was making furniture when a piece of wood slipped, causing his hand to go into a circular blade making 750 rotations a minute. He lost part of his thumb, and, in Milland's words, his tendons were "chewed to hell"; while surgeons restored 50 percent efficiency in his hand, this was not enough to allow him to pass a wartime medical (1974: 192–93).

Paramount may have had an overt European cohort, but this Hollywood film presents America as the "beloved that must rise, and not merely into the blue yonder like Tom's plane" (Dick 1985: 83). Moreover, while this message is aimed at America on the brink of war, the home countries of the actors delivering these lines were already at war, with Milland's family still in Wales. Dick notes a commonality between Chaplin's *The Great Dictator* (1940), Hitchcock's *Foreign Correspondent* (1940), and *Arise, My Love* in how they use imagery and discourse about "lethargy and political naiveté (the amnesiac baraber [sic], the blasé correspondent, the news-hungry reporter, the pilot of fortune who calls himself a confused liberal)." He calls each film "progressively more vocal in its insistence on a wake-up call for America" (1985: 83). In a backhanded compliment, Halliwell feels that Paramount "fell down on the job" of "its tradition of being unable to sell a film of quality," with this "bitter romantic comedy-drama" which "has laughs [but is] hardly a gay, glorious story" (1976: 176). However, given the grim atmosphere from the start, this was certainly not the aim. Dick suggests that while many deem *Foreign Correspondent* "the strongest of the anti-isolationist films; that distinction belongs" to *Arise, My Love* (1985: 80). He adds that it may seem less strange that Paramount made the film around the same time as *The Road to Singapore* (Victor Schertzinger, 1940), "if one remembers that in the years before Pearl Harbor, each studio did something atypical [world events encouraged it] but not entirely out of character" (1985: 80).[9]

This film certainly enabled Milland more character development than his prior roles and allowed him to display a wider range of performance skills. The role of Tom also helped him develop his comedy skills and reflect a more dangerous eroticism through his American flyer. Milland sounds slightly Americanized by clipping some words and uttering the occasional "yeah," but overall, his voice sounds more "naturally" British than the overly pronounced English accent he was required to employ in the past, which may have contributed to his early performances seeming stilted. Thus, after appearing in fifty films, Milland could confidently call himself a star at Paramount, even though he was still playing a secondary role to the studio's female leads.

Milland and Colbert were paired for the third and final time the following year in the comedy *Skylark* (Mark Sandrich), which Eames proclaims is "light, bright and forgettable" (1985: 155). While the story originated from a successful Samson Raphaelson play in which Gertrude Lawrence starred on Broadway, Eames notes the film "never soared very high, either on the screen or at the box-office" (1985: 155); it certainly did not have the critical or commercial success of *Arise, My Love*. After a decade in Hollywood, Milland is once more relegated to a secondary role with Colbert as the leading player, and there are even lengthy segments where Milland is absent, "replaced" instead by fellow Britisher Brian Aherne as he romances Colbert, much as Milland did several years earlier in *The Gilded Lily*. However, with the narrative opening on the Kenyons' fifth anniversary, with Lydia (Colbert) feeling increasingly neglected by her advertising executive husband, Tony (Milland), who is consistently absorbed in work, the film provided a different type of role for Milland and allowed him to further expand his range, if only slightly.

Lydia is annoyed when left to host their anniversary party alone while Tony, half-dressed and still in their bedroom, is desperately trying to devise a decent campaign to secure an important account. When Lydia complains of Tony's working incessantly, he irritably reiterates that it has allowed her to enjoy the lifestyle she has become accustomed to. She remains calm, but is visually distressed by his accusatory tone, and we are asked to side with her during these domestic disputes. Tony's "gifting" their private cook to his client causes Lydia to storm out and go for a late-night drive with a party guest, Jim Blake (Aherne). We remain with them throughout, returning to the house when only Tony and four guests remain.

It is only when Myrtle (Binnie Barnes) pointedly remarks that she saw Lydia and Jim leave together hours ago, cryptically noting that "they are not picking daisies," that Milland receives his first close-up of the film. Standing stiffly and leaning against the back of a chair, he demonstrates Tony's concern through a knitted brow, a slight opening of his mouth, and a clenching of his jaw. He also looks off and down, although he does not move his head, making it clear that Tony is lost in thought and no longer part of the conversation going on around him. It also suggests that he has been so engrossed in trying to impress his client that he did not notice his wife leaving the house, even at their anniversary dinner. During the scene, Milland is dressed in a familiar dinner jacket and black tie, adding to his constrained and uncomfortable positioning. In a two-shot, filmed in profile, Myrtle grins widely and looks at Tony flirtatiously through heavy eyelids as she informs him that she is the key stakeholder in her husband's company, before sultrily telling him that he might be able to convince her to sign a million-dollar deal with his firm if he will meet her the next day. He says nothing, merely bowing slightly as if addressing royalty in a way that suggests he is acknowledging both that he will meet her and that he will literally bow down to potential clients no matter the cost. Here, he is willing to almost prostitute himself to secure a deal.

Tony is standing in his pajamas and bathrobe in the front room when Lydia arrives home. Like a father waiting up for his teenage daughter, he coldly demands to know where she has been. When she confesses to acting atrociously, he quickly agrees but remains strangely aloof as she attempts to apologize. While Colbert wraps her arms around his neck, Milland keeps both hands firmly in his pockets and quickly breaks away from her with a stony face, Tony's irrational behavior leading Lydia, and us, to assume he is jealous and was worried for her safety. However, it soon transpires that he is angry because he believes Lydia may have cost him his deal, making this the scene in which Tony is the most unlikable as a character. Commanding that she calls Myrtle and apologize, he stares furiously down into her face, and whenever turning his back or looking away momentarily, Milland follows this by rapidly swinging back around to depict Tony's rage, bellowing and spitting out words of contempt for her. He angrily yells that this is "the beginning and the end of all that highfalutin, discontented wife business too," employing a superior manner and monitoring her side of the call. Milland's facial expressions and body language depict Tony's inner fury, but when told he need not worry about his commission, his face and voice instantly soften as he announces they should forget the whole thing—but Lydia is now furious. Announcing that they could take a trip away together, he puts his hand softly on her waist, kisses her cheek, and seductively says, "Let's talk about it upstairs, shall we?" before walking off and expecting her to follow, but she flinches at his touch and her face, turned away from him and towards us, suggests a combination of anger and humiliation. Grabbing the phone again, she calls for a taxi.

The Britishers meet for the first time when an incensed Tony barges into Jim's law office and demands to know where his wife is. Milland wears a hat and raincoat reminiscent of a movie detective while Aherne sits calmly behind a desk, wearing glasses, reading notes, and smoking a pipe, which adds to the humor of the scene. Tony is particularly animated here, pacing in an agitated manner and speaking in short but violent bursts, while the calm and composed Jim uses long and flowery sentences to reply, which increasingly annoys Tony. Milland appears larger and more dominant when he leans across the desk in a threatening manner towards a seated Aherne, but when the latter stands up, it becomes clear that he is slightly taller than Milland, which does not occur often but makes them a more even match as they face one another.[10] Jim uses sarcasm and repeatedly addresses Tony as "pal" and "chum," leading to an exasperated Tony yelling at him, which amuses Jim greatly and incites him to continue. When Jim begins telling elaborate stories about aprons and banjos, Tony stares at him with confusion, Milland alternating between one raised eyebrow and lowered eyebrows, a slightly gaping mouth, and several quick turns of his head to suggest that Tony is struggling to decipher Jim's ramblings. He vocalizes these facial expressions by blatantly informing Jim he is unsure "what the devil" he is talking about, an ideal idiom for this exchange. Jim remains calm while Tony increasingly displays his short temper, barking out words, and keeping his hands thrust in his pockets like a defiant child before he eventually storms out. In a near-reversal of this scene, Jim later arrives at Tony's house and furiously demands to know where Lydia is. Tony is now the one playing it cool, sardonically calling Jim "pal" and "chum" and repeating Jim's earlier lines back to him with a self-satisfied look on his face and relaxed body language. Jim is now furious, barking at Tony—who is enjoying this turn of fortune immensely. Adopting a mocking tone, Tony feigns ignorance about the private island Lydia has gone to before shrugging and indicating that there are loads of islands, amusingly listing Staten Island, Governors Island, and Coney Island in a series of throwaway comments.

Regaining control, or so he believes, upon seeing Lydia exit Jim's building, Tony rushes forward, grabs her umbrella, and forcefully marches her along the street. He comically gets the open umbrella stuck in the entranceway of the subway before knocking into people and causing chaos, and finally throwing the umbrella down in a complete rage. Putting two coins into the turnstile for Lydia and himself, she gets through but another man cuts in front of Tony, meaning he is stuck. As the train prepares to leave, he searches his pockets for change before jumping over the turnstile, causing the guard to yell that it is not the Olympic Games and recalling Milland and Colbert's first on-screen meeting during the subway altercation with the guard in *The Gilded Lily*. As the couple quarrel in the train carriage, several passengers become embroiled in their dispute. Tony looks haughty and nods arrogantly when they agree with him and becomes belligerent towards those siding with Lydia, again exposing his short temper and making him particularly unlikable here.

Friends convince a despondent Tony that he can save his marriage by falsely informing Lydia he has quit his job. Milland employs a series of doubtful facial expressions to show that Tony feels this plan is unfeasible. When he receives a call to tell him that Lydia is packing to leave him, Milland shows Tony looking jittery as he hangs up the phone, pausing with his hand on top of the receiver and glancing twice in quick succession at his friend. With a furrowed brow and stiff body, he briefly pauses before darting off to try and stop her from leaving. He begins his masquerade by tenderly announcing that he wants to be near her, but she is unconvinced by his overtly melodramatic display of affection that reads false to Lydia and the viewer. Milland then raises his eyes to the ceiling to signify that Tony is praying his deception will work. With his hands behind his back and his chin pointing upwards, he knits his brows together and rocks back on his heels to suggest Tony is getting into character. As if addressing a theatrical audience and not his wife standing near him, he avoids her eyes while declaring that he supposes it is too late, his voice rising at the end in a questioning way, rather than a definite statement, while aiding in indicating Tony's nerves. Looking down, he mutters something about quitting his job, while Milland's nervous actions indicate that Tony is not yet fully committed to his lie. Standing with his back to her, he states rather melancholically that he now feels "kinda scared," an unusual and unnatural way of speaking for Milland, indicating Tony is not quite himself in his deception.

While performing a series of dramatic and sweeping gestures, Tony comically steals a more natural glance at Lydia to gauge her response. Facing the camera and with his back to Colbert, Milland uses extreme and unconvincing facial expressions, much like pantomime, to confirm that Tony is both lying and is a "bad" actor. Milland purposely keeps his physical gestures stiff, while repeatedly looking down and tensing his jaw to denote Tony's apprehension. Deeply exhaling as Lydia approaches, Tony realizes his ruse is working, which leads to him becoming more confident and bolder with his lies. Conceiving fictional scenarios on the spot, he grins assertively while changing his posture, tone of voice, and facial expressions, and animatedly strolling around the house and flailing his arms as if acting out these imagined and improbable encounters. He even begins laughing at his own lies, his voice now strong and confident, and his movements looser and freer. Through his facial and bodily gestures, Milland also illustrates that Tony is paradoxically pleased and repelled that Lydia believes him.

The next morning, he descends the stairs whistling and smiling after a clearly pleasurable night; they kiss over the banister, and he even stops to smell flowers on the hallway table before sighing. However, his rapture is short-lived when a delighted Lydia rushes towards him and announces that he has been fired. His smile instantly disappears, and he visually convulses, swallows hard, and pulls her back towards him as he weakly asks what happened, suggesting the energy has instantaneously been sapped from his body. Looking sickly, Tony listens as she recalls her exchange with a client, and although horrified, he realizes he must keep up his façade while disguising his shock and worry if he is to save his marriage. Humorously, Milland lets his voice nervously break as Tony falsely announces that this is what he wants, but when Jim arrives and forces Tony to admit his lie, he walks slowly and defeatedly towards the window and looks out, his back turned to the others. Pleadingly telling Lydia he loves her and would do anything to keep her, she runs off crying while he lets his whole body go limp to suggest Tony knows this is the end of both his marriage and his career. Watching her leave, he sighs deeply as Jim sarcastically comments, "Sorry pal." Tony then seems to come out of a trance before announcing, in an understated way, that he is also sorry before unexpectedly and forcefully punching Jim in the face. With slightly messed up hair and tie, he kisses his knuckles while looking down at the unconscious Jim, his eyebrows raised and his other hand casually thrust in his pocket as if confirming, or reclaiming, his masculinity for the first time in a while.

After the Kenyons are divorced, Lydia begins a relationship with Jim. One evening, Lydia finds a tuxedo-clad Tony waiting in her hotel room before coldly informing him that he no longer has any effect on her, to which he gives a suspicious grin. As if to prove her wrong, he takes her in his arms and kisses her; she begins moving her hands slowly up his back before pulling away, flustered and breathing heavily. When he questions her previous statement, she announces that it is an involuntary reaction that proves she is normal. Quipping that he likes "them normal," he kisses her more passionately, bending her backwards before sitting her down and smiling victoriously as he reaches for his scarf and overcoat, conceitedly bidding her goodnight before walking out. She remains breathless in the chair, touching her mouth and looking stunned at the virility Tony has obviously just displayed.

Arriving on their secluded island, Tony stands alone outside a log cabin as Lydia approaches. Upon seeing him she tries to leave, but when he softly tells her he wants to talk to her she quickly changes tactics and flirtatiously announces that she wants to talk to him too, seductively entering the cabin. Her shift in behavior confuses Tony and us, but he dutifully follows her. As he attempts to light a fire, she begins touching the back of his neck, which causes him to turn around to look at her with an expression that is a combination of perplexity and delight, with one eyebrow raised as if he is uncertain why she is acting this way but that he is getting a thrill from it. When she turns the lights off, he again looks at her with a quizzically raised eyebrow, this time jerking his head backwards in a more visceral response. Removing her coat and sitting down, she leans back to accentuate her bosom before announcing that she might accept his offer to travel to South America with him and pose as his wife rather than remarry him, stating that she feels she owes him something for all the money he has spent on her. She begins playing with his collar, but he pushes her hand away, his shoulders visually becoming rigid as he moves back in his seat as if petrified. In an outraged voice, he questions why she would suggest such a thing and acts horrified when she pounces on him and kisses him. Struggling to free himself from her grip, he jumps to his feet and questions what has come over her. While she attempts to get him to sit beside her, he becomes stiff and curtly replies that he would prefer to remain standing. When she rushes over and grabs him around the neck, he battles to free himself from her grip but trips over a chair and crashes to the floor. His usually neat hair falls onto his forehead in a clump, and he extends an

Figure 5.4. A more casual Milland after his Tony Kenyon trips and falls in *Skylark* (Mark Sandrich, 1941).

arm to keep her back while telling her to leave him alone, Milland's Welsh accent particularly noticeable on the latter word. He sighs and holds his hand to his side as if injured, remaining on the floor while attempting to steady his breath. He appears dazed until he notices Lydia calmly walking away with her arms behind her back, and it finally dawns on him that she is putting on an act (figure 5.4). Deciding to get his own back, he looks at her suspiciously, stands up, and walks towards her with a glint in his eye. Persistently walking towards her and causing her to walk backwards, he announces that they will do things her way and that a divorce should not make any difference to their relationship. She now panics as he grabs her, thinking that her plan has backfired, struggling as Jim walks in and thinks Tony is attacking her. Tony releases her and when she confirms she wants him to leave, he dejectedly walks out of the cabin and her life.

Although Tony has taken a job in South America, Lydia finally breaks down and confesses that she still loves him. Catching Tony's ship during a stopover in Cuba, Lydia manages to board just as the gangplank is being raised. He is on deck and quietly says her name in disbelief before rushing over and kissing her, another happy ending with their problems apparently solved and the assumption that they will remarry. As Dick suggests, though, the ending is extremely abrupt, with Tony "on route [. . .] to help Latin Americans in their defense preparations (the film was released when World War II had already erupted in Europe) and Lydia arriving in Havana to join him," which may have worked "if there had been a reconciliation scene. But there was none." Dick concludes that Allan Scott wrote several exemplary scripts, but *Skylark* was not one of them, suggesting it was much better as a play than as a film (2008: 152). Perhaps people may not believe Colbert would leave Milland for Aherne. Also problematic is Tony being vilified for being diligent in his job to provide for his wife and Lydia coming across as ungrateful and brattish on several occasions. While none of them are truly likable characters, Jim is extremely loathsome, and Lydia is almost as abhorrent, so much so that one may wonder why Tony tries so hard to win her back. Everything needs to be on Lydia's terms, and even the final reunion is on her terms since Tony has taken his first step to starting a new life, but she follows him, unannounced, onto the restrictive environment of a ship. Nothing he does seems to be right in Lydia's eyes, which can become extremely frustrating for both Tony and the audience. Moreover, we are being asked to identify with Lydia since she is our protagonist and it is Colbert's film, but time and again, this proves too much to ask an audience.

In each pairing with Lamour and Colbert, Milland provides solid support in a film showcasing its female star. He consistently revealed himself as a consummate performer, never attempting to outact or steal the spotlight from his costar, and providing excellent support in each role. Adding to his bankability for Paramount, Milland gave each part his all, successfully conveying a range of emotions for his characters through facial expressions, gestures, vocal intonations, and physical actions that became familiar elements of his acting repertoire during this period. These films aided in developing Milland's star persona as a romantic lead, at times even in the "pinup" mold, while giving prominence to both dramatic and comedic elements of his image as he moved away from repeatedly portraying stereotypical Englishmen and was awarded meatier roles with better-developed characters. This verifies Milland's professionalism and dedication to his work, even when his character was not the film's focus, a pattern that would continue until the mid-1940s when he was awarded a greater number of starring vehicles. However, despite giving an Academy Award–winning performance in *The Lost Weekend*, a film intently absorbed in his character, he was immediately back to supporting regular costar Paulette Goddard in the costume drama *Kitty*. Milland made four films with Goddard, his most with any actress, yet even when he receives top billing, Goddard proves the nucleus of each film. As explored in the next section, Milland's professional and unyielding support for another leading lady is confirmed through his wide range of historical and contemporary roles opposite Goddard.

WAITING FOR GODDARD: PAULETTE AS MILLAND'S MOST FREQUENT COSTAR

Milland costarred with Paulette Goddard on four occasions:[11] in the contemporary films *The Lady Has Plans* and *The Crystal Ball* (Elliott Nugent, 1943), and the historical costume pictures *Reap the Wild Wind* (1942) and *Kitty*, the latter an atypical genre for him. Just three years his junior,[12] Goddard seemed a better fit for Milland than some of his other female costars, such as the older and more masculinized Marlene Dietrich in *Golden Earrings* or the much younger, almost childlike, Gail Russell in *The Uninvited*.[13] Each collaboration presents them as a believable couple by incorporating their performance skills, on-screen interactions, and complementary good looks. Despite their visual appeal as a couple, each film sees Milland relegated to supporting Goddard and her cinematic identity as a combination pinup and comedienne, even when he receives top billing. He delivers as professionally as ever, providing her with more than competent support in narratives overtly concerned with her characters. This section examines their pairings chronologically after briefly setting out the unusual historical and industrial context in which they were produced.

The partnership spanned from 1942 to 1946, which proved to be one of the most challenging periods for Hollywood. During a decade of uncertainty, the industry negotiated vast technological, economic, political, and social changes instigated by America entering World War II after the bombing of Pearl Harbor in December 1941 (Dixon 2006: 21). Schatz declares that some of the fresh faces who had replaced stars off fighting, such as Betty Grable, Frank Sinatra, Gregory Peck, Lauren Bacall, and Rita Hayworth, were "virtually unknown" beforehand (1997: 206). Interestingly, he lists Milland as one of these newcomers, and although he was not a major star before the 1940s, he had been active in Hollywood for over a decade. As noted, the success of *Three Smart Girls* and his jungle films with Dorothy Lamour had helped him become an identifiable cinematic figure in the mid-late 1930s, while *Arise, My Love* made him a "bona fide" star in 1940.

Having trained as a soldier in the cavalry and proved his gift for marksmanship with *The Informer*, Milland was a natural choice for active war duty. A licensed pilot, as noted earlier, he tried to enlist in the air force but was rejected after two severe accidents left him without full use of his left hand, the first on the set of *Hotel Imperial* (1939) and the second when making furniture with a circular saw (1974: 192–93). Milland had returned to work almost instantly after the second incident, during which he lost part of his thumb, admitting to considering himself a "glutton for work [. . .] until I tangled with Goddard." He appreciated her lack of false veneer that often accompanies stardom and referred to her as the most hardworking woman he had ever encountered: "wise, humorous, and with absolutely no illusions' (1974: 191). This praise suggests they may have worked well together because of their shared views on professionalism and a mutual lack of pretense.

COMIC ESPIONAGE: *THE LADY HAS PLANS*

Although marking her first screen pairing with Milland, Goddard was not the first choice for *The Lady Has Plans*, having replaced British actress Madeleine Carroll (Morella and Epstein 1985: 120). Given Carroll's immense success in Hitchcock's *The 39 Steps* (1935), she would have been a good fit for the role, although she arguably lacked the warmth that came from Goddard's southern appeal and that the part required. Although Milland receives top billing as reporter Kenneth (Ken) Clarence Harper, as the title suggests, it is Goddard's film. Moments of extreme comedy involving miscommunication, mistaken identity, and a battle of the sexes merge with tense and dramatic situations involving Nazis, spies, brutal murders, and the all-too-real threat of World War II. Eames feels the film "teetered uncertainly between comedy and drama and never managed to achieve either with any impact" and, while it has a good cast and some sparkle in the direction, there was just not enough of it (1985: 159).

The plot involves a criminal ring that murders a scientist and steals his plans for a radio-controlled torpedo. The plans are tattooed in invisible ink on the back of Rita Lenox (Margaret Hayes), who is to take the place of reporter Sidney Royce (Goddard) and auction them to the highest bidding country. Arriving in Lisbon before Rita, Sidney discovers a luxurious hotel suite containing Rita's luggage, full of expensive gowns, has been booked in her name. Chaos ensues when men of various nationalities demand to see her back, much to Sidney's confusion and dismay.

We hear Ken/Milland before we see him. Delivering a news report from Lisbon, his voice comes through a speaker in the US as Sidney is told she is listening to her challenging new boss. Ken has fired the last four reporters and sent them back, to use Sidney's words, "like ping pong balls," and she expects the same treatment. That the viewer is introduced to Ken from Sidney's point of view highlights almost instantaneously that it is her film, if the title did not already do so, but it is through Milland's familiar vocal intonation that the audience is permitted to determine the identity of her boss before he appears on-screen. A cut to Ken/Milland finishing his broadcast shows him standing casually with one hand in his pocket and the other holding the speech; his tie is loose and his jacket open. Although delivering the newscast with enthusiasm and professionalism, much like a screen performer, immediately after going off-air, he frustratingly notes the lack of news in town, fixing his tie and scowling at the men around him as he cynically deems the report "a lot of pure unadulterated hooey."

Given her masculine encoded name and the opulent hotel she is residing in, Ken quips that Sidney is probably the boss's "son" before adopting a confused manner when she answers the door. Raising an eyebrow suggestively, a trope of Milland's acting style, he comments that he hopes he is not interrupting anything. Wearing ordinary, nondescript daywear up to this point, Sidney has changed into one of Rita's floor-length sequined evening gowns, allowing her to appear particularly glamorous and feminine during her first encounter with Ken and leading him to make an incorrect judgement since it is the afternoon. He does a double take when she announces she is Sidney, and proclaims that she is a woman, looking her up and down before confirming "definitely" and turning away. Ken frustratedly snaps that he needs a leg man, but she proudly proclaims to be his leg man. He looks down at her shapely legs and mutters a nervous yes, costume and dialogue combining to allow focus to be placed firmly on Goddard's body.

Milland's good looks are highlighted when the US Embassy incorrectly inform Ken that Sidney is a murderess with stolen plans tattooed on her back to sell to the Nazis. He cautiously asks her to dinner at their request, but only with the reassurance that British Embassy member Ronald Dean (Roland Young) will be monitoring. The embassy requests that Ken romances Sidney to get hold of the plans, with Ronald reassuring him it should be easy for a "handsome dog" like him. Ken initially declines, pacing with his hands in his pockets with Milland using now familiar gestures of a raised eyebrow and the jutting out of his chin while casually throwing out a line, half-joking that he closes his eyes when kissing a girl and wants to ensure he can open them again. Milland impeccably delivers these lines to highlight Ken's fear, which he is covering up with humor. He slumps into a chair, but the newspaperman in him is eager to retrieve the plans and get a major scoop. Jumping up, he grabs his hat and ironically calls her the fair Borgia (clearly referring to Lucrezia) as he rushes out.

In a now-familiar tuxedo, black tie, and white carnation in his lapel, Ken asks Sidney to wear a backless gown before comically fighting with the waiters to seat her and remove her wrap. Standing behind her, he stares at her back for such an uncomfortably prolonged period that he compels the puzzled waiters to join in. When Sidney turns around, he stutters the excuse of admiring her gown and attempts to flirt using newspaper terms, such as calling her a "scoop." This undermines Sidney's position in the film and almost dehumanizes her, the men around her controlling the gaze and fetishizing her through their fixation on her back. The plot also appears to spoof more serious crime films of the *film noir* mold where the dangerous femme fatale is positioned as something to be investigated. But Sidney is wrongly and comically depicted as a dangerous woman, oblivious to why she is receiving so much unwelcome attention.

When Ronald suggests Ken spike Sidney's drink, before carrying her to her room to examine her back, the latter flatly refuses, sitting with his arms crossed and huffily looking away. Although Young and Milland were both British, their accents and matching tuxedos are where the similarities end. Milland towers over the 5'6" actor, and is much younger, more attractive, and broader than Young, looking particularly masculine as they sit side by side. Milland's posture of outstretched arms extends his positioning in the frame, and his broad shoulders help fill his tuxedo much more impressively than the meek Young with his small frame. Young is in his mid-fifties and applies the trademark timorous and stuttering manner he adopted for many screen roles, most famously as the title character in the Topper films.

Ronald tries to bribe the bartender to spike Sidney's drink, but when he spikes the two men's drinks instead, they quickly become intoxicated on a small glass of brandy while Sidney remains sober. Milland depicts Ken's reaction by arrogantly taking a sip before convulsing, grabbing onto the table, and worriedly asking if there was an earthquake while the other two remain completely still in a three-shot. He drinks the rest before pulling the glass away with wide eyes full of fear, his brows knitted together, and his teeth gritted as if he has just realized something is in his drink. Staring at the glass, Milland depicts Ken's attempts to regulate his face so that Sidney will not become suspicious. He begins staring at her as if Ken is trying to focus his eyes, his suaveness depleting by the second as he leans towards her before his elbow slips off the table. Sitting up again, he sucks his teeth, smacks his mouth, and folds his arms to attempt nonchalance before asking, with a slurred voice and a hint of an American accent, "You sure you feel alright, sister?" His conduct completely changes as he comically adopts the persona of a hardnosed detective in a film noir, only a drunk one, and Ronald is acting in a comparable manner. Embarrassed by their conduct, Sidney heads to her room. While being pursued by the Nazis, she realizes she has grabbed Ronald's key by mistake and enters his room.

The two inebriated men walk along the hotel corridor with their arms interlinked and singing at the top of their lungs. Milland's hair is now unruly, his clothes no longer pristine, and his sophisticated and suave disposition obliterated. As they drunkenly fumble with Ronald's key, they realize it is for Sidney's room. Stumbling into the suite and thinking there are twin beds due to their double vision, they fall fully dressed onto the double bed in unison. Hoping to photograph Sidney's back, the Nazis break in but wake Ken. Sitting up, Milland slurs when calling the photographer a "peeping Tom" before, in one perfectly executed sweeping motion, punching him in the face and lying back down. Noticing Ronald lying beside him, he drunkenly asks who he is before they amusingly introduce themselves, shake hands, and go back to sleep. When a ringing telephone wakes them, both men see a different part of the room containing Sidney's clothing. A cut from one to the other suggests they both believe they have spent the night with her. With a look of sheer delight, they slowly and simultaneously reach behind them until they make contact. Feeling each other's shirt sleeves, Milland furrows his brow and Young scratches his head as they slowly turn towards each other but say nothing. It is a silent scene perfectly played by the performers to illustrate the absurdity of their situation and uncertainty about what transpired the night before.

Looking even more disheveled than the previous night, and suggesting Ken's extreme hangover, Milland sits up in bed and tries to stand before delicately sitting back down as if his head will not allow him to stand fully upright. Finally getting to his feet, Ken announces, in not more than a whisper, that he will no longer help the embassy since he feels like death, sitting down again to nurse his throbbing head. When Sidney enters the room to reveal she is neither a murderer nor a spy, a continuity error occurs since the only element of Milland's appearance that is not pristine is that he has a few sections of loose hair falling onto his forehead. A hairstyle often used to add a dangerous but sexual attractiveness to a male performer and utilized on a somewhat regular basis for Milland across genres, his suit looks pressed, his bow tie is neatly tied, and the carnation is still in his lapel, even after a drunken night's sleep. Milland adds several grunts, "yeahs," and comical faces to his performance in the first forty minutes of the film, appearing relaxed and natural in the capacity of a newspaperman chasing a scoop. This is where the comedy ends, however, as the Nazis become more integrated into the characters' lives and an obvious threat to the country, as they would have been to audiences at the time.

When the embassy reveals the truth, Sidney convinces Ken to draw fake plans on her back, which he does so grudgingly. Their first intimacy is, sadly, a dangerous task as he begs her not to go to the Nazis and confesses his love for her. Putting herself in the role of a news story, she now actively and knowingly becomes the "scoop." Traveling alone to Nazi headquarters,

Figure 5.5. From comedy to noir, Milland hides in the shadows in *The Lady Has Plans* (Sidney Lanfield, 1942).

she allows them to photograph her back but is revealed as a fraud by a man who knows Rita. Concurrently, Rita has arrived at Sidney's room where Ken is still waiting. Although she pretends to be Sidney's friend, the keen journalist is not fooled. Pacing, he casually announces that Sidney finds the assignments quite difficult with her wooden leg; Rita agreeing with Ken's outlandish story confirms that she is lying, and a knowing look comes over his face. When she draws a gun on him, he tries to fool her by telling her there is a run in her stocking but she only sneers. He turns away as if defeated, casually shrugging and muttering about not being able to "blame a guy for trying" before rapidly, and quite shockingly, spinning around and punching the much smaller woman directly in the face, knocking her out before tying her up. It is revealed later that, not losing his sense of humor when faced with a murderess holding a gun, Ken has recovered the plans from Rita's back, wired them to Washington, and replaced them with the British wartime slogan "V for Victory."[14] Not only hinting at his British roots, which otherwise go unacknowledged, the scene demonstrates that although Ken helps women in need, as he does Sidney, his gentlemanly behavior does not extend to women like Rita, particularly in wartime.

One of Ken's colleagues is revealed to be working with the Nazis and plans for Ken and Sydney to be locked up "indefinitely." While Sydney panics, the more clearheaded and resourceful Ken devises a plan to get the guard to open his door. When he does, Ken promptly knocks him out, locks him up, and frees Sidney, thus temporarily becoming the active male to her damsel in distress. As they attempt their escape, the film adopts a fleeting sense of film noir with Milland hiding in the shadows with a gun (figure 5.5). Walking slowly through the resort full of spies with a newspaper in front of his face, he manages to reach a phone booth from which he delivers his live broadcast. This alerts the police, who descend on the retreat while the couple embrace in the confined, but romantic, phonebooth after Ken saves the day with the help of the brave and active Sydney.

Humor and screwball within an escapist world of luxurious clothing, beautiful stars, and a lush hotel decked out in true opulent Paramount style are combined here with the darker and more serious real-life issues affecting the world at the time. The film highlights the danger the Nazis posed to America, functioning as a cautionary tale offering the message that anyone can be a spy since, as Ken notes, they do not wear a sign. Bernard F. Dick calls it a clever pre-Pearl Harbor spy film and "espionage comedy marked by a touch of class—the white telephones" under a publicity photograph of Goddard in a tight evening gown and Milland in a form-fitting tuxedo (1985: 99). They are sitting on the floor of a plush room on a thick pile rug in front of a chaise longue and, with their heads together, each holds the receiver of a white telephone to their ear, depicting their roles as reporters,[15] a shortcut for the important work their characters are doing, while simultaneously presenting the performers as glamorous and beautiful stars. Milland's handsome but classic look is finished off with shiny, slicked-back hair, a white carnation in his lapel, and a large pinkie ring which suggests pure class and very much reflects both his star persona at the time and Paramount's lavish house style, as does Goddard's lightly colored satin gown and perfectly coiffured hair. Goddard's ability to be a beautiful but smart and active female who works suggests an equivalence in their relationship that reflected the shifts in gender roles during World War II as women began working in factories while many men were fighting overseas. However, although she is indisputably the star of the film and it is Sidney's story that we follow, Ken is still her boss and has a higher position in both society and the company as a white male.

Dick notes that comedies like this are based on the "up the ante" principle where the writer adds "as many devices as the plot can accommodate," and quite a few are packed into this film, from mistaken identity to bedroom farce to topical issues including specific wartime incidents (1985: 99). Goddard used her star image to help national drives as part of the war effort. She promised a kiss to the person who collected the most aluminum in Hollywood, and it was announced that it would be "no ordinary kiss but an exact duplicate" of the one she gave Milland in the film. According to Morella and Epstein, the winner was a small restaurant owner called H. B. Clifford, whose wife commented that he had never kissed her like that (1985: 122). This stunt was good for morale and the war effort as well as being positive publicity for both the film and the romantic coupling of Milland and Goddard as a new screen couple. The role of Ken seemed a natural fit for Milland's finesse with both light comedy and more serious drama, and the couple complement each other on-screen even as he permits Goddard to shine as the central character. Although they had shot *Reap the Wild Wind* first, it was released later, with Morella and Epstein declaring, that it was "of course a blockbuster" (1985: 121).

HIGH SEA ADVENTURE: *REAP THE WILD WIND*

Like Milland, Cecil B. DeMille spent much of his extensive cinematic career at Paramount, building his reputation early on in Hollywood history as the "most successful and flamboyant representative of the 'new morality' in all its manifestations" (Cook 2003: 138); concerned with liberalism in the 1920s, this new morality was about equality and freedom for all, regardless of gender, race, or sexuality. Helping to shape Paramount in its early days, DeMille was explicitly associated with the studio's "house style" and became production chief by 1935. David A. Cook calls him a "virtual incarnation of the values of Hollywood" during the 1920s, with "an uncanny ability to anticipate the tastes of his audiences and give them what they wanted before they knew they wanted it" (2003: 136). In 1914, while still at Famous Players-Lasky, DeMille directed Hollywood's first-ever feature-length Western, *The Squaw Man* (1914),[16] as well as several other films within the genre, including *The Virginian* (1914) and *Call of the North* (1914). It was the 1923 biblical epic *The Ten Commandments* that made DeMille "internationally famous"; costing over $1.5 million to produce (the equivalent of $24,745,740 in 2022), it was one of the era's most lucrative films (Cook 2003: 137). He replicated his success with religious spectacles over the decades, with films such as *The Sign of the Cross* (1932), *Samson and Delilah* (1949), and his final film, a remake of his own *The Ten Commandments* (1956). He was renowned for creating spectacles on screen, and *Reap the Wild Wind* paired Milland and Goddard in a historical adventure typical of DeMille. With three Academy Award nominations, it won Best Special Effects, while Milland won the *Photoplay* Award for Best Performer of the Month in May 1942.

Halliwell proclaims that "among producers, only Hitchcock has rivaled [DeMille] as a self-publicist"; his films consistently "sounded big, looked big and were billed big," his name more prominent in advertising than the title or its stars (1976: 28). Paramount reached a high in 1942, meaning that DeMille faced much competition even from within his home studio. However, as Eames asserts, DeMille again provided "the Big One of the Year" with *Reap the Wild Wind*. With over $2 million spent on creating storms and shipwrecks off the Florida coast, Eames calls it a "melodramatic adventure on a grand scale" (1985: 158). Acting as director and producer, it was only DeMille's second film released in Technicolor and he promoted historical authenticity via costumes, sets, props, and other visual elements to validate his films' historical "truth" (Blanke 2018: 137). The intricate historical setting portrayed through various aspects of the mise-en-scene makes *Reap the Wild Wind* especially noteworthy in this respect.

Portraying dandy sea lawyer Stephen Tolliver, Milland received top billing above John Wayne and Goddard during the film's original release, with Susan Hayward billed sixth. As is characteristic of Milland's pairings with Goddard, her Loxi is unquestionably the leading protagonist, but a reissue of the film just six years later saw Wayne receiving top billing followed immediately by Hayward, despite her playing a supporting role. Having Milland and Goddard moved down in billing highlights the fickleness of the industry and the public. However, while this restructured billing indicated that Hayward and Wayne were gaining in popularity while Goddard's star was on the wane, it seems more surprising that Milland was relegated to third billing since he had won his Academy Award two years earlier; Hayward would not win hers until 1959.[17]

Running just shy of two hours, the sea-faring epic begins by establishing its timeframe as 1840. The narrative concerns salvage masters and the threat to America's future on the sea. Starting with a storm at sea, Loxi Claiborne (Goddard) works as part of the dangerous, male-driven, salvage operation rescuing a ship. She nurses the severely injured captain, Jack Stuart (Wayne), back to health, and the two fall in love before he returns to sea. Upon learning that Tolliver runs the sailing ship line, Loxi plans to seduce him in order to help Jack. Her seduction does not take long, however, since it is obvious that the smitten Stephen has fallen for her.

Introduced at a lavish tea gathering in a sumptuously decorated drawing room, Stephen is captivated by Loxi the moment she arrives. When he attempts to make her laugh with a ventriloquism trick with his dog, Romulus, the spunky Loxi declares them a "wonderful pair of performing dogs" to the gasps of others, but the amused Stephen is not discouraged. As Loxi sings a salty sea ditty that shocks many of the guests, he intently stares at her. Leaning on the piano, Milland keeps his focus on Goddard the entire time and, although he hardly moves, his facial expressions perfectly encapsulate how Stephen views Loxi, much subtler and nuanced than his attempts at MGM.

Milland's eyes shine and his eyebrows raise a little as if in excited anticipation; dropping his chin, his mouth forms a half-smile as he examines her in wonderment and hangs on her every (bawdy) word, suggesting Stephen has never met a woman like her before and is wholly enchanted.

Her ability to be at once beautiful and earthy is a trait that Goddard shares with the character, setting her apart from the rest of the women in the room, particularly as far as Stephen is concerned. While the others in their dark, conservative clothing are seated further back in clusters, and thus begin to merge, the dark-haired Goddard in her green dress sits alone at the piano and is the focus of the room and the camera for both the diegetic and nondiegetic audiences, the spotlight clearly on her. She is the only woman to receive close-ups in this sequence, which are intercut with those of Milland as Stephen stares at Loxi, thus making us think there is something special about her above the many other women in the room, while also exhibiting her beauty in Technicolor to the audience. Indeed, while the partygoers look away in embarrassment at the language she uses, which also separates her from them, several women fan themselves and appear faint while others scan the room in disbelief, he never takes his eyes off her and seems to be relishing the whole experience. When Loxi's aunt eventually puts an end to her "vulgar" song, she proclaims it has twenty more verses and Stephen steps forward, flirtatiously assuring her he would love to hear them soon. Realizing that Stephen's interest in her might help her to win Jack the captaincy of the *Southern Cross*, the newest ship in the line, she flirts back and says she hopes so, hands him a flower, and walks off while he stares after her with great interest.

This film marked the first time Milland wore historical costuming onscreen, and he is most definitely presented as a dandy or fop with a great interest in clothes, in direct contrast to the simple, more manly, and utilitarian outfits worn by Wayne's Jack Stuart. During his first appearance, his light grey jacket is perfectly tailored across his broad shoulders with a cutaway waist and is accented by an extremely fussy ruffled shirt and blue-and-white dotted necktie; tight grey trousers highlight his figure. Even his pet dog wears a large blue satin bow around his neck that goes along with Stephen's style. Throughout his career, both on- and off-screen, Milland very often wore a pinkie ring, only here the usually plain gold piece is replaced by an elaborately chunky jade ring. He is clean-shaven and his hair is longer than previously, his curls swept back from his face and finished off with sideburns which were popular for men during the period of the narrative.

Writing about the fop, Peter McNeil and Vicki Karaminas note the figure is perceived as "an unnatural hybrid, containing a mingling of male and female attributes" (2009: 6), while Colin McDowell highlights this identity as an "over-fashionable man" presumed to have forfeited "too much of his masculinity" for the draw of the newest style (1997: 40). Roland Barthes sees dandyism as not only an ethos but a technique, where the latter guarantees the former ([1962] 2004: 67). Barthes further notes that the dandy must frequently devise idiosyncratic behaviors, a point illustrated by Milland's Stephen as he draws attention to himself at the tea gathering, cracking jokes, and performing ventriloquism with Romulus, all while impeccably groomed and immaculately dressed. However, he is also revealed to be a highly intelligent and perceptive sea lawyer who wants to see justice done. Therefore, Milland has several layers of acting to do in this film as a gendered hybrid figure that people do not take too seriously even though his sharp wit and tough masculinity emerge as needed. Indeed, Loxi appears to be more masculine than Stephen at times, especially near the start of the film, given her key role in a male industry and her fearlessly helping with wrecked ships. As a tough woman, she is also posed against her frailer and more stereotypically feminine cousin Drusilla (Hayward) who, in an important subplot, is in love with Dan Cutler (Robert Preston).

Loxi attempts to seduce Stephen as a way of helping Jack, spending almost all her time with him and feigning interest in him. Lying on a blanket near the water, Stephen is propped up on one elbow and once again holds Romulus. Dressed in another regal outfit, Milland wears a bright red coat and a matching red-and-white dotted necktie with a ruffled shirt; tight grey trousers with a red stripe down the side compliment his coat and figure. This time his curls are resting softly on his forehead rather than swept to the side, as Stephen tenderly proposes to Loxi. She is taken aback as her flirtations have been aimed only at securing a post for Jack, continuing to talk about the *Southern Cross* even when Stephen mentions their honeymoon. They are abruptly interrupted by a man telling Stephen that Jack has landed, and he notices the look of delight that comes across Loxi's face upon hearing Jack's name. In a particularly subtle piece of acting, Milland adeptly uses just his eyebrows and eyes to convey a wide and conflicting range of emotions, keeping the rest of his body and face immobile. Through Milland's deft performance, we know what is going through Stephen's mind in a few seconds of screen time that could easily be missed by a historical audience seeing the film just once in a theatre.

In a two-shot of Milland and Goddard, he observes her from out of the corner of his eye, and from his eyeline we see he is firstly looking at her eyes. Noticing that she is now smiling, his eyes move quickly down to her mouth while he simultaneously slightly raises his left eyebrow questioningly, as if he is wondering why Loxi is suddenly grinning. Lowering both eyebrows and

Figure 5.6. Milland's Stephen Tolliver gets wise to Goddard's Loxi in *Reap the Wild Wind* (Cecil B. DeMille, 1942).

diverting his eyes to the ground, as if momentarily considering the cause of her smile, he raises his eyebrow just a fraction again to demonstrate that Stephen has understood the real reason for her attentions and her frequent references to the *Southern Cross*. He moves his head down, his eyes cast to the ground and his face conveying hurt as he attempts to walk past her. When she forcefully stops him and asks him to listen to her opinion about the *Southern Cross*, he again raises an eyebrow and, perhaps to cover his hurt and disappointment, quips with a half-grin that the commodore is not the only one interested in Stuart's arrival. He elevates his already raised eyebrow even further, continuing to look at her from the corner of his eye as he walks away, his facial expression suggesting a combination of questioning, knowing, and accusatory reactions (figure 5.6).

Although lasting only a few seconds of screen time, this is a crucial moment in the narrative and comparatively understated compared to the sea-based action the film's publicity promoted, but it captures the development of Milland's acting skills and demonstrates the subtle and understated manner of his performances. Indeed, by using only his eyes and eyebrows, while keeping the rest of his face and body still, Milland conveys exactly what Stephen would be feeling and thinking in that moment. This subtlety directly contrasts with his performance with Romulus when we know Stephen is acting the fool to amuse those around him and become the center of attention. Thus, Milland must act Stephen's acting and take on the stereotypical traits of the dandy as people expect him to be, thereby giving them what they want through a forced performance. In an acting technique Milland honed over the years, this demonstrates that he was an actor able to use subtle gestures, body movements, and vocal intonations to show the cinematic audience his character is acting, while also being believable for the filmic audience who do not know he is acting. This is another mark of a good actor since he lets the cinematic audience know that his character is effectively "performing" for those around him. While using just his eyes and eyebrows was a successful method of expressing the inner thoughts of his characters, this subtle performance can be overwhelmed by more flamboyant actions or reactions of those around him, especially when paired with the much more animated Goddard.

When Jack is blamed for purposely causing the wreck, Stephen informs the commodore that the destruction was down to the Florida reefs and the Key West pirate wreckers who stole the cargo. It is well known that King Cutler (Raymond Massey) is behind it, but people are too scared to speak up, and the lack of witnesses and evidence greatly frustrates Stephen. Still dressed in his red coat and the youngest man in the room, Milland stands out from the older, more solemnly dressed men. The only other man wearing red sits at the end of a long semi-circular table while Milland is positioned near the center. While the others are seated, Milland stands for much of the scene, and his actively folding sheets of paper help draw the viewer's eye. While it may appear at first that Stephen is not taking the situation seriously, it is obvious that behind this façade he is clever, astute, and passionate about seeing justice done. When it is revealed that many have tried but failed to obtain proof against Cutler, Stephen volunteers to infiltrate his crew despite the danger involved.

Undermining his masculinity and reinforcing his position as a fop, one man laughs and says he "wouldn't last fifteen minutes in that pirate's nest," while another adds with a smirk that Stephen is "a lawyer, not a gunboat" who "wouldn't stand any more chance than a rat in a tar barrel." Although he tries to get the commodore to agree to give Jack the *Southern Cross*, they reach a compromise: if Jack is innocent, he can captain the ship. Loxi misinterprets this as Stephen trying to punish Jack because she loves him, calling the former cowardly, vicious, low, and cruel.

Loxi confesses she only flirted with Stephen to help Jack, cruelly declaring no woman would "even look at a namby-pamby popinjay like you," an insulting term for fop or dandy, after knowing just one "real man" like Jack. This exchange takes place at a formal gathering, Milland wearing his most decorative outfit yet: a dark suit, white ruffled shirt, white bow tie, and white gloves. Declaring that she must prefer the "rough ways of her Key West pirates" to his gentlemanly approach, he removes his gloves, takes her across his knee, and spanks her. She deems him a "sorry, insufferable nincompoop" before hearing a rumor that the two are engaged. She proclaims to the crowded room that she will marry a "real man" and not "a lace-ruffled, bullying jaybird like . . ."—whereupon she gestures to Stephen. Unable to finish, she runs into Jack's arms and the scene ends with Stephen removing his gloves again, only this time in a more confrontational manner. As he walks forward, we are to assume he is now removing them to fight Jack. Thus, Stephen is a combination of passive fop and active male, two distinct modes of masculinity intricately embodied within the same character and subtly executed by Milland.

The latter mode of masculinity begins to come to the fore when Loxi is marrying Jack aboard his ship. Hurriedly arriving in a carriage, Stephen jumps over the rail, throws off his cape—the first instance of his beginning to "shed" his dandy exterior—and demands Loxi return home. An extremely physical, action-packed scene follows when Jack pushes him before Stephen punches him to the ground. Loxi tries to attack Stephen with an implement, but he picks her up and throws her into the water, peering over the rail as Jack punches him. Although landing on his back on the deck, he manages to competently throw a rope around Jack's feet, as if roping a bull, an extremely masculine activity, pulling him back and punching him again before jumping into the water to retrieve Loxi.

When they arrive at the port, Loxi is extremely cold towards Stephen while he smiles at her. As he exits the ship, one of Cutler's men cuts a rope holding five barrels of molasses high above his head. Loxi shouts a warning, and he manages to jump over the side into some hay bales, Romulus still in his arms, as the barrels crash into the gangplank and destroy it. When she rushes over to ask how he is, he changes his expression from shock to delight, telling Romulus that they have finally made an impression. Seeing he is unhurt, she resumes her cold attitude and proclaims she was only worried about the dog. Although his dress is now less fussy, with a plain white shirt without frills, looser grey trousers, a navy-blue coat with tails and a cutaway waist, a matching blue tie around his neck, and a grey top hat, he is still immaculately dressed and there remains a flash of color with his red waistcoat. However, after jumping over the side his hat has come off, his hair is somewhat in disarray and molasses covers his trousers, coat, and face, foreshadowing the dirt and blood that will soon take its place.

As the film progresses, Milland's clothing gets less formal and slightly more utilitarian, suggesting that either Stephen is changing for the situations he finds himself in or that he is trying to become the "real man" Loxi desires. When Loxi learns that Cutler is planning to have Stephen shanghaied to a whaler, she convinces Jack to warn Stephen. Jack and Loxi arrive at the ship at the same time as Cutler's men and they fight on the same side, although there is still tension when the fighting ends. Loxi sits between them as she tends to Jack's wounds, sarcastically asking Stephen if he scared himself by fighting like that, but we have seen evidence of his perfectly adequate fighting skills. In this scene, the frilled shirt and necktie are gone, and he fights in a plain white shirt and red waistcoat, getting dirtier and bloodier throughout the physical altercation. The next scene sees the embroidered waistcoat replaced by a plain one in a muted shade of red, along with a simple open-necked white shirt that forms a low "V"; his curls are now loose and blowing in the wind. Even when more formally dressed while working as a lawyer, his waistcoat is now a subdued ecru color with a delicate floral tapestry design. His trousers are also ecru while his wide tie is black and his coat a deep brown. In the courtroom scene, after Jack has purposely wrecked the *Southern Cross* for Cutler, Stephen tries to obtain confessions from him and his men when Cutler, working as the opposing lawyer, accuses Stephen of the heinous crime. When one of the crew admits to hearing a woman scream as the ship hit it is discovered that Drusilla may have stowed away. Cutler challenges Stephen to prove that a woman's body is in the wreck by going on the almost impossible dive himself, and Jack volunteers to go with him.

As Jack and Stephen are being fitted in diving suits, Cutler tells Jack that if they find the body, he is to give a signal and they will cut Stephen's oxygen line. Loxi overhears and begs Jack not to add another crime to what has already been done. Stephen is confused and looks away when she approaches him, busying himself with the rope on his lap. When she sits down beside him and places her hand delicately on his, Milland immediately pauses, his left hand in midair as he looks at her with his mouth slightly open, showing Stephen is taken aback by the compassion Loxi is now displaying. When she asks him to forgive her, he moves his left hand on top of hers and begins to say her name longingly as they stare at each other. He remembers her love for Jack, composes himself, breaks the gaze, and looks down before completely changing his manner. Deciding to make a joke, he fiddles with his cuffs while telling her if he is late for supper to not let Romulus overeat. He then attempts a weak smile that quickly turns into a grimace as he is unable to keep up the façade. He tries another weak joke, but when she tearfully says his name, he grasps her hand again and they rest their heads comfortably together as a jealous Jack looks on.

The two men make the dive, and when Stephen finds Drusilla's body, Jack signals to the men in the boat to cut Stephen's oxygen line. Just as a knife is brought down on the line, Stephen's shipmate and friend, Captain

Philip Philpott (Lynne Overman), intervenes. What follows is the film's most famous scene, the climactic underwater fight featuring Milland, Wayne, and a giant squid made of red sponge rubber and operated electronically from a switchboard (Eames 1985: 158); Goddard's biographers referred to the mechanical squid as the film's real star (Morella and Epstein 1985: 117). Appearing out of nowhere, it wraps its tentacles around Stephen who struggles, trying to break free and begging for help, but it is a while before the observing Jack comes to his aid.

Milland describes DeMille as unquestionably one of the greatest showmen in the history of cinema, and who utilized a camera "better than anyone" (1974: 197). Taking ten days to shoot, the scene was staged in what was known as the "Big Tank" at Paramount Studios, which was around the size of a football field and twenty-five feet deep (Milland 1974: 197). Again highlighting DeMille's desire for realism, Milland notes that they were wearing extremely heavy but authentic nineteenth-century deep-sea diving outfits. The studio had built "a marine wonderland: the hull of a wrecked ship, strange and jagged rocks, a slowly moving aqueous forest. And caves, dark and frightening" (1974: 197). Discussing his childhood in Wales, Milland recalls playing in the water when his foot touched something soft below the surface. When it was revealed to be a woman's bloated corpse, this, understandably, gave him nightmares for an exceptionally long time (1974: 34). Explaining the impact of this discovery on his later life, he describes being fascinated by water, stating he loves it "with a passion and can never live beyond the sight of it. But I am terrified of it. I fear it. Not the water itself, but what lies beneath," adding that "the fear and horror were born that day" (1974: 33). Consequently, being dressed in restrictive diving gear while portraying a character searching underwater for a woman's body must not have been an easy undertaking. A massive wave approaches and Loxi demands they get the men up before noticing one has lost his lifeline. Unsure who has survived until they pull the unconscious Stephen to safety, Jack has sacrificed himself to save Stephen in the knowledge that he would probably be hanged for his crimes.

The film concludes with Loxi and Stephen on a barge together, ready to become reacquainted now that she knows he is not just the "namby-pamby popinjay" she previously asserted him to be. Although the frilled shirt and dotted necktie have made a return, they are paired with the brown coat, presenting him as a toned-down version of a fop. He continues his ventriloquism jokes, but Loxi no longer accuses him of not being a "real man." Taking his large hand in both of hers, she looks lovingly at him as she now instigates their relationship, while he tenderly places an arm around her as the film ends. Thus, throughout his first historical film, Milland begins by playing an apparently vacuous member of the nobility, a role he was used to playing, before proving his honesty, integrity, bravery, and interest in justice to both Loxi and the audience. She learns not to take people at face value, and he proves his tough masculinity when required, but he clearly prefers to act the gentleman, especially around women. Another intriguing point about Milland's star image is that just over an hour into the film, as Cutler's men approach, Stephen tells Jack to leave everything to him, demanding that he and Loxi "get below." While Milland's recognizably polished diction is evident throughout the remainder of the film, his South Wales accent sounds more pronounced in this line than anywhere else in his screen career.[18] A historical audience could easily miss this, especially with all the physical action occurring concurrently, and would have no way of increasing the volume or replaying the section to listen again. It is an interesting "slip" nonetheless and gives us an insight into how Milland may have sounded in his youth before his diction lessons.

PAULETTE CATCHES SOME RAY: *THE CRYSTAL BALL*

In contrast to the historical adventure *Reap the Wild Wind*, Milland and Goddard's third pairing was a modern comedy that is quite ridiculous and outlandish in parts. Milland may again receive top billing for *The Crystal Ball*, but it is Goddard's film once more. Although there was a lack of progression for Milland's star image, it allowed him to show his aptitude for light comedy, while conflictingly giving him even less agency than previous romantic pairings since his character is mostly controlled by others, most notably the two women played by Goddard and fellow Brit Virginia Field. It is also the film that most obviously presents him as an object of the gaze for these characters and, by extension, the audience, as the two women battle to take possession of him throughout. Although presented in this way in some of his earlier films, most notably his shirtless poses in the jungle films with Dorothy Lamour, here he is consistently presented as an object of desire throughout rather than just at select moments. Both women have a strong and open attraction to him. Goddard's character even concocts elaborate and fantastic schemes to get him to fall for her. While he does, and assumes it is his idea, or rather his "fate," she is the one who actively engineers their entire romance in a convoluted and underhanded way.

Like Sidney in *The Lady Has Plans*, Goddard's Toni Gerard has a predominantly male attributed name, the "i" at the end distinguishing it as the feminine rather than the masculine derivative "Tony," although they are verbally identical. This again immediately presents her as a figure of ambiguous gender possibilities, while aiding in highlighting her dominant, principally active position in the film as she plots to possess and control the destiny of Milland's Brad Cavanaugh from the instance she lays eyes on him. Toni is employed by fortune teller Madame Zenobia (Gladys George) as a decoy to help drum up business for the adjoining shooting gallery, run by Pop Tibbets (Cecil Kellaway). Concurrently, widow Jo Ainsley (Virginia Field), another male-attributed name, is visiting Zenobia accompanied by Brad, her lawyer and assumed lover. He decides to wait outside since, playing to fortune telling stereotypes, Brad cynically states he has no desire to meet a tall, dark man.

Disguised in a raincoat and sunglasses so she can return to the shooting gallery as a "new" customer, Toni's outfit connotes a private detective or spy while she observes the unknowing Brad from a street corner. Brazenly staring at him from the moment he exits the car, and the undeniable bearer of the gaze, she appears undiscouraged that he is with another woman. Goddard is filmed in a long shot as she watches intently over her glasses, eventually removing them for a better look, while Milland is positioned closer to the camera, thus allowing us the more intimate view that she craves. Goddard displays Toni's attraction by grinning widely and slowly walking backwards while absentmindedly eating peanuts from a paper bag. She continues to stare directly at him and is so distracted by his physical presence that she does not hear Pop calling to her. Despite her prolonged and penetrating stare, Brad is unaware of the impression he has made on this beautiful woman, who acts as a surrogate for the audience since we too are asked to look at and desire the tall, dark, and handsome Milland who mirrors Brad's comments about fortune telling clichés. Indeed, it is ironic that he manifests the very cliché he mocks but even more so that, despite her fraudulent work with Zenobia, it is Toni who falls for the actualization of her profession's formulaic line habitually foisted on paying customers.

While waiting for Jo to emerge, Brad suggests to his chauffeur, Biff Carter (William Bendix), that they try out the shooting gallery. Despite their social differences, Brad enjoys socializing with Biff, whom he considers a friend, thus adding to the likability of his character. Walking along with the much shorter and wider Bendix, their comparison adds to Milland's polished handsomeness, desirability, and machismo, as does his spotless sartorial style. The suit has, for over two centuries, symbolized successful and professional masculinity, as well as being "elegant and self-evident shorthand for heterosexual masculinity" in the way that it visually accentuates the masculine form to help broaden a man's shoulders and slim his waist (Thompson 2013:

394–95). This is certainly true of Milland here, sharply dressed in a dark tailored suit, white shirt, a slightly patterned dark tie, white handkerchief in his breast pocket, and dark trilby hat. Indeed, his style throughout is classic and sophisticated and would work as contemporary clothing today, save for the less popular addition of the hat.

Although the street is busy with men moving in all directions, Toni only has eyes for Brad, thus adding to his sexual appeal and signaling his distinctiveness for the audience. Moreover, Toni informed Zenobia that she has just come from a beauty contest where she came in second place since "blondes win everything." During this type of competition, judges would have been studying her face and body intently, similar to how she is currently scrutinizing Brad, thus equating them in their good looks. However, while Toni knowingly entered the contest to be looked at and judged, Brad does nothing to garner this attention and is merely waiting in the street unaware he is being observed. This places Toni in the more powerful and active, if uneasy, position of voyeur. The fact that he is being watched by a highly desirable woman further highlights his physical attractiveness, compelling the audience to recognize his striking appearance. Jo confirms this, instigating their romantic moments, none of which he prompts, thus proving both women are much more active than Brad.

While Brad offers Biff a dollar bet for fun, the latter insists on fifteen dollars so his girlfriend can get her tonsils removed. Brad easily wins the dollar but purposely loses the larger bet, pretending to have something in his eye. Once Biff exits, Brad shoots five tiny targets in a row with precision, demonstrating both his unwavering friendship and his dexterity with a gun. Toni and Brad parallel each other when they miss the targets, despite being proven good shots, echoing their "missing the target" of their romance at this stage. While he does so on purpose to help Biff, she is too busy looking at him to aim properly. Both holding a gun, therefore mutually in possession of the phallus, he employs a pistol while she uses a shotgun. Her gun being larger and more powerful symbolically echoes her dominance in the film without rendering him completely helpless or, metaphorically, castrated; this ensures that he remains an active male. Since Milland was a trained gunman, the camera remains stationary behind his back as he hits the targets and requires no cuts or edits as he turns away from the camera, shoots, and turns back after effortlessly completing the task; here, actor and character are melded into one. The oblivious Brad is the sole object of Toni's gaze throughout the sequence, and when Pop comments that his eyes must have gotten better, she dreamily replies, "Nice, aren't they?" while watching him leave. The more observant, and possessive, Jo returns and immediately notices Toni watching Brad. When

Figure 5.7. Blurring Milland's on- and off-screen personas with a publicity photograph labeled "Bradford Cavanaugh" in *The Crystal Ball* (Elliott Nugent, 1943).

she asks if he knows her, he looks towards Toni with bemusement, furrows his brow, and replies in the negative. While this allows him to become the bearer of the gaze momentarily, it is both at Jo's request and an impartial look.

When Toni stumbles across a photograph of Brad in a newspaper, it is a genuine publicity still of Milland distributed by Paramount, thereby further blurring actor and character (figure 5.7). As if trying to summon him, she places the image beside her and moves her hands over the crystal ball while emulating Zenobia. When Toni is sent to replace the injured fortune teller at an event at the exclusive Sheridan-Plaza Hotel, it just so happens that Brad is both a sponsor and in attendance. Despite Milland receiving top billing, Toni proves her capacity for controlling the narrative as the film's most active character by conducting extensive research on Brad beforehand. Boldly going to Brad's apartment, she erroneously informs Biff she is from the Office of Civilian Defense and asks whether Brad has any distinguishing marks that could be used as an identifier, such as a birthmark. Biff reveals the intimate detail that Brad has an unusually shaped set of buckshot scars on his backside, resembling a love heart, which he draws before revealing that only he and Brad know about this. At the gathering, Toni ingeniously, if cunningly, sets up her initial meeting with Brad by reading a woman's fortune and sending her into the room with Biff's drawing, explaining that she has a message for the man in the sketch. When an amused Brad asks to see the image, he immediately stops grinning and looks shocked. Milland moves his head back, widens his eyes, and, with a knitted brow, weakly but comically asks where she got it. When the woman asks if he knows the man, he stammers, "Oh no, no, certainly not, I, uh. . . ." He then excuses himself and rushes to Zenobia's tent. The event gave Paramount the perfect excuse to put Milland back in evening clothes, and he looks particularly handsome in this scene with the familiar attire of white tie and tails. Moreover, the alternating full-body, medium, and close-up shots highlight his elegance, attractiveness, and desirability, exemplifying why Toni is trying so hard to impress him.

Brad endeavors to look nonchalant while standing outside the tent, as if merely in the vicinity. Examining the drawing again, he rapidly hides it while glaring suspiciously at a woman attempting to look at it. Glancing around, he quickly dives inside the tent in one swift movement, Milland's facial and body gestures generating humor during this silent sequence as Brad attempts to remain unseen. Wearing a veil and disguising her voice, Toni sets up her swindle by predicting he will fall in love with a red-headed girl eating an apple in a restaurant the following day. He smugly informs her that this is an impossibility because he always eats in the men's grill of his country club on Saturdays, where no women are allowed, but is called to a restaurant to deal with a customer complaining about the establishment's hygiene. Brad stops by the restaurant to deal with the complaint, and although Toni is there eating an apple, nothing registers with him. She announces that she has no intention to sue, and a relieved Brad offers to buy her lunch elsewhere. While driving, it dawns on him that she is a redhead eating an apple, and Milland makes several facial gestures which suggest Brad's disbelief and shock before he smiles and repeats, "Well, I'll be darned." Toni proves her dominance by taking control and going after what she wants: Brad. Later, while driving, he places his arm around the back of her seat, suggesting a developing romantic interest in her, or at least that she has set it up for him to think he feels this way, as he asks her for a date and assumes he is the dominant party. Toni repeatedly lies to Brad, but only because she wants to ensnare him, and is horrified to discover Zenobia tricked Jo into taking an option on a piece of property that the US government was interested in. Since Brad was handling the deal, he is arrested for sabotage, but the police soon uncover the crime ring and let him go.

In the final scene, he appears in the doorway of her room as she is packing, staring angrily at her with his legs crossed at the ankle and his back leaning against the doorframe. Demanding that she follow him to the other room, she obediently complies, and this rapid reversal of their roles makes their relationship more acceptable in terms of gender politics for films of the era. Pointing abruptly at the crystal ball, he demands to know what she sees in it, and she meekly confesses to seeing nothing. Asking how she knew about his buckshot scars, she notices Biff gesturing not to tell and vaguely announces, "You know, a vision." Milland puts both hands on the table and leans down into her face, finally taking control and looking particularly dominant here, much more so than at any other point in the film. Brad irritably proclaims, "Sure, I know a vision. I see her everywhere I look. Did you know that?" before turning away. Milland walks around the table and towards the camera; in a medium-long shot, he flails his arms around while the camera follows him as he circles the table. Brad announces he tries not to think about Toni because she is a "cock-eyed little liar," again looking into her face for emphasis, while Milland's voice sounds faintly Americanized as he speaks this line. Still furious, he now stands at the opposite side of the table, breaking his gaze before walking behind her and adding, "But it's no good because . . ." before trailing off. Milland is shown in a medium close-up as his face softens and his brows interlace while Brad softly concludes, "Because I'm in love with her, Toni," using the third person while looking tenderly down at her. Finally coming together now that their gendered positions have been established, they kiss in a long shot as Jo tries to get to him. Biff pulls the blind down on Jo and, symbolically, on her relationship with Brad. Brad may finally appear as if he is in charge at the end, thus allowing their relationship to go forward naturally, but Toni chooses to refrain from admitting the truth, with the support of Biff, so perhaps she is still the dominant party as she has been throughout the film. Incidentally, the buckshot wounds are the result of an accident during the predominantly masculine pastime of hunting, again linking the characters via the phallic symbol of a gun, while also intimately connecting the pair since they are on Brad's bottom, while simultaneously suggesting his incompetence in the sport to acquire such an injury and his toughness to endure it. Moreover, although Toni has been in a beauty contest and is obviously an extremely attractive woman, she is not presented in the same to-be-looked-at way that Milland is throughout the film and as she is in several other films. In fact, her activeness and power in being able to drive the narrative forward for so long leads to her complicating, and almost queering, the film's gender balance once more while we, and Brad, will never know if his love for her really comprises of his autonomous feelings or not.

EIGHTEENTH-CENTURY FOP: *KITTY*

Following the success of *Gone with the Wind* (Victor Fleming, 1939) and preceding *Forever Amber* (Otto Preminger, 1947), *Kitty* (1945) was Paramount's first foray into adaptations of controversial historical novels, as well as Milland and Goddard's final screen pairing. Mitchell Leisen commenced his career in the silent era under DeMille, and Morella and Epstein proclaim him ideally suited to this lush adaptation since it was the kind of film he did "to perfection" (1985: 139). Based on Rosamond Marshall's phenomenally successful "bodice-ripping" 1943 novel, which relates the story of a prostitute using men to rise through society, the film was required to tone down much of the book's sexual references and coarse language. As a result, the Paramount picture is a sanitized version with a Pygmalion-style plot that allowed it to fit with the Production Code and Hollywood censors (Doherty 2007). Goddard receives top billing this time, and her Kitty Gordon is unquestionably the main character. Indeed, Milland's Sir Hugh Marcy appears intermittently throughout the film even though he is a more constant presence in the novel.

The film presents Kitty as a "guttersnipe" from London's Houndsditch Slums, but in the novel she is a prostitute from a brothel on Halfmoon Street in London's Mayfair, interestingly located a fifteen-minute drive from Milland's Albany Street army barracks. Hugh is a somewhat colorless role, making this the least developed of Milland's pairings with Goddard. On the other hand, Goddard's title character transforms throughout. Returning to the role of a fop and supporting Goddard's character, in the manner of *Reap the Wild Wind*, implies an intense sense of regression around Milland's career and image after his triumph in *The Lost Weekend*. Perhaps this casting was due to his firm connections to upper-class Britishness and nobility on-screen. However, while Stephen Tolliver is a likable character who is both amusing and fights for justice, as a romantic lead Hugh is unusually selfish, deficient in redeeming qualities and rather detestable. This enabled Milland to develop an antihero quality on-screen, which had come to the fore in his previous film, *The Lost Weekend*, and reached its peak during his portrayal of Satan in *Alias Nick Beale* so he was perhaps chosen for this reason, since he was able to give Hugh some depth of character while also looking desirable in tight historical costuming. Milland describes his role as an eighteenth-century fop, "complete with powdered wig, beauty spot, silk breeches, and buckled shoes, who made his living as a procurer and pimp" (1974: 221).

The novel and film are comparatively divergent, with deviations in characterization, content, and conclusions. Told from Kitty's point of view, when she first sees Hugh in the novel, she calls him handsome and a fop. They maintain a sexual relationship throughout, both before and during her marriages, but she eventually realizes their lovemaking has become routine rather than an active desire and sends him away. Therefore, they do not end up together in the end. Hugh is introduced on page sixteen, and immediately takes Kitty home, sneaking her past his landlady so they can make love.

Figure 5.8. The tailor, and cinematic audience, observe that Sir Hugh Marcy's (Milland) clothes fit perfectly, despite his protests otherwise, in *Kitty* (Mitchell Leisen, 1945).

Indeed, most of the time Hugh appears in the novel, it is to sleep with Kitty or plan a life of luxury using her money from other men, so he is hardly a gallant hero.[19] However, the big-screen Hollywood version must have the romantic lead prosper, even if he is a (sanitized) cad, and concludes with Kitty running into Hugh's arms, which affirms him as her true love despite the dreadful way he treats her throughout.

The film opens in 1783, when Kitty, with a dirty face, no shoes, and dressed in rags, attempts to steal from artist Thomas Gainsborough (Cecil Kellaway). Seeing potential in her beauty, he asks her to clean up so he can paint her portrait. Hugh and his cousin Brett (Patric Knowles) visit Gainsborough's studio and are immediately captivated by the mysterious model. Hugh is the victor when they fight over her, but he registers shock when she emerges in her rags, before cruelly laughing. Telling her he waited three hours because he thought she was "someone else" (in other words, someone of breeding), she climbs in his carriage while he looks irritated. Depicting Hugh's discomfort in Kitty's presence, Milland sits rigidly and stares forward, his nose in the air, and his voice full of disdain and conceit in a complete shift of attitude. Eventually offering her a job in his scullery, she looks quizzically at him before confessing to never having met anyone like him before and calling him a "proper gent." He arrogantly looks her up and down before coldly replying, "Thank you, I'm sure you know the real thing," indicating her promiscuity and "real" occupation the film only alludes to.

Hugh and his aunt, Lady Susan Dowitt (Constance Collier), are both aristocrats with titles but also penniless after he was ejected from the foreign office following a scandal involving a woman, a string of pearls, or both. Suggesting his status as a ladies' man and rake, Kitty is told that one thing Hugh is good at is getting women to speak up for him. When a tailor attempts to collect payment, Hugh greets him condescendingly and refuses to pay, dishonestly denouncing the suit as inferior. The shocked and confused tailor examines the perfect craftsmanship which Hugh is currently wearing, and which fits Milland's figure perfectly. We are asked to judge its fit when he stands on a chair close to the camera and proclaims the coat is loose at the arms and the waistcoat is too tight (figure 5.8). His aggressive manner results in the tailor apologizing and reassuring him it will be fixed, again underscoring Hugh's contemptible and deceitful personality, and his ability to lie much more convincingly than *Skylark*'s Tony Kenyon. This scene in particular allowed Milland to show a different facet to his acting, a disreputable historical rake and somewhat of an antihero with very few redeeming features. This pattern continues throughout the film, especially in Hugh's treatment of Kitty.

When the Duke of Malmunster (Reginald Owen) shows interest in Gainsborough's portrait, Milland grins eerily to reveal that Hugh is hatching a plan. Concocting an elaborate backstory for Kitty, as Hollywood studios did for many of their stars, he states that she is Kitty Gordon of Devon and the ward of his aunt. Hugh desires revenge on the duke, referring to him as "the old buzzard" who had him thrown out of the foreign office, and proceeds to train Kitty in social graces so he can marry her off to the duke.

Dressed in an elaborate silk waistcoat, white shirt with flouncy sleeves, and extremely tight trousers, the outline of Milland's buttocks is particularly evident as he faces away from the camera and is positioned in the center of the frame. He stands silently but dominantly over the two women as Susan teaches Kitty how to serve tea, but when she drops her "hs" he goes into a rage and furiously screams, "No, no, no." His anger results in a single piece of hair falling onto his forehead, adding to his sexual appeal, while the rest of his long dark hair is pulled back in a large bow. He is short-tempered, hostile, and so relentlessly cruel that he makes the otherwise tough Kitty weep. Although he momentarily softens his voice and dries her eyes, this is just so she will practice again. Hardly essential life skills, Hugh deems it essential that women know how to pour tea and even stops Susan from teaching Kitty how to write because he deems knowing how to dress well a

Figure 5.9. Milland's Sir Hugh Marcy tries to train Kitty in the "language of the fan" in *Kitty* (Mitchell Leisen, 1945).

much more vital skill. In a more comical scene, Hugh attempts to teach Kitty the language of the fan, informing her that women are armed with fans like men are with swords. Milland looks ridiculous while imitating a woman; covering half his face and pretending to flirt, his large face and hands juxtapose with the delicate lace of the object he is holding (figure 5.9). When Kitty tries to emulate him, he leans in and tells her she should make a man crazy to want to get on the other side of the fan while she looks dreamily at him, swooning as his face almost touches hers, thus suggesting Hugh's sexual magnetism. Drawing back to show her how to perfect the "angry flutter," a wide shot reveals all three humorously fluttering their fans angrily, with Hugh looking distinctly out of place.

Despite his superior nature and vicious treatment of her, upon learning that Hugh is in debtor's prison, Kitty marries wealthy industrialist Jonathan Selby (Dennis Hoey) and uses the dowry to free him. Although she has sacrificed her happiness to help him, Hugh is furious. Telling her he was saving her for the duke, he selfishly hollers that she has ruined his chances of getting back into the foreign office. Having to hide due to his debt, he makes Kitty steal Jonathan's money for him, but Jonathan slaps Kitty and knocks her down before her faithful maid kills him. Hugh is elated at Jonathan's death, almost seducing Kitty into marrying the duke so he can get his job and reputation back. Although in love with Hugh, she selflessly marries the duke to help him.

Another way the film sanitized the novel to get past the censors was to have Kitty become pregnant by Jonathan shortly before his death, but inform the duke that it is his child. This shocks everyone since the duke is rather elderly—although we know older men can father children. In the novel, Kitty is not pregnant when Jonathan dies, and she marries the duke before discovering he is impotent. Since the duke wishes for an heir, Hugh impregnates Kitty so that she can pretend the duke is the father. In both the film and novel, just as Kitty gives birth, the duke drops dead, leaving her a widow twice over but also a duchess of extreme wealth. Referring to her as "Kitten," the ever-selfish Hugh comes to her room and casually asks her to gift him a castle, since he needs a place in the country; obnoxiously and insincerely replying, "Thank you dear," when she does. Rubbing his chin, Hugh notes that he could take her even higher up the social ladder since the Prince of Wales has shown an interest in her, but she has finally had enough. Storming over to him, she asks if he is blind or just does not care. Appearing confused, Milland stands with his hand half-elevated while voicing his lack of understanding, his knitted brow suggesting Hugh is being genuine for once. When she confesses her love for him, he oddly and impartially replies that they have only ever had a business arrangement before adopting his superior manner once more.

When he asserts that he created her and made her into something she is not, much like the construction of a star persona, she replies that she also created him, got him out of prison, and made him into what he is today, so they are even. Selfishly recognizing that he may be losing his meal ticket, he alters his demeanor by smiling and announcing that they should be friends, the best of friends, but she demands that he leave. Laughing at the slip she makes back into her "real" Cockney accent, he cruelly mocks her before she slaps his face. He slaps her back and walks out, a Hollywood shortcut for characters secretly being in love while exhibiting Hugh's aggression and unlikability.

Hugh is examining a new portrait of Kitty in Tom's studio when paint gets on his sleeve. Displaying his persistent arrogance, he removes it with a series of small, angry swipes which indicate he cannot tolerate even the slightest mark on his person or character. Watching the newly engaged Kitty and Brett from the corner of his eye, he smirks at his own jokes and continues to belittle Kitty. However, when the couple departs, Hugh turns and slowly walks back to Tom, his arrogance abruptly superseded by a look of bewilderment. When Tom asks whether he is surprised that someone of Brett's taste and refinement should appreciate Kitty, Hugh despondently replies that he has only just begun to appreciate her himself. Milland raises his voice at the end of the sentence, making it sound like both an exclamation and a question, suggesting Hugh cannot quite believe what he is saying. Looking back at the portrait, he turns to Gainsborough and states, more desperately, that he is serious. When Tom dismisses Hugh's words, telling him it cannot be serious if it transpired in the last ten minutes, Milland turns slowly towards the camera and, in a state almost resembling a trance, mutters that men have died in less time. Studying Kitty's portrait, he remarks with wide-eyed realization that she is no longer pretending to be a lady but has actually become one. Hugh has also been masquerading for years in clothes he cannot afford, pretending his social position is higher than it is, thereby making him as bad as, if not worse than, Kitty. Tom warns Hugh that he blew his chance with Kitty and to let her be happy with Brett. Clearly as sure of himself as ever, Hugh pompously remarks that she would be happier with him as if she should come running to him now that he has finally decided he wants her.

Visiting Kitty's home, Hugh hollers at her servants and demands to see her before barging into her bedroom unannounced while she is dressing. Although he confesses to being "selfish, cruel, and probably very stupid," he will not explicitly state that he loves her. Growing defensive, Hugh childishly asks if Brett is any better looking than him, pouting when she replies that they are both good looking. When he quips that they both have titles, she turns and looks directly at him, taking complete control of the situation as she tells him that they all have titles and hers is the best of all. Losing his cool, he proclaims in an exasperated and overtly English way, "Dash it, Kitty [. . .] I won't have you being in love with Brett," as if forbidding her natural sexual attraction to another man, a man who does not treat her cruelly.

In a final contemptible act, Hugh invites Old Meg, Kitty's former madam, to enlighten Brett about Kitty's past during a lavish ball. When a deeply hurt Kitty asks Hugh why he did this, he steps forward and announces it is because he loves her, finally saying the words, although cruelly adding, "Knowing what you were, I still love you." Hugh watches Brett with raised eyebrows in excited anticipation while Meg talks, but when the kind and understanding Brett informs Kitty that she is still the woman he fell in love with, Hugh once more looks dejected. For the "happy ending" to be successful, we must sympathize with Hugh during this brief soul-searching moment as he painfully admits that he is not worthy of her, suggesting he is finally humble and genuinely in love.

During this scene, Hugh and Kitty wear light-colored, complementary outfits that associate them as a couple; Hugh is in his most glitzy and elaborate outfit yet, while Brett's dark and plainer outfit highlights his difference and makes him resemble an outsider. Although Hugh is noble for once and tries to walk out of Kitty's life, she announces to the understanding Brett that she has always loved Hugh and always will and that they belong to each other. The Prince of Wales has just arrived and is shocked to see Kitty running past him and into Hugh's arms. Declaring women to be extraordinary, he asks why a "charming creature" would "throw herself away on such a bounder," while Tom agrees that Hugh is very much beneath her. Hugh stops and looks back at her before she falls into his arms. He spins her around and kisses her passionately, ensuring the Hollywood "happy ending" that is vastly different from its source material.

Kitty is, very obviously, Goddard's film once more, arguably more so than any of her previous pairings with Milland since the focus is almost consistently on Kitty as she steers the narrative through her colossal rise in society. Other than hinting at his ability to play a seductive antihero and presenting him intermittently as object of the erotic gaze, *Kitty* offers little to advance Milland's career or star image, perhaps even detracting from the attraction of his previous pairing with Goddard in *The Crystal Ball*. Although highlighting his physique in tight costuming, the historical ensembles do not work for him as well as modern suits and evening clothes, and he looks uncomfortable and foolish for much of the film. Milland rarely receives close-ups of his face or lingering shots of his body throughout, while Goddard receives numerous close-ups and full-body shots while dressed in a range of gowns, which become more expensive-looking and elaborate the higher Kitty climbs, thus putting a strong focus on Goddard's visual appeal. Despite the attention she receives from numerous men, however, Kitty only ever loves Hugh, thus suggesting to the audience that there is something unique and incredibly appealing about him. However, Hugh is extremely unlikable as a romantic Hollywood lead, judgmental of others, and unable to see his own flaws. A socially masculine man of the era with a contempt for following societal rules, Hugh lives well beyond his means and uses his (worthless) title while attempting to blend into the upper crust of society to which he feels he belongs. A rake with a contemplable attitude, he uses his charisma to charm people into doing his bidding.

During the film's release, Goddard "was, of course, the centerpiece in the ads" (Morella and Epstein 1985: 146); the theatrical poster carried the tagline, "Paramount's lavish revelation of the life and loves of the first of the flaming gold-diggers!" Not only does Goddard's name appear first, but the enormous central illustration is of the actress dressed in green satin, looking over her shoulder, and her red hair piled high. A small, disembodied image of Milland appears behind her, with an even smaller image of Knowles's face behind him. Indicating how the marketing grabbed the public's attention, *Kitty* was an "immediate, huge hit" (Morella and Epstein 1985: 149), with *Life* magazine picking it as its Movie of the Week. The publication called it "one of the lushest pictures to come out of Hollywood since the pre-War days" and declared that Milland had turned in "another accomplished performance" (1985: 149); while this is debatable, it does prove his professionalism and dedication to every role. One of the top-grossing films of the year, it made almost $4 million (the equivalent of almost $52 million today), while also becoming the most successful film of Goddard's career (1985: 149). As Eames highlights, *Kitty* proved to be the peak of Goddard's stardom, while Paramount's technical experts "captured the period atmosphere down to the last wig and wink" allowing it to recoup "every cent of its high cost, and then some" (1985: 175).[20]

Since this final pairing followed Milland's critical highpoint—his award-winning leading role in the bleak drama *The Lost Weekend*—*Kitty* represented something of a regression of his star status and considerably restricted the acting skills he had so recently shown to have honed on-screen. As the next chapter explores, had he not won an Academy Award for *The Lost Weekend*, Milland may have been overlooked for starring roles in many of his later successes, such as *So Evil My Love*, *The Big Clock*, and *Alias Nick Beale*, all of which allowed him to expand his performance skills even further, and may have been unremittingly destined to support Paramount's female stars.

CHAPTER SIX

REACHING A PARAMOUNT
THE LONG CLIMB TO *THE LOST WEEKEND*

Mainly due to its immense theatre chain and a war-induced market boom, Paramount experienced the same kind of industry domination during World War II that it had twenty years before. Its theatres, which had been a "drag on its finances" during the Depression, now became a source of massive profits (Cook and Bernink 1999: 16). During the war years Paramount's most profitable stars were Bing Crosby, Barbara Stanwyck, and Milland (Edmonds and Mimura 1980: 227).

Despite being a constant presence in cinema from the end of the silent era, Milland's career began slowly and reached a peak with his sixtieth film, *The Lost Weekend*, before tapering off again. What is truly fascinating, however, is that the peak years of his extensive career were also Hollywood's most powerful years. Beginning his career in Britain in 1929, Milland relocated to Hollywood in the early days of the studio system and, as explored in previous chapters, following nearly a decade of bit parts, supporting roles, and leading roles in minor productions, his first real taste of stardom came in 1940 with Paramount's *Arise, My Love*. The screenplay was written by Charles Brackett and Billy Wilder, and when Wilder directed his first feature film, *The Major and the Minor*, two years later, he cast Milland opposite Ginger Rogers. As with most of his films, it was a star vehicle for the leading lady and Milland had no more than a supporting role. In 1945, however, Wilder gave Milland his best remembered and most critically acclaimed role as an alcoholic writer in *The Lost Weekend*. An almost constant presence on-screen, this time it is without a doubt Milland's film, but required his acting to be fully believable if he were to get the controversial subject across to audiences without swaying too much towards either melodrama or satire, which he managed impeccably, as this analysis chapter explores and which his Academy Award win fortifies.

Gerd Gemünden declares that Wilder's films, in general, "register exile in all its complexities and contradictions," often depicting "experiences of nonbeing and loss" while repeatedly being told from the viewpoint of an outsider or underachiever (2008: 3). These include Fred MacMurray's "insurance salesman turned criminal" in *Double Indemnity* (1944), William Holden's "mediocre screenwriter prostituting himself to an aged star" in *Sunset Boulevard* (1950), and Milland's "drunk betraying his friends and family" in *The Lost Weekend* (2008: 3). While Wilder's "disenchanted views of sordid human fragility" has resulted in his films being labeled as "cynical, bitter, and misanthropic," Gemünden argues that they simply tell the unvarnished truth about distasteful elements of human conduct (2008: 3). He suggests that nobody exits a Wilder film feeling comfortable; "ideologically unpredictable, Wilder spares no one and nothing" with a harshness and betrayal of sympathy that has been interpreted as contempt for audiences. A fundamental pleasure of these films, though, is "the highly controlled audacity that has accounted for their longevity; they still excite and irritate today" (2008: 25). Joseph McBride adds that anyone searching for "sentimentality or easy consolation" from Wilder's films tends to be disappointed since they "often straddle a high wire between grimness and entertainment" (2021: 292). Milland gives a particularly corporeal and visceral performance, using and abusing his own body to make the audience feel tense and uneasy throughout, while highlighting the problem of alcoholism.

Suggesting the groundbreaking nature of the film and its importance in cinema history, the December 19, 1945 issue of *Motion Picture Daily* featured an impressive eight-page advertisement for *The Lost Weekend*. Printed in eye-catching black, white, and red, it stands out from the standard newsprint used throughout the rest of the publication. While the first page boldly declares, "There has never been a picture like this," the next two pages concern its monetary status and record-breaking attendance in New York. The following four pages explore the film's "unparalleled praise" from critics, declaring that while they could fill a book with its positive reviews, they have included just a selection due to the wartime paper shortage. The final page of reviews focuses on Milland and his performance, featuring a groomed and smartly dressed studio portrait of Milland in a small circle, or intended "O" for Oscar, at the top of the page and a still of him in character at the bottom. Bold type across the top of the page declares, "The nation's critics promise you one of the great screen performances of all time," while the bottommost text calls Milland the "star of the year in the hit of the decade." Between these images are two columns featuring snippets of reviews from thirteen well-known critics and publications, including film fan magazines *Screenland*, *Motion Picture and Movie*, women's magazines *McCall's* and *Mademoiselle*, and rival gossip columnists Hedda Hopper and Louella Parsons. Within these reviews, the terms "Oscar" and "Academy Award," as well as Milland's own name, are frequently printed in bold and upper case to catch a casual reader's attention. Kate Cameron, the film critic with "the largest newspaper circulation" in the US (Anon. 1967: 46), proclaims in the *New York Daily News* that Milland "gives one of the outstanding performances of this or any other year," while *McCall's* declares his to be the best performance of the year. Lee Mortimer of the *New York Mirror* deems Milland to have "turn[ed] in a masterpiece of Academy Award stature," while *Movie* magazine makes an almost identical statement with the term "Oscar-winning caliber." A Hollywood reporter for five decades, Sidney Skolsky anoints Milland "a cinch for the Oscar," while *Newsweek* stresses his performance is "already being talked about as Academy Award material." Hopper agrees by calling it "an engraved invitation for an Academy Award," while Parsons remarks that Milland has "proven himself a great, great actor" and wonders how "any other actor can surpass him, he's that good," and they were soon to be proven right.

THE BACKGROUND

During the war and postwar period, many stars who had established their careers in lighter fare in the prewar era began moving into darker roles, portraying more morally ambiguous characters in genres including Westerns, crime, and social problem films. Actors returning to Hollywood from active war duty tended to have a newfound mature masculinity which worked well for these roles, such as Tyrone Power in *Nightmare Alley* (Edmund Goulding, 1947), Robert Taylor in *Undercurrent* (Vincente Minnelli, 1946), and James Stewart's Westerns with director Anthony Mann. It was when "paranoia, pessimism and social angst" of the postwar years achieved full maturity (Schatz 1997: 235)—as did many of Hollywood's romantic leads.

This darker version of Hollywood reflected America's changing society and depicted the public's sense of bleakness and persistent anguish (Dixon 2006: 9). Mainstream Hollywood films began to depict more sordid areas of life for the first time in Code-era history (Byars 1991: 112), a new wave of social realism films dealing with controversial issues affecting society at the time. Topics explored in these films included antisemitism in *Gentleman's Agreement* (Elia Kazan, 1947), the difficulty of transitioning back into peacetime after war in *The Best Years of Our Lives* (William Wyler, 1946), and insanity in *The Snake Pit* (Anatole Litvak, 1948). All but the latter won the Best Picture Academy Award, thus bringing with them a new kind of critical acclaim in the mid-1940s. Chris Cagle (2007) views these as Academy Award-seeking "prestige" films, while *The Lost Weekend* appears to have been the film that heralded in this trend, thus helping the studios to understand it as a future strategy. This new amoral, cynical world is perhaps best reflected in *The Lost Weekend* as one of the earliest Hollywood films to present a bleak, unrelenting portrayal of alcoholism as a problem concerning modern American society.

Although finding historical box-office statistics can prove challenging, the US Census Bureau appears to be one of the most reliable sources. Peter Lev uses this to determine that in 1940 around eighty million people attended US cinemas weekly; the figure reached an unprecedented ninety million in 1946. Proving impossible to maintain, by 1960 these figures had dropped to around forty million (2003: 7). With around 1,400 houses, Paramount owned the largest theatre chain in the US, and during the 1940s the studio emphasized A-pictures and long runs, resulting in profits of $39.2 million in 1945 and $28.2 million in 1946, the highest by far of any Hollywood studio (Lev 2003: 16). Thus, the peak years of Hollywood's fortunes and Milland's critical and commercial acclaim coincide. Moreover, Paramount was the largest and most profitable studio in Hollywood at the same time Milland's star power was at its highest and when he won his only Academy Award.

THE CONTROVERSY

In 1922, the Hays Commission fashioned a set of moral rules that Hollywood's filmmakers had to follow. The forerunner to the 1934 Production Code, section I, part 4 stated that "*the use of liquor* in American life, when not required by the plot or for proper characterization, will not be shown" (Dixon 2006: 152). When the US entered World War II, the OWI (Office of War Information) instructed Hollywood to redefine America's social health by stressing the promise, not the problems, of a democratic society. This resulted in protagonists' psychological difficulties being presented as solitary and not directly caused by society, thus alcoholism, unemployment, prostitution, orphaned children, migrant workers, and lynching, topics that had flourished in the Depression-era "social problem" films, suddenly became taboo in wartime (Dixon 2006: 151).

The year 1945 was a watershed year for alcoholism in film with the release of *The Lost Weekend*. The film not only marked a shift in how alcohol was portrayed but it was the first to "challenge restrictions of showing drinking on screen," thus instigating the breakdown of Hollywood's Production Code (Dixon 2006: 152). One of the year's top-grossing films, it presented "the standard by which subsequent films about alcoholism would inevitably be judged" (Dixon 2006: 152). Earlier films concerning alcohol abuse had only alluded to drinking, including the pre-Code *Merrily We Go to Hell* (Dorothy Arzner, 1932), *A Star is Born* (1937), and *Swing High, Swing Low* (Mitchell Leisen, 1937). However, the creation of Alcoholics Anonymous in 1935, the National Council on Problems of Alcoholism in 1937, and the National Committee on the Education of Alcoholism in 1944 led to both a better understanding of alcohol abuse and a gradual easing of these regulations. The National Council aimed to increase the recognition of alcoholism as both a disease and a public health problem, while noting that alcoholics deserve help in treating the illness. Given the power of cinema, activists for the National Council urged Hollywood to produce films that embodied these ideas, and between 1945 and 1963, nearly thirty films were made which focused on an alcoholic and his/her struggles with substance abuse.

From the mid-1940s, Milland's screen work took a literary turn, with many of his films based on recently published novels. Not only was there *Kitty*, discussed in the previous chapter, but *Ministry of Fear*, based on Graham Greene's 1943 novel, *The Big Clock*, from Kenneth Fearing's 1946 novel, and, as explored here, *The Lost Weekend*, based on Charles Jackson's 1944 novel. Although Wilder's cinematic interpretation of Jackson's controversial book shares the same title, the film avoids several issues from the original text, including Don's childhood trauma, his homosexual experimentation with a school friend, his idolization of a fellow male student, sleeping with women only when drunk, and his continuous and torturous repressed homosexuality, which is given as the reason for his alcoholic binges. In the film, Don's drinking is blamed on writer's block and the inability to start his novel because homosexuality remained a taboo subject in 1940s Hollywood. McBride notes that, while the film was predictably criticized for eliminating the sexual insecurity that plagues Don, its absence strengthens the film. No attempt is made in the film to provide a psychological account of Don's alcoholism, presenting it instead in "enlightened modern terms as a physical disease" rather than the author's "trite, defensive pseudo-explanation" of the reasons behind Don's drinking (2021: 459). The film was described as not attempting to "sugarcoat the grim tale of a man tortured by drink" but just stating the reality rather than preaching (Masden 1969: 72); "gripping, stark, dispassionate, stripped of any glamour, a vision of dipsomaniac hell" (Heritage 2012: 295) and a "searing, relentlessly downbeat [...] pioneering postwar 'social problem' film" (Cook and Mierke 1999: 15), the film is a harrowing presentation of the disease of alcoholism, especially when considering the period in which it was made.

Jackson's "provocative novel [...] was not pleasant. Neither was the film," which Paramount was hesitant about from the start (Masden 1969: 67). Although a bestseller, Maurice Zolotow notes that every star and studio had spurned the "downbeat" novel since, "you did not make a heart-wrenching story about a drunk. [...] Drunks were funny characters. [...] Who pays money to see a guy having DTs in the Bellevue alcoholic ward?" (1977: 126). Similarly, Mark Bailey deems it "easily" the frankest look at the ravages of alcohol in the studio era, highlighting Paramount's concerns about its bleakness and whether anyone would want to see it (2014: 80). Despite the studio's hostility, Axel Masden quotes Wilder as saying it "eventually turned into one of those oddball successes that you only have every ten years or so" (1969: 67). Eames confirms this, stating that "this work of art was almost withheld from the public view permanently" since some of Paramount's most authoritative figures loathed the film, while the opinion cards from its California preview were mostly disparaging (1985: 176). Paramount even seriously considered accepting $5 million offered by a syndicate of distilleries who wanted the film destroyed and never released, believing the "suppression of such a powerful anti-booze document was worth that much to their business" (Eames 1985: 176).

Moreover, while representatives from whiskey firms thought that a screen depiction of a "five-day binge would prejudice audiences against their product," Prohibition groups contended that the film would incite drinking. Eventually, however, the whiskey producers decided the film would benefit better brands since Don drinks the cheapest stuff he can buy, and the Prohibitionists were satisfied that it taught a lesson about the vices of alcohol (Masden 1969: 69). In fact, any thoughts of shelving the film were halted after a New York screening for critics "aroused overwhelming enthusiasm" for the script, direction, and Milland's performance, and it was subsequently released to international acclaim (Eames 1985: 176). While British censors planned to ban the film unless drastic cuts were made, Paramount saw this as a chance for global publicity and gave it a London premiere, leading to a spree of admiration for the film. Moreover, despite the wartime paper shortage, Blake Bailey declares it received more commentary than any film since *Gone with the Wind* (2013).

Wilder purchased Jackson's novel at a kiosk in Chicago, read it twice on the train and arrived in Los Angeles determined to turn it into a film regardless of its then-controversial topic (Bailey 2013: 1). Wilder was convinced that the actor who took on the role of Don Birnam would win an Academy Award, but Hollywood's leading men did not necessarily agree, with the likes of Robert Montgomery and Cary Grant turning it down. Bailey concludes that it eventually went to "Welshman Ray Milland, who refused to heed an all but universal warning that he was committing 'career suicide'" (2013: 1–2; Masden 1969: 72). Even during shooting, "the studio, newspapers and friends of the principles were against it," with Milland and Wilder being extensively warned about their future in cinema (Masden 1969: 72). Upon release, however, "the tune changed," with *Life* labeling it the film of the year (Masden 1969: 72). Halliwell declares it both a "piece of showmanlike cinema" and an "exposé film which got the exposé treatment [and] collected a mantlepiece full of awards," while declaring that Wilder propelled Milland "to the top in this cleverly designed movie" (1976: 186). Edmonds and Mimura feel that Milland "proved he was more than a light comedian" and "richly deserved" his Academy Award. Moreover, "although a depressing tale of the miseries of an alcoholic, the picture was enormously successful" (1980: 227).

THE PERFORMER

Three elements of characterization go into creating a star performance: the actor, the character, and the star image (Naremore 1988: 158). Milland, or rather Alfred Reginald Jones, is the corporal presence bringing his distinct voice, accent, and vocal quirks to the role, along with his acting techniques, and physical attributes as a 6'2" white British male of medium build, who lost weight for the role. Secondly, there is the character. In this case, Charles Jackson had created the character of Don Birnam long before Milland was cast or a film version was even considered. Jackson's character was also somewhat autobiographical, before Birnam was reimagined by screenwriters Wilder and Charles Brackett. Finally, the star image is made up of what came before for the actor in terms of their previous screen work and off-screen biography. In the case of Milland, this included sixteen years' worth of work in Britain and Hollywood, covering fifty-nine films of varying budgets in which he portrayed extras, supporting players, and leads in light comedies and sometimes dramas. Milland repeatedly portrayed stereotypical upper-class British gentleman or suave Americans, often appearing impeccably dressed in military uniform, tailored suits, and evening dress. In terms of biography, as noted, there was continued confusion about Milland's national identity in the press about whether he was Welsh, English, or Irish. He married an American shortly after arriving in Hollywood, and now had two children (a biological son and an adopted daughter) and, while there had been no scandal about him in the press, he did appear regularly in film fan magazines' gossip columns.

Milland had featured as the cover star for a select number of publications throughout his career, though not as many as some other male stars at the time, most notably Tyrone Power (Kelly 2023b). While sometimes appearing alone, most often he featured alongside a female costar in a publicity still, advertising their newest release more widely to film fans and potential paying customers. He appeared sporadically on international publications in countries like Brazil, Sweden, Belgium, France, Italy, and Mexico, and secured limited coverage across US publications. This included alongside Colbert on *Movie Life* (December 1940) and *Screenland* (September 1941) and alone on *Screen Pictorial* (May 1938). In the latter, he smiles in an open and friendly manner while holding a cigarette and is dressed impeccably in a grey suit and tie. It was on the British magazine *Picture Show*, however, that he principally featured as a cover star. Indeed, between 1935 and 1954, he was featured (with a female costar, as was this magazine's practice) seventeen times, additionally appearing with Goddard on the *Picture Show Annual* of 1943.[1] The first occasion was on June 22, 1935, alongside costars Colbert and MacMurray, wearing evening clothes, and in a still from *The Gilded Lily*, his first substantial film role, as discussed in chapter two. The final time he appeared on the cover was on August 28, 1954, alongside Grace Kelly in a still widely used publicity shot for *Dial M for Murder*. The latter marked the end of his "stardom years" as well as his only publicized "scandal" when the two stars embarked on a very public affair;[2] but this episode was still in his future when *The Lost Weekend* was cast.

Milland had worked at Paramount for over a decade by this point, and although not one of its leading stars of the highest echelons, he had several publicity portraits in circulation that projected the polished, well-dressed gentlemanly appeal that had made him a popular leading man for so long. Thus, the character of Don Birnam was a sharp change in direction for Milland from his previous work and established persona, helping to alter the type of roles he was given going forward, as well as adding more depth to his screen image. As I argue elsewhere, while Christine Becker (2008) has suggested the public refused to "buy" Milland's characterization of a college professor in his first television sitcom, *Meet Mr. McNutley*, the "bumbling college professor in comedic situations had been an-oft repeated element of his filmic persona, far more so than his alcoholic in *The Lost Weekend*" (Kelly 2022: 4). The believability of an actor *for* a role and, most importantly, *in* the role is crucial for the success of both. Milland, known as a lightweight comedian and occasional romantic lead, was undoubtedly a gamble when cast as Birnam, but it paid off for all involved.

Milland recalls that Buddy DeSylva, head of production at Paramount, sent a copy of Jackson's novel to his home along with a note instructing him to read and study it because he was going to play Don. Attempting to read in bed, he awoke feeling peculiarly anxious and with the book beginning to repel him. Retreating to his boat, *Santana*,[3] to study it, he drove home feeling "subdued and just a little leery of the project." Not only was it dissimilar to any story he had read before that was to be turned into a film, but it was downbeat and absent of any light moments. He calls alcoholism a topic he was completely ignorant about, and an issue people tended to respond to with uneasy laughter and push "under the rug." Feeling he was overdoing it if he had two drinks in a month, Milland calls alcohol something he just never thought about; even at social gatherings, drunk people made him extremely anxious since he never knew how to interact with them (1974: 211). What made him particularly uneasy about the film was that it concerned the disease of alcoholism, the addiction itself, and not the "social drinkers or the party drunks" who were already abundant in Hollywood; he had even played a few himself. Furthermore, while Jackson was gay and the book deals frankly with issues around homosexuality, Milland declares himself to be a "raving heterosexual" (1974: 212).

Wilder and Paramount knew that getting the right actor for Don was imperative, since the role required someone able to be weak but sympathetic so that viewers would be with him even as he slid into deprivation. Although Wilder believed Milland capable of pulling this off (Chandler 2002: 124), the actor notes his own skepticism in his memoir. Aware the film would "garner a few huzzahs as a social document," Milland knew it would require some considerable acting on his part, and his nerves increased as the start date approached. He had serious doubts that he was skilled enough to do the "gem of a script" justice (1974: 213). Mark Bailey concedes that Milland had his reservations, although he knew the role could be a "game changer" for him; for one thing, he "wasn't sure he had the acting chops. [. . .] Mostly, though, the guy just didn't drink very much" (2014: 80), while Blake Bailey calls Milland "a near teetotaler" whom Jackson had to coach on "the ways of drunkenness" (2013: 2). While Milland knew that performing the DTs (delirium tremens) from alcohol withdrawal would be harrowing, he confessed that this bothered him less than the drunk scenes, which he was afraid he would overdo, thus making them appear amateurish (1974: 214). Since 80 percent of the story concerns Don's search for alcohol, "the terrible physical craving, the degradation and the complete moral break-down," Milland decided to perform the two scenes where Don is actually "under the influence" for his in-laws to gauge their response (1974: 213). In what sounds like a screwball comedy plot, and a doubtlessly embellished story, Milland recalls downing a large quantity of Old Mammoth Cave bourbon whiskey, left over from the early days of the war, and immediately feeling unwell. Since the film was to be shot in reverse, Paramount had requested he lose eight pounds so that he looked haggard when filming commenced, so he had dropped from 168 to 160 pounds. As he read from the script, his seventy-pound dog pushed him into a lit fire, leading him to rush to the bathroom to throw up from one end while "smoking and smoldering" from the other. Waking at dawn the next morning, Milland poetically describes feeling "the wages of sin" and thinking it would have been the best time to start the film since makeup artist Wally Westmore could never improve on what was reflected in his mirror (1974: 213–14). Announcing that he could not even look at a drink for six months, this contributes to the trope of getting drunk and deeply regretting it at various stages of his adult life evident throughout his memoir.

THE BUILD-UP

Off-casting allowed studios to invoke audience expectations while simultaneously giving them something a little different. It could widen an actor's box-office potential by modifying his/her image, while augmenting ideas of their being an excellent performer (Maltby 1995: 255). This was certainly successful for Milland in *The Lost Weekend*, demonstrated by the rave reviews he received, his performance surprising many, and leading to his winning an Oscar for his first truly offbeat role. Maltby declares that advertisements regularly suggested audiences would see a star "as you've never seen her [sic] before" (1995: 255). Indeed, a print advertisement for *The Lost Weekend* features a book and the words "the daring, sensational book now on the screen!" while another incorporates an open book featuring Jackson's name and a large image of Milland's disembodied head emerging from it, the words "Strange! Savage! Sensational!" printed over his brow. Next to his image it adds, "the picture that dares to bare a man's soul . . . as it rips five relentless . . . unforgettable days . . . straight from the powerful pages of the sensational best-seller that millions talked about in shocked whispers." Although it was hardly straight from the pages of the novel, given the number of elements the film omits, this advertisement allowed Milland to be presented to audiences in a vastly different way than he had previously, while Paramount could link their new film to an already established and popular novel.

Wilder wanted to cast José Ferrer but, despite playing an American character, Paramount insisted on "the handsome and distinguished Milland chosen in part for his accent (he was Welsh by birth) and demeanor" (Dixon 2006: 153), although he does adopt a more Americanized accent in this film, particularly through the clipping of words and repeating "yeah." The studio argued that "an attractive-looking hero" like Milland would make audiences "feel that if he were not an alcoholic he would be a worthwhile human being" (Zolotow 1977: 130), qualities they obviously felt Ferrer lacked. Moreover, by casting Milland, Paramount hoped some of his "inherent likeability would rub off" on Don (Bailey 2014: 80). Bailey suggests that the film became "an instant classic [and the] likeable Milland had succeeded in showing that humanity remains even in our darkest moments" (2014: 80). While Ward Calhoun argues that Milland portrayed Don "masterfully [and his] harrowing descent into blackoutville plays out like a booze-fueled nightmare" (2010: 262), an unconvinced Roy Pickard suggests Milland's "sparkling eyes and roguish smile didn't really belong in the lower depths of New York and the murky world of the alcoholic," but Wilder's "courageous casting" led to his Oscar win at a time when "few in Hollywood regarded him as anything more than a lightweight leading man" (1996: 244). Indeed, as shown, he was never really allowed to prove himself as a dramatic actor until this point. Eames declares it an "amazingly sensitive and moving portrait of an alcoholic on a three-day bender' (1985: 176), while Madsen proclaims Milland's "pitiful, congenital drunk" not only his best performance but one he had to, unfortunately, live with for years (1969: 69). Indeed, in an interview with *Life* magazine just after making the film, Milland notes that barkeepers, sailors, and passers-by frequently heckled and derided him, columnists persistently devised jokes about him, and he received pathetic letters from drunks (March 11, 1946). Over thirty years later in his memoir, he notes that he was erroneously considered an alcoholic from that point forward, both a credit to, and curse of, his convincing performance.

Wilder experimented with a slow pace as a way of enriching the dramatic effect of Don battling "his craving in some of his calmer moments, then yielding. When he succumbs, nothing stands in his way" (Masden 1969: 69). It was a slowness that relied heavily on Milland's acting proficiency and plausibility in the role. Although some of Jackson's novel was altered, Eames affirms that it does not lose any of its potency but gained something from the "visual realism of John Seitz's camera," particularly in the streets of Manhattan and Don's "delirium-haunted" apartment (1985: 176). Correspondingly, as Zolotow argues, it was uncommon for a Hollywood film to have so little dialogue and such "powerfully focused images" which present the film as a "realistic tour of hell" (1977: 129). This covers Don's visits to Third Avenue, Fifty-second Street, the bars, the pawnshops, and Bellevue Hospital, all of which are explored below.

THE OPENING

The film opens with helicopter shots of Manhattan, while Milos Rosza's "eerie theme" plays (Zolotow 1977: 129). The camera focuses on the peculiar sight of a whiskey bottle hanging by a string outside an apartment window, before moving past the bottle and entering the bedroom of brothers Don (Milland) and Wick Birnam (Philip Terry). In a seemingly normal scene, Milland's back is to the open window as he packs a suitcase on his bed, but he looks slightly agitated as he takes quick glances towards the bottle, making us aware that Don is conscious of its presence in this curious location. Here, he appears no different from the Milland of other films, dressed in the same white shirt, braces, and striped tie that had appeared in previous films. We learn that the brothers are packing for a weekend trip, and it becomes immediately apparent that Wick is unaware of the bottle's presence while Don is attempting to hide it. We see Don begin to panic when Wick makes the simple remark that he is packing five shirts since they may not return until Tuesday, thereby enjoying a long weekend away, while Don uncomfortably quips, mostly to himself, that it certainly sounds long. Although already a tall man, Milland's closeness to the camera gives the impression that he is too small for the frame, as he "restlessly moves around the room" in this scene, which appears to use natural lighting (Dixon 2006: 153). Pacing the small space between the single beds, the cramped bedroom emphasizes a feeling of claustrophobia and appears to mirror Don's dread of facing a weekend away from alcohol. When Wick asserts that the country will be good for him, with its buttermilk and fresh water from a well, Don moves his eyes upwards, throws his shirts abruptly into the suitcase, and cuts Wick off by demanding he stop talking about "liquids. Very dull liquids"—words that Milland angrily spits out.

Facing away from Wick and towards the camera, Don pauses as if getting into character and instantly changes his whole demeanor, pretending to be nonchalant about the trip, but we know better. To convey Don's façade to the audience, Milland deliberately relaxes his shoulders by almost shaking them out while simultaneously making his voice higher and more "singsong" to appear lighthearted and suggest his (artificial) excitement for the trip. When he announces he is taking his typewriter so he can begin drafting his novel, it is a more familiar Milland for audiences aware of his previous screen persona. The half-grin and free body movements, such as throwaway hand gestures, were often used by the actor to convey the relaxed nature of his characters, but for Don they are constructed and inauthentic, and the audience knows it. Turned away from Wick, and busying himself with his suitcase, we know from Milland's facial expressions that Don is lying when he tells Wick his typewriter is at the back of the living room closet. This lets him stall since he knows it is under his bed. Immediately after Wick leaves the room, he turns abruptly towards the window and, in an extremely animated manner, pulls the bottle up in hurried desperation, wraps it in a sweater, and frantically tries but fails to unhook the string. As Wick reapproaches the cramped bedroom, Don lowers the bottle gently back down and returns to his constructed relaxed manner while pulling the typewriter out from under his bed with a supposedly casual "sure, sure, here it is," turning again from Wick and giving a death stare to the wall. Absentmindedly dusting the side of the case with his fingertips, his back again to Terry, Milland's eyes dart around and his shallow breathing conveys Don's panic as he wonders how he can get the bottle without observation. Unsuccessful in his quest and unsure how to get Wick back out of the room, Don returns to his offhand and brusque manner, again indignant about the trip. The confined space adds to the sense that Don is constantly under Wick's surveillance, reflecting his panic of obtaining the whiskey bottle without being detected. Furthermore, the cramped area makes us feel like we are in the room with them, and we sense Don's panic since Milland is closer to the camera and able to show Don's vulnerability and true feelings throughout at close range. His back is almost constantly to Terry, who is more distant from the camera, and therefore us, his stolid expressions throughout proving harder to read. This indicates Wick's control and authority over Don, like a prison guard, which is exactly how Don feels about the situation.

While the opening of Jackson's novel only mentions Don's girlfriend, Helen, by name, in the film she visits the men to bid them goodbye before their trip and to give Don some books, cigarettes, and chewing gum. Completely absent from the film is Don's Scottie dog Mac, perhaps as a way of allowing more focus to be on Milland and his performance without other distractions, while also creating a more obvious sense of isolation and hopelessness for Don. When Helen (Jane Wyman) tells them she has two tickets to a concert but is going alone, Milland's body remains motionless,

Figure 6.1. The already claustrophobic space for Don (Milland) and Wick (Philip Terry) increases when Helen (Jane Wyman) joins them in *The Lost Weekend* (Billy Wilder, 1945).

his hands casually in his pockets, but his eyes dart around and his mouth suggests Don's excitement at the prospect of being able to get the bottle if Wick accompanies Helen. He casually suggests his brother go while he continues to pack, and they can then catch the later train. He moves towards the camera and the bottle once more, the three of them now in the already cramped space and the sense of claustrophobia and desperation increasing as Don tries to get them to leave (figure 6.1). The audience, rather unwillingly, shares in Don's guilt, and we almost will them to go so that he can retrieve the bottle, despite knowing this is wrong.

To help diffuse Don's anger at being watched, Wick reluctantly agrees before noticing the cigarette he tossed at the window has landed on the windowsill. Once more, we are put in an uncomfortable position: not wanting Wick to see the bottle as he moves past Don and Helen, who are kissing goodbye, towards the window and us. When Don realizes where Wick is going, he breaks away from Helen to watch, his eyes moving down silently but horrified towards the location of the bottle and back to his brother, who is now pulling the bottle up. His body gives nothing away as Milland remains in the bending position he assumed to kiss Wyman, frozen to the spot, but he looks physically sick standing behind Wick as the scene unfolds and Helen looks on. Trying to preserve the perception of casualness once more, he forces a grin and dismissively remarks he was unaware of the bottle's presence or how it even got there, which we, and probably Wick and Helen, know to be untrue. Turning to Helen, he takes both her arms and attempts to assure her that he did not know it was there, and even if he had, he would not have touched it. Using a tender and pleading voice, he asks her to believe him, but again we know our protagonist is lying. Throughout the scene, Don pays much more attention to the bottle than he ever does to Helen, a beautiful woman in love with him, which is extremely telling about where his focus lies and how much alcohol is controlling his life, having become his greatest desire. Although helplessly and pitifully looking past Helen while watching Wick tip the contents down the sink, in the next instant he is belligerent and defensive when he declares that Wick is accusing him of trying to get them out of the apartment because of the bottle, which he resents "like the devil," but it is true, and we realize quickly he is not to be trusted. They finally leave Don alone as a way of defusing the situation.

Immediately after they leave, he moves towards the door to listen before turning around with a hand nervously raised to his face, partially covering his mouth, as he glances around the apartment. Turning back to the door, he pulls the chain across before moving somewhat unnaturally and animal-like through the rooms in search of hidden alcohol. We hear Wick reassuring Helen that Don has no money so cannot go out and buy alcohol nor will any shops or bars give him credit. He has searched every inch of the apartment and tells her, almost in awe, of "the places he can figure out" to hide bottles. This again suggests Don's untrustworthiness and shrewdness while also highlighting his illness. This is exemplified when Don rushes to the bathroom, removes a razorblade from the cabinet and throws aside the laundry basket next to the bathtub. Falling to his knees, he uses the blade to hurriedly remove the grate and reach as far inside the hole as he can, his whole arm disappearing as he desperately moves it around with a look of panic on his face. Finding the space empty, he realizes Wick has discovered his hiding place and wearily drops his head onto his right hand, which is resting on the bathtub, tightening it into a near fist. Standing, he rushes to the vacuum cleaner in the hall and feels up and down the bag. Finding it empty, he tosses it aside and rushes back to the living room, touching the walls as he goes, again suggesting the narrowness of the apartment and the claustrophobia he feels within it. Dragging the couch out from the wall, he throws himself onto it and reaches his hand behind, once more finding it barren and obvious that Wick got there first. Throughout this scene, Milland's gestures and facial expressions depict the mixed emotions Don is battling internally: a combination of desperation, panic, frustration, dejection, and helplessness, allowing the audience to understand, through Milland's wordless actions, Don's severe problem with alcohol.

Sitting up slowly, he looks stunned and confused as he rubs the back of his right hand across his brow just as someone tries to open the door. Standing up slowly and creeping towards it, the chain still across to prevent it opening fully, he again has the appearance of an animal rather than a man. Softly asking who is there, when there is no answer, he repeats the words again more forcefully and the cleaner answers. Telling her to come back on Monday, he agitatedly turns from her, his mind on other things. Even though she is outside the apartment and cannot see his face, he has turned his back on her, perhaps instinctively since this is what he is used to doing to hide his true feelings from those around him. He moves around restlessly, but when she asks if Wick left her money, he suddenly pauses and becomes very attentive. Almost spinning around to face the door, his eyes move around frantically as he realizes there may be money in the house. At one point, his eyes even move in one direction while his head moves in the other as he questions her about where Wick would have left the money. Informing him it would be in the sugar bowl, he instantly walks to the kitchen and removes the lid to the bowl. Beginning to pour the sugar cubes into his hand, he notices a ten dollar bill folded in the lid which he stares at, before removing and unfolding it. Despite her being outside and unable to see him, he oddly hides the note behind his back like a child as his voice becomes lighter and almost excited while falsely telling her that Wick must have forgotten and she will be paid on Monday. This is the second time he has mentioned Monday, a telling sign he has no intention of remaining in the country until Tuesday. Don has no feelings of remorse or change of heart, even when she announces that she needs the money to buy groceries; the moment she leaves he moves through the flat, grabbing his hat and placing it on his head as he walks, hurriedly putting on his jacket and staring at the money as if he cannot believe it is in his hands. Although this should be a moment of excitement for Don, since the money will get him what he wants, he looks at it grimly before staring past it as if lost in thought of what it will do to him or what people will think. He does not ponder this long, however, and heads to the nearest liquor store for two bottles of their cheapest rye.[4]

THE BENDER

Don begins his journey into the abyss of his "lost weekend" by entering the liquor store. The camera is placed behind a row of bottles, blocking our view of fully seeing Milland as he approaches and covering part of his face as if Don and the contents of the bottles are now one. Behind him we see traffic and pedestrians, but Don figuratively and literally turns his back on this ordinary life that is taking place outside, blocking it out by closing the liquor store door. Looking sheepish and ashamed while approaching the counter, Milland's eyes are cast downwards until he adds a quick and fleeting glance towards the assistant, looking down again before asking for two bottles of rye in a way that teeters between a statement and a question, suggesting Don is unsure if they will be sold to him. When the assistant says he is sorry, he immediately looks at the man, switches to indignance and demands to know what he is sorry about in a blunt tone. When he reveals that Wick told him Don is to get no more credit, he aggressively grabs for the money, victoriously holds it out and restates his order. Establishing that he has no interest in how alcohol tastes, just in its effects, when asked what kind he wants, Don cynically replies he will take the cheapest since "liquor's all one anyway." Grabbing the bottles, he rubs the tops with his thumbs and lies again, saying it is to fill his cigarette lighter, before angrily walking out. On the street, and with the bottles safely in a brown bag, his wide eyes dart around his surroundings and he smiles conceitedly while purchasing three apples from a fruit seller to cover the bottles. Greeting two older women, one notes he is "the nice young man who drinks," while the other tuts and shakes her head. Holding what now looks like a bag of groceries, Don enters Nat's bar for the first time in the narrative.[5] Milland uses by-now familiar gestures, facial expressions, and vocal intonations as Don starts off witty and friendly, playing the fool by asking for Nat's (Howard Da Silva) hand in marriage. Although Nat also initially refuses to serve him, when Don produces money, grins, and tells him this time they can "barter on a cash basis," Nat pours him a straight rye and his bender begins.

Milland quickly builds up Don's character in a remarkably convincing fashion, with believable changes in mood and temperament, his mind racing with conflicting thoughts and the cunning ways Don attempts to conceal and obtain alcohol, born from his sense of desperation and need. This is also the only time in the film that Don resembles the familiar star image Milland had built up across many of his prior films, although this is a tortured version of that image. As with many of his previous characters, in this introduction Don is clean-shaven, his hair styled, and is wearing a clean and ironed white shirt and tie. Moreover, while many of Milland's characters were easygoing in the past, here he must play this insouciance as forced in order to reflect how Don is really feeling internally, which does not match up with his outer projection when there are others around. Indeed, Don performs normality for Wick and Helen, but for the audience Milland (the actor) performs Don (the character) performing, so there are several layers to his performance. At times it is almost as if we are viewing an actor (Don) readying himself for a role, such as in the previous scene with the typewriter. His manner changes after a quick pause to help him change gears, which Milland must outwardly project so that we know Don is acting but throughout this the mechanisms of Milland's own acting need to remain invisible. Don is not an actor, but Milland is, so he must outwardly present his character's constructed performance for the diegetic audience, while simultaneously exhibiting Don's conflicted inner feelings to the nondiegetic audience. The difficulty of this cannot be overstated since they are extremely dissimilar from one another, much like a piano player whose right hand is playing something quite different from the left, but which must occur simultaneously and in harmony so that the audience sees the real "Don."

Throwing the money on the bar, Milland uses now-familiar exaggerated eye movements and a wide grin while requesting a drink, depicting another elaborate public performance from Don, whose audience now is Nat. Upon seeing the reality of the glass being placed before him, however, Don's manner changes and he forgets to perform. He instantly stops talking, the grin gone and his eyes cast downwards while intensely studying the glass and what it signifies. Placing his hand on the counter, as close to the glass as possible, he resembles a frightened child afraid their new toy will be taken away from them. He simultaneously takes a subtle but sharp intake of breath, which could be easily missed amongst everything else going on in the frame. Even though it takes mere seconds for the shot glass to be filled, he begins tapping his fingers impatiently on the bar before deciding to reach for the glass. Since Nat is still pouring, there is marginal hesitation, demonstrated by the slight pulling back of his hand synchronized with a twitch around the right side of his mouth, which resembles something of a smile but reads more like a sneer, appearing before he licks his lips in anticipation and grabs the glass as soon as it is full. As he raises it to his lips, he catches Nat's eyes, which are staring at him, and he pauses with the glass close to his lips, his eyes raising up to meet Nat's stony-faced exterior. Throughout this scene, the stationary camera is placed behind De Silva's back, allowing us to not only clearly see Milland's facial expressions and bodily gestures, but positioning us behind the bar with the bartender so that we too become enablers for Don's drinking.

Putting the glass back down without taking a sip, his indignant pride is perhaps stronger than his need for alcohol at this point. Nat busies himself at the cash register while Don takes out a cigarette as if trying to play it cool. He puts the wrong end in his mouth before flipping it over, an action that will be repeated throughout the film, staring at the drink from behind the lit match while focusing his complete attention on it. Holding the match for a few seconds while it burns close to his fingertips, in one rapid sweeping motion he violently tosses it to the ground, grabs the glass, and downs the lot. Dropping his head and screwing up his face, the shot cuts to behind Milland's back as he lets out a small gasp, his head still down, his shoulders tense, and his hand almost vicelike as the knowing Nat observes from the large mirror behind the bar. Just as Don has done throughout the film with those around him, here Nat has his back to Don, but unlike Don, the mirror gives him the advantage of seeing the action playing out behind him. In his novel *Across the River and into the Trees*, Ernest Hemingway notes that this staple piece of barroom décor is "placed behind bars so a man can tell when he is drinking too much" ([1950] 2004: 58), and it becomes a point of literal and metaphorical self-reflection for Don. Alcohol can also be seen as the film's allegorical "femme fatale" that seduces him and makes him unfaithful to "good girl" Helen, after promising her he will stay away from alcohol, acting as a way of framing and interpretation that the film makes possible in a way the novel does not, given its theme of homosexual repression. Thus, while he once more becomes alcohol's prey, he deeply regrets his decision, as is shown by his actions when he takes this first drink but is too weak to resist. She continues to control his every waking moment in both his thoughts and actions. She becomes the obsession that he cannot leave alone, even though he knows she is no good for him.

When Nat tries to wipe down the bar, Don actively stops him, requesting he be allowed his "little vicious circle," another literal and metaphorical reference and almost like a battle wound worn with both pride and horror. Staring at it, he appears lost in his thoughts as he philosophically contemplates the perfect geometric nature of a circle, which has no beginning and no end. As if waking from a daydream, he lifts his head to ask Nat what time it is, before squinting towards what we assume is a clock in the corner of the room. He is now back in the present and aware of his surroundings. He asks Nat to let him know when it is 5:45 p.m., because he is going to the country with his brother, although he loads the word "brother" with sarcasm. He then grins while showing Nat the two bottles of rye hidden under the apples, proudly informing him of his plan to "smuggle these two time bombs past the royal guard." Stating that he is going to roll one in a newspaper so that Wick discovers it right away, which he wants him to do, he will place the other in Wick's suitcase, so he ironically transports it himself. Removing it when Wick is dealing with the caretaker, he plans to hide it in the hollow of a tree, informing Nat that he may not touch a drop of it but just needs to know it is there. Nat pours him another drink as Don begins to sweat, his brow and upper lip glistening. When Gloria (Doris Dowling), a young woman often in the bar with gentlemen and clearly coded as a prostitute, walks past Don she touches the back of his neck and tells him he is "awfully pretty." He smiles and comments that she probably says that to "all the boys," perhaps emasculating himself or attempting to appear more youthful for the young Gloria, but more likely just being his usual cynical self and mocking her. She replies in the affirmative, before adding that with Don it is "on the level," thus revealing she is also a character keeping up an outward façade.

Don begins to tell Nat what happens when he drinks, acknowledging that it affects him physiologically, shrinking his liver and pickling his kidneys, before rhetorically asking, "But what does it do to my mind?" The camera films Milland head-on as he sits at the bar, looks up at De Silva, and begins a monologue with an excited but manic look on his face. Expressing how alcohol helps his creativity, Don metaphorically informs Nat that it "tosses the sandbags over the side so the balloon can soar," moving his hand in an upward gesture. Widening his eyes, he declares that all at once he is above the ordinary and becomes competent, repeating more forcefully "supremely competent." Using his face and hands to illustrate what he is saying, he stands while declaring, "I'm one of the great ones." As if giving a lecture, he proclaims that when he drinks, he is Michelangelo "sculpturing the beard of Moses," referring to the famous fourteenth-century marble sculpture, moving his right thumb in an S shape as if creating the artwork. Bringing his left hand forward to replace the right thumb, he holds a nonexistent paintbrush as he moves his hand up and down as if there is a canvas before him, adding that he is Van Gogh "painting pure sunlight. I'm Horowitz playing 'The Empire Concerto.'"[6] Staring unblinkingly as he moves slightly closer to Nat, he adds, "I'm John Barrymore before the movies got him by the throat," grabbing his own neck as he alludes to the celebrated stage actor of several Shakespearean productions and commonly perceived as the greatest American stage actor of all time but much less successful in cinema, especially near the end of his career. Ironically, Barrymore's life and ability to get work were plagued by the alcoholism he had struggled with since he was fourteen, and he died in 1942, just three years before the film was made, from alcohol-related cirrhosis of the liver and kidney failure, complicated by pneumonia, at the age of sixty.

Having covered the arts of sculpture, painting, music, and acting, Don has demonstrated how cultured he is in just a few statements. He then switches gear to explore Western folklore by saying he is Jesse James, a celebrated outlaw of the Old West and an antihero, which it could be argued that Don also is. Despite his knowledge of the arts, Don says he is "Jesse James and his two brothers, all three of them," but he only had one brother: Alexander Franklin James, known as Frank. (His other sibling was his sister, Susan

Lavenia James.)[7] He makes the statement rapidly, as if galloping along in an exciting Western scene, before stopping, lifting his pointing finger slowly, raising his brow and adding "I'm W. Shakespeare" in a clear and concise voice, suggesting that playwright William needs no further explanation than his first initial and surname. As a writer, finishing with Shakespeare, probably the most celebrated author in history, is both appropriate and telling about how alcohol gives Don (false) confidence in his ability to create. He adds that when he drinks, he no longer sees Third Avenue out the window but instead the Nile, the barge of Cleopatra floating past. Still in high spirits, he fittingly and eloquently begins to recite from Act 2, Scene 2 from Shakespeare's *Antony and Cleopatra*: "Purple the sails, and so perfumed that/The winds were lovesick with them; the oars were silver/Which to the tune of flutes kept stroke. . . ." We move from Milland's face, as Don melodically quotes from the play, to the bar from which he lifts another glass of whiskey which is now accompanied by six "vicious circles," four overlapping and two separate.

A brief cut shows Wick and Helen arriving at the apartment to find Don gone before we return to the same spot in the bar, but now there are twelve "vicious circles." The thicker ones indicate the glass has been set down several times in the same place, thereby providing a visual shortcut for Don's incessant drinking in the interim. Further suggesting a later time, the bar is busier, but Don continues to recite Shakespeare, having now switched to Act 4, Scene 1 from *The Tempest*. Heard off-screen, Milland's melodic voice quotes, "The cloud-capp'd towers, the gorgeous palaces / The solemn temples, the great globe itself," before Nat interrupts and advises Don to go home. His back to the bar, Don ignores him and continues his performance for no one in particular. He adds, "Yea, all which it shall inherit, shall dissolve," before Nat reiterates that he should go home. Stopping abruptly, and without turning around, he asks what time it is, as if too afraid to look for himself. When Nat confirms it is 6:10 p.m., he spins around and berates Nat for not telling him, even though he has multiple times. Don grabs the brown bag and the apples scatter, the disguise uncovered, as he rushes out without his change. Clutching the bag, the film takes on more of a film noir atmosphere as he wipes his mouth with the back of his hand and half-walks/half-runs down the now-dark city street.

Don enters the apartment building and begins climbing the stairs before hearing footsteps. Retreating, Milland lunges out of the rear exit in a way that suggests Don is trying to be light on his feet. Observing Wick getting into a taxi to take him to the train for his weekend away, he sees Helen pacing just outside the open door while peering into the night awaiting Don's return. A close-up of Milland shows several beads of sweat on his brow as Don

Figure 6.2. A sweating Don (Milland) hides outside the screen door of the apartment waiting for Wick and Helen to leave in *The Lost Weekend* (Billy Wilder, 1945).

silently opens the door and sneaks upstairs unnoticed (figure 6.2). Entering the apartment, Milland lets his tense shoulders drop the moment he locks the door. Turning around and removing his hat, he immediately walks to the chair by the window and sits the first bottle on the table. Gripping the second, he throws the paper bag on the floor while searching for a place to hide it. Initially trying to conceal it behind books on a shelf, it proves to be too tall; although he then moves towards the fireplace, Milland's expressions suggest Don considers this too obvious. Peering up from his crouched position by the fire, he grabs a chair and places it on the coffee table, before climbing up and sitting the bottle in the ceiling light. His actions suggest this is a new hiding space, since he hesitates at first, places the bottle in carefully to check it will be fully concealed, while momentarily hovering his hand below the lamp as if contemplating whether it will take the weight of the bottle. Realizing it has worked, he smiles and climbs down, projecting Don's smugness at his own ingenious plan. Returning to the first bottle, he pours a glassful before placing both the glass and the uncorked bottle on the table. He removes his jacket and tosses it aside without once taking his eyes from the glass. Sitting down, he leans his head on the back of the chair and looks up, a strange smile coming over his face and his breathing rapid and heavy. Loosening his tie, he continues to grin manically as if unable to believe he is finally alone in the apartment with the bottles unobserved. He looks back at the whiskey with his eyebrow raised just as the camera moves in for an extreme close-up of the glass and, despite its sitting stationary on the table, ripples appear which resemble the sea or ocean, thus suggesting Don is truly drowning in this liquid, and that we are drowning with him, as the scene fades into blackness.

Opening the apartment door the next morning, Don carefully steps over the milk and newspaper deliveries before peering over the banister to confirm Helen is gone; he descends the stairs and heads straight for Nat's. The establishment is empty apart from Nat, who is fixing himself some coffee, bacon, and eggs. Don grabs a stool, sits down, and requests a drink, becoming increasingly impatient when the already occupied Nat fails to serve him immediately. He appears repelled at Nat's suggestion that he eat something, both gesturing and demanding he take the food away. Without any hesitation this time, Don downs the drink the instant it is placed in front of him before requesting another. Nat stresses that it is still morning, but Don soberly responds that this is when alcoholics need it most, calling it medicine at this time. In another melodramatic monologue, he describes an alcoholic's terror of waking to see daylight and being uncertain if it is dawn or dusk. He stresses that if it is dawn "you're dead," because the bars are closed and liquor stores do not open until 1 p.m. He pauses before adding, rather chillingly, that Sunday is the worst of all since the stores do not open at all and the bars are closed until 1 p.m. Milland employs oscillations to his voice throughout this speech, used to suggest not only Don's increased frustration and agitation, but the idea that he is reliving harrowing experiences from his past. When Nat casually inquires where the bottles from the previous night went, he suddenly becomes extremely animated. Flailing his hands around, and now with a huge grin, he proclaims himself rich and a capitalist with untapped reserves, slamming the glass down three times and pointing to it to indicate he wants another drink.

Don is in good spirits when Gloria re-enters the bar, and he announces that he will take her to see *Hamlet* playing on Forty-fourth Street. Becoming theatrical and haughty once more, he informs her that one should always see Shakespeare on an empty stomach before downing another drink. Requesting "one last one," Milland uses a singsong voice as Don asks Nat to "pour it softly, pour it gently, and pour it to the brim." Nat finally snaps back at Don for his treatment of both Gloria and Helen and tells him to get his liquor at another bar. His head down and his face hidden behind his hat, Milland begins moving his head from side to side, which suggests Don's shame and regret. He nervously fidgets with his sleeve before slamming his fist on the counter and telling Nat to shut up and pour him another drink. When Nat asks how Helen got mixed up with him, Don declares their story to be the basis for his novel. Becoming animated and theatrical yet again, the recognizable timbre of Milland's voice asserts the novel to be "morbid stuff [. . .] nothing for the book of the month club, a horror story" and the "confessions of a booze addict, the logbook of an alcoholic," jerking his head as he emphasizes each critical word for dramatic effect. As Nat pours his drink, Don muses that it will simply be called *The Bottle* (in Jackson's novel it is *The Glass*). Lifting the glass, Milland employs no reaction this time, indicating that the more Don drinks the less it affects him. Pausing momentarily, he informs Nat that the story is in his head but that he will tell him the first chapter which began three years ago, as the film moves to a flashback of Don and Helen's first meeting.

Even here Don is linked to the theatrical world, since their "meet cute" occurs inside a theatre after their cloakroom tickets are mixed up and they end up with each other's coats. Watching the stage performers drinking from bottles of champagne, Don uses a handkerchief to wipe sweat from his brow, licks his lips, and anxiously leaves the auditorium to retrieve the bottle in the pocket of his raincoat. Given the wrong coat, he must wait for Helen to exit the show to exchange with her. Helen's is revealed to be the animal print coat she has been seen wearing throughout the film, which plays a crucial role in the climactic scene. It is fitting that Don ends up with it since he is at times presented like an animal; perhaps this is why she is attracted to them both. Their first conversation even revolves around the unusual coat, which demonstrates Helen is a special sort of woman, while Don's is a nondescript, mass-produced men's raincoat that the cloakroom had been full of—one reason why it was so difficult for him to locate. Walking outside together, when the bottle falls out and smashes, he lies even then, saying it was to make a hot toddy for a sick friend. The next flashback conveys the time Don was meant to meet Helen's parents but, overhearing them discuss him in the hotel lobby, he panics and manages to sneak unseen to a telephone booth. Helen is in his eye view as he tells her over the phone that he will be late and to go ahead without him—another lie.

Wick later enters the apartment to find Don drunk on the sofa. Turning on the light, Don bellows at him to turn it off, covering his eyes and confessing he had a drink to be able to face Helen's parents, but that it led to several more, as is his pattern. As if tending to a child, Wick loosens Don's tie while he begs Wick to call Helen and make an excuse for him. Asking Wick to join him in his lie, Don sounds almost childlike as he repeatedly asks if he will phone Helen and tell her anything, ending dramatically by saying, "Tell her I'm sick, tell her I'm dead," as Milland squeezes his eyes shut and turns his head away. Helen comes to the apartment to check on Don, and Wick tells him to wait in the next room. Wick hides the empty bottle under the couch, but it rolls out and Helen asks if it is Don's. When Wick lies and says he is the drinker in the family, it spurrs Don to emerge and face Helen, saying she would find out eventually. Condescendingly commenting that the glass looks ridiculous in Wick's hand, he grabs it and turns around, one hand in his pocket and the other casually holding the glass to demonstrate his comfort with it, like a musician with their chosen instrument. When Helen comments that most people drink sometimes, Don quips that most people can take it or leave it alone whereas he cannot take it or leave it alone, subtly trying to highlight his issue. When she appears confused, he looks down into her face and rather sinisterly states, "I'm not a drinker, I'm a drunk." With a sneer on his face, Milland spits out the words while moving his upper body as Don emphasizes his point. When Helen suggests there must be a reason behind his drinking, he informs her it is because of what he is, or rather what he is not and always wanted to be: a writer. In the lengthy monologue that follows, Don tells Helen and the audience why he drinks, while Milland expertly employs a wide range of facial expressions and vocal intonations to get Don's lengthy but sordid story across, never breaking character or appearing implausible.

In lieu of the homosexuality of Jackson's story, McBride notes the film proposes a "different kind of anguished psychological secret, Don's crippling insecurity that manifests itself in writer's block." He further suggests that Wilder and Brackett's depiction of Don as a "hopelessly mediocre talent who believes he drinks to palliate his creative anxiety contributes powerfully to their portrait of addictive torment" (2021: 459), certainly demonstrated in this scene. Sitting by the window, Don places the glass down before drunkenly announcing that he reached his peak at the age of nineteen. Writing like Hemingway, he sold a story to a newspaper that was reprinted in the *Reader's Digest*, leading him to drop out of college since, he rhetorically asks, "Who wants to stay in college when he's Hemingway?", linking himself to another author, this time it is a modern, then-living American writer whose work was produced mostly between the 1920s and 1950s and who, like Don, often went on alcoholic binges. Don explains that his mother bought him a typewriter, which becomes a trope throughout the film, and he moved to New York to pursue his dream, but he failed to find success. When a voice within him told him he was not good enough, he had a couple of drinks, stating that this was where his problem began. Poetically and with the earmark of a true writer, he brings this voice to life by describing it as clear, thin, and like "the E string on a violin," almost whispering the words as if he can still hear its melodic sound in his ear. He declares alcohol made him think more clearly, allowing the story to take shape in his head: "the tragic sweep of the great novel beautifully proportioned." Before he could get it down on paper, however, the effects wore off and the story evaporated as quickly as it came. Throughout this monologue, the camera remains mostly stationary while filming Milland in close-up and slightly from above, suggesting we are in Helen's position while Don gives his explanation to both her and us. Here, Milland moves only his head and face when speaking, letting his eyes do much of the talking as if to show Don is lost in his past experiences, staring at nothing in particular while recalling specific details. Noting that being unable to write was followed by despair, which he drank to counterbalance, he hauntingly but amusingly adds that when this did not work, he would drink to counterbalance the counterbalance. Don is clearly experiencing a range of complex and varied emotions, with Milland successfully using an array of facial expressions and subtle variants in the cadence of his voice to create believability for Don's story and avoid his becoming a comic drunk or portraying only a surface reading. He slightly slurs his words at times to remind the audience of Don's present inebriated state, but never enough to reduce him to a character part or make it seem Don is unaware of his surroundings.

Thinking somewhat lucidly, he informs Helen that there are two Don Birnams: Don the writer and Don the drunk, indicating schizophrenia or a split personality. Indeed, when quoting "Don the drunk," Milland actively adopts a different vocal inflection, one almost resembling the stereotypical voice of a witch in a fairytale as he discusses this Don telling him to take his typewriter to the pawn shop in exchange for money for "another binge, another bender, another spree," the same words that end the film and the recurrence of "another" suggesting the never ending cycle. Pausing, he covers his face with his hand and reverts to his natural voice as he says, in an almost Shakespearean way, and perhaps now as "Don the writer" that these are "such humorous words." He even confesses to buying a gun with which he intended to shoot "Don the drunk" on his thirtieth birthday but that, ironically, "Don the drunk" insisted on having a drink first so the gun was exchanged for whiskey, and he was no longer able to carry out the task. Now standing and becoming extremely animated as he talks angrily about being no good as a writer and widely viewed as Wick's freeloader, he throws down his cigarette and demands Helen leave, not just the apartment but him. He gets heated while gesturing to the door, telling her not to come back now that she knows the truth. Announcing that she is not going anywhere and, given their height difference, asking him to bend down so she can kiss him, he remains standing erect before defiantly draining the glass and staring at her, although slightly weaving on his feet. She wipes the whiskey from his lips, reaches up and grabs his face between her hands, and kisses him, taking control because he will not cooperate.

Returning to the present, Don informs Nat he is going home to begin his novel and excitedly leaves the bar. In the apartment, he sits down at his typewriter and types:

THE BOTTLE
A Story by Don Birnam
To Helen With All My Love

Smiling as if proud he has finally started his novel he moves to the next line, his fingers twitch above the keys ready to begin typing, but nothing is forthcoming. Taking his cigarettes from his pocket, he grabs matches before looking back at the page questioningly. Again, the cigarette is the wrong way round and he corrects this before lighting it, rubbing his forehead, removing his hat, and leaning forward to look at the page again before standing up. Placing a hand in his pocket, he smokes while pacing the room, rubbing his face and ear as he goes, as if trying to think. Turning towards the camera, he sees the empty whiskey bottle on the table in the foreground, visibly shudders, and turns away abruptly. However, he slowly turns back around to look at it before covering his mouth in a thoughtful way, demonstrating that Don has just remembered there is another bottle hidden in the apartment. Almost casually, he begins to reach behind the books on a shelf and looks into the fireplace, which we can only assume is where he tends to hide alcohol from Wick. Claustrophobia begins to set in again as he moves from room to room, each action becoming more frantic and urgent than the last. In the bedroom, he pulls up his mattress before heading to the couch in the living room, dragging it out from the wall only to find nothing. He begins to talk to himself, asking where he put the bottle, before desperately throwing a floor lamp out of his way and returning to the bookshelves where he now aggressively knocks row after row of books onto the floor in his quest. Climbing over an armchair, his back is slightly hunched, and he resembles a prowling animal once more, making his way to the closet as he recklessly throws out shoes, tosses boxes off the shelves, and feels through the pockets of coats. He moves to the middle of the room, looking around urgently but unable to remember where he hid the bottle. Any thoughts of writing are now obliterated. He sits in the chair near the window, breathing heavily. Noticing a matchbook on the table advertising the bar Harry and Joe's, which has the slogan "Where good liquor flows" alongside a drawing of a martini glass, the camera zooms in on the matchbook and the next scene sees Don sitting in this very establishment.

McBride declares the film one of many examples of Wilder's "obsession with masquerading and the secrets of people's hidden lives," replacing the "self-protective lying of closeted gay life" from Jackson's novel "with the perpetual denial that characterizes an alcoholic's desperate existence." Thus, "rather than hiding lovers" Don hides bottles (2021: 459).[8] Exploring the vast array of "scams and frauds" present in Wilder's films, McBride calls

The Lost Weekend a film about a man "constantly deceiving himself and everyone around him by trying to hide his addiction" (2021: 502). Indeed, Don hides his alcoholic state from those around him as well as physically hiding bottles, but I would argue that he also masquerades as a writer, since he calls himself one but has never actually produced anything. Stating that he sold a story to the *Reader's Digest* at the age of nineteen, in the flashback he informs Helen he has started novels and short stories but never finished any of them. Moreover, he is thirty-six at the time of the narrative, and yet his novel(s) remains only in his head, and when he sits down to write it, he cannot get a word out other than the title.

Don sits alone at a table in the nightclub, appearing half-asleep while leaning his head on a leather bench behind him, unshaven and beginning to appear unkempt by this stage. An empty glass sits in front of him, but when he looks at his check, he seems shocked. Taking money from his pocket, he sneakily examines it beneath the table before worriedly putting it away. However, instead of confessing to his lack of funds, he foolishly orders another drink. Desperately looking around the room as if searching for an escape route, his eyes fall on the unattended handbag of the woman next him who is turned away, drinking with her boyfriend and listening to the pianist. In an attempt not to draw attention to himself, Don slowly reaches over and gently pulls the monogrammed clutch across the bench, tucks it beneath his jacket, and returns to a casual pose as he leans back to smoke. When his drink arrives, he asks where the washroom is. He enters and manages to distract the attendant while searching through the purse. Locating ten dollars, he begins walking casually but cautiously back to his seat but stops abruptly when noticing the couple's table has been abandoned. When challenged about the purse, he appears mortified and hands it over at once, along with the ten dollars he claims to have "borrowed," as if unable to utter the word stolen. Giving the waiter all the money he has on him, Don announces he will come back and pay his debt but is forcefully thrown into the street and told never to return. As the pianist begins singing "Somebody stole a purse," encouraging the patrons to join in, he turns to them and repeats twice that he is not a thief, the words additionally helped by Milland's perfect enunciation, a strong contrast to how purse thieves are often depicted in cinema since they tend to be from the lower echelons of society. This exemplifies just how far Don has fallen in his attempts to obtain a drink.

Returning to his apartment building, the camera films him from behind as he reaches the top of the staircase, swaying and hitting both sides as he goes. Slowly wandering inside, he hangs his hat on a hook just inside the door but falls headfirst against the wall, suggesting this minimal action has sapped him of his remaining strength. Steadying himself on the wall, he staggers through the torn-up apartment before throwing himself heavily down on the sofa. The camera moves in for a close-up of Milland's face as he grimaces and squeezes his eyes shut, suggesting both Don's extreme pain and his humiliation. Loosening his tie as if it is choking him, he wipes a hand across his face before opening his eyes from his prostrate position and blinking several times at the ceiling. The camera shifts to his point of view: the shadow of the bottle in the ceiling lamp. The camera returns to him as he lets out a small gasp resembling a combined laugh and cry, a blend of triumph and idiocy. Rising from the couch, he stares at the ceiling while reaching for the chair, unsteady and tripping as he goes. Given his inebriated state, he warily stands on the chair on the table this time, pulling out the bottle with a wide grin and cradling it as he steps down, as if he has just won a prize. The moment his feet touch the ground he immediately pulls the cork out and, without even reaching for a glass this time, raises the bottle to his lips and gulps it down as if it were nothing stronger than Coca-Cola.

The subsequent scene opens with an extreme close-up of Milland's eye, which moves around to suggest Don is trying to get his bearings. Momentarily going out of focus before he closes his eyes, it is as if we are experiencing the sensation of waking up from Don's viewpoint. We hear a diegetic telephone ringing, the sound of which has obviously woken him, and the shot is unforgivingly unfiltered and far from glamorous in its depiction of a Hollywood star. The dark shadows under Milland's eyes are apparent, as is every line on his face, his freckles, and blemishes, including a small hole beside his nose, potentially a childhood chickenpox scar. The camera moves out to present his unshaven face and tousled hair and even further out to show he is in bed but still wearing his suit and tie. Rubbing his eyes, he rises slowly and exits the bedroom while holding onto the doorframe for support. Approaching the telephone in the foreground, he stands in the center of the frame while weakly attempting to grab the back of a chair to steady himself, suggesting this short journey has been too taxing for Don in his present state. His arms appear too weak to support his body weight, and they slip from the top of the chair down either side as his head and upper body fall forward in an exhausted or defeated state. Still leaning on the chair, and knowing it is Helen who is calling, he wills the phone to stop ringing by talking to it. Steadying himself first with the chair and then the table, he picks up both bottles of rye and holds them over the glass; while a dribble exits one, the other is dry. Drinking this down, he turns with his hands in his pockets and looks around the room before pulling a single coin out, staring at it, and putting it away. Obviously in need of another alcohol fix and wondering how he can achieve this, he turns from left to right and then left again like an animal confined to a small cage. Suddenly freezing when his eyes fall upon the typewriter, he rushes towards it, pulls out the sheet of paper from the night before and hurriedly puts on the lid. Grabbing it, he moves to get his hat but, as he places it on his head, he must again steady himself on the wall, first with his arm and then his back as he strives to get the typewriter up into his arms. Looking down, he shakes his head and begins talking to himself; nearly in tears, he softly utters, "I'll never make it. I'll never make that pawn shop, it's a block and a half away." Milland grimaces again to convey to us that Don's body is in agony. Lost in his thoughts, perhaps mentally taking the "impossible" journey, the dialogue is used to inform the audience of Don's plans since he is alone. The phone begins ringing again, bringing him back to the present and spurring him on to go. Slowly leaving the apartment, he steadies himself on the banister since, given his present state, there is a high chance of his falling down the stairs, thus foreshadowing a key incident that occurs slightly later.

THIRD AVENUE

McBride suggests that the film being set in prewar 1937, rather than the current wartime of its 1945 release, means that while it digs "deeply into the physical and psychological torment of an alcoholic, [it] seems oddly distanced from other social issues" (2021: 440). Set a year later than Jackson's novel, he declares viewers could be forgiven for missing the film's timeframe, since the only date visible is in the flashback sequence at the theatre, where a poster advertises the 1934–35 season. However, it can also be argued that the date is almost certainly irrelevant to Don since, as McBride correctly notes, the events of his weekend "take place in hermetic settings mostly unrelated to the greater world surrounding him" (2021: 441). Therefore, it is perhaps ironic that, unbeknownst to Don, he makes his journey up Third Avenue on Yum Kipper, also known as the Day of Atonement, with Don's own punishment or penance being that all of the pawnshops are closed so he cannot pawn his typewriter to buy alcohol. Masden proclaims that the pawnshops being closed the day Don chooses to walk fifty blocks with the typewriter meant the "whiff of anti-Semitism in Jackson's book is kept intact" (1969: 67); however, it was not a choice for Don but rather a necessity when all else had failed him, and both his liquor and money had run out. McBride suggests that this sequence, where Milland's Don resembles a dead man walking, has a somber "evocation of death camps" as he "wanders through a New York landscape mysteriously empty of Jews" until he is informed it is a "Jewish holy day" (2021: 282). He adds that Wilder, a

German exile, had an "obsession with living death as reflections of his hidden anguish over the Holocaust" and his sense of "survivor's guilt" when he was unable to save his mother (2021: 243). McBride declares that he is a "'living deadman' a terminal form of the masquerade," stemming from "the need of the exile and the Jew to deal with the threat of oblivion through adaptation and/or disguise, while facing the bitter truth that "to survive is to be buried alive inside the deaths one did not die" (2021: 243–44).

Wilder's lifelong feelings of being an exile and Jewish outsider in various societies links him to "the Wandering Jews of folklore" and led to him delving into the "trauma caused by those feelings of helplessness, rage, and alienation" in his films (McBride 2021: 244). Thus, it was during the war and its immediate aftermath that this theme was strongest in his work, and Wilder's protagonists "must deal with that guilt and either overcome it (usually through love) or let its consequences devour them" (2021: 243). This occurs with MacMurray's Walter Neff in *Double Indemnity*, Holden's Joe Gillis in *Sunset Boulevard*, Kirk Douglas's Chuck Tatum in *Ace in the Hole* (1951) and Milland's Don, the latter being the only one who (perhaps just) survives, but whom we assume will go on another bender in the not-too-distant future, while Gillis is already dead when the film begins. Moreover, Zolotow declares that while there has been much celebration of the 1960s and 1970s antihero films, "when Dustin Hoffman, Jack Nicholson and other naturalistic stars came into view," this was actually "an old story with Wilder," referring to Neff, Gillis, Tatum, and Birnam as "the original anti-heroes in American film [. . .] except nobody praised [Wilder] for his anti-heroes" (1977: 179).

Wilder fought hard to innovatively film the exterior shots in New York during Don's long walk on Third Avenue (Masden 1969: 69). Milland notes that most of the scenes were filmed by hidden cameras through vacant store fronts, holes cut in the canvas tops of delivery trucks and inside a piano packing case "strategically placed on the sidewalk before dawn." Thus, "nobody paid any attention to a drunken bum staggering along Third Avenue looking for a pawnshop for his battered typewriter. [. . .] To them I was normal" (1974: 217). Beginning his journey up Third Avenue, Don passes Nat's Bar, looking longingly in the window but unable to enter quite yet since he has no money and a typewriter to pawn. Passing familiar buildings, his eyes move around rapidly but his body appears less alert. Indeed, despite his desperation to reach the pawnshop, he maintains an almost leisurely stroll, the typewriter held at his left side and his right hand slightly swinging as he walks. But this is perhaps the fastest he is able to go, consistently mouth-breathing despite his slow pace. Clearly knowing the location of the pawnshop, which suggests that he makes visits often, he clenches his jaw upon reaching it,

Figure 6.3. Don's (Milland) long walk up Third Avenue as he tries to pawn his typewriter in *The Lost Weekend* (Billy Wilder, 1945).

lifts the typewriter, and turns to enter, but looks surprised when met with a closed shutter. Pulling at the shutter, he desperately asks a bystander if it is Sunday; she informs him it is Saturday but the store may be closed due to a bereavement. Dropping his head slightly, he turns to look back towards Nat's as if contemplating returning home before turning and continuing down the street. Stopping in the foreground and lowering his chin, as if readying himself for the journey ahead, he falteringly takes off again. We watch Don approaching another pawnshop from behind its shutter, seeing the anguish on his despair-ridden face as he comes towards us and peers in, his gaping mouth turned down in a grimace as he anxiously wipes his face and brow. We remain behind the shutter, watching normal life going on, as Don walks past, detached from his surroundings. Stopping to rest, he falls heavily into an iron girder supporting the Third Avenue Bridge, panting and unable to stand upright without support. Staggering to yet another closed pawnshop, he sees the establishments around it are open and again pulls at the shutter as if this will miraculously help. His knees buckle and he rests his face against the shutter; other pedestrians do not even glance his way as they hurry past. The typewriter now in his right hand, possibly to distribute the weight, he reaches his left hand up and grabs hold of the shutter which steadies him and aids in driving him forward as he practically limps along on his journey.

A montage of images showing more closed pawnshops and street signs are intercut with a medium close-up of Milland walking. Although the camera is consistently in front of the actor, it never films him from a distant or detached position, but instead moves with him as he walks, giving it a handheld, almost documentary-like feel and suggesting we are with Don as he makes his arduous journey. Looking even more disheveled now, his face shines with sweat, and he has heavy facial hair growth since he has not shaved in days (figure 6.3). Wearing the same clothes throughout, and even sleeping in them, their unkempt and soiled state add to Don's overall appearance. This is far removed from the fitted suits and tuxedos Milland commonly wore on-screen, often while drinking socially at a nightclub or party—a life completely alien to Don. Wiping his mouth as if it is bone-dry, perhaps not completely by chance he stumbles over his own feet while passing a funeral parlor, thus alluding to Wilder's concept of the deadman walking. Shifting to a medium shot as Don continues his journey, he is beyond tired and now looks genuinely fatigued. Barely able to keep his eyes open, he lifts the typewriter up to carry it under his left arm, his head dropping and his whole body constantly pulling to the right as he walks, suggesting vertigo or delirium and that every part of him aches tremendously. Additionally, his head violently rolls about as if it is now too heavy for his neck. This scene in particular makes for extremely uncomfortable watching as we voyeuristically peer into this troubled man's world but are powerless to help. In fact, this segment helps cement Gemünden's opinion that nobody exits a Wilder film feeling comfortable. The actor appears his most frail here, particularly in the full-body shots, where his clothes are seen hanging loosely on his frame. Any aspect of his past suaveness or joviality are completely nonexistent while Don struggles to carry the (seemingly) increasingly heavy typewriter as he almost drags himself along the street. Milland was able to channel Don's physical and mental feelings into his face and body, the power of the scene hugely dependent on Milland's acting ability and his aptitude in credibly embodying both Don's physical and metaphorical journeys.

Don finally finds a pawnshop where the owner is present, although it too is closed. Resting his back against the shutter, he steps away and attempts to stand unaided in a manner reminiscent of someone learning to ice skate and moving precariously into the center of the rink for the first time. We hear the diegetic sound of his shoes scuffing on the sidewalk as if he can now barely lift his feet as a woman enters the shot, glances momentarily at him, and moves on without stopping. Observing Don's swaying body and rocking head as he cradles the typewriter, the store owner turns and asks what is wrong with him. In almost a whisper, he asks why all the pawnshops are closed before declaring, in an animal-like wail, "they're all closed, every one of them." Told they are closed for Yum Kipper, a Jewish celebration, Don gestures towards other stores and asks why Kelly's and Gallagher's are also closed. The man tells him they are closed out of respect for their Jewish colleagues who, in return, do not open on St. Patrick's Day as a mark of respect for the Irish cultural and religious celebration. Don grimaces and almost moans the words, "That's a good joke. That's funny. That's very funny." His voice and facial expressions are far removed from the words he is saying and suggest he is emotionally, physically and mentally spent. As he moves the typewriter from under his left arm to his right side, the weight of it, even heavier given his weak state and the length of time he has been carrying it, almost pulls him out of the left side of the frame, while the man stares after him with what appears to be a combination of confusion and sympathy.

Having literally circled the town, thus acted out his own "vicious circle" foreshadowed by the stain on the bar, Don enters Nat's in his worst state thus far. Nat is playing a dice game with two other men close to the camera at the far side of the bar, which Don has occupied in all his scenes there thus far. We are positioned at the far end of the bar, almost with the men, and with a clear view of the front door. Don struggles through the door backwards, holding the typewriter at his chest with both hands. Raising his eyes momentarily to meet Nat's, he drops the typewriter and himself headfirst onto the bar. Nat, at the right of the screen, and the men at the left all turn their heads to look at Don, and we are positioned between them with Don directly in front of us as if we are also part of this gathering. Raising his head just long enough to call Nat's name, like a sick child crying out for its mother in the night, he drops it again, his face now resting on his hand atop the typewriter.

Nat slams down the cup the dice are in, obviously annoyed at seeing Don again, especially in this state, but calmly approaches and asks what he wants, respectfully calling him Mr. Birnam. The man with great ideas, who was spouting Shakespeare not long ago, is now a shadow of a man, all of his self-respect gone. Hunched over, his head in his hands, he lifts it occasionally to converse with Nat before dropping it again. This is the lowest point Don has yet reached as he begs Nat for just one drink. Milland applies a wide range of speech patterns here, expertly suggesting the complex range of emotions Don is experiencing through his troubled voice which goes from tearful to resentful when Nat asks why he is not home writing his book, before breaking when informing Nat he will pay when he can, the "can" hardly audible as if even speaking is too much effort for him now. Here the script, written by successful, professional, and prolific writers Wilder and Brackett, draws attention to Don's lack of words. He drops his head again as he hyperbolically asks Nat not to let him die by refusing him a drink. When Nat firmly announces Don has no credit, he raises his head, grits his teeth, and more forcefully proclaims that he is asking for charity and begs for a drink. Holding up the bottle, Nat angrily, but philosophically, replies that "one's too many

Figure 6.4. Begging Nat for a drink, Don (Milland) does not have the strength to even lift the glass, drinking it off his typewriter case in *The Lost Weekend* (Billy Wilder, 1945).

and a hundred is not enough" while filling a shot glass. The camera moves to a close-up of Milland, unshaven and sweating as he grabs the glass with a half-smile/half-grimace. His hand shakes as he lifts the glass and places it on the typewriter. Staring at it like a loved one and, unable to even lift it to his mouth, he awkwardly pulls the typewriter closer to him and lowers his head towards the glass, drinking from the flat surface of the typewriter case (figure 6.4), ironically bringing together the constantly battling forces of the typewriter and the alcohol, making them one in the same just as "Don the writer" and "Don the drunk" are both Don Birnam. Shuddering, he drops his head onto the typewriter, his hand still gripping the glass and slightly convulsing as we hear Nat firmly telling him that is all he is getting.

Don's eyes look hollow and haunted as he pleads for another drink; screwing his face up, he begs through gritted teeth, and even offers Nat his typewriter. Since Don declares that his inability to write is his reason for drinking, it seems strange that he would wish to exchange the object that would help with his writing. Dropping his head onto the typewriter, he repeatedly and woefully begs Nat, who continues to refuse. Without any more commotion, Don slowly gets to his feet, lifts the typewriter, and turns towards the door, struggling with the door handle before lunging into the street. Unsteady on his feet, he shuffles and sways, his mouth open as if gasping for air, but as he starts to walk past a wooden Indian he stops and looks at it, remembering that Gloria lives in this apartment building. Bursting through the door, he begins to climb the stairs to her apartment, struggling to get his footing at the very bottom, the weight of the typewriter alone almost bringing him to his knees. Grabbing the banister, he begins to ascend as we watch from the top of the staircase, a fade-out and a return to Don at the top suggests it has been a long and arduous journey since the audience is aware that this filmic technique is deployed to suggest a considerable amount of time has passed.

Breathing heavily, Don impatiently rings Gloria's doorbell before she appears in her nightwear, which tells the audience how late it is, and berates Don for standing her up. The camera films Milland from a low angle, highlighting his now very thin face, beaded with sweat and full of anguish. Exhibiting Don's agony and exhaustion, Milland rests his head against the wall with his mouth open, intermittently groaning and grimacing through clenched teeth. Highlighting their opposing social positions, Gloria mockingly refers to him as Mr. Don Birnam, Esq., and notes his "ritzy friends," but she now holds power over him simply by having a few dollars. She demands he leave when he requests money from her, but he suddenly moves forward and kisses her. Shocked at first, she then begins to kiss him back, reaching up and touching the back of his hair that she so often admires. Thereafter, she is calmer, speaking softly before going to get him money. Although never mentioned in the film, it is obvious that Gloria is a prostitute; here, however, it is Don who falsely seduces Gloria to obtain money from her, thus prostituting himself for a drink. Knowing she likes him but obviously feeling nothing for her contributes to Don's antihero status since it potentially jeopardizes his relationship with Helen. When Gloria gives him the money, he kisses her hand, attempting to be gallant and gentlemanly despite his present appearance. Turning, he begins descending the stairs as a young girl rushes up, running a stick along the banister. He steps aside but loses his balance, desperately grabbing at a wall-mounted lamp in an attempt to stabilize himself; but the fixture comes loose, and he falls downstairs screaming. The camera shows Don's viewpoint as we tumble down the stairs with him, the pattern on the stairs coming up to meet us. A cut to the girl shows her watching in horror, before we see the tall and thin Don falling violently, landing on his back on the ground below with his eyes closed and the typewriter thrown from him.

BELLEVUE

The scene that follows the incident on the staircase, Don's literal and metaphorical fall to the dangerous depths of his condition, is the film's most disturbing. It fades in on an extreme close-up of him sleeping and, considering these images were projected on a massive screen for historical audiences in

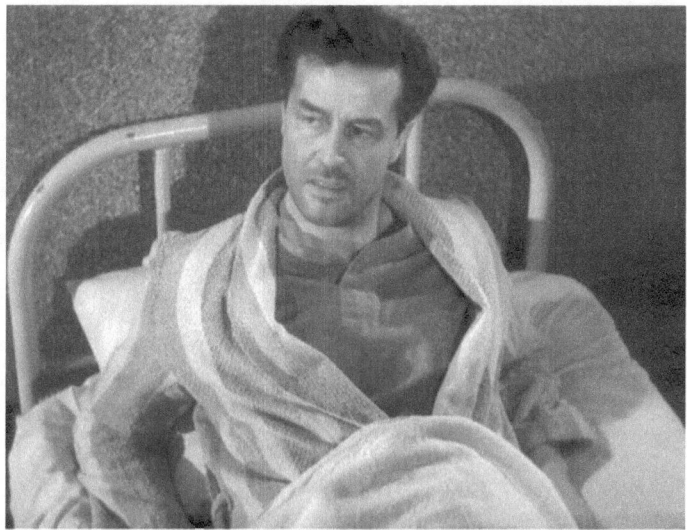

Figure 6.5. Don (Milland), in threadbare terrycloth bathrobe and narrow iron bed, wakes up in Bellevue's alcoholic ward in *The Lost Weekend* (Billy Wilder, 1945).

theatres, shots like this were magnified and unforgiving, especially given the bleak subject matter, the ghastly nature of the real-life environment, and the events which transpire within the scene. Milland notes that the camera "comes so close that nothing can be hidden and fakery isn't possible," and would not have worked without Wilder's "prying, probing, intuitive touch of genius, and Brackett with his kindly calm and sociologist insight." Additionally, Milland proclaimed Jackson "a bright, erratic problem child, telling me the horrors he had been through" that led to his writing (1974: 218).

Masden calls the sequence in Bellevue one of the grimmest scenes ever filmed; when the lights go out in the ward, Wilder "treats his audiences to the full force of the horrors of delirium tremens" (1969: 72). Likewise, Zolotow declares it a "terrible nightmare" scene, suggesting audiences may feel further discomfort knowing that Wilder showed a fake script, with a toned-down version of what he actually shot, to the superintendent when gaining access to film there (1977: 130). To aid his performance, Milland requested he spend a night in Bellevue's psychiatric ward as he was informed that this was where "really far gone alcoholics were confined until [...] sufficiently dried out." Given hospital pajamas and a "threadbare terrycloth bathrobe," a costume he also sports in the film (figure 6.5), he was assigned a narrow iron bed (Milland 1974: 215), the depiction of which is particularly stark and ugly in the film.

Milland's grim observations no doubt aided his performance and, writing almost thirty years later, he recalls that two of the men were strapped to their beds while another talked "incessantly, just gibberish." He notes a multitude of smells, the dominant one being a "cesspool. And there was the sound of moaning, and quiet crying" (1974: 215). Continuing his harrowing description, he recollects being woken abruptly by a door slamming near his bed as two male nurses brought in a man who kept up "a high, keening wail" and screamed that his bed was on fire, while others "began growling in the foulest language imaginable." Across the room came "a long ululating howl" like "coyotes make at night in the high deserts of Arizona. Suddenly the room was bedlam. I knew I was looking into the deepest pit" (1974: 215). Once more like a screenplay, and no doubt embellished by Milland, he recalls deciding to leave the ward at 3 a.m. without dressing and immediately running into a policeman. Observing his hospital bathrobe, he claims the policeman did not believe he was "lapping up some atmosphere for a movie," grabbed him, stamped on his bare feet, and returned him to the hospital; he was only allowed to leave after receiving substantiation from the head nurse (1974: 216). Although his disturbing experience made him never want to see "that horrifying place again," the Bellevue segment was the first to be shot in New York (1974: 217).

The scene begins with Milland fractionally opening his mouth and then his eyes, slowly at first and then more widely. Looking at the ceiling from his prostrate position, he frowns slightly to show these are unfamiliar surroundings for Don. A cut to his point of view shows a stark white ceiling with shadows resembling prison bars covered by mesh. Still following Don's viewpoint, the camera slowly moves towards a wall and door depicting the entrance to a ward. We see rows of basic iron beds, which add to the atmosphere of a hospital setting, while a diegetic sound like a pig squealing is consistent throughout. Don and the audience both realize the noises are emitting from the man lying next to him; sweating profusely, he stares upwards, convulsing and constantly making horrific noises that do not sound human. A two-shot reveals their beds are mere inches apart, and it is here we see that Don is wearing a hospital robe. Appearing confused and distressed, he investigates the man's face before turning away with sympathy or perhaps self-reflection about his own potential future state if he allows himself to continue drinking. The camera films Milland from above as he glances towards the foot of the bed before freezing; another man stands staring at him, while nervously pulling at threads on his robe. Propping himself up onto his elbow, Don looks directly at the man and asks him twice where they are, but he does not answer, shuffling away as male nurse Bim Nolan (Frank Faylen) enters the ward and approaches Don's bed to check his vitals.

When Don indignantly asks why he is in the alcoholic ward, referred to by Bim as "hangover plaza," the nurse glibly replies that his blood registered as "straight applejack 96 proof." Don arrogantly proclaims himself to be as well as Bim but is noticeably shaky on his feet while attempting to leave. As a uniformed guard locks the heavy metal door, Don turns and asks, more softly, if he is in prison, to which Bim informs him it is a hospital-jail hybrid as he leads Don back to the ward. Milland nervously rubs the back of his head, while Bim knowingly tells Don he will be back, since he can "pick an alkie with one eye shut, you're an alkie." He describes some of the "regulars" to Don: a man who comes every month "like the gas bill," one who has returned forty-five times, and yet another who has been coming since 1927, some of them beginning to drink because of Prohibition. Don looks both repelled and fascinated as Bim talks, moving forward with morbid curiosity to take a closer look and perhaps wondering if he will become one of them.

Don sits on the bed with his head hung as Bim attempts to get him to drink something, presumably a sedative, since there is "liable to be a little floor show" later that may disturb him. Don looks up, eyes wide, and repeats the words "floor show" as a question while appearing terrified; Milland undoubtedly projecting his recent experience into his performance. The camera moves to film from behind Milland's head from his seated position and towards Faylen, now ominously towering over him as Bim asks Don if he has ever had the DTs. Don immediately drops his head again, answering with a defiant "no" as if trying to block this thought out. Grinning sinisterly, Bim tells him, "You will, brother," while Don shakes his head vigorously and says he will not, but it seems he is trying to convince himself more than Bim, once more foreshadowing a subsequent scene. The camera continues to film Faylen from this lower position while Bim explains the terrors of the ward at night and how the DTs work, potentially for the audience since Milland notes that he had never seen anyone with DTs and that not many people have (1974: 215). Bim states that it begins with little animals, not stereotypical pink elephants; gesturing to the man from the foot of Don's bed, he notes that he thinks beetles are crawling all over him each night. The camera has shifted to film Milland from above as he screws up his eyes and falls slowly back onto the bed looking defeated; his eyes remain shut, while his rigid body suggests that Don is considering how both the night and his future will unfold. Chillingly, Bim informs both Don and the audience that the DTs can only occur in the dark since "delirium is a disease of the night."

Don lies awake, his wide eyes shining in the darkness as they rapidly scan the room in a horrified manner. He looks towards a man coughing further down his row, before a piercing scream from the other side of the room makes him sit bolt upright. The man Bim told Don about has thrown his blanket off and is screaming repeatedly, slapping his bed, and standing to get away from the "beetles" that only he can see. Don stares at him silently, paralyzed with fear, while two male nurses rush in, pull the man down on the bed, and call for both restraints and the doctor. Another man then lets out a roar and a manic laugh as the ward turns into chaos similar to what Milland described of his own experience. Cuts between the men, the nurses, and Don as he sits motionless but aghast add to the bedlam, as the shadow from the mesh door falls on Milland's face, covering it with a strange pattern that changes each time the door swings open. The noise reaches a crescendo as a nurse with a trolley of implements and a doctor enter to attend to the still-screaming man. Just then Don notices the doctor's overcoat on the bed nearest the door; his face lights up as he looks right and then left at the staff, who are all currently occupied with frantic patients. While two nurses take the first man out to the violent ward, the doctor and another nurse tend to the second, Don takes his chance amid this commotion; quickly creeping from his bed, he walks with his back hunched over and grabs the coat before leaving the ward. Managing to rush past the guard, currently helping the nurses get the belligerent patient into the elevator, he enters the stairwell and puts on the coat, pulling the collar up as he casually leaves the building before half-walking/half-running down the street. Again, a coat belonging to someone else is a catalyst in helping Don on his journey; here, it becomes a literal journey when we briefly see him boarding a train.

Back in town, he immediately investigates the window of the closed liquor store, wiping his mouth and longingly staring at the bottles; he even looks back at them as he crosses the road, as if taking a second look at a beautiful woman he has encountered. He waits across the street until the owner opens the store, immediately returning and threatening him over a quart of rye. Having no money, he informs the man he will get it one way or another, grabs it from his hand, and leaves. The lights are still on when he enters his apartment, the table lamp on its side, and he turns them off as he looks around at the disarray he previously caused, surveying the scene as if he is seeing it for the first time. He sits in the chair by the window, uncorks the bottle, pushes the empty bottle out of the way, and grabs a glass from the table. He pours a glass, although we do not see him drinking it here, as the camera pans to the ringing telephone.

BAT AND MOUSE

The scene fades back in on the telephone, only this time it is dark, and the camera moves in reverse back to Don in the chair. Still wearing the coat, his face shining with sweat, he wakes up as we hear a mouse squeaking off-screen. Raising his head and then tilting it to the side, he stares open-mouthed. There is a cut to Don's viewpoint of a mouse appearing through a hole in the wall of his apartment, as the camera moves in for an extreme close-up. A lighthearted, almost cartoonlike, nondiegetic tune plays over a series of cuts between Don and the mouse, beginning with him slightly chuckling at the creature and concluding with a heavy-eyed, tired-looking Don watching it affectionately. A slight flapping sound can be heard as the music changes to desperate and dramatic and, as Don looks up, his expression alters completely while his eyes widen frantically. There is a cut to a bat, which appears to have entered the open window. Don watches it, ducking down in his chair as it flies past him through the room, his mouth gaping as he turns his head away. Watching as the bat swoops in and consumes the mouse, he stares for a moment before shrieking and looking away. Glancing back just as blood drips down the wall, he screams repeatedly, covering his face and averting his eyes before looking back at the horrifying scene. This embodiment of Don's DTs, in which the bat plunges at the "gibbering mouse," is highlighted by Zolotow as the film's "most unbearable and poignant sequence" (1977: 130). We can also read it as Don as the mouse and the bat as the alcoholism that consumes him, or the bat as "Don the drunk" who kills "Don the writer," thus the screams of agony Don emits suggest that part of him is dying. Since this is the final time we see Don drink in the film, this scene could also be seen as an exorcism, his piercing screams a sign that he is finally letting the demons escape his body in a boisterous, unpleasant, but necessary way so that he may heal.

Following his hysterical outburst, Don slumps low in the chair. Frozen to the spot in fear, his body does not move save from the rapid and shallow breathing which causes his chest to repeatedly rise and fall as if hyperventilating. This sight is far removed from the image of a glamorous movie star (figure 6.6); his eyes are wide and manic as he continues to stare at the wall, sweat now pouring down his face and his hair plastered to his head. When Helen demands he let her in the apartment, he covers his mouth with his hand as if trying to muffle the sound of his rapid breathing. Since he ignores her pleas, the landlady asks the janitor to bring the passkey while Don stares at the door. Trying to stand up so that he can bolt the door, he immediately falls, knocking furniture over, and, still breathing heavily, is forced to crawl across the room on his hands and knees, dragging himself along the floor towards the door in a demeaning position: this is the lowest he can sink. Although making it there in time, he gets the chain in his hand but does not have the strength to pull it across and the janitor opens it for Helen. He is propped against the door when she enters and looks up at her before covering his eyes with the back of his hand, his elbow outstretched rather dramatically—a gesture that can be read as a mixture of shame, his not wanting her to see him in his present state, and a reaction to the shaft of light coming through the window, which is far too bright for his eyes. As before, he tells her to go away, but she will not. Helping him to his feet, she turns on the light and is shocked to see both the state of the room and of him but does not let him see this. She tries to keep cheerful as she tells him once he has bathed, shaved, eaten, and slept he will feel better. However, when she leads him towards the bathroom he jerks away and cries '"no," telling her about the hole in the wall, the mouse, and the bat. Looking towards the wall, she tells him there is nothing there and encourages him to look for himself (figure 6.7). With trepidation he slowly moves towards the wall which has no hole, no blood—nothing. He looks at it, lifts his hand to touch it, and runs it down the clear wall, even checking the palm of his hand for blood, a gesture reminiscent of Lady Macbeth as she goes mad in *Macbeth*, yet another Shakespeare play, only she sees the blood that is not there so maybe Don is not quite beyond saving yet. Looking at his hand and realizing it was all in his mind, he throws his head back and begins to cry, continuing to weep as Helen leads him away. She sits him down before turning the light on, but he is staring forward unblinkingly as he murmurs about Nat and Bim being right: that it starts with little animals.

The next morning, Don appears from his bedroom clean-shaven, with neat hair and wearing different clothes for the first time in the film. Helen is asleep on the couch when he grabs her leopard coat, the one responsible for their first meeting, and rushes out of the flat without a word. Helen wakes up and calls to him, but he ignores her, and when she meets him in the street, he has already pawned it. They discuss the importance of the coat as a symbol of their relationship before he curtly tells her to stop being sentimental and tries to walk past, but she forcefully stops him. Maybe Don wants her to hate him so that she will leave and will not have to endure the situation anymore, or perhaps he wants her to forget him but the coat is a constant reminder. Standing in the rain, Helen tells him she has stopped being sentimental, that it is all over and dead. He is unable to look her in the eye, staring shamefully at the ground as she continues her rant by informing him that for three years everyone warned her against him but she thought she understood his core, but now realizes his core is a sponge, and that he will do "anything ruthless, selfish, dishonest" to feed that sponge. Ironically, given his behavior throughout the film, he requests that she does not make a scene. When she asks for the pawn ticket he shakes his head rapidly and nervously, firmly stating, "Not now." He seems agitated and preoccupied, just wanting to get past her, and when she tells him he can get as drunk as he likes, he calmly and defeatedly thanks her as he walks past with his hands thrust in his pockets.

Figure 6.6. Don (Milland) paralyzed with fear after seeing the bat attack the mouse in *The Lost Weekend* (Billy Wilder, 1945).

Figure 6.7. Helen (Jane Wyman) tries to help a distraught and unkempt Don (Milland) after his bout of the DTs in *The Lost Weekend* (Billy Wilder, 1945).

Although it appears that Don is rushing off somewhere, and while both Helen and the audience are to assume that it is to buy alcohol, when Helen enters the pawnshop, she discovers Don exchanged the coat for the gun he pawned on his thirtieth birthday. This is the gun he noted earlier was to kill

"Don the drunk," but which would also kill "Don the writer." Back in the apartment, we have the privileged knowledge of seeing Don calmly write a suicide note before taking the gun into the bathroom, staring into the mirror, and holding it up to his chin, as if considering how it will look, which is a strange gesture. Perhaps in these moments of complete desperation we see the intricate details the most, because as he looks in the mirror his eyes move slightly down as he notices the button on one side of his collar is undone; he does it up before giving a weak half-smile at his reflection. He and we hear the off-screen sound of someone opening the door. He panics and tries to find a place to hide the gun before placing it in the sink. It is Helen, relieved to see him alive. She uses the excuse of wanting to borrow a coat since it is raining; he gives her his raincoat and morbidly ponders their exchanging coats again at the end, with him forever getting "the best of the bargain." Deciding his drinking is better than his death, she tells him there is some leftover whiskey, but he uncharacteristically refuses it. This is a completely changed man from the rest of the film; previously, all he could think about was obtaining and consuming alcohol. Now he is thinking clearly, but only for the moment, because he has formulated the greater plan of ending his life. He questions why she is trying to get him to drink, speaking coldly to her while repeatedly attempting to get her to leave the apartment. However, when she holds a glass up to him, he softens, telling her she is very sweet while gently pushing the drink away. Saying goodbye, he bends to kiss her, the first time without her having to tell him to bend down, but when she does not respond he says, "Don't let me bend for nothing." He looks confused when she tells him she will get him all the alcohol he wants before declaring she would rather see him drunk than dead. He looks alarmed that she has discovered his plan but does not let her see this; turning away, he speaks out of the side of his mouth with the (seemingly) casual remark, "Who wants to be dead?" She demands he stop before rushing to grab the gun after seeing it reflected in a shaving mirror. Startled, he races after her and brusquely tells her to give it to him; easily overpowering her, he grabs her arm and twists it behind her back before retrieving the gun.

THE RESOLUTION

The film's final few minutes become a message about alcoholism and how to deal with it, whether it is yourself or someone you love who is suffering from it. Helen becomes the voice of reason to Don's damaged man. When she asks why he is going to commit suicide, he tells her it is better for everyone, for him, for her, and for Wick. When Helen tells him that is not true, he barks, "Okay, me then, selfish again," as he grabs her by the arm and marches her to the door. Gesturing to the gun, he tells her that it is merely a formality since Don Birnam already died several times over the weekend: "of alcohol, of moral anemia, fear, shame, DTs." Milland spits each word out angrily and loads them with meaning for the viewer since we have shared in his shameful journey. When Helen suggests that "Don the drunk" died over the weekend but now wants to kill "Don the writer," he angrily tells her not to go back to "a fancy figure of speech," that there is only one Don and "he is through." Given his state, this aggressive confrontation has been too much for him, his eyes start to get heavy, his words are less forceful, and he falls headfirst against the door. When she tries to help him, he pushes her away and remarks that he still has enough strength left. He is short-tempered and just wants her to leave him as he cannot keep promises, has no purpose, no talent, and no writing left in him. He asks if she wants a miracle just as Nat comes to the door with his typewriter and, referring to Don's earlier speech, tells him he found it floating on the Nile after Don's fall down the stairs. Helen views this as his miracle, with Nat acting as his guardian angel, and tells him this is the sign he needs to write.

Don follows Helen slowly into the flat and sits down, a distressed look on his face as he tells her he cannot write with his shaky hands and a brain "all out of focus," looking down in a defeated manner—the opposite of the spunky, upright Helen. She tells him to get all the ugly feelings down on paper that he wants to forget, to get rid of them that way, and to sign it "to whom it may concern," adding that it concerns so many people, thus directly relating to the social condition of the country, especially during wartime and directly afterwards. Helen heads to the kitchen to make them breakfast while Don shouts from the other room that he could not even get the first line of his novel written. She cheerily informs him that he could not write the beginning until he knew the ending but stops when she sees him stand up and wander over to the glass of whiskey she poured earlier. She watches in horror as he lifts it in his left hand, looking down into the glass as the music swells. He takes the cigarette from his mouth and drops it in and Helen smiles with a sense of relief, telling him he can now write the beginning because he knows the ending. Sitting on the couch, he begins to talk about his unwritten book as a finished product, saying he will send copies to Nat, Bim, and the doctor who lent him his coat, acknowledging those he feels have helped him during his weekend. He then lets a short audible breath out through his nostrils, as if to signal irony, as he smiles and considers Wick standing in front of a bookshop, seeing "a big pyramid" of his books and saying, "That's by my brother, you know." He opens his eyes wide and stares forward, moving his hands to show the volume of books that will be there as if completely lost in the moment and actually seeing the scene play out—Wick now having something to be proud of Don for, and Don no longer living in the shadow of the brother who has paid his way for so long. He tells Helen he is going to get the whole weekend down minute by minute, beginning a speech about the weekend which we assume will be the opening lines of his novel. He looks to the side, as if thinking what he is going to say, Helen listening intently by his side as he tells her he will begin with the way he started packing his suitcase, but his mind was not on the trip, the weekend, or the shirts he was packing. The scene fades back into the opening scene we saw in real time as Don packs while being distracted, as he adds, metaphorically and in Milland's perfect diction, "My mind was hanging outside the window, it was suspended just about eighteen inches below. And out there in that great big concrete jungle I wonder how many others there are like me. Poor bedeviled guys on fire with thirst. Such comical figures to the rest of the world as they stagger blindly toward another binge, another bender, another spree."

In 2011, the National Registry of Film chose *The Lost Weekend* as one of its films to be preserved as a cultural, artistic, and historical treasure, referring to it as "a landmark social-problem film [with] an uncompromising look at the devastating effects of alcoholism." They see the film as a blend of expressionistic film noir style and documentary realism combined to immerse viewers in Don's "harrowing experiences," and which was not only one of the best films of the decade but established Wilder as one of America's leading filmmakers.[9] Paramount enjoyed enormous success in the mid-late 1940s, setting industry records in 1945 with their profits of $15 million, the equivalent of about $270 million in 2025. At the war boom's peak in 1946, Paramount earned record profits of almost $40 million, roughly twice that of their major competitors (Schatz 1997: 334; Cook and Bernink 1999: 16). Thus, the peak of Paramount's fortunes was also the peak of Milland's professional career as it was in 1946 that he won his only Academy Award. In fact, 1946 was the most profitable year in Hollywood's history, with gross takings of $1750 million (Higham and Greenberg 1968: 15). This was the time of the somewhat inexpensive quality picture, black-and-white psychological melodramas generally with small casts and indoor settings, with changing definitions of "quality" in Hollywood films (Cagle 2007). *The Lost Weekend* was at the start of this shift. It was also the year *The Lost Weekend* won Best Picture, Best Director, Best Screenplay, and Best Actor. Higham and Greenberg argue that overall, the 1940s can be viewed as the paragon of Hollywood's feature film and, "its last great show of confidence and skill" prior to essentially yielding creatively to the "paralyzing effects" of the collapse of the studio and star systems (1968: 18).

Milland would never recapture this on-screen glory, and neither would the studio. The war boom ended abruptly around 1947 due to various social and economic factors, including the baby boom, suburban migration, and the rise of television. Equally devastating for the studio was the Paramount Decree, an antitrust ruling which forced Paramount (the first company named in the suit) and Hollywood's other major studios to relinquish their theatre chains, which had been imperative to their business, and strictly limit the sales policies which had allowed them control over the industry for decades (Cook and Bernink 1999: 16). Therefore, we can read *The Lost Weekend* as a post-Paramount Decree style film that arrived slightly early. Towards the end of the decade, Paramount took another "staggering blow" by losing control of its theatre chain, consequently losing a considerable assured market for its productions (Edmonds and Mimura 1980: 237). Indicating that the "old days of vast grosses" and Hollywood's distribution of entertainment worldwide had come to an end, by February 1949 the industry was producing just half of its usual number of films (Higham and Greenberg 1968: 17). Hence, while 1946 may have been Hollywood's most lucrative year, 1949 was its poorest in a long time.

Many years after *The Lost Weekend*, actress Piper Laurie turned down *Days of Wine and Roses* (Blake Edwards, 1962),[10] stating that she was too apprehensive to portray an alcoholic since Milland and Susan Hayward (in *I'll Cry Tomorrow* [Daniel Mann, 1955]) had already done it so "brilliantly" (2011: 194). Tom and Sara Pendergast assert that the surprise shown by the critical establishment at Milland's aptitude suggests that "nothing much had ever been expected of him," but he delivered a performance of "increasing depth, vitality, variety, and originality" (2000: 830). According to David Thomson, however, Milland's execution was "far too self-destructive, too dreamily trapped in the dire romance of booze, to be saved by the happy ending appended to the film" (1994: 512). He adds that, although Milland "suddenly revealed himself as an actor capable of showing all the flaws in attractiveness," this "promise was not taken up by his employer, largely because the bleakness of *The Lost Weekend* was so far ahead of its time" (1994: 512).[11] Milland noted the most crucial element of winning the award was that he was no longer considered merely a "movie star [...] in the usual magazine concept," as he had been for several years prior, but now accepted as an actor "with dramatic merit. It was a wonderful feeling" (1974: 225). This statement suggests not only the fleeting notion of fame, but the undermining of a performer as a mere "movie star" who can be more about presence on screen than acting capability.

The role was not only the peak of his career, commercially and critically, but the one he continued to be associated with throughout, and after, his lifetime. During his first appearance as a mystery guest on the television show *What's My Line?* (CBS, 1950–67) on October 31, 1954, Milland attempted to disguise his voice by adopting a Spanish accent, but panelist Fred Allen soon asked, "Did you . . . become famous suddenly one season for appearing in a film called *The Lost Weekend*?"—causing Milland to mumble that he "never get[s] away with anything." Out of context, this seems like an unusual response to his identity being revealed on a game show, but at the time he had just filmed *Dial M for Murder* and his affair with costar Grace Kelly had been made public, almost ruining his image and his marriage, so may have been an (unconscious) assertion of this incident. When Milland returned as a mystery guest over a decade later, appearing on the November 12, 1965, episode, the audience audibly gasped at his first answer, which was very close to his own voice, and which was commented on by presenter John Daly after his identity was revealed. While panelist Bennett Cerf agreed with Daly, fellow panelist Tony Randall notes he did not notice "an English accent," to which no one corrected him. When Arlene Francis questioned if he was a popular motion picture actor, he replied with "not anymore" and when Cerf asked, "Is there one particular picture for which you're quite famous?" Milland responded, in a gruff voice, "I'm afraid so." Cerf then probed if he was in "a very famous picture called *The Lost Weekend*?" before correctly identifying Milland. At this point, the actor was in rehearsals for the play *Hostile Witness*, which opened on Broadway in early 1966; three years later, Milland both directed and starred in a motion picture version of the play.

If the Best Actor Academy Award win did not gain him international fame, it did at least open the doors for him receiving more demanding roles, and he capably portrayed several morally ambiguous characters and blatant antiheroes in the subsequent decades, including Hugh Marcy in *Kitty* directly following *The Lost Weekend*, a sartorial Victorian seducer and murderer in *So Evil My Love*, a would-be wife-killer in *Dial M for Murder*, a murderous thief in *The River's Edge* (Allan Dwan, 1957), and even Satan himself in *Alias Nick Beale*. The final analysis chapter examines Milland's performances in the two most enduring films from the second half of his career, his best-known antihero in *Dial M for Murder* (1954) and his brief return to the big screen in 1970 with *Love Story* (Arthur Hiller).

CHAPTER SEVEN

OSCAR AFTER PARTY

While Richard Dyer (1998) suggests that all star images consist of an ordinary/extraordinary paradox, this tension is especially peculiar in relation to Milland's star persona. His very "ordinariness" is perhaps a factor in why he did not become a major star or an overnight success like some of his contemporaries. However, it also allowed him a long and varied career across several genres and eras as a dependable and bankable performer, if not a top-tier star. Likewise, aside from his rather public affair with Kelly in the early 1950s, Milland's off-screen persona was also presented as exceptionally normal. He was married to the same woman from his early twenties until his death at the age of seventy-nine. Yet, Milland's Britishness added an element of exoticism to his Hollywood image, while his underlying Welshness offered a complexity that allowed him to progress past the superficial, despite studios' compulsion to cast him as stereotypical upper-class Brits at the start of his Hollywood career. It can be argued that Milland's bid for extraordinariness began around the time he won his Academy Award for a darkly offbeat role that showed his potential to be a much more capable and stimulating actor than he had, thus far, been permitted to demonstrate.

Milland repeatedly proved himself a dependable and adaptable actor who, despite no formal training, was able to move seamlessly across a vast range of genres and decades. This is evidenced throughout his career as he moved effortlessly between British and Hollywood cinema, theatre, radio, and television, and even between performing and directing across seven different decades. While never recapturing the glory of *The Lost Weekend*, he did continue to enjoy varying degrees of commercial and critical success throughout the rest of his career. Some of these films were poorly made and others poorly received, both at the time and in the present. The final film Milland acted in, the cheaply made *The Sea Serpent* (Amando de Ossorio, 1985), is rated just 1.5 stars on Encyclopedia.com, and 3.8 stars out of 10 on IMDB, with almost a quarter being one-star reviews.[1] A somewhat unknown film today, this is reflected by the fact that it only has one critic and three audience ratings on the popular site Rotten Tomatoes, with the most recent being from 2015. This lack has resulted in the film not receiving a percentage, which is highly unusual.[2] In comparison, *The Lost Weekend* has a critic rating of 97 percent and an audience score of 90 percent, with over 5,000 reviews, although those criticizing the film call it dated, with cheap special effects, and corny acting. Of the seventy-seven critics, only two rated the film "rotten," with C. A. Lejeune of *The Observer* calling it dull and Mike Massie arguing that the film's subject matter supersedes the characters and means it does not go beyond a public service announcement.[3] However, Milland did continue to be a working actor for the rest of his career, transitioning to a character actor with ease as he moved between genres and characterizations across his career. Whether in high production Hollywood films like *Love Story*, or low-budget independent films, he always gave convincing and consistently competent performances.

DIAL M FOR MILLAND

Although Warner Brothers' *Dial M for Murder* is one of the few Milland films still celebrated, as noted, discussions tend to focus on director Alfred Hitchcock, costar Grace Kelly, or the film's experimental use of 3-D in the 1950s, while Milland is left out of most conversations. Moreover, although receiving solo top billing in the credits and on theatrical posters, visual representations of Milland are mostly absent from the latter, which largely focus on Kelly dressed in a nightgown, either holding a telephone or struggling with her attacker with the telephone in the foreground. One exception is the French poster for the film, titled *Le Crime etait Presque Perfect* (*The Crime was Almost Perfect*), featuring a head-and-shoulders illustration of Milland in profile on the left, dressed in a tuxedo and holding a telephone to his ear, while Kelly is shown on the right, mid-attack. Creating added interest, while simultaneously hinting at the film's resolution, a sizable blue key, much larger than the illustration of either actor, separates the two images, suggesting both a cinematic split-screen paralleling the action and indicating the centrality of the key to the plot. The words "le plus parfait suspense d'Alfred Hitchcock" ("the most perfect suspense of Alfred Hitchcock") are seen on the head of the key, while the poster's background is a blend of reds and yellows, as if awash with fire, and circling the image of Milland. Red is the primary color used on most posters depicting Kelly, connoting a crime of passion or referencing the red lace dress she wears when her character Margot is first seen carrying out her illicit affair with Mark Halliday (Robert Cummings) in the apartment she shares with her husband, Tony (Milland). Moreover, while her nightgown is pale blue in the film, on most posters it is depicted as yellow, again contrasting with the surrounding red, while lobby cards usually had a blue frame and her nightdress colored a light shade of pink, suggesting an advanced sense of vulnerability and femininity for the character and star.

This was Milland's first and only on-screen pairing with Kelly, and his second, much later, film with Cummings, who receive second and third billing, respectively. Each of the principal performers was deeply involved in television at the time of filming. After increasingly moving into television after over two decades in cinema, Milland took a break from filming his weekly sitcom *Meet Mr. McNutley* (CBS, 1953–55) to make this film, with the reverse being true for Kelly. Her screen career had begun in 1950 when she appeared in an episode of *Believe It or Not* (NBC, 1949–50), three episodes of *Actor's Studio* (ABC, 1948–49; CBS, 1949–50), and an episode apiece of *Big Town* (CBS, 1950–54; NBC, 1955–56), *The Clock* (NBC, 1949–51, CBS, 1951–52), *The Prudential Family Playhouse* (CBS, 1950–51), and *Nash Airflyte Theatre* (CBS, 1950–51). She made her cinematic debut in a minor role in *Fourteen Hours* (Henry Hathaway, 1951), and, between appearing in several other television shows, portrayed Gary Cooper's new bride in *High Noon* (Fred Zinnemann, 1952) and Ava Gardner's rival for Clark Gable in *Mogambo* (John Ford, 1953) before being given her first big-screen starring role in *Dial M for Murder*. For his part, Hitchcock began directing in cinema's silent era and, like Milland, had worked in his native Britain before moving to Hollywood. His television series *Alfred Hitchcock Presents* ran from 1955 to 1961, spanning seven seasons and 268 episodes, followed by ninety-three episodes of *The Alfred Hitchcock Hour*, from 1962 to 1965, with Milland starring in the first episode of the second season, "A Home Away from Home."

Robert Cummings, who portrays American writer Halliday, and Margot's lover, not only costarred with Milland back in 1939, when they battled over Sonja Henie in *Everything Happens at Night* (Irving Cummings) but, along with Milland, was one of Hollywood's first male stars to have a regular television series with *My Hero* (NBC, 1952–53) and, later, *The Bob Cummings*

Show (NBC, 1955–59; CBS, 1961–62) and *My Living Doll* (CBS, 1964–65). Like Milland, although Cummings continued to appear in a limited number of theatrical releases, from the 1950s until his retirement in 1979 he was seen more often on television, either in his own series, made for television movies or as a guest star on other popular sitcoms, among them *Bewitched* (ABC, 1964–72) and *Here's Lucy* (CBS, 1968–74).

As both an American and a woman, Kelly may be deemed "Other" since the rest of the cast were all British males (Welsh, English, and Scottish)— aside from Cummings, whose Mark is an American. Kelly had worked on her Philadelphia accent while in drama school in New York, often sounding more British than American on-screen and in interviews. Since she is portraying a British character here, her accent sits somewhere between Milland's upper-class British and Cummings's middle-American accents, again conflictingly placing her between the two leading men. No matter their nationalities, Milland's characters always sound British since, like his peer Cary Grant, Milland never fully adopted another accent in any of his roles; however, as discussed earlier, he would often clip his words when portraying American characters. Given that Tony is an affluent Brit and former Wimbledon tennis champion,[4] Milland projects a stronger British accent here than he had in years,[5] making sure that every word is enunciated flawlessly and with an upper-class tone that leaves us in no doubt of his privileged background.

With its limited cast, confined space, and restricted kinetics of the film's performances, it is perhaps no surprise to learn that *Dial M for Murder* originated as a two-act play and was adapted for the screen by its playwright, Frederick Knott. The play premiered at London's Westminster Theatre in June 1952, just two years before the film was released. In October of the same year, the play made its Broadway debut at the Plymouth Theatre (now the Gerald Schoenfeld Theatre) in New York. While Milland's "languid tennis champion" Tony Wendice features in Peter Conrad's *The Hitchcock Murders* (2000: 100), he engages, or rather blackmails, another man to kill his unfaithful wife, using an elaborate plan rather than carrying out the murder himself.

The film begins with an establishing shot of an affluent-looking residential street in London with a police officer patrolling the area,[6] thus foreshadowing how important the police will soon become in the protagonists' lives. We then cut to the living room of the Wendices' apartment, where much of the action takes place. Suggesting a scene of marital bliss, Tony is standing over Margot, who is seated at the breakfast table, as he kisses her and gives her a slight pat on the shoulder before moving on. Although kissing her on the lips, it is a chaste and somewhat staged kiss, alluding to the film's origins as a play and the façade the pair are presenting as a loving married couple, both to each other and the outside world, since we soon learn that Margot has a lover and Tony is planning her demise. Tony is so engrossed in looking through the mail that he knocks over the salt and pepper shakers as he sits down. Quickly placing them upright, he throws salt over his left shoulder. Since Milland achieves this in such a smooth and naturalistic motion, we cannot be sure if this tiny gesture is scripted or accidental. However, the superstitious associations of spilt salt and bad luck foreshadow how the next few days will unfold for the couple.[7]

The next scene sets up Margot's illicit affair taking place in her own home as she is locked in the embrace of her lover Mark, sharing a passionate kiss significantly different from her earlier kiss with Tony. In her first scene with Milland, Kelly wore a pale pink bathrobe with floral embroidery, a specifically domestic and demure outfit befitting a wife. Here, her vibrant red lace dress connotes Margot's underlying passion and her positioning as a scarlet woman but one who, like the material, is feminine and delicate. Divulging to Mark, and therefore to us, that she has not yet told Tony about their affair, she does reveal that one of Mark's love letters went missing when her handbag was stolen, and she subsequently received a blackmail threat stating that the letter would be sent to Tony if payment is not made.

As they kiss again, Tony's key is heard in the lock off-screen. In a creative shot reminiscent of the famous image of Herbert Marshall's and Kay Francis's shadows projected onto a bed in Ernst Lubitsch's pre-Code *Trouble in Paradise* (1932), Hitchcock displays Kelly's and Cumming's shadows on the back of the door as they nervously move in opposite directions just as Milland steps through, Tony's corporeal presence placed firmly between the two specters. Smiling and apologizing for his lateness, he kisses Margot's forehead and shakes Mark's hand before engaging the latter in small talk, seemingly unaware of what has unfolded before his arrival. The first sense of unease reverberating from Tony occurs when Milland adopts an exceedingly wide grin when facing the other performers.

The way he displays his teeth is reminiscent of a toothpaste advertisement and is strangely unsettling as he consistently talks through the smile. The audience is given the privileged view of his dropping the smile while his back is turned to the others and replacing it before facing them again. He adopts deliberate, almost stilted movements with his head and body and continues to smile while dispatching the pair to the theatre without him, saying that he has work to do and quipping that they can sell his ticket for a drink. Tony's smile appears forced and inauthentic, and the instant he closes the door, Milland allows it to vanish entirely.

Clenching his jaw and turning around, he crosses the apartment to draw the curtains before sitting at the desk and reaching for the telephone. He falsely but arrogantly introduces himself as "Fisher," declares he has twisted his ankle, and proceeds to give a convoluted story about wishing to buy the man's car if he drops by that night. During this call, we witness Tony putting on yet another act with apparently prosaic statements and feigned laughter. After replacing the receiver and moving around the flat, his actions are far less contrived and mannered. Milland's naturalistic movements allow him to display the instantaneous transformation in Tony when alone and to suggest the character's manipulative nature towards others. It is when he removes a pair of white gloves from the brown paper bag he brought home that we truly realize Tony is not as naïve as initially assumed, with the prior friendly and carefree persona he exhibited now exposed as the act of a dangerous man. Milland so skillfully alters his facial expressions and demeanor that the audience quickly shifts from sympathizing with Tony, as the seemingly "wronged husband," to growing increasingly suspicious of him.

He grabs a walking stick and tries it out before smiling; another prop to aid Tony's act. Like Margot and Mark, he initially panics when he hears a knock on the door but composes himself quickly, seizes the cane, and adopts a faux limp. Smiling as he opens the door, it soon transpires that Tony has summoned Lesgate (Anthony Dawson) on false pretenses. Having previously discovered they attended Cambridge together two decades prior, he limps over to the wall to remove a black-and-white photograph featuring the men, alongside several others, dressed in formal attire at a reunion dinner.[8] Exposing his knowledge that the man was formally Charles Swann and has a criminal past, Tony admits to stealing Margot's handbag and writing the blackmail note while calmly, almost psychotically, endeavoring to blackmail Swann into murdering her.

Tony's encounter with Swann lasts over twenty-two minutes. Milland speaks much of the time as he subtly and expertly depicts Tony's increasing gain of control, leading Swann to reluctantly agree to his narcissistic terms. He talks consistently and rather rapidly for over a minute without any cuts, the camera following him as he sits and stands. There is one minor cut to show Swann's reaction to Tony's thoughts on murdering Mark and Margot, but he continues to talk uninterrupted for a while longer. Swann occasionally interjects with short phrases or questions.

Sitting in an armchair, Milland leans on the cane, an oft-used prop in his early Hollywood career to depict his Britishness or "Otherness." He then moves in a semicircle from the chair to standing at the fireplace before sitting on the sofa with his profile to the camera, rising again before perching on

Figure 7.1. The pompous Tony Wendice (Milland) amid blackmailing a man into killing his wife in *Dial M for Murder* (Alfred Hitchcock, 1954).

the arm of the chair and looking down at Swann, resembling a bird of prey ready to pounce. Throughout, he informs Swann of Margot's infidelity in a somewhat lighthearted way, keeping his voice playful, smiling intermittently, making slight gestures with his hand, and occasionally shrugging his shoulders. However, it is largely his vocal intonation that Milland plays with here, emphasizing certain words, pausing for dramatic effect, spitting out some phrases, and filling others with venom. This continues for several minutes before Swann interrupts, Milland having returned to his original position in the armchair as Tony begins to extort Swann. The camera shifts to filming him from below, which adds more confidence, dominance, and menace to the suave, slick, calm, and calculated Tony (figure 7.1). Milland keeps his body movements to a minimum and his voice steady and impeccably controlled while detailing the murder plan to the nervous and reluctant assailant, providing Tony with a supplementary ominousness. He blinks rapidly at times, looks obnoxiously at his nails, and casually stands with his hands in his pockets while relaying how he can frame Swann for the murder. As Tony details his elaborate plan, the camera films the apartment and Milland from above as he walks through the murder for Swann as if it is a dress rehearsal in a theatre and he is providing the stage directions.

After convincing Swann to commit the crime, Tony must obtain Margot's latch key and persuade her to stay home the following night, both of which he successfully accomplishes. While attempting to place the key under the

Figure 7.2. Tony (Milland) panics when he hears the "perfect murder" going wrong through the phone in *Dial M for Murder* (Alfred Hitchcock, 1954).

hall carpet, so Swann can let himself in, Mark is blocking his way, both physically and metaphorically, and Tony must invent an excuse to go back and speak to Margot. Casually leaning on the stairs, he places the key under the carpet without the others noticing before leaning forward to kiss her, more passionately this time, patting her on the face and telling her goodbye, thus expecting her to be dead the next time he sees her but without exhibiting remorse or hesitation.

Although Tony is another of Milland's affluent Britishers, he is a much more sinister one and, as the villain, is soon exposed as the actual "Other" of the film. Tony even stands in stark contrast to Hitchcock's most famous murderer: Anthony Perkins's Norman Bates in *Psycho* (1960), who barges in, murders messily, and panics afterwards, all with a sense of high intensity. Predating Bates by six years, Tony is cold and calculated and remains almost motionless while ensuring that he has several alibis on the night of the premeditated murder, including Mark, before telephoning his house during a formal dinner to initiate the procedure (figure 7.2). Conrad suggests the telephone acts as the "repository [of Tony's] guilty secret" while equating his dialing of the number to "pressing his fingers to the trigger of a gun" as he listens to his wife "gasping and gurgling" while being choked (2000: 239). However, Tony's intricate prearranged murder goes wrong when the struggling Margot reaches for her sewing scissors, ironically handed to her by Tony before he left, and plunges them into Swann's back, thus killing her assailant instead of being killed.

The fact that most of the action takes place in the Wendices' apartment, which should be a safe environment for Margot, and that the domestic items of her stocking and scissors become murder objects is simply macabre. When Tony calls the police to report Swann's death and is asked if it was accidental, he replies that he does not know. When further asked if he knows who could have done it, a close-up depicts Milland lifting his head and looking towards Kelly, indicating that Tony has quickly devised a new plan to portray Margot as a murderer. Sending Margot to bed before moving silently around the flat with the sinuous grace of a cat, Tony sets up a new murder scene with Margot as the perpetrator. Burning the scarf that Swann used on Margot, he removes her stockings from her sewing basket and hides them before placing the blackmail letter into Swann's pocket to imply a motive. He then calmly sits by the fire and takes out his silver cigarette case, raising an eyebrow and crossing his legs to suggest Tony's calm and somewhat psychotic disposition as he awaits the arrival of the police, all perfectly and chillingly executed by Milland in a naturalistic and understated way.

Mark uncovers the truth and attempts to report Tony's guilt to Chief Inspector Hubbard (John Williams). However, Tony offers his exposed crime merely as Mark's "fantastic story," recounting the details with mockery and hubris, while sarcastically presenting authentic details of his crime as a ludicrous and far-fetched narrative concocted in the mind of an American fiction writer. When Tony later asks whether the police would have believed Mark's outlandish story, which was also the reality, Hubbard laughs and replies "not a chance." Margot is found guilty of murder, and the day before she is to be hanged, Hubbard shakes Tony's hand and bids him farewell for the final time. Despite exhibiting dignity and humility while thanking the inspector, the instant Tony closes the door his cracks begin to show for the first time. With his hand still on the doorknob, Milland pauses momentarily before releasing his tension, letting his whole body sink to indicate Tony's tremendous relief at assuming he has got away with his crime. He drops his arms rapidly, swinging them loosely at his sides while simultaneously dropping his head. Opening his mouth with a sigh and closing his eyes in sheer relief, he pours himself a drink before half-smiling and half-grimacing as he drinks it down in one and quickly leaves the flat. Although Tony has never dropped his façade of being a doting husband around Hubbard, the inspector grows increasingly suspicious and returns to the flat after he leaves, having switched raincoats with Tony and taken his key.

A small but highly significant domestic item, the key plays a major part in the narrative and proves to be Tony's undoing, leading to his capture by the police. Opening the door with the fatal key he planted for Swann, Tony at once realizes his mistake when faced with his wife, her lover, and Hubbard. He knows, as do we, that his apartment key will soon be replaced by one for a prison cell, which he will have no control over. It is worth exploring Milland's nuanced performance in this scene in detail, since his body gestures and, most notably, his facial expressions are imperative to making the scene work without the aid of any dialogue for his character.

During this tense final scene, we watch the others watching Tony through the window as he becomes the focus of both the diegetic and nondiegetic audiences. Silently framed by the glass, overtly resembling an image on a television screen, Hubbard gives commentary on Tony's movements to Margot and Mark while the camera cuts from Williams looking out the window to the reactions of Kelly and Cummings and finally to Milland, who is now outside the domestic space.

Milland's series of microscopic movements are vital to unaffectedly revealing Tony's realization that he has been trying the wrong key, thereby revealing his scheme to kill Margot. Although Hubbard comments on Tony's general movements, it is also apparent through Milland's performance what Tony's thought process is. Arriving outside the flat, his mouth is downturned in a frown as he searches for the key in the raincoat and then in his suit jacket and trouser pockets, flipping the coat from one hand to the other as he does so. It is only when he looks again at the raincoat, examining the label and the front of it that he realizes he has Hubbard's coat, and heads to the police station to exchange it for his own. Returning with Margot's handbag and a handful of books she left behind, he unsuccessfully tries the key from her purse before going back outside. Examining the key with a puzzled expression, he flips it like a coin before gazing back at the flat. Glancing at the key again, he steps into the street before stopping abruptly and looking at the handbag, as Hubbard narrates that "he's trying to remember when he put the key back in there." Staring at the bag again, he casually lifts his hand off it and returns to the street as Hubbard suggests that he has given up and is walking off. However, a cut to Milland shows him just outside the gate, standing tensely with his back to the camera as he looks intently down at the key. Turning slowly back towards the flat, his brows are furrowed and his mouth slightly open as he diverts his gaze back at the key in his outstretched hand. With his mouth still open, he lifts his head to look at the flat and drops it again towards the key as Hubbard dictates Tony's thought process, stating, "Of course, that's Swann's key. Now he's got it, he's coming back fast. He's remembered."

We rejoin Milland in the hallway as he rushes towards the stairway; lifting the carpet, he slides the key out, looking down at it and towards its former hiding place before raising one eyebrow in a perplexed manner and placing the key in the lock. Switching the light on before noticing Margot and Mark at one side of the flat and Hubbard at the other, he stares at them with wide eyes and a gaping mouth before, more swiftly than previously, turns and opens the door but is faced with another officer directly outside. Slowly shutting the door, he composes himself by pulling at his jacket and clicking his tongue while exhibiting an obnoxious expression. As if getting back into character as Tony Wendice, he pastes on a grin and ominously nods to Mark that it "might work on paper," as if continuing their conversation about the perfect crime from the night before. He moves towards Hubbard and congratulates him in a lighthearted and seemingly nonplussed way, as you would congratulate an acquaintance who has recently been engaged or promoted. He hands the inspector the key before pouring himself a drink, concentrating on the measure before casually offering one to the horrified Margot and Mark as if hosting a dinner party. Turning to Hubbard, he utters the film's final line off-camera, "I suppose you're still on duty, inspector?" As he does so, Hubbard dials the emblematic telephone.

The film presents a chilling and controlled performance from Milland, who competently expresses the complex layers of Tony's personality, from his calculated ruthlessness to unguarded moments when he is alone. Milland also impressively moves seamlessly between scenes with lengthy dialogue, such as the extensive details he conveys to Swann, and those with no dialogue, particularly those leading up to Tony being caught. It is a powerful and chilling performance from Milland that deserves more attention in accounts of psychotic and calculated cinematic villains.

AGING CINEMATIC PATRIARCH

Given his strong link to Hollywood's glamorous past and the star value of his name, many of Milland's late career films credit him as "AND RAY MILLAND," which helped give them a sense of quality and value. In 1970, his portrayal of Oliver Barrett III, the father of Ryan O'Neal's Oliver Barrett IV, in the smash hit *Love Story*, based on Erich Segal's novel of the same name, helped introduce Milland to a new generation of filmgoers largely unaware of his leading man past and assisted in reviving his career at the age of sixty-three. It can also be considered the actor's final hurrah for Paramount Pictures, his home studio for over two decades and where he had enjoyed his most notable professional triumphs. The film took an impressive $106.55 million at the US box office and another $30 million worldwide. Currently listed at number 727 of the biggest moneymakers in cinematic history, *Love*

Story is positioned directly below the James Bond film *GoldenEye* (Martin Campbell, 1995) and above *Kramer Vs Kramer* (Robert Benton, 1979).[9] In a separate list of all-time international box office for Paramount Pictures, *Love Story* is the oldest film in the top 225,[10] with only four earlier films also in the top 380 releases—*Vertigo* (Alfred Hitchcock, 1958) [363], *Once Upon a Time in the West* (Sergio Leone, 1969) [368], *The Lady Eve* (Preston Sturges, 1941) [375],[11] and *Roman Holiday* (William Wyler, 1953) [377].[12]

Philip Gillett notes the film's box-office success evidenced a persistent "market for high romance" while making it accessible to younger viewers by presenting characters of their own age on screen. However, he adds, "changing attitudes to youth culture, sex and marriage were by no means uniform across Britain or America, which should prompt caution in making generalizations" (2019: 66). Likewise, at the 1971 Royal Film premiere in London, Milland, who contemptuously describes his character as an "ordinary everyday louse of a father," advised that the film's lack of nudity counteracts "some of the pornography we're seeing." This assertive statement on mainstream cinema's shift away from wholesome family entertainment implies why he turned predominantly to television before accepting a role in a film he calls a "return to standards." Showing his unpretentiousness, when interviewer Michael Parkinson asks Milland if he has seen the film yet, the actor looks around him before moving towards the microphone and quietly and, somewhat ashamedly, answering "no" before elaborating that, although he attempted to see it twice, the lines were around the block and he was too embarrassed to go in ahead of other patrons. During this brief segment, a rare televised interview with Milland, the actor proves himself eloquent, engaging, genuine, and very "un-star-like." Additionally, he exhibits humor and authenticity, making himself relatable, especially to the British audience, when he silently pretends to punch a younger man who has repeatedly bumped into him from behind during the interview, without the latter seeing.

This segment was uploaded on YouTube by Thames Television, a franchise holder for the British ITV television network between 1968 and 1992. A quick look at the comments section reveals how viewers feel about Milland. Several comments call him a brilliant or excellent actor, while another suggested, "If genuine, his refusal to jump the long queues at a cinema to see the film shows a welcome degree of modesty." The lengthiest statement includes the following observations: "I love that guy. Charming, obviously brilliant, and endlessly fascinating [. . .] it was impossible for me to believe that he WASN'T Ryan's dad in that movie. Completely encompassed the role." Another interesting point of discussion in the comments section is Milland's Welsh accent, or lack thereof, with most of these commenters stressing their own Welsh identity. While some imply that Milland completely lost his accent, even during his early years in Hollywood, others argue it is still apparent here, if only faintly. One declares that, like Milland, he is from Neath and "can pick up his Welsh accent. . . . just," while another responds that his accent is "still there [. . .] just softened a bit though from years living in the US." Similarly, while one user argues it is "hard to detect a Welsh accent on him", another declares that "if you listen carefully you can hear it in certain words. Even in *The Lost Weekend* [. . .] I catch the welsh [*sic*] accent it in [*sic*] a few of his line readings" although, ironically, his character is American in this film. Another commenter does not appear to grasp the film industry's proclivity for providing stage names for performers, asking why he changed his birth name "to so-called "Ray Milland? Ashamed of his Father [*sic*] maybe?!"; this further suggests the actor had agency in choosing a name rather than an employer deciding he needed a stage name more distinct than the most common surname in Wales, shared by 200,000 people or around 6 percent of the population (McElduff 2008). Other users remark on his aging; one even suggesting he looks seventy-five rather than sixty-five, perhaps because he no longer wore a hairpiece and was almost completely bald.[13]

Milland may not appear extensively on-screen in *Love Story*, but Barrett's domineering nature means he unfailingly controls those around him even when not present, causing Oliver to be consistently angry and to refer to him as "the son of a bitch." Moreover, Milland does an excellent job of delivering an understated but robust performance as an aging patriarch, and one less angry than his domineering wheelchair-bound Jason Crockett of the environmental horror film *Frogs* (George McCowan, 1972) two years later.

Oliver is playing ice hockey for Harvard when he gets embroiled in a fight and removed from the game. As his father witnesses the trouble unfolding from the crowd, cuts between O'Neal and Milland help to visually convey the duo's tense relationship. Seated in the front row, he wears a grey overcoat, trilby hat, and dark red scarf, the latter mirroring the bloody gash smeared across Oliver's face following the physical altercation. The instant Oliver notices his father in the crowd the camera quickly zooms in on Milland, suggesting Oliver's panic and distress that he has witnessed this scene. Looking grimly at Oliver before glancing around, Milland's facial expression appears haughty and indignant, with an added depth alluding to Barrett's embarrassment and disappointment. Milland averts his eyes with a look of shame, but this slowly progresses to a display of hurt when spectators on either side of him begin booing his son. This screen image is reminiscent of the younger Milland in films like *The Lost Weekend*, thus offering an aging and similar-but-different persona for a new decade and viewing demographic.

Figure 7.3. The fraught relationship of father and son Oliver Barrett III (Milland) and Oliver Barrett IV (Ryan O'Neal), as evidenced in *Love Story* (Arthur Hiller, 1970).

Leaving the venue, the two men walk together while engaged in an awkward conversation, with father asking all the questions and son replying in as few words as possible. Moreover, while Oliver calls him "father" twice, he addresses him as "sir" seven times, employing the latter mostly at the end of his curt replies, thus providing an overt indicator of their strained relationship. The camera is placed in front of the actors, both with their hands thrust defiantly in their pockets, as they walk through the snow, connoting their cold relationship. Looking down while conversing, they occasionally glance in each other's direction but never make eye contact (figure 7.3). Halting at Barrett's car, the two finally turn to face each other, Oliver not only refusing his father's offer to get him into Harvard Law School but declining a ride in his car and dinner at his house. The two shake hands as they say goodbye, a hollow and unaffectionate gesture one may undertake when meeting a stranger or acquaintance. The two actors give excellent portrayals of their characters' uncomfortable encounter, as well as a sense of relief that they are parting. Although Milland appears intermittently throughout the film, it is increasingly evident that Barrett has never truly bonded with his son.

In his next appearance, Oliver takes his working-class girlfriend, Jennifer Cavilleri (Ali McGraw), to meet his snobbish parents. A huge mansion on extensive grounds, as they approach the house Jennifer exclaims, "Holy shit." She notes that she did not realize Oliver's family was this rich and then declares that it is too rich for her. They encounter a probing and unpleasant Barrett in his ornate and affluent encoded house, each room overtly displaying his money and how he presents himself to others. Milland shows

Barrett's malicious side through his abrupt and deprecating treatment of Jennifer in his home. Although he spitefully threatens to cut Oliver off from any financial support if he should marry her, the pair wed directly following graduation and he becomes even more distant from his father as a result.

They live in a cramped apartment while scraping enough together to get Oliver through law school as Barrett languishes in his immense house. However, when Jennifer becomes terminally ill, Oliver swallows his pride and visits his father to borrow money. As soon as Barrett writes the check, Oliver grabs it and leaves, unable to tell his father the real reason he needs the loan or spend more time with him than required. Watching as he leaves, Milland lets his guard down in several stages, showing Barrett physically and emotionally sinking lower as he does so.

The film concludes with Barrett arriving at the hospital to ask why Oliver did not tell him the truth, followed by Oliver informing his father that Jennifer has died. Without words, Milland registers Barrett's shock, following this with a subtle movement of his eyes to the ground as he lets his face drop before saying he is sorry. While Oliver walks off, Barrett looks after him with sadness in his eyes, projecting a sense of loneliness and isolation from the son he is unable to comfort in his darkest hour.

Eight years later, the pair reprised their roles in the sequel *Oliver's Story* (John Korty, 1978), based on Erich Segal's novel from the year before and with the narrative taking place just eighteen months after *Love Story*. Although the film did not perform well at the box office, *Variety* argues that *Love Story* is "a tough act to follow, but *Oliver's Story* manages to hold its own" (Anon. 1977). Although far less successful than its predecessor, it is noteworthy for allowing Milland much more character development as father and son reconcile, finally bonding over their shared grief and learning new information about each other. As *Variety* points out, the film's "most moving segments" are not those between the young couple, played by O'Neal and Candice Bergen, but instead the few brief scenes between O'Neal and Milland, concluding that it is "a tribute to both performers and Korty's direction that this most basic of conflicts is resolved here in a genuinely satisfying manner" (Anon. 1977), with Milland now permitted to portray Barrett in a much more sympathetic manner, particularly when the two men share an emotional exchange in the domestic space of the kitchen.

Having begun his Hollywood career in bit parts in the 1930s, Milland ended it the same way, the difference being that he was now a former Hollywood star whose presence in a production, however brief, had this association and his star name attached to it. He was often billed with "AND Ray Milland" or as a "special guest" in the credits in roles including other strong patriarchal figures either personally, as the authoritarian family head, as depicted in *Love Story*, *Frogs*, *Escape to Witch Mountain* (John Hough, 1975), *The Attic* (George Edwards, 1980), and *Our Family Business* (Robert L. Collins, 1981); or professionally, as in *Oil* [Mircea Dragan, 1977], *Gold* (Peter R. Hunt, 1974), *Slavers* (Jürgen Goslar, 1977), and the futuristic *Battlestar Galactica: Saga of a Star World* (Richard A. Colla, 1978).

As with his early career, Milland frequently portrayed doctors and educators in his post-stardom years, including in *X: The Man with the X-Ray Eyes* (Roger Corman, 1963), *Daughter of the Mind* (Walter Grauman, 1969), *The Thing with Two Heads* (Lee Frost, 1972), *The Big Game* (Robert Day, 1973), *The Student Connection* (Rafael Romero Marchent, 1974), *Mayday at 40,000 Feet!* (Robert Butler, 1976), *Cruise into Terror* (Bruce Kessler, 1978), *Survival Run* (Larry Spiegel, 1979), *The Darker Side of Terror* (Gus Trikonis, 1979), *Cave In!* (Georg Fenady, 1983), and his final film, *The Sea Serpent* (1985). This also extended into television with his roles in *The Alfred Hitchcock Hour* (CBS, 1962–65; S2 E1), *Night Gallery* (1969–73; S2 E1), and *The Hardy Boys/Nancy Drew Mysteries* (ABC, 1977–79; S2 E17 and S2 E18). Indeed, while Milland had been one of the earliest film performers to successfully transition to television in the 1950s, he frequented the small screen far more regularly than cinema screens in the final decade of his career, appearing as a guest star in, among many others, the still-popular series *Charlie's Angels* (ABC, 1976–81; S2 E24), *The Love Boat* (ABC, 1977–86; S3 E1 and S3 E2), *Columbo* (NBC/ABC, 1971–2003; S1 E2 and S2 E2), and *Hart to Hart* (ABC, 1979–84; S3 E12 and S5 E8).[14] Additionally, he intermittently had roles in series named after large corporations, such as *Schlitz Playhouse* (CBS, 1951–59, S6 E25),[15] the beer which later sponsored Milland's most successful venture on television, *Markham* (CBS, 1959–60).[16]

In Milland's penultimate screen performance, he portrays the Home Secretary in the made for television movie *Sherlock Holmes and the Masks of Death* (Roy Ward Baker, 1984),[17] starring English actors Peter Cushing and John Mills as Holmes and Doctor Watson, respectively. A position previously held by Arthur Wellesley, the First Duke of Wellington, and Sir Winston Churchill, the Home Secretary is the head of the Home Office and is, therefore, one of the most senior and influential positions in the UK, for whom a key responsibility is law enforcement in England and Wales. Established in 1782, the Home Secretary is appointed by the UK's ruling monarch and reports directly to the prime minister. Being cast in this quintessentially British role not only definitively associated the elder Milland with an ongoing power on-screen, but once more strongly linked him with Britain, especially London, at the close of his career and over half a century since he last resided there as a soldier for the King's Royal Horse Guards.

CONCLUSION

This book is the first in-depth examination of the somewhat problematic progression of Ray Milland's career trajectory and star persona, predominantly leading up to and including his Academy Award–winning performance in his sixtieth film, *The Lost Weekend*. While the concluding chapter discussed his career after his most celebrated role, the preceding chapters explored his complex and "hidden" working-class background and Welsh national identity, his restless early background, and eventual military employment in London's Royal Horse Guards—which serendipitously secured him his first paid work in British cinema. While Milland discussed acting as a job rather than a passion during his early career, he eventually moved to Hollywood, where, after a few hiccups, he remained for the duration.

While investigating the evolution of Milland's screen image from "upper-class Brit" to respected dramatic performer, this book has examined some of the ambiguities and tensions inscribed within fundamental class-, gender-, and sexuality-related components of an amalgamated image. It has also dealt with Milland's struggle to reach a high point in his career and the many obstacles he faced to get there. Firstly, Hollywood erased his roots of being from a working-class Welsh village, and he was instead forced to adopt the studios' long-established stereotype of a Brit: an upper-class Englishman. While this enabled Milland to secure various roles at the start of his career, both as a supporting player and leading man, it erased his utterly unique national identity in Hollywood cinema at the time. Moreover, after bringing him from Britain to America, MGM let Milland go after a few roles as a bit part player and extra since they appeared unsure of how to market him as a star image. His early image as a suave Britisher in Hollywood not only denied his early British career as manual laborers on-screen but limited his roles to bland and almost sexless Brits offered as being less attractive to women than a series of virile American leading men. Thus, his early gentry and royalty were safe but unexciting and denied him the ability to develop as an attractive and desirable leading man.

Milland's remarkably durable screen career covers vastly different socio-cultural and political periods, not to mention geographic locations and technological industrial advancements. Making his screen debut in Britain in 1929, Milland started acting at a crucial intersection between the end of the silent era and the advent of sound—in fact, the final cut of Milland's first film, *The Flying Scotsman*, combines the two and was the first of few working-class roles for him. Principally working in Hollywood from 1931 onwards, Milland was therefore an integral component of the industry throughout the entirety of the studio era and well beyond it. In 1934, after his rather shaky start with MGM, which included several loan-outs to other studios and a brief return to British cinema, Milland signed with Paramount Pictures, where he would remain under contract for a remarkable twenty-one years. Long regarded as a consistently competent and bankable, if lightweight, leading man, even after winning an Oscar for his intensely emotive interpretation of alcoholism he continued being cast in lightweight roles supporting female performers.

Leading to a long, if undynamic, career, Milland eventually became one of only a handful of stars who worked across silent and sound cinema, pre-Code, Code-era, and post-Code cinema, and from the days of Hollywood's studio and star systems until after their disintegration. Like many actors in 1930s Hollywood, he began working in a narrow range of genres dominated by drama and comedy; but this would change in the following decades, and he extended his repertoire into genres including musicals, Westerns, war films, horrors, crime films, and eventually low-budget sci-fi. His career ended in 1985, shortly before his death, during which time he was working within what is now known as New Hollywood or the age of the Blockbuster. Additionally, while working across television, radio, and the stage, his final performance was in *The Gold Key* (Richard G. Kutok, 1985), in the unusual medium of a "made for video" mystery game, released on VHS, which promised one player a reward of $100,000 for solving the mystery. He also stands out as an actor turned producer and director across film and television, usually directing himself, another underexplored facet of his career.

Despite these divergences, it is 1940s Hollywood which defines Milland as a leading man and crowd-drawing star. Nevertheless, his Oscar in 1946 did nothing to guarantee him "better" or more diverse roles, and his career continued on an even keel afterwards, which perhaps led to a less dynamic, yet extremely long-lasting, career that never truly petered out. While Richard Dyer discusses the "structured polysemy" of stardom (1998: 3), perhaps

Milland was too varied and constantly good across so many roles and genres to become an identifiable enough star image, except to be forever associated with *The Lost Weekend* and alcoholism. An animated Milland even appears in the Warner Brothers short *Slick Hare* (I. Freleng, 1947), paying his bar tab with a typewriter and being given change in tiny typewriters, an in-joke for film fans and cementing his strong association with this film. This ensured him regular employment and exposure throughout his lifetime, if not a sensational entry in the history books; some of his later horror and sci-fi films have even become camp or cult classics, including *Premature Burial* (Roger Corman, 1962), *X: The Man with the X-Ray Eyes* (1963), and *Frogs*, which were all recently released on Blu-ray.[1]

With his youth and stardom years behind him, Milland was able to make a smooth transition into character parts from the late 1960s onwards, which he approached with as much conviction and assurance as he had any of his previous leading man roles. Moreover, he appeared able to objectively assess his career in relation to his own inevitable aging and maturing body, while adjusting to industrial and societal changes by taking on roles more suited to his physical appearance and actual age in films employing both technological advancements and more controversial plots. Thus, it appears that Milland moved with the times instead of trying to nostalgically hold onto his lost youth, as some stars did. This exposed him to a new generation of filmgoers and television viewers during the final decades of his career, only now he was being introduced to audiences as an elder statesman, most notably when portraying Ryan O'Neal's father in the 1970 smash hit *Love Story*. Even after he had entered his late sixties and seventies, Milland appeared in several action-adventure films, with varying degrees of involvement in the physical action. These films showcased a new generation of action performers, such as the pre-James Bond Roger Moore in *Gold* (1971), and covered a range of subjects including slavery, crime rings, the greed of large corporations, and the state of America's youth, topics that are always timely and relevant.

Focusing on different facets of Milland's career trajectory and star image, this book has considered his almost unique position as a Welsh-born actor working as a leading man throughout Hollywood's classic era and beyond, illustrating the usefulness of Milland as a particularly interesting case study. Not only one of the earliest Welsh actors to find success in Hollywood but the first in history to win the Best Actor Oscar, he nevertheless remains curiously uncelebrated compared to other Welsh performers like Richard Burton and Anthony Hopkins. After winning his Academy Award, however, Paramount sent Milland and Adolph Zukor to do a series of film showings in Europe. Reflecting his Hollywood journey in reverse, the shows began in London and moved to Cardiff, the capital city of Wales, where Milland declares he was given "a roaring welcome and the key to the city," while referring to himself as "hometown boy makes good!" (1974: 229).

BEYOND THE SILVER SCREEN

When a performer with longevity dies, an obituary can take their whole life and career into consideration. In Milland's case, this included a career in British and American cinema from 1929 to 1985, television from the 1950s onwards, extensive appearances on radio, limited performances on stage, and even a "made for video" mystery game. Despite covering decades of pre-Code, Code era, and New Hollywood for a range of major studios and independent companies in the capacity of actor, director, and producer, when Milland died of lung cancer at the Torrance Memorial Medical Center in California, the most dominant theme across all obituaries was, predictably, his role in *The Lost Weekend*, with most also referencing his Academy Award win for the same film. This confirms that, despite the film arriving at the midpoint of his career, Milland had become consistently associated with it throughout his life, and now beyond. Also noteworthy, reminiscent of the confusion around his nationality in early fan magazines, *The New York Times*, *Los Angeles Times*, and *Chicago Tribune* incorrectly reported Milland's age as seventy-eight, while *The Washington Post* listed him at eighty-one.[2] Peter B. Flint's report of Milland's death in *The New York Times* receives around a third of a page in the middle of the publication and begins by describing Milland as "the urbane actor who won an Academy Award and many other honors for his riveting portrayal of a sympathetic alcoholic" (1986: 30). Featuring images of the young Milland with Dorothy Lamour, one from shortly before his death, and another in his alcoholic stupor in *The Lost Weekend*, the second paragraph is dedicated solely to the film, describing it as "starkly realistic" and "still forceful," while noting it "broke many enduring movie taboos." Flint calls Milland's performance "so compelling that for years, many people confused the actor with the role he had brought to life. It propelled him into the popular folklore as a national symbol of alcoholism" (1986: 30). While the *Los Angeles Times* suggests he portrayed "a dipsomaniac young writer so convincingly that he even fooled some friends into thinking he actually had become an alcoholic" (Anon. 1986), *The Washington Post* simply calls his performance "agonizing and convincing" (Weil 1986). Notably, each publication acknowledges Milland's nationality to varying degrees, with Flint calling him a "sharp-featured, debonair Welshman" who "portrayed nimble, self-assured characters. [. . .] He was widely regarded as one of the most competent and intelligent film actors, one who never gave an inferior performance" (1986: 30). This reflects a review of *Night Into Morning* from thirty-five years prior, which deemed him "the kind of capable actor who can not [sic] give a bad performance, and his characterization [. . .] is thoughtful and sincere" (Anon. 1951: 12).

While celebrity funerals can become media frenzies, Milland shunned the limelight in death just as he had in life. Leaving instructions that there was to be no funeral, he requested that his cremated ashes be scattered in the Pacific Ocean, just off the coast of Redondo Beach in Los Angeles County, California. As noted in the introduction and accordingly taking this book full circle, Milland reveals in his 1974 memoir that, despite always viewing himself as a Welshman and never forgetting his Welsh roots, when returning to his hometown in the 1950s to attend his former headmaster's funeral, he felt like an outsider. However, he also cites feeling an almost identical sensation at a Hollywood party around the same time (1974: 13). Accordingly, it seems fitting that a transatlantic star who felt disconnected from both his home and adopted home requested his ashes to be scattered in the expansive ocean. Not only did this eliminate any enduring base or marker for people to visit after his passing, but this final act attached a permanence to his persistent restlessness and complex national identity, allowing him to belong nowhere and every place.

FILMOGRAPHY

The 39 Steps (Alfred Hitchcock, 1935)
Ace in the Hole (Billy Wilder, 1951)
Alias Mary Dow (Kurt Neumann, 1935)
Alias Nick Beale (aka *The Contact Man*) (John Farrow, 1949)
Aloma of the South Seas (Alfred Santell, 1941)
Ambassador Bill (Sam Taylor, 1931)
Are Husbands Necessary? (Norman Taurog, 1942)
Arise, My Love (Mitchell Leisen, 1940)
The Attic (George Edwards, 1980)
The Awful Truth (Leo McCarey, 1937)
The Bachelor Father (Robert Z. Leonard, 1931)
Battlestar Galactica: Saga of a Star World (Richard A. Colla, 1978)
Beau Geste (William A. Wellman, 1939)
The Best Years of Our Lives (William Wyler, 1946)
The Big Broadcast of 1937 (Mitchell Leisen, 1936)
The Big Clock (John Farrow, 1948)
The Big Game (Robert Day, 1973)
Blackmail (Alfred Hitchcock, 1929)
Blonde Crazy (Roy Del Ruth, 1931)
Blue Horizon (Alfred Santell, 1942)
Blue Scar (Jill Craigie, 1949)
Bolero (Wesley Ruggles, 1934)
Bought! (Archie Mayo, 1931)
Brigadoon (Vincente Minnelli, 1954)
Bringing Up Baby (Howard Hawks, 1938)
Bulldog Drummond Escapes (James P. Hogan, 1937)
But the Flesh Is Weak (Jack Conway, 1932)

California (John Farrow, 1947)
Call of the North (Cecil B. DeMille, 1914)
Captain's Courageous (Victor Fleming, 1937)
The Captive Heart (Basil Dearden 1946)
Cave In! (Georg Fenady, 1983)
Charlie Chan in London (Eugene Forde, 1934)
Circle of Danger (Jacques Tourneur, 1951)
The Citadel (King Vidor, 1938)
Cleopatra (Joseph L. Mankiewicz, 1963)
Close to My Heart (William Keighley, 1951)
The Clue of the New Pin (Arthur Maude, 1929)
The Corn Is Green (Irving Rapper, 1945)
The Crimson Circle (Frederic Zelnik, 1929)
Cruise into Terror (Bruce Kessler, 1978)
The Crystal Ball (Elliott Nugent, 1943)
The Darker Side of Terror (Gus Trikonis, 1979)
Daughter of the Mind (Walter Grauman, 1969)
Days of Wine and Roses (Blake Edwards, 1962)
Dial M for Murder (Alfred Hitchcock, 1954)
Dinner at Eight (George Cukor, 1933)
The Doctor Takes a Wife (Alexander Hall, 1940)
Double Indemnity (Billy Wilder, 1944)
Dynamite (Cecil B. DeMille, 1929)
Easy Living (Mitchell Leisen, 1937)
Ebb Tide (James P. Hogan, 1937)
Embassy (Gordon Hessler, 1972)
Escape to Witch Mountain (John Hough, 1975)
Everything Happens at Night (Irving Cummings, 1939)
Flying Down to Rio (Thornton Freeland, 1933)
The Flying Scotsman (Castleton Knight, 1929)
Foreign Correspondent (Alfred Hitchcock, 1940)
Forever Amber (Otto Preminger, 1947)
Forever and a Day (Edmund Goulding, Cedric Hardwicke, Frank Lloyd, Victor Saville, Robert Stevenson, Herbert Wilcox, and René Clair, 1943)
Fourteen Hours (Henry Hathaway, 1951)
French Without Tears (Anthony Asquith, 1940)
Frogs (George McCowan, 1972)
The Gay Divorcee (Mark Sandrich, 1934)

Gentleman's Agreement (Elia Kazan, 1947)
The Gilded Lily (Wesley Ruggles, 1935)
The Girl in the Red Velvet Swing (Richard Fleischer, 1955)
Gold (Peter R. Hunt, 1974)
Golden Earrings (Mitchell Leisen, 1947)
GoldenEye (Martin Campbell, 1995)
Gone with the Wind (Victor Fleming, 1939)
The Great Dictator (Charles Chaplin, 1940)
Her Jungle Love (George Archainbaud, 1938)
High Noon (Fred Zinnemann, 1952)
Hostile Witness (Ray Milland, 1969)
Hotel Imperial (Robert Florey, 1939)
How Green Was My Valley (John Ford, 1941)
I Want to Live! (Robert Wise, 1958)
I Wanted Wings (Mitchell Leisen, 1941)
I'll Cry Tomorrow (Daniel Mann, 1955)
Il Conformista (Bernardo Bertolucci, 1970)
The Imperfect Lady (aka *Mrs. Loring's Secret*) (Lewis Allen, 1946)
Informer, The (Arthur Robison, 1929)
Irene (Herbert Wilcox, 1940)
It (Clarence G. Badger, 1927)
It Ain't Necessarily So (Graham Johns and Jeremy Bubb, 1986)
It Happened One Night (Frank Capra, 1934)
It Happens Every Spring (Lloyd Bacon, 1949)
Ivanhoe (Herbert Brenon, 1913)
Jamaica Run (Lewis R. Foster, 1953)
The Jazz Singer (Alan Crosland, 1927)
The Jungle Princess (Wilhelm Thiele, 1936)
Just a Gigolo (Jack Conway, 1931)
King of Kings (Nicholas Ray, 1961)
Kitty (Mitchell Leisen, 1945)
Kramer vs. Kramer (Robert Benton, 1979)
The Lady Eve (Preston Sturges, 1941)
The Lady from the Sea (Castleton Knight, 1929)
The Lady Has Plans (Sidney Lanfield, 1942)
Lady in the Dark (Mitchell Leisen, 1944)
Land of My Fathers (Fred Rains, 1921)
Last Days of Dolwyn (Emlyn Williams, 1949)
The Last King of Wales (George Ridgwell, 1921)

The Last Tycoon (Elia Kazan, 1976)
Let's Do It Again! (Alexander Hall, 1953)
A Life of Her Own (George Cukor, 1950)
Lisbon (Ray Milland, 1956)
The Little Welsh Girl (Fred Paul, 1920)
The Long Arm (Charles Frend, 1956)
Look What's Happened to Rosemary's Baby (Sam O'Steen, 1976)
The Lost Weekend (Billy Wilder, 1945)
Love in the Welsh Hills (Bernard Dudley, 1921)
Love Story (Arthur Hiller, 1970)
The Major and the Minor (Billy Wilder, 1942)
A Man Alone (Ray Milland, 1955)
The Man in Grey (Leslie Arliss, 1942)
The Man Who Played God (aka *The Silent Voice*) (John G. Adolfi, 1932)
Many Happy Returns (Norman Z. McLeod, 1934)
Mayday at 40,000 Feet! (Robert Butler, 1976)
Men with Wings (William A. Wellman, 1938)
Merrily We Go to Hell (Dorothy Arzner, 1932)
Ministry of Fear (Fritz Lang, 1944)
Miss Tatlock's Millions (Richard Haydn, 1948)
Mogambo (John Ford, 1953)
Moulin Rouge (E. A. Dupont, 1928)
My Fair Lady (George Cukor, 1964)
My Favorite Wife (Garson Kanin, 1940)
The Mystery of Mr. X (Edgar Selwyn, 1934)
Night After Night (Archie Mayo, 1932)
Night into Morning (Fletcher Markle, 1951)
Nightmare Alley (Edmund Goulding, 1947)
North by Northwest (Alfred Hitchcock, 1959)
Oil (Mircea Dragan, 1977)
Oliver's Story (John Korty, 1978)
Once Upon a Time in the West (Sergio Leone, 1969)
Orders Is Orders (Walter Forde, 1933)
Our Family Business (Robert L. Collins, 1981)
Passion Flower (William C. DeMille, 1930)
Payment Deferred (Lothar Mendes, 1932)
Piccadilly (E. A. Dupont, 1929)
The Plaything (Castleton Knight, 1929)
Polly of the Circus (Alfred Santell, 1932)
Premature Burial (Roger Corman, 1962)

Prince of Foxes (Henry King, 1949)
Proud Valley (Pen Tennyson, 1940)
Quick, Let's Get Married (William Dieterle, 1964)
Reap the Wild Wind (Cecil B. DeMille, 1942)
The Return of Sophie Lang (George Archainbaud, 1936)
Rhubarb (Arthur Lubin, 1951)
The River's Edge (Allan Dwan, 1957)
The Road to Singapore (Victor Schertzinger, 1940)
Roberta (William A. Seiter, 1935)
Roman Holiday (William Wyler, 1953)
Romance (Clarence Brown, 1930)
Rosemary's Baby (Roman Polanski, 1968)
The Royal Romance of Charles and Diana (Peter Levin, 1982)
A Run for Your Money (Charles Frend, 1949)
The Safecracker (Ray Milland, 1958)
Safety in Numbers (Victor Schertzinger, 1930)
Samson and Delilah (Cecil B. DeMille, 1949)
Say It in French (Andrew L. Stone, 1938)
Scarface (Howard Hughes, 1932)
The Sea Serpent (Amando de Ossorio, 1985)
Sherlock Holmes and the Masks of Death (Roy Ward Baker, 1984)
The Sign of the Cross (Cecil B. DeMille, 1932)
The Silence of the Lambs (Jonathan Demme, 1991)
The Singing Fool (Lloyd Bacon, 1928)
Skylark (Mark Sandrich, 1941)
Slavers (Jürgen Goslar, 1977)
Slick Hare (I. Freleng, 1947)
The Small Voice (Fergus McDonell, 1948)
Smash-Up: The Story of a Woman (Stuart Heisler, 1947)
Snake Pit, The (Anatole Litvak, 1948)
So Evil My Love (Lewis Allen, 1948)
So This Is London (Thornton Freeland, 1939)
Something to Live For (George Stevens, 1952)
Son of India (Jacques Feyder, 1931)
The Squaw Man (Cecil B. DeMille, 1914)
The Squaw Man (Cecil B. DeMille, 1931)
A Star Is Born (William A. Wellman, 1937)
Star Spangled Rhythm (George Marshall, 1942)
Strangers May Kiss (George Fitzamaurice, 1931)
The Student Connection (Rafael Romero Marchent, 1974)

Sullivan's Travels (Preston Sturges, 1941)
Sunset Boulevard (Billy Wilder, 1950)
Survival Run (Larry Spiegel, 1979)
Suspicion (Alfred Hitchcock, 1941)
Swing High, Swing Low (Mitchell Leisen, 1937)
The Ten Commandments (Cecil B. DeMille, 1923)
The Ten Commandments (Cecil B. DeMille, 1956)
Terror in the Wax Museum (Georg Fenady, 1973)
Test Pilot (Victor Fleming, 1938)
The Thief (Russell Rouse, 1952)
The Thing with Two Heads (Lee Frost, 1972)
This Is the Life (Albert de Courville, 1933)
This Is the Night (Frank Tuttle, 1932)
Three Smart Girls (Henry Koster, 1936)
Tiger Bay (J. Lee Thompson, 1959)
Today We Live (Ralph Bond and Ruby Grierson, 1937)
Top Hat (Mark Sandrich, 1935)
Tropic Holiday (Theodore Reed, 1938)
Trouble in Paradise (Ernst Lubitsch, 1932)
The Trouble with Women (Sidney Lanfield, 1947)
Twentieth Century (Howard Hawks, 1934)
Typhoon (Louis King, 1940)
The Uncanny (Denis Héroux, 1977)
Undercurrent (Vincente Minnelli, 1946)
The Uninvited (Lewis Allen, 1944)
Untamed (George Archainbaud, 1940)
Valley of Song (Gilbert Gunn, 1953)
Variety Girl (George Marshall, 1947)
Vertigo (Alfred Hitchcock, 1958)
The Virginian (Cecil B. DeMille, 1914)
Walk, Don't Run (Charles Walters, 1966)
Way for a Sailor (Sam Wood, 1930)
The Well Groomed Bride (Sidney Lanfield, 1946)
A Welsh Singer (Henry Edwards, 1915)
We're Not Dressing (Norman Taurog, 1934)
When Knighthood Was in Flower (Robert G. Vignola, 1922)
White Cargo (J. B. Williams, 1929)
Wings (William A. Wellman, 1927)
Wise Girl (Leigh Jason, 1937)
Wolves (Albert de Courville, 1930)

A Woman of Distinction (Edward Buzzell, 1950)
X: The Man with the X-Ray Eyes (Roger Corman, 1963)
Zulu (Cy Endfield, 1964)

TELEVISION

Actor's Studio (ABC, 1948–49; CBS, 1949–50)
Alcoa Premiere (ABC, 1961–63)
The Alfred Hitchcock Hour (CBS, 1962–65)
Believe It or Not (NBC, 1949–50)
Bewitched (ABC, 1964–72)
Big Town (CBS, 1950–54; NBC, 1955–56)
The Bob Cummings Show (NBC, 1955–59; CBS, 1961–62)
Bracken's World (NBC, 1969–70)
Charlie's Angels (ABC, 1976–81)
The Clock (NBC, 1949–50, CBS, 1951–52)
Columbo (NBC/ABC, 1971–2003)
Cool Million (NBC, 1972–73)
The Dream Merchants (CPT, 1980)
The DuPont Show of the Week (NBC, 1961–64)
Ellery Queen (NBC, 1975–76)
Fantasy Island (ABC, 1977–84)
The Ford Television Theatre (NBC/ABC, 1952–57)
General Electric Theater (CBS, 1953–62)
Goodyear Theatre (NBC, 1957–60)
The Hardy Boys/Nancy Drew Mysteries (ABC, 1977–79)
Hart to Hart (ABC, 1979–84)
Here's Lucy (CBS, 1968–74)
The Love Boat (ABC, 1977–86)
Markham (CBS, 1959–60)
Meet Mr. McNutley (aka *The Ray Milland Show*, CBS, 1953–55)
My Hero (NBC, 1952–53)
My Living Doll (CBS, 1964–65)
The Name of the Game (NBC, 1968–71)
Nash Airflyte Theatre (CBS, 1950–51)
Night Gallery (1969–73)
The Prudential Family Playhouse (CBS, 1950–51)
Rich Man, Poor Man (ABC, 1976)

Schlitz Playhouse (aka *Schlitz Playhouse of the Stars*, CBS, 1951–59)
Screen Directors Playhouse (NBC, 1955–56)
Seventh Avenue (NBC, 1977)
Suspicion (NBC, 1957–58)
Testimony of Two Men (WPIX/KSTW, 1977)
What's My Line? (CBS, 1950–67)

NOTES

INTRODUCTION

1. Although Reginald Alfred Jones is the name used for Milland in both the official record for England and Wales Births, 1837–2006, and the 1911 Census for England and Wales, in his 1974 memoir he claims to have been born Reginald Alfred John Truscott-Jones. The only record for an Alfred Truscott-Jones in Neath is an 1871 birth, registered in the 1871 England, Wales, and Scotland Census and possibly a relative.

2. These films are *A Man Alone* (1955), *Lisbon* (1956), *The Safecracker* (1958), *Panic in the Year Zero!* (1962), and *Hostile Witness* (1969), the latter of which he had performed on stage.

3. Milland has twelve televisual directorial credits. He directed and appeared in four episodes of *General Electric Theatre*: "That's the Man!" (1956 [S4, E29]), "Never Turn Back" (1957 [S5, E16]), "Angel of Wrath" (1957 [S5, E32]), and "Battle for a Soul" (1958 [S7, E7]), while directing Tallulah Bankhead in *Eyes of a Stranger* (1957 [S6, E10]) and his *Alias Nick Beale* costar Audrey Totter in *The World's Greatest Quarterback* (1958 [S7, E5]). Milland also directed and starred in *The Ford Television Series* episode "Catch at Straws" (1956 [S5, E1]), the *Schlitz Playhouse* episode "The Girl in the Grass" (1957 [S6, E25] and the *Goodyear Theatre* episode, "A London Affair" (1959 [S2, E9]). Furthermore, he directed Edmond O'Brien in the *Suspicion* episode, "Death Watch" (1958 [S1, E34]; his *Dial for Murder* costar John Williams in the *Thriller* episode, "Yours Truly, Jack the Ripper" (1961 [S1, E28]), and Dorothy Malone in an episode of *The Dick Powell Theatre* titled "Open Season" (1961 [S1, E14]).

4. Other noteworthy studies on the cultural identity of film performers include Gill Plain's 2006 monograph on John Mills and his British identity and Susan Hayward's *Simone Signoret: The Star as Cultural Sign* (2004), which explores the actress's personification of Frenchness.

5. In March 1981, Milland tragically lost his own son, Daniel, when the forty-one-year-old committed suicide via a gunshot wound to the head, issued from a 22-caliber rifle. Unlike his father, newspaper reports state that the younger Milland was unable to keep a job and was unemployed and heavily intoxicated at the time of his death (Anon. 1981a). Less than two months later, French actor Louis Jourdan lost his twenty-nine-year-old namesake son to a drug overdose, ruled a suicide after drug misuse led to manic-depressive behavior

and long-term unemployment (Anon. 1981b). That same year, actress Mary Tyler Moore's twenty-four-year-old son, Richard, died in a similar fashion as Daniel Milland, but his death was eventually ruled accidental after the shotgun he was holding unintentionally went off (Anon. 1981c). Some of Milland's acting peers had lost children to suicide the previous decade, including Gregory Peck in 1975 and Paul Newman in 1978. Prior to this, Milland's contemporary Charles Boyer had lost his twenty-one-year-old son, Michael, and in 1978, two days after Boyer's wife of forty-four years, British actress Pat Paterson, died of cancer, the distraught seventy-eight-year-old actor committed suicide (1978: 5).

6. Milland and Wright were paired three times: in *The Trouble with Women* (1947), the historical drama *The Imperfect Lady* (1946) and *Something to Live For* (1952).

7. Milland and Rogers costarred twice more, in *Lady in the Dark* (1944), another Rogers vehicle in which Milland supports her, and later in *Quick, Let's Get Married* (William Dieterle, 1964).

CHAPTER ONE.
WELSH NATIONAL IDENTITY AND CINEMATIC REPRESENTATIONS

1. Wikipedia's list of Welsh male actors can be viewed here: https://en.wikipedia.org/wiki/Category:Welsh_male_film_actors [accessed June 9, 2021].

2. As the first Welshman in history to win a Best Actor Academy Award and one with such a long career in the industry, Milland is oddly absent from this list which includes lesser-known performers such as Bernard Fox (best known as Dr. Bombay on the TV series *Bewitched*) and Peg Entwistle, an aspiring actress born just a year after Milland and who became infamous in death as the "Hollywood Sign Girl" after committing suicide by jumping from the letter H on the Hollywoodland sign in 1932 at the age of twenty-four. Wikipedia's full list of notable people from Port Talbot can be viewed here: https://en.wikipedia.org/wiki/Port_Talbot [accessed April 1, 2022].

3. The name originates from the English word for "Nedd," the original name for the River Neath.

4. As a child, Milland attended Gnoll Hall Primary School, which was later demolished and is now the site of Neath Police Station. A newly built and slightly renamed Gnoll Primary is now located nearby.

5. The hotel is located on The Parade.

6. Neath's Gnoll House and Country Park have a similarly rich history, with Gnoll Estate's earliest recorded owners being the Earls of Pembroke after it was gifted by Queen Elizabeth I.

7. Spanish for lair or home ground.

8. Eventually, Luisa informed him the split was because his thirty-four-year-old mother wished to see the world after having given birth to five (four surviving) children in seven years (Milland 1974: 37). There is no explanation of why she left Milland behind.

9. Milland was very close to his three sisters and had a brother who tragically drowned at the age of three. Although a significant detail, Milland does not discuss this any further.

10. Now Mahikeng, South Africa.

11. Perhaps influencing his own relationship with his wife Muriel (Mal), to whom he was married from 1932 until his death (despite admitted affairs), Milland reveals that his grandfather was married twice and, in Wales, that is "looked upon rather like leprosy" (1974: 18). His grandfather fathered two girls with his first wife (Milland's aunts, Emma and Luisa) and eight boys with his second (Milland's father being the seventh son). While Emma had one daughter and Luisa remained unmarried, his father and each of his seven brothers had four to five children each, prompting Milland to declare that "Wales is just crawling with my relatives" (1974: 18).

12. Prices increased from 2s 4d. to 6d.

13. The only reference I can find to this film is an entry on the BFI website: https://www2.bfi.org.uk/films-tv-people/4ce2b6e4cace5 [accessed April 28, 2022].

14. The trivia section on Milland's IMDB page suggests an alternative origin for his stage name, stating that it was "from a riverside street called Milland Road in Neath, where he resided prior to becoming an actor" (see https://www.imdb.com/name/nm0001537/bio?ref_=nm_ov_bio_sm [accessed 19 April 2022]). Although there is no source to support this claim, a Milland Road does exist in Neath, close to the Neath River and a ten-minute walk from the location of his old primary school, so would no doubt be a street he was familiar with.

15. For more information on this and other coal mines in Wales, see the Southern Miners Research Society, a registered charity dedicated to preserving the mining history of Wales.

16. The BBC's coverage of the blue plaque unveiling can be viewed here: https://www.bbc.co.uk/news/uk-wales-11041219 [accessed April 26, 2022].

17. According to Patrick Humphries, Milland was considered for the role of Caesar in *Cleopatra* before Rex Harrison was cast, which would have meant two Welshmen were wooing Elizabeth Taylor's title character. Other potential candidates included elite British leading men Laurence Olivier, Ralph Richardson, Michael Redgrave, John Gielgud, James Mason, Basil Rathbone, David Niven, George Sanders, and Leo Genn (2023: 70). Furthermore, before Harrison was cast as Professor Henry Higgins in *My Fair Lady* (George Cukor, 1964), Humphries cites Milland as one of those initially considered, alongside Michael Redgrave and Noel Coward (2023: 161). Given Milland's vocal quality, visual appeal, and star persona, alongside his credible depictions of professors in *The Trouble with Women*, *It Happens Every Spring* (Lloyd Bacon, 1949), and *A Woman of Distinction*, he would have been a perfect fit for the role. Indeed, he did star as Higgins on stage in 1964, with the play opening on June 23 at the Highland Park Theatre in Los Angeles. Furthermore, there are obvious parallels between Higgins and his portrayal of architect Stanford White in *The Girl in the Red Velvet Swing* (Richard Fleischer, 1955). Based on a true story, White makes over Evelyn Nesbit (played by Joan Collins), a young model and chorus girl he is obsessed with, before he is killed by her obsessively jealous husband, Harry Thaw (Farley Granger).

18. Jenkins was Burton's surname at birth.

19. Unfortunately, no such study exists on cinemas in South Wales.

20. In the August 1931 issue, *Screenland* also claimed Milland had been born in Ireland, adding that his experience on the London stage "accounts for his grand British accent" (Anon.: 126). In December 1931, a *Screenland* article titled "Found! New Men in

Hollywood" states that, while he was born in Ireland, he was educated in Cardiff, Wales. It notes that he was a boxer but omits the fact that this occurred during his time in the army (20). Furthermore, the article tells a dramatic story which is claimed to have taken place during Milland's time working on *The Informer* and led to his getting a shot at the lead in another film (presumably *The Flying Scotsman*). When the director refused to let him leave, Milland allegedly picked up a gun and threatened to kill the director, who also then lifted a gun. As the pair faced off, the Prince of Wales walked on the set and Milland was released from his contract. Milland tells the story quite differently and much less dramatically. He notes that he was working on *The Informer* when he was asked to do a screen test for another film, got the role, and completed the work on *The Informer* during his breaks (Milland 1974). Milland's version of the event appears to be more likely, since he was just starting out at the studio it is doubtful that he would have been allowed to continue working there if he had threatened the life of the director with a loaded gun.

21. Savile Row is a street in London's affluent district of Mayfair, which has long been associated with expensive and bespoke men's tailoring.

22. It would appear Milland was to play Allen Macklyn in the film, a role that was ultimately played by Ralph Bellamy.

23. Before 1542, Wales employed a patronymic naming system in which children's surnames emanated from their father's first name. Accordingly, when Henry VIII proclaimed that the Welsh people must have traditional surnames, those whose fathers had the common name "John" became "Jones," which clarifies why Jones remains the most common surname in Wales (Windsor 2023). For more details on Wales and its use of surnames, see Kieren Windsor's "Wales Guidebook" at the following link: https://walesguidebook.com/about-wales/welsh-surnames-explained/ [accessed March 20, 2024].

24. Milland also had a cameo as "himself" on the set of an unnamed film in *Miss Tatlock's Millions* (Richard Haydn, 1948), while Veronica Lake almost collides with him on the Paramount lot in *Sullivan's Travels* (Preston Sturges, 1941).

CHAPTER TWO. STUMBLING INTO ACTING

1. Reflecting the elegance and importance of "Passing Out" day, Milland recalls being "mounted and in full regimental regalia, with saddles covered in black sheepskin, gold stirrup buckles, silver chains, breastplates, and pipeclayed surcingles, the horses shining and prancing" (1974: 55).

2. A famous British stage performer from one of the oldest theatrical families in history, Stanley Lupino was the father of actress, director, producer, and screenwriter Ida Lupino and actress/dancer Rita Lupino.

3. Milland notes that half of the bill at the London Palladium came from the US.

4. Constance Talmadge was an American silent film star and the sister of actresses Norma Talmadge and Natalie Talmadge.

5. Neagle and Milland costarred twice: in *Irene* and *Forever and a Day* (Edmund Goulding, Cedric Hardwicke, Frank Lloyd, Victor Saville, Robert Stevenson, Herbert Wilcox, and René Clair, 1943).

6. Milland would later direct Bankhead in an episode of *General Electric Theatre* in 1957.

7. Milland does not reference this film in his memoir.

8. I can find no mention of Denison Clift directing a film on location in Pitlochry or any reference to Clift working with Raine. After *Piccadilly*, Raine's only other 1929 film was *The Hate Ship*, directed by Norman Walker and shot at Elstree Studios.

9. This is the original version of the more famous 1935 remake directed by John Ford and starring Victor McLaglen.

10. For performing this off-screen trick, Milland received £160 for eight weeks' work, the equivalent of around £12,535 (or $15,970) today.

11. The restored version of the film recently released by the BFI (British Film Institute) includes both the silent version and what the inlay calls the "rare sound version."

12. Milland is credited as "Sharpshooter" in the booklet accompanying the DVD and Blu-ray dual format version of the restored film released by the BFI.

13. Sound on a disc.

14. Soundproofing was a major concern. Celotex, comprising of crushed sugar cane, lined the timber framework and heavy flannelette covered the walls to muffle the noise. The floor was covered with coconut fiber (Warren 1983: 43).

15. Milland receives a brief mention in Warren's book under a photograph of him in profile and with his dark, shiny hair slicked back. Looking dapper but relaxed in a dark suit and tie, his hand rests on his chin and the caption reads: "Welsh-born Reginald Truscott-Jones became a great favourite in Britain and Hollywood as Ray Milland" (1983: 46).

16. Network Distributing was an independent UK company founded in 1997 and disbanded in 2023. It specialized in classic British films and television series and the obscure *The Lady from the Sea* was released as part of its British Film collection.

17. Given the timeframe, the film was most likely *Dynamite* (Cecil B. DeMille, 1929).

18. This date comes from his official 1938 petition for US nationalization.

19. The official document for Milland's 1938 application for US naturalization states that he traveled under the name "Raymond Alton Milland" (the only mention of Alton I could find). His birth name is listed as Reginald Alfred Jones, which is how he has signed the document. His last place of residence is listed as London, while his nationality is given as Welsh. It confirms his birthdate as January 3, 1907, despite discrepancies in print over the years, while his occupation is given as "Motion Picture Actor."

CHAPTER THREE. SECOND FIDDLES AND THIRD WHEELS

1. Both IMDB and Wikipedia note that Owsley died of a heart attack aged thirty-six, with neither mentioning a horse. Realizing Milland may have been mistaken about which actor the horse had killed, I attempted to find out if it had been another actor, but my research came up negative.

2. Similar in looks and audience appeal, Montgomery was cast by MGM in British-based roles which would have proved a better fit for Milland, such as *The Mystery of Mr. X* (Edgar Selwyn, 1934). A murder mystery set in London, some sources claim Milland played an extra, but this appears to be incorrect. Upon close examination, the only time Milland

could potentially have been in the film is the courtroom scene, but no men of Milland's height and build are seen on-screen. Moreover, since he was signed to Paramount by 1934, it is highly doubtful he would have been lent out to MGM to play an extra.

3. Although Milland does not specify the name of the castle, it would appear to be St. Donat's Castle, located in Glamorgan. A medieval castle, Hearst did not purchase it until 1925, the same year that Milland turned eighteen.

4. Over forty years later, Milland refers to Ross as not only still an extremely close friend but now one of the most respected surgeons in California (1974: 133). What Milland does not mention is that Ross had married Hollywood actress Hazel Brooks in June 1967. Similar in looks to Milland and just two years his junior, Ross had dated British actress Merle Oberon in 1955, while Brooks was the widow of MGM art director Cedric Gibbons, whom she had married in 1944, when he was fifty-four and she was nineteen (Anon. 1944: 17). However, the couple remained together until his death in 1960. After thirty-one years of marriage, Ross died in 1999 at the age of ninety, while Brooks died five years later in 2002. Her burial plot in Section H, Lot 117 of Calvary Cemetery, California, lists her as "Hazel Gibbon Ross."

5. He adds that, after being introduced to his future wife, he dropped into his seat "with a thud, looking and feeling very odd" (1974: 137). Going outside, he felt "bemused" but with the "tiniest touch of panic" since he had "never felt any really deep emotion; no one had ever touched me inside. I had been self-sufficient or, more correctly, self-centered and solitary." But now he had "suddenly [. . .] met someone I wanted terribly to impress and I didn't even know her name" (1974: 138). It is possible that his emotional state and his experiencing what appears to be real love for the first time is why his acting began improving around this time.

6. The marriage lasted despite rumors of several affairs. While Milland admits to some in his memoir, he never names the women, and his alleged affair with Grace Kelly provided his only public scandal.

7. Studios wanted to keep their most popular romantic leading men bachelors as long as possible, but fan magazine *Photoplay* printed an article sensationally titled "Hollywood's Unmarried Husbands and Wives" in 1938 which targeted MGM's top male stars Gable and Taylor and their respective relationships with Lombard and Stanwyck. The studios were so "terrified of accusations of immorality" in their stars that they arranged for the couples to marry quickly to avoid any further scandal (Barbas 2001: 99).

8. In his 1974 memoir, Milland cannot recall if the film was called *Blonde Crazy* or *Larceny Lane*, which proves his good memory since it was known as both. While *Larceny Lane* was the film's working title in the US, it was released under both names in the UK.

9. Milland would later portray a famous (retired) tennis player in *Dial M for Murder* (1954).

10. Milland notes Cagney owned a "Gloucester schooner called the *Martha*," while he was the proud owner of *Santana* (1974: 143).

11. When cast in *Bolero*, Milland pretended to have broken his ankle and requested his job at the Shell station to be held for a month, saying, "I figured that if I flopped in the picture I'd have something to fall back on [. . .] But I needn't have worried" (1974: 165).

CHAPTER FOUR. THE BRIT EFFECT

1. Perhaps as a nod to *Wings*, Wellman directed Milland and Fred MacMurray in another film about flying: *Men with Wings*.

2. The full Merriam-Webster dictionary definition of paramount can be viewed here: https://www.merriam-webster.com/dictionary/paramount#:~:text=paramount.%20noun.%20Definition%20of%20paramount%20%28Entry,2%20of%203%29%20%3A%20a%20supreme%20ruler [accessed February 20, 2022].

3. Highlighting his position as the son of a rich Englishman, Mike declares Robert's father "owns all the coal in England."

4. Incidentally, Milland later appeared as the cover star on Italian magazine *Bolero Film* on January 11, 1948, and January 2, 1949.

5. An argument between Raft and producer Barnet Glaser delayed the schedule so Milland received an extra $300 (Milland 1974: 164).

6. Milland received $300 a week for five weeks' work.

7. *Dinner at Eight* (George Cukor, 1933) was an MGM all-star vehicle starring John Barrymore, Wallace Beery, Marie Dressler, Jean Harlow, and Lionel Barrymore.

8. According to Milland, Kaufman offered him twenty-four weeks with no layoffs for the first two periods of his contract, which pleased him immensely since most contracts at the time were for forty weeks a year (1974: 169).

9. Some sources claim Milland was 6'1" but he states he was 6'2" (Milland, 1974: 52).

10. Deanna Durbin, Nan Grey, and Charles Winninger reprised their roles, while Helen Parrish replaced Barbara Read as Kay.

CHAPTER FIVE. IT'S A WOMAN'S WORLD: SUPPORTING PARAMOUNT'S FEMALE STARS

1. Over four decades later, the song was still part of her nightclub act (Lamour 1980: 176).

2. Corman directed Milland in *Premature Burial* and *X: The Man with the X-Ray Eyes*, while Milland directed an episode of *Boris Karloff Presents* titled "Yours Truly, Jack the Ripper" (S1 E28), which aired on April 11, 1961, about Jack the Ripper still being youthful in the 1960s.

3. Milland's first color film was *Ebb Tide* (James P. Hogan, 1937).

4. Sometimes Alexandreia.

5. Milland recalls the tattooist "wiping off the blood with a rag that was none too clean," and he remained unconscious for ten days and had an extended recovery period before being allowed to travel back to Wales (1974: 43–44).

6. Astaire and Rogers provide the secondary romance in *Roberta* (1935), with Irene Dunne as the top-billed star, but receive higher billing than Dunne's love interest Randolph Scott, so this is similar, but not precisely the same, as *Tropic Holiday*.

7. Another Hollywood release from the previous year, Spencer Tracy won his first Best Actor Academy Award for *Captains Courageous*, beating March for *A Star Is Born*.

8. Milland portrayed another, now aging, Hollywood studio employee in *The Last Tycoon* (Elia Kazan) in 1976. Set in 1930s Hollywood, the film is set in the Golden Age of Hollywood, the time period when Milland was starring in pictures opposite Lamour.

9. Milland reprised his role in a radio version of *Arise, My Love* in the spring of 1942, opposite Loretta Young.

10. Aherne was two inches taller than Milland.

11. Both also appeared briefly but separately in Paramount's all-star *Star Spangled Rhythm* and *Variety Girl*.

12. Goddard was born in 1910.

13. Born in Germany in 1901, Dietrich plays a gypsy who dominates Milland's character in *Golden Earrings*, while twenty-year-old Gail Russell starred opposite thirty-seven-year-old Milland in *The Uninvited*. Their seventeen-year age gap is extremely apparent and almost distasteful, especially since he treats her like a child before developing romantic feelings for her.

14. V for Victory was a BBC run campaign which originated on July 18, 1941, and was strongly associated with then-British prime minister Winston Churchill. It has been deemed "the most successful propaganda campaign in history," and several candid photographs of Churchill giving the V for Victory sign in the streets of London still circulate (for more on this and images of Churchill see Zimmerman's writings at the following link: https://www.defensemedianetwork.com/stories/the-v-for-victory-campaign/ [accessed May 16, 2024]).

15. Milland played several reporters on-screen, each with ease and suggesting they were a good fit for his star persona and acting style. He also portrayed a reporter later on stage in *The Front Page* with the Parker Playhouse in Fort Lauderdale, Florida, in 1969. Written by former reporters Ben Hecht and Charles MacArthur, the comedy made its Broadway debut in 1928 and has very recently entered the public domain (2024). The play was adapted to cinema several times, including most famously as *His Girl Friday* (Howard Hawks, 1940), starring Milland's future costar Rosalind Russell and his closest transatlantic contemporary, Cary Grant. Indeed, it is not hard to envision Milland in the role of Walter Burns, either with Russell, Paulette Goddard, or even Claudette Colbert in the role of Hildy Johnson.

16. DeMille remade this film several times, and it was his third version in 1931 that provided Milland with his first Hollywood screen test but which came to nothing.

17. Although Hayward's first nomination came in 1948 when she played an alcoholic in *Smash-Up: The Story of a Woman* (Stuart Heisler, 1947), after three more nominations, she eventually won for *I Want to Live!* (Robert Wise, 1958).

18. Another "slip" of his Welsh accent occurs sixty-nine minutes into *The Gilded Lily* (1934) when he utters a second "go on" when stopping for refreshments at a pub.

19. While Hugh is English, Wales is also mentioned in the book when a man announces that Welshmen sing as other men eat and breathe.

20. There were plans to pair Milland and Goddard in at least three other films, none of which transpired for various reasons. While Paramount announced them for *The Lady Eve* (Preston Sturges, 1941), it was later recast with Barbara Stanwyck and Henry Fonda

(Morella and Epstein 1985: 111). As this would have marked their first on-screen pairing, it is possible the studio wanted bigger star names to sell their product during a particularly challenging time for the industry. Although a perfect vehicle for the pair and their style of comedy, the recasting proved extremely successful, with the film now regarded as one of the best screwball comedies ever made. Goddard was later cast in *The Well Groomed Bride* (Sidney Lanfield, 1946) but withdrew due to pregnancy, although she later miscarried (Morella and Epstein 1985: 142). She was replaced by British-born actress Olivia de Havilland in her only pairing with Milland, and de Havilland does well in this zany physical comedy—a genre she did not often appear in, although she lacks the earthy, all-American appeal of Goddard.

In a rare example of Milland resisting the studio, thus demonstrating his intuitive understanding of cinematic potential, he recalls that he made every film assigned to him without complaint until finally "rebelling" in 1948 by refusing a picture. He calls the film "a turkey called *Bride of Vengeance*. Can you believe that title?" (1974: 200); referring to its working title, *A Mask for Lucrezia*, as much better, over thirty years later he declares, "But the story? Whew! I can still smell it" (1974: 200). A lush and expensive film concerning the Borgias and the Duke of Ferrara, it starred Goddard and was assigned to Paramount's top director, Mitchell Leisen. Two nights before receiving the script, Milland alleges to seeing Twentieth Century-Fox's *Prince of Foxes* (Henry King, 1949), which told the same story, only much better. Since *Bride of Vengeance* debuted in April 1949 and *Prince of Foxes* was released in December 1949, perhaps, Milland is misremembering some of the information or timeframe in which these events occurred. Nevertheless, it highlights Milland's perception and ability to tell a poor film from its initial script. He claims to have spent two hours at the front office desperately trying to be let out of the assignment, choosing to take a two-month suspension without pay, his only suspension in his twenty-one years at Paramount, rather than make the film (1974: 201). Morella and Epstein call it jinxed from the start, starting with Milland's refusal. An advertising campaign was built around "Paulette [Goddard] and sex" (1985: 173), in a crude attempt to generate interest. Despite Milland's desired absence from the film, the studio's advertising campaign references their previous pairing, noting, "Not since the famous *Kitty* has Paramount brought you Paulette Goddard in a picture as spectacular as this adventure-filled story of the strangest bridal night in history," but the film closed within a week of opening in New York (Morella and Epstein 1985: 173). Milland corroborates this, stating that the critics "lacerated it unmercifully, and after five days of being in release it was yanked" (1974: 205). Milland states that Paramount took the failure particularly badly, leading to Goddard, director Leisen, producer Richard Maibaum, and "the unfortunate leading man who replaced me" (John Lund) all being let go, while the assistant director was demoted (1974: 205). Indeed, Goddard did leave Paramount that year, followed, in 1951, by Leisen—who had started working at the studio in 1933 and directed eight of Milland's films. Lund departed shortly afterwards in 1952. Thus, although usually an obedient and punctual worker, Milland's gut instinct around this film was accurate. Furthermore, the studio's insistence on another Milland/Goddard pairing shows the success of their partnership.

CHAPTER SIX. REACHING A PARAMOUNT: THE LONG CLIMB TO *THE LOST WEEKEND*

1. When working with ephemeral material such as film fan magazines, some dating from almost ninety years ago, modern researchers are at the mercy of individuals who chose to save and preserve these "disposable" items. Therefore, I acknowledge here that Milland may have appeared on more than seventeen covers of *Picture Show*, or other publications, but I did not come across them during my many years of conducting and collating this research. Moreover, since vast numbers of magazines were pulped during World War II paper drives, it is possible that whole issues have been lost to modern researchers before digitalisation was an option for preservation.

2. Milland's affair with Kelly almost ended his long-standing marriage, while he confessed to Kelly's sister that he wanted to marry the actress. However, after wife Muriel reminded him that all their property was in her name and both actors were advised it would destroy their reputations, the affair ended.

3. A. M. Sperber and Eric Lax call *Santana* a "Marconi-rigged yawl [. . .] an aristocrat of the sea, fifty-five feet of mahogany, teak, polished brass, and sail—a championship racer with below-deck quarters. [. . .] The boat had been built in 1935 for the heir to a California oil fortune and then was owned by a succession of actors" including George Brent, Dick Powell, Humphrey Bogart, and Milland. Well-known in the sailing world, the yacht was considered "a delight to the seaman's eye. Her decks run long and clean. [. . .] There's no sign of the seams [. . .] just a flawless white skin, smooth and hard as a ball bearing" (1997: 326). Milland portrays a skipper in *Jamaica Run* (Lewis R. Foster, 1953) and captains a ship in the self-directed/self-produced *Lisbon* (1956), while extensive action takes place aboard ship in *Ebb Tide* (1937) and *Reap the Wild Wind* (1942).

4. In Jackson's novel, Wick leaves Don a dollar for the cleaner, and Don finds an additional twenty dollars hidden in an envelope while reading art books and James Joyce's *Dubliners*.

5. In Jackson's novel, the bartender is called Sam.

6. Russian pianist and composer Vladimir Horowitz famously played a rendition of Ludwig van Beethoven's final piano concerto "The Piano Concerto No. 5 in E-flat major, Op. 73," popularly known as the "Emperor Concerto."

7. Following his father's death, James's mother married Benjamin Simms in 1852 and Dr. Reuben Samuel in 1855. This final union produced four children: Sarah Louisa, Fannie Quantrell, John Thomas, and Archie Peyton, the latter died in 1875, aged eight, when a grenade exploded during a raid on the family farm (Gardner 2014).

8. In Milland's much later spoof, alongside Bob Hope in a special televised on April 10, 1972, his now aged character calls himself a "girlaholic" and has several young women hidden around his flat, including one, rather suggestively, hidden up his fireplace (where Don had originally searched for his missing bottle).

9. Details of the National Film Registry and other 2011 entries can be viewed here: https://www.loc.gov/item/prn-11-240/ [accessed June 17, 2022].

10. Lee Remick starred opposite Jack Lemmon.

11. There are several inaccuracies in Thomson's entry, including Milland's birth year, his university education (incorrectly stated as King's College, London, rather than King's College, Cardiff), the timeline of his British career, and some of his films' plots.

CHAPTER SEVEN. OSCAR AFTER PARTY

1. The ratings breakdown can be viewed here: https://www.imdb.com/title/tt0088089/ratings/?ref_=tt_ov_rt [accessed February 8, 2024].

2. All Rotten Tomatoes reviews for *The Sea Serpent* can be viewed here: https://www.rottentomatoes.com/m/sea_serpent/reviews [accessed February 8, 2024].

3. All Rotten Tomatoes reviews of *The Lost Weekend* can be viewed here: https://www.rottentomatoes.com/m/lost_weekend/reviews [accessed February 8, 2024].

4. In *Say it in French* (1938), his character was a famous golfer.

5. Englishness was also key to Milland's earlier pairing with Robert Cummings in *Everything Happens at Night* (1939).

6. Set in London, it was shot entirely on Warner Brothers' Burbank Studios' soundstages in California (with some back projection footage of London supplied by a second unit). The location is the affluent residential area of Maida Vale in central West London, which is located near Paddington Station and St. John's Wood. In the nineteenth century, mansion flats were built here and, in March 2024, apartments listed for sale in the area cost £1.3–£4 million, with houses beginning at £13 million. While Maida Vale underground station does exist, the Maida Vale police station of the film is fictional, with the closest actual police stations being Paddington Green and Harrow Road. Moreover, while Tony gives his address as 61A Charrington Gardens, this street does not exist, but 61 Harrington Gardens does. It appears that Swann voices his confusion, since Tony corrects him on the telephone by repeating "Charrington" and emphasizing the "Ch."

7. Since salt was a difficult commodity to acquire in ancient times, spilling it was considered bad luck. It later became a superstition associated with religion, particularly Catholicism, since it was thought that the Devil stands at our left shoulder and encourages us to sin. While spilling salt allows evil spirits in, throwing some over your left shoulder will blind the Devil and ward off wickedness. Leonardo da Vinci's painting *The Last Supper* depicted Judas as having knocked the saltcellar over and, since the Bible informs us that Judas betrayed Jesus, salt became associated with lies and disloyalty (Wasserman 2003).

8. Hitchcock is seen sitting across from Milland in the photograph, thus allowing the director to make his famous cameo "within" the apartment without disrupting the narrative.

9. For a complete list, see the following link: https://www.the-numbers.com/box-office-records/domestic/all-movies/cumulative/all-time [accessed March 19, 2024].

10. For the complete list, see the following link: https://www.the-numbers.com/box-office-records/international/all-movies/theatrical-distributors/paramount-pictures [accessed March 19, 2024].

11. The Western *Once Upon a Time in the West* (Sergio Leone, 1969) and screwball comedy *The Lady Eve* (Preston Sturges, 1941) were made almost two decades apart, both star Henry Fonda.

12. The political drama *Il Conformista* (Bernardo Bertolucci, 1970), released the same year as *Love Story*, appears in position 369.

13. Michael Parkinson's interview with Milland, and viewers' comments, can be viewed at the following link: https://www.youtube.com/watch?v=22Sh7SA31Y4 [accessed March 19, 2024].

14. Milland also appeared on lesser-known shows *Ellery Queen* (NBC, 1975–76; S1 E0); *Fantasy Island* (ABC, 1977–84; S2 E7), *Bracken's World* (NBC, 1969–70; S1 E15), *Cool Million* (NBC, 1972–73; S1 E2), *The Name of the Game* (NBC, 1968–71; S3 E2), *Screen Directors Playhouse* (NBC, 1955–56; S1 E23), and *Alcoa Premiere* (ABC, 1961–63; S1 E11), the latter presented by Fred Astaire.

15. Others are *The Ford Television Theatre* (NBC/ABC, 1952–57, S5 E1), *General Electric Theater* (CBS, 1953–62), and *Goodyear Theatre* (NBC, 1957–60, S2 E9), the latter in the episode titled "A London Affair" in keeping with Milland's British heritage, and which he also directed. He also featured in the miniseries *Rich Man, Poor Man: Books I and II* (ABC, 1976–77), *Testimony of Two Men* (WPIX/KSTW, 1977), *Seventh Avenue* (NBC, 1977), and *The Dream Merchants* (CPT, 1980).

16. For more on Milland and product advertisement on television and in print, see Kelly 2022.

17. Milland played a similar role as The Ambassador in *Embassy* (Gordon Hessler, 1972).

CONCLUSION

1. Although not as strongly associated with the horror genre as some of his peers, like many aging actors of his generation, Milland appeared in an eclectic range of horrors in the final phase of his career. This included *Terror in the Wax Museum* (Georg Fenady, 1973) and *The Uncanny* (Denis Héroux, 1977). He also appeared in *Look What's Happened to Rosemary's Baby* (Sam O'Steen, 1976), a made-for television sequel to *Rosemary's Baby* (Roman Polanski, 1968), while his final film was the low-budget horror-adventure *The Sea Serpent*. Milland's best-known and most critically revered horror was *The Uninvited* (Lewis Allen, 1944), a ghost story set in Cornwall, England.

2. Like early fan magazines, discrepancies in Milland's height occur across his obituaries.

BIBLIOGRAPHY

Aldhouse-Green, Miranda, and Ray Howell. 2017. *Celtic Wales*. Cardiff: University of Wales Press.
Anon. 1931a. "Presenting Possible Hollywood Headliners." *Screenland*, May.
Anon. 1931b. "New Men Wanted in Hollywood." *Screenland*, August.
Anon. 1936. "Ribbing Ray." *Picturegoer*, December 12.
Anon. 1937a. "Let George Do It!" *Picturegoer*, October 16.
Anon. 1937b. "Give Us Real Heroines!" *Picturegoer*, September 18.
Anon. 1944. "To Wed Art Director." *Boston Globe*, August 22.
Anon. 1945. "There Has Never Been a Film Like Paramount's *The Lost Weekend*." *Motion Picture Daily*, December 19.
Anon. 1950. "Studio Size-Ups: Behind the Scenes of Film Productions." *Film Bulletin*, November 6.
Anon. 1951. "'Night into Morning' Somber Tale of Tragedy." *Monthly Film Bulletin*, June 4.
Anon. 1967. "Kate Cameron Rolls Last Reel as a Critic of Films for News." *New York Times*, January 1.
Anon. 1977. "Oliver's Story." *Variety*, December 31.
Anon. 1978. "Boyer a Suicide." *Los Angeles Times*, August 28.
Anon. 1981a. "Actor Ray Milland Son's Death is Ruled a Suicide." *Desert Sun*, March 26.
Anon. 1981b. "Louis Jourdan Jr. Is Found Dead." *New York Times*, May 14.
Anon. 1981c. "Actress' Son Dies." *Washington Post*, October 15.
Anon. 1986. "Ray Milland Dies of Cancer: Actor Won Fame for 'Lost Weekend' Role." *Los Angeles Times*, March 11.
Asher, Jerrold. 1943. "Portrait of an Individualist." *Photoplay*, July.
Atwater, James. 1953. "Ray Milland Once Walked Alone," *Radio-TV Mirror*, July.
Bailey, Blake. 2013. *Farther and Wilder: The Lost Weekends and Literary Dreams of Charles Jackson*. New York: Alfred A. Knopf.
Bailey, Mark. 2014. *Of All the Gin Joints: Stumbling Through Hollywood History*. Chapel Hill: Algonquin Books.

Balio, Tino. 1993. *Grand Design: Hollywood as a Modern Business Enterprise, 1930–1939.* New York: Charles Scribner's Sons.

Barbas, Samantha. 2001. *Movie Crazy: Fans, Stars, and the Cult of Celebrity.* New York and Hampshire: Palgrave.

Barlow, David, Philip Mitchell, and Tom O'Malley. 2005. *The Media in Wales: Voices of a Small Nation.* Cardiff: University of Wales Press.

Basinger, Jeanine. 1994. *American Cinema: One Hundred Years of Filmmaking.* New York: Rizzoli.

Baslette, Kirtley. 1938. "Hollywood's Unmarried Husbands and Wives." *Photoplay,* December.

Becker, Christine. 2008. *It's the Pictures That Got Small: Hollywood Film Stars on 1950s Television.* Connecticut: Wesleyan University Press.

Berry, David. 1994. *Wales and Cinema: The First Hundred Years*, Cardiff: University of Wales Press.

Birchard, Robert S. 2021. *Cecil B. DeMille's Hollywood*, Lexington: University Press of Kentucky.

Blandford, Steve. 2000. "Introduction." In Blandford, ed. *Wales on Screen.* Bridgend: Poetry Wales Press.

Blanke, David. 2018. *Cecil B. DeMille, Classical Hollywood, and Modern American Mass Culture: 1910–1960.* London: Palgrave Macmillan.

Bolton, Lucy, and Julie Lobalzo Wright, eds. 2016. *Lasting Screen Stars: Personas that Endure and Images that Fade.* London: Palgrave Macmillan.

Bordwell, David, and Kristin Thompson. 2003. *Film History: An Introduction*, third edition. New York and London: McGraw-Hill.

Branston, Gill. 2005. "What a Difference a Bay Makes: Cinema and Welsh Heritage." In Jo Littler and Roshi Naidoo, eds. *The Politics of Heritage: The Legacies of "Race."* London: Routledge.

Breen, Max. 1937. "Ray Milland's Ups and Downs." *Picturegoer,* September 4.

Burton, Alan, and Steve Chibnall. 2013. *Historical Dictionary of British Cinema.* Plymouth: Scarecrow Press.

Burton, Richard. 2012. *The Richard Burton Diaries*, New Haven and London: Yale University Press.

Byars, Jackie. 1991. *All That Hollywood Allows: Re-Reading Gender in 1950s Melodrama.* Chapel Hill and London: University of North Carolina Press.

Cagle, Chris. 2007. "Two Modes of Prestige Film." *Screen* 48, no. 3: 291–311.

Calhoun, Ward. 2010. *Must-See Movies: The Essential Guide to the Greatest Films of All Time.* London: Carlton.

Chandler, Charlotte. 2002. *Nobody's Perfect: Billy Wilder, A Personal Biography.* New York and London: Simon and Schuster.

Chibnall, Steve. 2007. *Quota Quickies: The Birth of the British "B" Film.* London: BFI.

Coleman, Allison, Ian Courtney, John Davies, Iestyn George, and Miles Fletcher. 2004. *100 Welsh Heroes.* Aberystwyth: The National Library of Wales.

Conrad, Peter. 2000. *The Hitchcock Murders.* London: Faber and Faber.

Cook, David A. 2016. *A History of Narrative Film*, fifth edition. New York and London: W. W. Norton.

Crane, Diana. 2000. *Fashion and Its Social Agendas: Class, Gender and Identity in Clothing.* Chicago and London: University of Chicago Press.

Dance, Robert. 2011. *Glamour of the Gods: Hollywood Portraits.* London: National Portrait Gallery.

Davies, John. 2006. *A History of Wales.* London: Random House.

Davies, Marion. 1975. *The Times We Had: Life with William Randolph Hearst.* New York: Ballantine Books.

de Cordova, Richard. 2001. *Picture Personalities: The Emergence of the Star System in America.* Illinois: University of Illinois Press.

Dick, Bernard F. 1985. *The Star-Spangled Screen: The American World War II Film.* Kentucky: University of Kentucky Press.

Dick, Bernard F. 2001. *Engulfed: The Death of Paramount Pictures and the Birth of Corporate Hollywood.* Kentucky: University of Kentucky Press.

Dick, Bernard F. 2008. *Claudette Colbert: She Walked in Beauty.* Jackson: University Press of Mississippi.

Dick, Bernard F. 2011. *Hollywood Madonna: Loretta Young.* Jackson: University Press of Mississippi.

Dillon, Franc. 1934. "Dashing Adventurer." *Picture Play*, November.

Dixon, Wheeler Winston. 2006. *American Cinema of the 1940s: Themes and Variations.* Oxford: Berg.

Doherty, Thomas. 2007. *Hollywood's Censor: Joseph I. Breen and the Production Code Administration.* New York: Columbia University Press.

Dyer, Richard. 1998. *Stars*, second edition. London: BFI.

Eames, John Douglas. 1985. *The Paramount Story.* London: Octopus Books.

Edmonds, I. G., and Reiko Mimura. 1980. *Paramount Pictures and the People Who Made Them.* New York: A. S Barnes.

Elroy, Ruth. 2016. "Minor Cinema: The Case of Wales." In Yannis Tzioumakis and Claire Molloy, eds., *The Routledge Companion to Cinema and Politics.* London: Routledge.

Evans, Gareth D. 2000. *A History of Wales, 1906-2000.* Cardiff: University of Wales Press.

Eyman, Scott. 2020. *Cary Grant: A Brilliant Disguise.* New York and London: Simon and Schuster.

Fagen, Herb. 2003. *The Encyclopedia of Westerns.* New York: Facts on File.

Fearing, Kenneth. 1946. *The Big Clock.* California: Harcourt Brace.

Fevre, Ralph, and Andrew Thompson, eds. 1999. *Nation, Identity and Social Theory: Perspectives from Wales.* Cardiff: University of Wales Press.

Flint, Peter. B. 1986. "Ray Milland Dies; Won Oscar for 'Lost Weekend.'" *New York Times*, March 11.

Fontaine, Joan. 1978. *No Bed of Roses.* New York: William Morrow.

Gardner, Mark Lee. 2014. *Shot All to Hell: Jesse James, the Northfield Raid, and the Wild West's Greatest Escape.* New York and Glasgow: HarperCollins.

Gemünden, Gerd. 2008. *A Foreign Affair: Billy Wilder's American Films.* New York and Oxford: Berghahn Books.

Gillett, Philip. 2019. *Film and the Historian: The British Experience.* Newcastle upon Tyne: Cambridge Scholar Publishing.

Girelli, Elisabetta. 2014. *Montgomery Clift, Queer Star*. Detroit, MI: Wayne State University Press.

Glancy, Mark. 2020. *Cary Grant, The Making of a Hollywood Legend*. Oxford: Oxford University Press.

Gomery, Douglas. 2005. *The Hollywood Studio System: A History*. London: BFI.

Greene, Graham. 1943. *Ministry of Fear*. London: William Heinemann.

Halliwell, Leslie. 1976. *Mountain of Dreams: The Golden Years of Paramount Pictures*. New York: Stonehill Publishing.

Harding, James. 1987. *Ivor Novello*. London: W. H. Allen.

Hayward, Susan. 2004. *Simone Signoret: The Star as Cultural Sign*. London: Continuum.

Hefner, Brooks E. 2014. "Milland Alone: The End of the System, Post-Studio Stardom, and the Total Auteur." *Journal of Film and Video* 66, no. 4: 3–18.

Hemingway, Ernest. (1950) 2004. *Across the River and into the Trees*. London: Arrow Books.

Heritage, Andrew. 2012. *Great Movies: 100 Years of Cinema*. Bath: Parragon.

Higham, Charles, and Joel Greenberg. 1968. *Hollywood in the Forties*. New York: A. S. Barnes.

Hirschhorn, Clive. 1981. *The Warner Bros. Story*. London: Octopus Books.

Hoyt, Eric, Paul McDonald, Emily Carman, and Philip Drake. 2015. "Introduction: On the Legal Lives of Hollywood." In McDonald, Carman, Hoyt, and Drake, eds., *Hollywood and the Law*. London: BFI.

Humphries, Patrick. 2023. *Cleopatra and the Undoing of Hollywood: How One Film Sunk the Studios*. Cheltenham: The History Press.

Jackson, Charles. 1944. *The Lost Weekend*. New York: Farrar & Rinehart.

Jenkins, Graham. 1988. *Richard Burton, My Brother*. New York: Harper and Row.

Kelly, Gillian. 2019. *Robert Taylor: Male Beauty, Masculinity and Stardom in Hollywood*. Jackson: University Press of Mississippi.

Kelly, Gillian. 2021. *Tyrone Power: Genre, Gender and Image in Classical Hollywood Cinema*. Edinburgh: University of Edinburgh Press.

Kelly, Gillian. 2022. "Dial M for Markham, McNutley and the Milland Show: Remaking and Reimagining Ray Milland's Established Cinematic Image for 1950s Television." *TV/Series*, no. 20: 1–17.

Kelly, Gillian. 2023a. "The Competent Welshman in *The Flying Scotsman* (1929): Ray Milland in (Semi-)Silent British Cinema." *Immagine: Note di storia del Cinema*, no. 23: 125–44.

Kelly, Gillian. 2023b. "Tyrone Power: International 'Cover Boy.'" In Tamar Jeffers McDonald, Lies Lanckman, and Sarah Polley, eds., *Stars, Fan Magazines and Audiences: Desire by Design*. Edinburgh: University of Edinburgh Press.

Kobal, John. 2019. *The Lost World of DeMille*. Jackson: University Press of Mississippi.

Lamour, Dorothy. 1980. *My Side of the Road*. New Jersey: Prentice-Hall.

LaSalle, Mick. 2002. *Dangerous Men: Pre-Code Hollywood and the Birth of the Modern Man*. New York: St. Martin's Press.

Madsen, Axel. 1969. *Billy Wilder*. Bloomington and London: Indiana University Press.

Maltby, Richard. 1995. *Hollywood Cinema: An Introduction*. Oxford: Blackwells.

Marshall, Rosamond. 1943. *Kitty*. Cleveland: World Publishing Company.

Mason, James. 1981. *Before I Forget*. London: Hamish Hamilton.

McBride, Joseph. 2021. *Billy Wilder: Dancing on the Edge*. New York: Columbia University Press.

McElduff, Fiona, Pablo Mateos, Angie Wade, and Mario Cortina Borja. 2008. "What's In a Name? The Frequency and Geographic Distributions of UK Surnames." *Significance* 5, no. 4: 189–92.

McGilligan, Patrick. 1975. *Cagney: The Actor as Auteur*. New Jersey: A. S Barnes.

McKay, James. 2020. *Ray Milland: The Films, 1929–1984*. Jefferson, NC: McFarland.

Mercer, John. 2015. *Rock Hudson*. London: BFI.

Morella, Joe, and Edward Z. Epstein. 1985. *Paulette: The Adventurous Life of Paulette Goddard*. New York: St. Martin's Press.

Morella, Joe, and Edward Z. Epstein. 1986. *Loretta Young: An Extraordinary Life*. New York: Delacorte Press.

Milland, Ray. 1974. *Wide-Eyed in Babylon*. New York: William Morrow.

Miskell, Peter. 2006. *A Social History of the Cinema in Wales, 1918–1951: Pulpits, Coal Pits and Fleapits*. Cardiff: University of Wales Press.

Monger, Christopher. 2000. "Foreword." In Steve Blandford, ed., *Wales on Screen*. Bridgend: Poetry Wales Press.

Mook, S. R. 1931. "Found! New Men in Hollywood." *Screenland*, December.

Morgan, Michelle. 2016. *Carole Lombard Twentieth-Century Star*. Gloucestershire: History Press.

Naremore, James. 1988. *Acting in the Cinema*. Los Angeles and London: University of California Press.

Naremore, James. 2022. *Some Versions of Cary Grant*. London: Oxford University Press.

Noble, Peter. 1951. *Ivor Novello: Man of the Theatre*. London: Falcon Press.

Oller, John. 1997. *Jean Arthur: The Actress Nobody Knew*. New York: Limelight.

Ott, Frederick C. 1972. *The Films of Carole Lombard*. New York: Citadel Press.

Pendergast, Tom, and Sara Pendergast. 2000. *International Dictionary of Films and Filmmakers 3—Actors and Actresses*, fourth edition. London and New York: St. James Press.

Perrins, Daryl. 2019. "The Cinema Has Two Tongues: The Cinema Cultures of Wales." In John Hill, ed., *A Companion to British and Irish Cinema*. New York: John Wiley & Sons.

Pickard, Roy. 1996. *Oscar Stars from A to Z*. London: Headline.

Plain, Gill. 2006. *John Mills and British Cinema: Masculinity, Identity and Nation*. Edinburgh: Edinburgh University Press.

Richards, Helen. 2003. "Memory Reclamation of Cinema Going in Bridgend, South Wales, 1930–1960." *Historical Journal of Film, Radio and Television* 23, no. 4: 341–55.

Richards, Helen. .2005. "Cinema as an Attraction: Representations of Bridgend's Cinema Exhibition History in the *Glamorgan Gazette*, Wales, 1900–1939." *Historical Journal of Film, Radio and Television* 25, no. 3: 427–53.

Schatz, Thomas. 1997. *Boom and Bust: American Cinema in the 1940s*. New York: Charles Scribner's Sons.

Shakespeare, William. (1611) 2008. *The Tempest*. Oxford: Oxford University Press.

Shakespeare, William. (1623) 2015. *Antony and Cleopatra*. Oxford: Oxford University Press.

Shipman, David. 1992. *Judy Garland: The Secret Life of an American Legend*. New York: Hyperion.

Slattery-Christy, David. 2006. *In Search of Ruritania: The Life and Times of Ivor Novello*. Self-published, Christyplays Publications.

Slide, Anthony. 2010. *Inside the Hollywood Fan Magazine: A History of Star Makers, Fabricators and Gossip Mongers*. Jackson: University Press of Mississippi.

Spicer, Andrew. 1999. "The Emergence of the British Tough Guy: Stanley Baker, Masculinity and the Crime Thriller." In Steve Chibnall and Robert Murphy, eds., *British Crime Cinema*. London and New York: Routledge.

Spicer, Andrew. 2023. *Sean Connery: Acting, Stardom and National Identity*. Manchester; Manchester University Press.

Stanton, Gareth. 2002. "New Welsh Cinema as Postcolonial Critique?" *Journal of Popular British Cinema*, no. 5: 77—89.

Stead, Peter. 2002. *Acting Wales: Stars of Stage and Screen*. Cardiff: University of Wales Press.

Thomas, Sarah. 2018. *James Mason*. London: BFI.

Thompson, Lauren Jade. 2013. "Suiting Up and Stripping Off: The Male Makeover." In Stella Bruzzi and Pamela Church Gibson, eds., *Fashion Cultures Revisited: Theories, Explorations and Analysis*. London and New York: Routledge.

Underhill, Duncan. 1939. "Welsh—But No Welsher (Ray Milland)." *Motion Picture*, February.

Wasserman, Jack. 2003. "Leonardo da Vinci's Last Supper: The Case of the Overturned Saltcellar." *Artibus et Historiae* 24, no. 48: 65–72.

Warren, Patricia. 1983. *Elstree: The British Hollywood*. London: Columbus Books.

Webb, Gareth. (1999) 2005. *Ivor Novello: Portrait of a Star*. London: Haus Publishing.

Weil, Martin. 1986. "Famed Actor Ray Milland Dies at 78." *Washington Post*, March 10.

Weiler, A. W. 1952. "Spy Melodrama at the Roxy." *New York Times*, October 16.

Whitehead, Tony. 2007. "World Cinema in Wales." *New Readings*, no. 8: 1–9.

Williams, Michael. 2003. *Ivor Novello: Screen Idol*. London: BFI.

Williams, Michael. 2013. *Film Stardom, Myth and Classicism: The Rise of Hollywood's Gods*. Basingstoke: Palgrave Macmillan.

Williams, Michael. 2018. *Film Stardom and the Ancient Past: Idols, Artefacts and Epics*. Basingstoke: Palgrave Macmillan.

Williams, Raymond, ed. Daniel Williams. 2003. *Who Speaks for Wales? Nation, Culture, Identity*. Cardiff: University of Wales Press.

Woodward, Kate. 2006. "Traditions and Transformations: Film in Wales during the 1990s." *North American Journal of Welsh Studies* 6, no. 1: 48–64.

Woodward, Kate. 2012. "The Desert and the Dream: Film in Wales since 2000." *Journal of British Cinema and Television* 9, no. 3: 413–33.

Woodward, Kate. 2016. "Off-Road and Off-Beat: *Gadael Lenin*, American Interior and the Transnational Focus of Welsh Art Cinema." *Journal of British Cinema and Television* 13, no. 2: 292–311.

Zeitlin, Ida. 1940. "Beginning Ray Milland's Romantic Life Story." *Screenland*, November.

Zolotow, Maurice. 1977. *Billy Wilder in Hollywood*. New York: G. P. Putnam's Sons.

INDEX

Ace in the Hole, 189
Actor's Studio (TV series), 209
Aherne, Brian, x, 40, 121–23, 128, 244n10
Alcoa Premiere (TV series), 248n14
Alfred Hitchcock Hour, The, 209, 222
Alias Mary Dow, 98
Alias Nick Beale, 31, 34, 151, 158, 206
Allen, Fred, 206
Allen, Gracie, 38, 78, 82
Aloma of the South Seas, 111
Amami, Eugenie, 46
Ambassador Bill, 6, 30, 76–77, 79, 96
Annabella, 60
Are Husbands Necessary?, 98
Arise, My Love, 78, 92, 112–21, 129, 159, 244n9
Arlen, Richard, 75
Arliss, George, 60
Arthur, Jean, 74, 75
Ashton, Charles, 11
Astaire, Fred, xii, 107, 243n6, 248n14
Attic, The, 222
Auer, Mischa, 92
Awful Truth, The, 22

Bacall, Lauren, 129
Bachelor Father, The, 24, 58–59, 66
Baker, Stanley, 4, 11, 12, 16, 19–20, 21, 32
Balcon, Michael, 17
Baldwin, Stanley, 102
Bankhead, Tallulah, 40, 237n3, 241n6

Bannerman, Margaret, 37
Barnes, Binnie, 92, 94, 107, 122
Barrie, Nigel, 41–42
Barrymore, John, 178, 243n7
Barrymore, Lionel, 40, 243n7
Battlestar Galactica: Saga of a Star World, 222
Beau Geste (1939 film), 75
Beery, Wallace, 50, 55, 243n7
Believe It or Not (TV series), 209
Bellamy, Ralph, 240n22
Bendix, William, 146
Bennett, Constance, 61–63, 64, 91
Bennett, Richard, 61
Benny, Jack, 78
Bergen, Candice, 221
Bernhardt, Sarah, 72
Best Years of Our Lives, The, 162
Bewitched, 210, 238n2
Bickford, Charles, 48, 52–53
Big Broadcast of 1937, The, 38
Big Clock, The (1943 film), 41, 158, 163
Big Clock, The (novel), 163
Big Game, The, 222
Blackmail, 40, 44
Blonde Crazy, 63–66, 80, 242n8
Blondell, Joan, 63–65
Blue Horizon, 111
Blue Scar, 15
Bogart, Humphrey, xiii, 246n3
Bolero, 6, 70, 75, 79–82, 95, 96, 242n11

Boris Karloff Presents, 243n2
Bought!, 61–63, 64, 91
Bow, Clara, 38, 73, 75, 78
Boyer, Charles, 238n5
Bracken's World, 248n14
Brackett, Charles, xvi, 159, 165, 183, 192, 195
Brent, George, 246n3
Bride of Vengeance, 245
Brigadoon, 23
Bringing Up Baby, 34
Brody, Estelle, 38, 39, 41, 42, 50, 66
Brook, Clive, 52, 74
Brooks, Hazel, 242n4
Brooks, Louise, 75
Bubb, Jeremy, 9
Buchanan, Jack, 40
Bulldog Drummond Escapes, 16
Burns, Bob, 82, 99, 106, 108, 111
Burns, George, 38, 78, 82
Burton, Richard, xvii, 3, 4, 5, 11, 16, 17–19, 21, 22, 32, 47, 225, 239n18
But the Flesh Is Weak, 54, 56

Cagney, James, 63, 65, 66, 80, 242n10
California, xiii
Call of the North, 136
Calvert, Phyllis, 33
Cantor, Eddie, 111
Captains Courageous, 108, 243n7
Captive Heart, The, 16
Carroll, Madeleine, 40, 130
Cave In!, 222
Cerf, Bennett, 206
Chaplin, Charles, 121
Charlie Chan in London, 76
Charlie's Angels (TV series), 222
Chevalier, Maurice, 74, 75, 97
Churchill, Winston, 102, 222, 244n14
Circle of Danger, x, xiii, 12–14
Citadel, The, 14, 15
Cleopatra, 18, 239n17
Clift, Denison, 41, 241n8
Clive, E. E., 16
Clock, The (TV series), 209

Close to My Heart, xiii
Clue of the New Pin, The, 44
Colbert, Claudette, xvi, 74, 75, 79, 87–92, 96, 97, 98, 112–28, 166, 244n15
Collier, Constance, 153
Collins, Joan, 239n17
Colman, Ronald, xii, xiv, 52
Columbo, 222
Connery, Sean, xii
Cool Million (TV series), 248n14
Cooper, Gary, 74, 75, 78, 209
Corman, Roger, 102, 243n2
Corn is Green, The, 15
Coward, Noel, 239n17
Crabbe, Buster, 69
Craigie, Jill, 15
Craven, Edward, 87
Crawford, Joan, 50
Crimson Circle, The, 44
Crisp, Donald, 15
Crosby, Bing, 73, 74, 78, 82–83, 87, 97, 111, 159
Cruise into Terror, 222
Crystal Ball, The, 129, 145–50, 157
Culver, Ronald, xv
Cummings, Robert, 209–10, 216, 247n5
Cummins, Peggy, 16

Da Silva, Howard, 175
Dalton, Timothy, 4
Daly, John, 206
Dare, Phyllis, 37
Darker Side of Terror, The, 222
Daughter of the Mind, 222
Davies, Marion, 16, 24, 57, 58–59
Davis, Bette, 15
Days of Wine and Roses, 205
de Havilland, Olivia, 245n20
Del Rio, Dolores, 107
Del Ruth, Roy, 65, 66
DeMille, Cecil B., 51, 73–74, 78, 136–37, 144, 151, 244n16
Denning, Richard, 111
Dial M for Murder, 5, 30, 31, 34, 44, 166, 206, 208–17, 242n9

INDEX

Dick Powell Theatre, The, 237n3
Dietrich, Marlene, xiii, 73, 74, 97, 98, 129, 244n13
Dinner at Eight, 82, 243n7
Doctor Takes a Wife, The, 32
Donat, Robert, 14
Dorsey, Jimmy, 82
Double Indemnity, 160, 189
Douglas, Kirk, 189
Dowling, Doris, 177–78, 181, 194
Dream Merchants, The, 248n15
Dressler, Marie, 243n7
Dunne, Irene, 243n6
Dupont, E. A., 41
Durbin, Deanna, 92, 243n10
Dynamite, 241n17

Ealing Studios, 16, 17
Easy Living, 75
Ebb Tide, 243n3, 246n3
Edwards, Henry, 10
Edwards, Meredith, 16, 19
Ellery Queen (TV series), 248n14
Elstree Studios, 38, 39–42, 241n8
Embassy, 248n17
Emmanuel, Ivor, 19
Entwistle, Peg, 238n2
Errol, Leo, 82, 83, 85, 86
Escape to Witch Mountain, 222
Evans, Clifford, 16
Evans, Edith, 10
Evans, Madge, 51
Everything Happens at Night, 209, 247n5

Fairbanks, Douglas, 78, 102
Fantasy Island, 248n14
Faylen, Frank, 196–97
Fearing, Kenneth, 163
Ferrer, José, 169
Feyder, Jacques, 51
Field, Virginia, 145, 146
Fields, W. C., 73
Fitzgerald, Barry, 15
Flying Down to Rio, 107

Flying Scotsman, The (1929 film), xiv, 3, 9, 19, 31, 40, 43, 44–45, 47, 59, 67, 70, 105, 224, 240n20
Fonda, Henry, 244n20, 247n11
Fontaine, Joan, 6
Forbes, Ralph, 58
Ford, John, 241n9
Ford Television Theatre, The, 237n3, 248n15
Foreign Correspondent, 121
Forever Amber (1947 film), 150
Forever and a Day, 240n5
Fourteen Hours, 209
Fox, 76
Fox, Bernard, 238n2
Francis, Arlene 206
Francis, Kay, 52–53, 211
Frawley, William, 80
French Without Tears (1940 film), xv
Frogs, 219, 222, 225

Gable, Clark, xv, 57, 60, 87, 117, 209, 242n7
Garbo, Greta, 24, 50
Gardner, Ava, 209
Gareth Hughes (2000 film), 17
Gay Divorcee, The, 107
General Electric Theater, 237n3, 241n6, 248n15
Genn, Leo, 239n17
Gentleman's Agreement, 162
George, Gladys, 146
Gering, Marion, 74
Gibbons, Cedric, 242n4
Gielgud, John, 26, 239n17
Gilbert, John, 55
Gilded Lily, The, 87–92, 96, 112, 121, 124, 166, 244n18
Girl in the Red Velvet Swing, The, 239n17
Gleason, James, 69
Goddard, Paulette, xvi, 96, 97, 98, 111–12, 128, 129–58, 166, 244n12, 244n15, 244n20
Gold, 222, 225
Gold Key, The, 224
Golden Earrings, xiii, 129, 244n13
GoldenEye, 218

Gone with the Wind (1939 film), 74, 150, 164
Goodyear Theatre (TV series), 237n3, 248n15
Goya, Mona, 45–46
Grable, Betty, 129
Granger, Farley, 239n17
Granger, Stewart, x, 32–33
Grant, Cary, x, xv, 25, 32–35, 39–40, 54, 59, 165, 210, 244n15
Gray, Gilda, 41
Great Dictator, The, 121
Greene, Graham, 163
Greenwood, Charlotte, 69
Grey, Nan, 92, 95, 243n10
Griffith, Corinne, 50
Griffith, Hugh, 16

Haines, William, 57
Hale, Binnie, 41, 69
Hall, Jon, 111
Hands Across the Table, 27
Hanson, Lars, 43
Harding, Lyn, 16
Hardy Boys/Nancy Drew Mysteries, The (TV series), 222
Harker, Gordon, 69
Harlow, Jean, 50, 52, 243n7
Harrison, Rex, 239n17
Hart to Hart, 222
Hate Ship, The, 241n8
Hayes, Margaret, 130
Hayward, Louis, 92
Hayward, Susan, 137, 139, 205, 237n4, 244n17
Hayworth, Rita, 129
Hearst, William Randolph, 59, 242n3
Hemingway, Ernest, 177, 183
Henie, Sonja, 209
Henry, Jay, 83–85
Her Jungle Love, 98, 103–6
Here's Lucy, 210
High Noon, 209
Hitchcock, Alfred, 5, 33, 40, 44, 121, 130, 136, 208–9, 210, 211, 214, 247n8
Hoey, Dennis, 154
Hoffman, Dustin, 189
Holden, William, xiii, 34, 160, 189
Hope, Bob, 73, 74, 78, 97, 111, 246n8

Hopkins, Anthony, 4, 16, 20, 32, 225
Hostile Witness (1966 play), 206, 237
Hostile Witness (1968 film), 3, 237
Hotel Imperial (1939 film), x, 120, 129
Houston, Donald, 16
Houston, Glyn, 16
How Green Was My Valley (1941 film), x, 15
Hughes, Gareth, 17
Hughes, Roddy, 16
Hutton, Betty, 97

I Want to Live!, 244n17
I Wanted Wings, 111
Il Conformista, 248n12
I'll Cry Tomorrow, 205
Imperfect Lady, The, 238n6
In Search of Gareth Hughes, 17
Informer, The (1929 film), 42–44, 70, 129, 240n20
Irene, 22, 98, 240n5
It (1927), 78
It Ain't Necessarily So, 9
It Happened One Night, 87
It Happens Every Spring, 32, 34, 239n17
Iturbi, José, 22
Ivanhoe (1913 film), 11

Jackson, Charles, 163, 164, 165, 167, 168, 169, 171, 182, 183, 185, 188, 195, 246n4, 246n5
Jamaica Run, 246n3
Jannings, Emil, 74
Jazz Singer, The, 44
Johns, Glynis, 16
Johns, Graham, 9
Johns, Mervyn, 16, 19
Johnson, Kay, 48
Jolson, Al, 44
Jourdan, Louis, 237n5
Joyce, James, 246n4
Jungle Princess, The, 98–102
Just a Gigolo, 54, 57

Kellaway, Cecil, 146, 152
Kelly, Grace, 5, 166, 206, 207, 208–11, 215, 216, 242n6, 246n2
Kerr, Deborah, 4

King, John "Dusty," 95
King of Kings, 31
Kitty (1945 film), 98, 128, 129, 150–58, 163, 206, 245n20
Kitty (novel), 150, 151–52, 155, 163
Knight, Castleton, 42, 43–44, 45
Knowles, Patric, 152, 157
Kramer vs. Kramer, 218

Ladd, Alan, xiii, 97
Lady Eve, The, 218, 244n20, 247n11
Lady from the Sea, The, 9, 19, 31, 40, 45–46, 59, 105, 241n16
Lady Has Plans, The, 98, 129, 130–36, 145
Lady in the Dark, 22, 98, 238n7
Laemmle, Carl, 11
Lake, Veronica, xiii, 74, 97, 111, 240n24
Lamont, Molly, 101
Lamour, Dorothy, xvi, 96, 98–112, 117, 128, 129, 145, 226, 243n1, 244n8
Land of My Fathers, 10
Lang, Fritz, xiii, 5
Larceny Lane. See *Blonde Crazy*
Last Days of Dolwyn, 15
Last King of Wales, The, 11
Last Tycoon, The, 244n8
Laughton, Charles, 41, 66–68, 74
Laurie, Piper, 205
Lawrence, Gertrude, 74, 121
Lebedef, Ivan, 51
Leisen, Mitchell, 51, 150, 245n20
Lemmon, Jack, 246n10
Leonard, Robert Z., 59
Let's Do It Again!, 22
Levant, Oscar, 22
Lewis, Jerry, 3
Lewis, Ronald, 16
Life magazine, xii, 157, 169
Life of Her Own, A, 70
Lisbon, 3, 237n2, 246n3
Little Welsh Girl, The, 10
Litvak, Anatole, 74
Livesey, Roger, 16, 19
Lockwood, Margaret, 33
Lombard, Carole, 27, 60, 70, 78–85, 242n7
Long Arm, The, 16

Longden, John, 40
Longfellow, Malvina, 11
Look What's Happened to Rosemary's Baby, 248n1
Lost Weekend, The (1945 film), xi, xiii, xvi, 4, 6, 16, 20, 48, 54, 75, 78, 98, 128, 151, 158, 159–206, 208, 219, 223, 225, 226, 247n3
Lost Weekend, The (novel), 163, 164, 165, 167, 168–69, 171, 177, 182, 183, 185, 188, 246n4, 246n5
Love Boat, The, 222
Love in the Welsh Hills, 10
Love Story, 206, 208, 217–21, 222, 225, 248n12
Lubitsch, Ernst, 74, 211
Lukas, Paul, 74
Lund, John, 97, 245n20
Lupino, Ida, 240n2
Lupino, Rita, 240n2
Lupino, Stanley, 37, 240n2
Lyon, Ben, 61, 63

MacDonald, Jeanette, 75
MacMurray, Fred, 27, 87, 89, 90–91, 112, 160, 166, 189, 243n1
Madoc, Philip, 4
Maibaum, Richard, 245n20
Major and the Minor, The, xiii, 159
Mamoulian, Rouben, 74
Man Alone, A, 3, 237n2
Man in Grey, The, 33
Man Who Played God, The, 60
Mann, Anthony, 161
Many Happy Returns, 38
March, Fredric, 75, 79, 108, 243n7
Marks, Howard, 4
Marriott, Moore, 42, 45
Marshall, Herbert, 52, 74, 211
Marshall, Rosamond, 151
Martin-Harvey, John, 38
Marx, Chico, 22
Marx Brothers, 97, 111
Mason, James, x, 32–33, 34, 239n17
Massey, Raymond, 141
Mayday at 40,000 Feet!, 222
McCormack, Colin, 4
McCrea, Joel, 74

McGraw, Ali, 220
McLaglen, Cyril, 43–44, 45
McLaglen, Victor, 40, 45, 50, 74, 241n9
Meet Mr. McNutley, 28, 32, 166, 209
Meilir, Rhodri, 4
Men with Wings, 243n1
Mendes, Lothar, 68
Merman, Ethel, 82, 83, 85
Merrily We Go to Hell, 163
MGM (Metro Goldyn Mayer), x, xv, xvi, 24, 25, 26, 33, 45, 47–48, 49–52, 54, 55, 57, 59, 60, 66–68, 73, 75, 88, 102, 111, 113, 137, 223, 224, 241n2, 242n4, 242n7, 243n7
Ministry of Fear (1944 film), xiii, 5, 98, 163
Ministry of Fear (novel), 163
Miss Tatlock's Millions, 240n24
Mix, Tom, 50
Mogambo, 209
Montgomery, Robert, 52, 55, 56, 165, 241n2
Moore, Roger, 225
Morgan, Charles, 4
Morgan, Kenneth, xvi
Moulin Rouge (1928 film), 41
Mrs. Loring's Secret. See *Imperfect Lady, The*
My Fair Lady (1964 film), 239n17
My Favorite Wife, 34
My Hero (TV series), 209
My Living Doll (TV series), 210
Mystery of Mr. X, The, 241n2

Name of the Game, The (TV series), 248n14
Nash Airflyte Theatre (TV series), 209
Neagle, Anna, 22, 39, 240n5
Negri, Pola, 74
Nesbit, Evelyn, 239n17
Newman, Paul, 238n5
Nicholson, Jack, 189
Night After Night, 78
Night Gallery (TV series), 222
Night Into Morning, xiii, 32, 227
Nightmare Alley (1947 film), 161
Niven, David, 40, 239n17
North by Northwest, 33

Novarro, Ramon, 17, 51
Novello, Ivor, xvii, 3, 16, 17, 25, 29, 32, 40, 51, 56, 82

Oberon, Merle, xiv, 242n4
O'Hara, Maureen, 15
Oil, 222
Oland, Warner, 74
Oliver's Story, 221
Olivier, Laurence, 239n17
Once Upon a Time in the West, 218, 247n11
O'Neal, Ryan, 217, 219–20, 221, 225
Orders Is Orders, 69
O'Sullivan, Maureen, 66
Our Family Business, 222
Overman, Lynne, 103, 144
Owen, Reginald, 153
Owsley, Monroe, 52, 241n1

Panic in Year Zero!, 3, 237n2
Paramount Decree, 205
Paramount Pictures, x, xi, xiv, xv, xvi, 3, 16, 33, 38, 54, 56, 59, 70, 71–75, 77–79, 80, 82, 83, 87, 89, 92, 93, 96, 97–99, 107, 109, 111–12, 113, 120, 121, 128, 135, 136–37, 144, 148, 149, 150, 151, 157, 158, 159, 162, 164, 166, 167, 168, 169, 204, 205, 217, 218, 224, 225, 240n24, 242n2, 244n11, 244n20
Parrish, Helen, 243n10
Passion Flower, 52–54, 55
Paterson, Pat, 238n5
Payment Deferred, 41, 66–68
Peck, Gregory, 129, 238n5
Perkins, Anthony, 214
Peterson, Dorothy, 61
Pickford, Mary, 73, 78
Pidgeon, Walter, 15
Plaything, The, 42
Polly of the Circus, 54, 57–58
Powell, Dick, 246n3
Power, Tyrone, xv, 60, 161, 166
Premature Burial (1962 film), 225, 243n2
Preston, Robert, 111, 139

Prince of Foxes, 245
Proud Valley, 14–15
Prudential Family Playhouse, The, 209
Psycho (1960 film), 214
Puglia, Frank, 113

Quartero, Nina, 58, 59
Queen Elizabeth (1912 film), 72
Quick, Let's Get Married, 238n7

Rabal, Paco, 31
Raft, George, 70, 78, 79–82, 243n5
Raine, Allen, 10
Raine, Jack, 41, 241n8
Rand, Sally, 80
Randall, Tony, 206
Rathbone, Basil, 239n17
Rattigan, Terence, xv
Ray Milland Show, The. See *Meet Mr. McNutley*
Raye, Martha, 99, 106, 107, 111
Raymond, Gene, 107
Read, Barbara, 92, 94, 95, 243n10
Reap the Wild Wind, 60, 74, 129, 136–45, 151, 246n3
Redgrave, Michael, 239n17
Remick, Lee, 246n10
Return of Sophie Lang, The, 98
Rhubarb, xiii, 75
Rich Man, Poor Man, 248n15
Richardson, Ralph, 239n17
River's Edge, The, 206
Road to Singapore, The, 121
Roberta, 243n6
Roberts, Rachel, 11–12, 20
Robeson, Paul, 9, 14–15
Robison, Arthur, 42
Roc, Patricia, 12
Rogers, Charles "Buddy," 75, 79
Rogers, Ginger, xiii, 22, 98, 107, 159, 238n7, 243n6
Rogers, Will, 76
Roman Holiday, 218
Romance, 50

Romero, Cesar, 51
Rosemary's Baby (1968 film), 248n1
Royal Romance of Charles and Diana, The, 32
Ruggles, Wesley, 70
Run for Your Money, A, 16
Russell, Gail, 129, 244n13
Russell, Rosalind, 14, 244n15

Safecracker, The, 3, 237n2
Safety in Numbers, 79
Samson and Delilah (1949 film), 136
Sanders, George, 239n17
Say it in French, 75, 247n4
Scarface (1932 film), 78
Schlitz Playhouse, 222, 237n3
Scott, Randolph, 243n6
Scott, Walter, 11
Screen Directors Playhouse, 248n14
Sea Serpent, The, 208, 222, 247n2, 248n1
Seventh Avenue (TV series), 248n15
Shearer, Norma, 56
Sherlock Holmes and the Masks of Death, 222
Sidney, Sylvia, 78
Sign of the Cross, The, 136
Silence of the Lambs, The (1991 film), 20
Silent Voice, The. See *Man Who Played God, The*
Sinatra, Frank, 129
Singing Fool, The, 44
Skylark, 121–28, 153
Slaughter, Tod, 38
Slavers, 222
Slick Hare, 225
Small Voice, The, 12
Smash-Up: The Story of a Woman, 244n17
Smith, C. Aubrey, 58, 74, 87
Snake Pit, The, 162
So Evil My Love, 30, 31, 34, 75, 158, 206
So This is London, 33
Something to Live For, 6, 238n6
Son of India, 51
Song You Gave Me, The, 32
Squaw Man, The (1914 film), 136
Squaw Man, The (1931 film), 51

St. Leger, Margot, 37, 38, 60
Stahl, John, 74
Stamp-Taylor, Enid, 37
Standing, Guy, 74
Stanwyck, Barbara, xiii, 60, 159, 242n7, 244n20
Star Is Born, A (1937 film), 108, 163, 243n7
Star Spangled Rhythm, 111, 244n11
Stewart, James, 32, 161
Strangers May Kiss, 54–55, 56
Student Connection, The, 222
Sturges, Preston, 73, 74
Sullivan's Travels, 240n24
Sunset Boulevard (1950 film), 160, 189
Survival Run, 222
Suspicion (1941 film), 34
Suspicion (TV series), 237n3
Swanson, Gloria, 78
Swing High, Swing Low, 163

Talmadge, Constance, 39, 240n4
Talmadge, Natalie, 240n4
Talmadge, Norma, 240n4
Taurog, Norman, 82
Taylor, Elisabeth, 5, 18, 239n17
Taylor, Rhys, 4
Taylor, Robert, xv, 60, 161, 242n7
Ten Commandments, The (1923 film), 78, 136
Ten Commandments, The (1956 film), 136
Terror in the Wax Museum, 248n1
Terry, Philip, 170–72
Test Pilot, 117
Testimony of Two Men (TV series), 248n15
Thaw, Harry, 239n17
Thief, The, 32, 56
Thing with Two Heads, The, 222
39 Steps, The (1935 film), 130
This Is the Life, 69
This Is the Night, 33
Thomas, Jameson, 41, 87
Three Smart Girls, 92–95, 99, 102, 129
Three Smart Girls Grow Up, 95, 243n10
Tiger Bay (1959 film), 12
Today We Live, 11
Todd, Thelma, 33

Top Hat, 107
Tracy, Spencer, 243n7
Tree, David, xv
Tropic Holiday, 98, 106–11, 243n6
Trouble in Paradise, 211
Trouble with Women, The, xiii, 32, 34, 238n6, 239n17
Turner, Lana, 70
Twentieth Century, 79
Twentieth Century-Fox, 113, 245n20
Tyler Moore, Mary, 238n5
Typhoon, 111

Uncanny, The (1977 film), 248n1
Undercurrent, 161
Uninvited, The (1944 film), 22, 129, 244n13, 248n1
Universal, 11, 73, 92, 95, 113
Untamed (1940 film), 32

Valentino, Rudolph, 17, 51, 78
Valley of Song, 12
Variety Girl, xiii, 34, 244n11
Vertigo (1958 film), 218
Virginian, The (1914 film), 136
von Sternberg, Josef, 74
von Stroheim, Erich, 74

Walk, Don't Run, 34
Warner Brothers, xv, 44, 48, 60, 61, 63, 73, 77, 113, 208, 225, 247n6
Way for a Sailor, 6, 54–55
Wayne, John, xii, 60, 137–38, 144
Wayne, Naunton, 16, 19
Well Groomed Bride, The, 245n20
Welles, Orson, 31
Wellman, William A., 75, 243n1
Welsh Singer, A, 10
We're Not Dressing, 30, 38, 79, 82, 83–87, 95
West, Mae, 73, 74–75, 78
Westmore, Wally, 79, 168
What's My Line? (TV series), 206
When Knighthood Was in Flower, 16
White, Stanford, 239n17
White Cargo, 44

Wilcoxon, Henry, 74
Wilder, Billy, xiii, xvi, 5, 74, 113, 115, 159–60, 163, 164, 165, 167, 169, 183, 185, 188, 189, 191, 192, 195, 204
Williams, Emlyn, 16
Williams, John, 215, 216, 237n3
Williams, Rhys, 15
Wings, 75, 243n1
Winninger, Charles, 92, 243n10
Wise Girl, 98
Wolves (1930 film), 44
Woman of Distinction, A, 32, 98, 239n17
Wong, Anna May, 40, 41
Wray, Fay, 75
Wright, Teresa, xiii, 238n6
Wyman, Jane, 22, 171, 172, 201

X: The Man with the X-Ray Eyes, 222, 225, 243n2

Young, Loretta, 244n9
Young, Roland, 74, 131–33

Zeta-Jones, Catherine, 4
Zukor, Adolph, 72–73, 74, 77, 225
Zulu, 19

ABOUT THE AUTHOR

Photo courtesy of the author

GILLIAN KELLY is the author of *Robert Taylor: Male Beauty, Masculinity, and Stardom in Hollywood* (University Press of Mississippi, 2019), which was shortlisted for Monograph of the Year at the BAFTSS Awards in 2020, and *Tyrone Power: Gender, Genre and Image in Classical Hollywood Cinema* (Edinburgh University Press, 2021). She has written extensively on Hollywood stars, masculinity, and country music for academic journals and edited collections. Her previous work on Ray Milland includes the journal articles "Dial M for Markham, McNutley and the Milland Show: Remaking and Reimagining Ray Milland's Established Cinematic Image for 1950s Television" in *TV/Series* (2022) and "The Competent Welshman in 'The Flying Scotsman': Ray Milland in (Semi-)Silent British Cinema" in *Immagine. Note di storia del Cinema* (2023).

www.ingramcontent.com/pod-product-compliance
Lightning Source LLC
Chambersburg PA
CBHW022002220426
43663CB00007B/925